ESSENTIALS OF INFORMATION SYSTEMS FOR MANAGERS

ESSENTIALS OF INFORMATION SYSTEMS FOR MANAGERS

GABRIELE PICCOLI

Università di Sassari

WILEY

John Wiley & Sons, Inc.

Vice President and Publisher   *Don Fowley*
Executive Editor   *Beth Lang Golub*
Editorial Assistant   *Elizabeth Mills*
Marketing Manager   *Christopher Ruel*
Senior Photo Editor   *Lisa Gee*
Senior Production Manager   *Janis Soo*
Associate Production Manager   *Joyce Poh*
Assistant Production Editor   *Annabelle Ang-Bok*
Cover Photo   *Don Bishop/Getty Images, Inc.*
Cover Design   *Harry Nolan*

This book was set in 10/12 Times Roman by Laserwords Private Limited and printed and bound by Courier Westford.

This book is printed on acid free paper.

Founded in 1807, John Wiley & Sons, Inc. has been a valued source of knowledge and understanding for more than 200 years, helping people around the world meet their needs and fulfill their aspirations. Our company is built on a foundation of principles that include responsibility to the communities we serve and where we live and work. In 2008, we launched a Corporate Citizenship Initiative, a global effort to address the environmental, social, economic, and ethical challenges we face in our business. Among the issues we are addressing are carbon impact, paper specifications and procurement, ethical conduct within our business and among our vendors, and community and charitable support. For more information, please visit our website: www.wiley.com/go/citizenship.

Library of Congress Cataloging-in-Publication Data

Piccoli, Gabriele.
   Essentials of information systems for managers : text only / Gabriele Piccoli.
      p. cm.
   Includes bibliographical references and index.
   ISBN 978-1-118-05711-7 (pbk.: acid free paper)
 1. Management information systems. 2. Business—Data processing. I. Title.
   HD30.213.P523 2012
   658.4′038011–dc23
                                    2011042844

Printed in the United States of America

10 9 8 7 6 5 4 3 2 1

To Margaret: The finest teammate I could have asked for.

To Laura Jean and Erik who always help put it all in perspective.

PREFACE

THE PHILOSOPHY OF THIS BOOK

This book is inspired by the notion that today, forty years into the "information age," general and functional managers must be able to *actively* and *knowledgeably* participate in discussion and decisions about information systems and information technology. I have designed this book from the ground up, based on what has worked and proven useful to advanced undergraduate, master of management and executive management students I have taught over the past twelve years in the US and in Europe. Thus, the topics this book covers, its writing style, and the examples, mini-cases, and full-length cases I use, are all carefully chosen to be both *relevant* and *engaging* to an audience of students who may or may not plan to become information systems specialists.

I have found in my interactions with executives of large and small firms that both general and functional managers in modern businesses need to be able to do two things when it comes to information systems decisions:

1. Evaluate the plethora of modern information technology and trends—from a strategic, not a technical standpoint—in order to be able to identify and use the technology/technologies that will generate value for the organization.

2. Become effective partners of the information systems function. To this end they need to be familiar with those areas where they will have to come in contact with information systems professionals.

The main foci of this book are therefore the strategic role of information systems in the modern firm and the design and implementation of IT-dependent strategic initiatives. Over the years I have come to believe that Masters and Executive MBA students, as well as undergraduates who concentrate in information systems, need less of a "breadth book" that offers an overview knowledge of technology and technology issues, and much more of an "analytics tools-focused" book that offers them frameworks and tangible guidance on how to ensure that their firms benefit from information systems and technology efforts. I designed and wrote this book to provide such a toolkit for them.

Thus, this is not a text *about IT* and *how IT works*. This is a book about the information system and information technology resource and how these should be optimally deployed to achieve an organization's objectives. In other words, this book treats IT like any other organizational resource: An asset that general and functional managers alike need to understand enough to be able to plan for, select, deploy, and effectively manage with a keen eye to its strategic potential so as to be able to create and appropriate value for their organizations.

HOW THIS BOOK IS ORGANIZED

The book follows a progression designed to engage skeptical students while creating a sound long-term basis for decision making. I have been particularly sensitive to the audience with both the expository approach and content selection. The book uses a more colloquial and engaging writing style than traditional textbooks, with many examples and quotes centering on decision-making by both general and functional managers. My students, as well as many of my colleagues' students, have told us that this book has the colloquial style of a consulting report rather than the dry writing style of a textbook. This is important feedback for me as it confirms my hunch that once the "dry reading" obstacle is removed, students can see what the course is really all about: A critical subject matter for modern managers, delivering a set of tangible and practical skills that will help them be an asset for their organization. The opening mini-cases, written from the perspective of functional or general managers, reinforce this approach by clearly showing the relevance of the chapter's content while helping to foster discussion and generate momentum at the start of class.

The book's content is organized into four sections; four stepping stones that build upon one another in a sequential manner. Part I covers essential definitions and provides the conceptual foundation for the following chapters. Part II describes how new technologies have changed, and continue to change, the competitive landscape and social environment thus creating both opportunities and new threats for established firms and start-ups. Part III carries the defining content of this book, offering actionable frameworks to help managers envision how to develop value-adding IT-dependent strategic initiatives and to gauge whether they can be protected so as to reap benefits in the long term. Part IV concludes the text by focusing on how to create and implement information systems at the core of any initiative. It also discusses common systems and major trends as well as security, privacy and ethical considerations.

Finally, the book provides a number of full-length end-of-chapter cases, written by myself and colleagues, that were expressly designed to use the frameworks and debate the issues covered in the chapter. This tight parallel between content and cases has worked very well in my classes because students immediately see the applicability of the theories and concepts covered.

SUPPORTING RESOURCES

For this book, I have developed an extensive set of support resources, all available on the instructor's companion website (http://www.wiley.com/college/piccoli). They consist of the standard set of materials including PowerPoint presentations for each chapter and a test bank (to supplement the study questions at the end of each chapter). An instructor's manual containing teaching notes for each of the opening mini-cases, along with tips and suggestions on how to use them to jump-start class with a high-energy discussion, is also available. Each of the full-length cases has a complete teaching note with the analysis of the case, a teaching plan and a set of PowerPoint slides for case discussion debrief.

ACKNOWLEDGEMENTS

While mine is the only name on the cover of this book, and while I take responsibility for any errors or inaccuracies, a book like this one is really a joint effort. The ideas and concepts, teaching philosophy, pedagogical approaches, tools and techniques covered came about through observation of, and discussion with, the many colleagues I have had the good fortune of interacting with over the years. Amongst the most influential, I want to acknowledge Blake Ives, Roy Alvarez, Erica Wagner, Dick Moore, Kathryn Brohman, Rick Watson, and Mark Talbert. Each of them has helped me shape the courses I have taught, and ultimately, the content of this book.

I would also like to acknowledge the contribution of the many students over the last twelve years who have brought a positive attitude and an open mind to the Information Systems Management course; those who have challenged my own understanding of the concepts in this book, as well those who pushed me to find better ways to introduce and discuss them. I would also like to acknowledge the many companies, their management and employees, who recognize that we can't have relevant education without their full engagement and support. These people have kindly volunteered their time to discuss many of the ideas explored in this book with me. Many have also agreed to allow their companies' examples and experiences to serve as case studies, and welcomed my colleagues and me to share their knowledge.

I want to acknowledge the help of Deborah Bauder and Jeff Shampnois, who were invaluable assets in the research and editing phases of this project. Deb and Jeff sheltered me from many of the most time consuming and tedious elements of this endeavor with professionalism and energy. I would also like to thank the colleagues who took time from their busy schedules to review the first and second editions of the manuscript and to offer valuable and constructive feedback. From the first edition:

Louis Beaubien, Providence College

Ed Christensen, Monmouth University

John Kohlmeier, DePaul University

Blake Ives, University of Houston

Roberto Mejias, Indiana University

Graham Peace, West Virginia University

Cynthia Ruppel, University of Alabama, Huntsville

Paul Licker, Oakland University

Richard McCarthy, Quinnipiac University

Paul Pavlou, University of California, Riverside

John Scigliano, Nova Southeastern University

Michael Wade, York University

Erica Wagner, Portland State University

Ted Williams, University of Michigan, Flint

From the current edition:

Patrick Becka, Webster University, Louisville

Leida Chen, Creighton University

J. Michael Cummins, Georgia Tech

FJ DeMicco, University of Deleware

David Dischiave, Syracuse University

Rassule Hadidi, University of Illinois, Springfield

Raymond Henry, Cleveland State University

Jeff Howells, University of Georgia

Shin-jeng Lin, Le Moyne College

Rodger Morrison, Troy University

Barbara Ozog, Benedictine University

Jeffrey Pullen, University of Maryland

Malu Roldan, San Jose State University

Last, but certainly not least, I would like to acknowledge the staff at John Wiley & Sons. Without them this book would have never become a reality. Beth Lang Golub, who originally saw the opportunity for this book to be written and was instrumental in its development; Elizabeth Mills, who saw the lengthy writing process through and was an indispensable source of suggestions and guidance; Annabelle Ang-Bok, who managed the production process and ensured that the manuscript took on its final printed form in time; Lisa Gee who found new, interesting and high-quality images for the book. Thank you also to Patty Donovan for composing the original book layout, to Chris Ruel for his marketing guidance and to all others involved in the production and marketing of the book at Wiley.

FOREWORD

There tend to be two major approaches to teaching information systems. The technology perspective instructs students about hardware and software, and the focus is very much on information technology. The transformative approach assists students to identify how information systems can transform an enterprise's relationships with its key stakeholders, such as customers and suppliers. Under the transformative approach, the emphasis is on the information systems an enterprise can create and the value they can then unleash. Anyone can buy information technology, but it takes skill, vision, and persistence to create a transformative information system that can radically change an enterprise and even a society.

Gabe is a key member of the transformational school of Information Systems. His academic research and work with practitioners, the results of which are incorporated in this book, are directed at understanding and exploiting the transformative power of information systems. He has studied many examples of transformation, as you will find when you read some of the insightful cases in this book and the highly useful frameworks he presents. As you read this book, you will discover why information systems have been the major change engine for many enterprises and economies over the last five decades. Nothing else has had anywhere near the same influence on the way we live today.

As you develop your managerial skills, it is important that you realize that to become an organizational leader, you will need to demonstrate that you can design, lead, and execute transformational projects. Most of the morphing assignments you take on will require an intimate understanding of technology in organizations. Irrespective of which particular field is your area of concentration, you will find that at some point you will need to become deeply steeped in understanding how you can exploit one or more information technologies to create a new information system to generate a competitive advantage or superior customer experience. How well you integrate people, procedures, and information technology to create an information system will determine your success. This book is about developing your skills to successfully participate in, and possibly lead, an information systems-enabled project to create new opportunities for customer service and organizational growth. Read the book carefully, reflect on the frameworks and cases, incorporate the key insights into your model of the world, and above all, apply the knowledge gained to improve your organization's performance.

Richard T. Watson
Rex Fuqua Distinguished Chair for Internet Strategy
University of Georgia
Athens, GA, USA

As we all know, the required master level Information Systems course is a very difficult one to teach. I always admire the few faculty teaching this course who can transcend the reluctance, prejudice and general disinterest too many of us confront from our students. Gabe is one of the talented few. He has enjoyed significant success teaching the required Information Systems course over the years, receiving teaching awards for his work with both Masters and Executive MBA students. In my foreword to the first edition I had said: "Hopefully, this book will arm the rest of us with some of Gabe's teaching magic." Now that we are in the second edition I can report that I have talked to a number of colleagues who teach the required MBA, Executive MBA and upperclassmen in undergraduate courses who have confirmed that this book has worked quite well for them.

I can now be confident in saying that this book will be a great addition to your arsenal, allowing you to leverage the enthusiasm of students already interested in the material, while energizing those who come in the door with a negative bias toward an "IT course." This book can make your course more compelling to your students thanks to Gabe's very approachable writing style, the wealth of examples he uses, the opening mini-cases that quickly create excitement and buzz, and the many unique full-length cases (several of which we wrote together). Most helpfully, Gabe has identified both the foundation and leading edge content that is most relevant to Management students. With this book you will find it much easier to demonstrate the relevance of Information Systems to your students and to create a positive learning environment in your classes.

Blake Ives, Ph.D.
C. T. Bauer Chair in Business Leadership
C. T. Bauer College of Business
University of Houston

CONTENTS

Foundations

In Part I, we lay the foundations for the study of information systems. Although the press and commentators devote much attention to information technology (IT) and the (often substantial) IT investments that organizations make, modern general and functional managers don't have the time, or often the inclination, to become IT experts. After all, that's why organizations hire and pay information systems and IT professionals.

Yet with information technologies becoming increasingly present in both business and society at large, modern general and functional managers can no longer abdicate their obligation to make decisions about this crucial organizational resource. The good news is that you can be an effective manager without knowing a huge amount about IT, without knowing in detail how the technology works, and without having to keep up with the barrage of new technologies that are constantly being commercialized. To be an effective general or functional manager, a proficient user of the IT resource, and a productive partner of the firm's information systems and technology professionals, you need a strong grounding in the fundamentals of information systems (IS) management and decision making.

As we describe in Chapter 2, information systems are sociotechnical organizational systems that encompass technology, the people who will be using such technology, and the business processes they execute to accomplish their daily tasks and carry out business activities. User managers can rely on IT professionals when it comes to choosing among programming languages or the appropriate structure of a new database being implemented, but general and functional managers must be able to design the appropriate information systems for their organization, plan and budget for the use of IT resources, and analyze whether or not a given information system creates a competitive advantage that can be protected.

This is not a book about IT and how it works. This is a book about information systems and the IS decisions that general and functional managers are routinely called on to make. In Part I we lay the foundations upon which you will build your information systems knowledge. Specifically,

- *Chapter 1: Introduction.* The first chapter defines some basic terms and makes the case for why general and functional managers must be intimately involved in information systems decision making.

- *Chapter 2: Information Systems Defined.* The second chapter defines what an information system is (the central concept in this book), places this definition in the organizational context, and draws the crucial distinctions between IT and IS.

- *Chapter 3: Organizational Information Systems and Their Impact.* The third chapter categorizes the different information systems found in modern organizations and provides the vocabulary you need in order to communicate with other managers and the information systems professionals in your firm. This chapter also provides you with a foundation to consider the impact of various information technologies on the organization.

Information Systems and the Role of General and Functional Managers

What You Will Learn in This Chapter

This chapter focuses on the role that general and functional managers play in the organizational use and management of information systems. The chapter also describes the meteoric rise to prominence of information technologies and the role advanced IT plays in the modern organization.

In this chapter you will learn:

1. To define the terms general manager, functional manager, and end user. You will also learn to articulate the difference between these concepts.

2. To define the role of the modern chief information officer (CIO).

3. To identify organizational and information technology trends that have led to the current popularity of IT-based information systems.

4. To identify why it is important for general and functional managers to be involved in information systems decisions.

5. To identify, and avoid, the risks that arise when general and functional managers decide to abdicate their right (and duty) to make important information systems decisions.

MINI-CASE: FACING TERMINATION?

The silence was beginning to become uncomfortable as you searched for words to answer the question from your chief executive officer (CEO). The boardroom had never looked so big, and it seemed her words were still echoing: "How could it get to this? You sat here telling us how this new software program would dramatically improve our marketing efficiencies and customers' repurchase frequency. It has been over two months, and the bloody thing isn't even working!"

As you searched for the right way to respond, the events leading up to this moment flashed through your mind. It was over two months ago when you sold the board on the benefits of a new salesforce automation tool. You had just been promoted to vice president of marketing, taking over from Tom Vecchio. Tom was an old-fashioned salesperson, with a huge personality and an incredible memory. He was employee number four when the company launched, back in 1982, and had been instrumental in its early growth via personal networking—phone calls, rounds of golf, and birthday calls. He had surrounded himself with very similar people. You understood that culture, you had been one of the young guns a few years ago, and now you had replaced the master.

But things had changed in your industry, competition was much tougher, and markets were now global. "How could a firm the size of this one run sales and marketing without any IT support?" you wondered once promoted. How ironic that you'd be the one to usher in the "new IT-enabled world." You had managed never to concern yourself with all that techie computer stuff. You were a pretty good user: e-mail, Web, some Excel... the usual. But now your bonus depended on the performance of the whole function, not just the number of contracts you closed, and it seemed you had been getting all the heat about efficiencies that they could not put on Tom... they could scream all they wanted, he was untouchable. But you weren't!

It all seemed to have fallen into place when you went to the National Convention of the Sales Executives Association. At one of the booths you had seen VelcroSoft and the salesforce automation product VelcroSFA. There was a lot of buzz around their product both at the conference and in the press. The attendant at the booth told you about all of the great features of VelcroSFA: automated recording of information at each stage in the sales process, automated escalation and approval, contact management, lead sharing for team selling, and in-depth reporting. It could even integrate with human resource systems for immediate computation of commissions, reduced data entry, and increased speed.

After you returned to the office, you read some more material about VelcroSFA and called a couple of friends who had installed it in their organizations. It seemed to be the right application. You showed the brochure to some of the best-performing salespeople. They did not seem impressed, and they raised a bunch of issues. Joe, one of the old-timers, said, "The Rolodex did wonders for me throughout my career; what do I need a computer for?" Joe never liked you anyway since you had taken Tom's spot, you thought. Amanda, a younger associate, seemed more positive: "I'm willing to give it a shot, but it seems quite convoluted. I'm not sure I need all those functionalities." You recall thinking that they would change their mind once they saw their commissions go up because the software would allow them to spend more time with customers. You did not like computers after all, but you liked the software more as you found out more about it. They would, too.

Jenny Cantera, the IT director, had pledged her help with the installation and, after looking at the brochure, had said, "Should take a weekend to install this application and write the interface to the HR system. I'm busy with the implementation of the new accounting system for the next three or four weeks, but I should be able to do this afterward." You had some doubts about Jenny. She was very smart and technically gifted, but she was the very first IT director in your firm and she had little experience in the position.

The board had been sold pretty easily on the purchase, even though at $55,000 it was a sizable investment for your firm. You had used the return on investment (ROI) calculations provided by VelcroSoft. Granted, VelcroSoft personnel were very aggressive with assumptions underlying their calculations, but with a bit of effort on everyone's part you truly believed you could achieve strong results. As soon as you got the go-ahead, you contacted the vendor and obtained the installation package. Everything had gone perfectly up to that point, but your fortune seemed to turn right after.

First, you had the software installation disks sitting on your desk for over a month. Jenny was running into unexpected trouble with the accounting software. Once she finally got around to implementing your product, she took one weekend to complete the installation and created the user accounts. The interface to the HR application was not operational yet—something about a "software conflict," you did not quite understand. However, you pressed on. Over the following week, you had encouraged your sales rep to "play around with the applications." You had even sent an e-mail with the subject line "Up and running in the brave new world of Sales Force Automation!" But response had been cool at best. Only a few accounts had been accessed, and overall the people you spoke to said they were too busy and would look at the software once the quarter closed.

Last weekend, when Jenny wrote the interface to the HR systems, all hell broke loose. On Monday (yesterday) the HR database was locked and the HR system was down. Jenny was scrambling to bring it back up, and she was now saying she may have to reinstall the program. She had already uninstalled VelcroSFA, and at this point it looked like the application would not be a priority for a while. You did not really mind; you had bigger fish to fry... you were concerned about getting fired.

DISCUSSION QUESTIONS

1. Who do you think is to blame for the current state of affairs?
2. What do you think is the most critical mistake you made over the last two months? What were the principal mistakes made by others involved?
3. How could these mistakes have been avoided, if at all?
4. Should you take this opportunity to say goodbye to everyone and resign now? If not, what should you say in response to the CEO's question?

 ## INTRODUCTION

It is hard these days to escape the hype and publicity surrounding information technology (IT) and its business applications. IT has become more affordable and pervasive than ever before; just think about the wide array of technologies that you use for work and pleasure on any given day. You may own an iPad, a PlayBook, or a Galaxy Tab (Figure 1.1), most likely you own a personal computer and a Smartphone, and perhaps you even have a game console, such as the Microsoft Xbox or Nintendo Wii.

At work you are likely a heavy user of word processing and spreadsheets, as well as some more specialized applications such a customer relationship management or business intelligence software. You may even have been talented enough to create your own Android apps (Figure 1.2) or launch your own startup.

More generally, for business, not-for-profit and governmental organizations, IT has become a critical resource that draws significant investments. The recent recession put pressure on spending, but expenditures remained significant, particular in some sectors. As Gartner reported: "From a cross-industry perspective, IT spending per employee continues to fall compared with the 2008 and 2009 levels, and, at $12,350, dropped 2.9% in 2010. This decrease is not universal,

Figure 1.1 Competing tablets

Figure 1.2 The Android operating system *Source*: © Pillyphotos/Alamy

and information-intensive industries have seen an increase." (Figure 1.3).[1] As important as technology is to today's general and functional managers, don't be misled, this is not a book about IT and how it works. Nor is this a book written exclusively for IT professionals. This book is written from the standpoint of, and to serve the needs of, the modern manager.

GENERAL AND FUNCTIONAL MANAGERS

A manager is a knowledge worker of modern business and not-for-profit organizations who is in charge of a team, a functional area (i.e., functional managers), a business unit, or an entire organization (i.e., a general manager). These individuals are typically trained in management schools, and particularly in larger organizations and entrepreneurial ventures, they often hold a master's degree in management or business administration.

General and functional managers have, through schooling and on-the-job experience, developed strengths in a business area such as operations, marketing, finance, human resources, accounting, and the like. Those of you who plan on a career in business consulting will develop a similar set of functional expertise. However, with the unrelenting pace of IT innovation and its widespread adoption in organizations, the personal success of managers and of their area of responsibility increasingly depend on making optimal decisions about the use and management of information. Information is a critical organizational resource. As Thomas Watson, Jr., the legendary chairman of IBM, recognized 50 years ago, "All the value of this company is in its people. If you burned down all our plants, and we just kept our people and our information files, we should soon be as strong as ever."[2]

To manage information effectively, the modern firm must adopt and use information systems and information technology resources. Selecting, designing, and managing these resources

---

[1]IT spending and staffing report, Gartner Inc. (2011)

[2]Quinn, S. B. (1992). *Intelligence Enterprise: A Knowledge and Service Based Paradigm for Industry.* New York, NY: Free Press, p. 244.

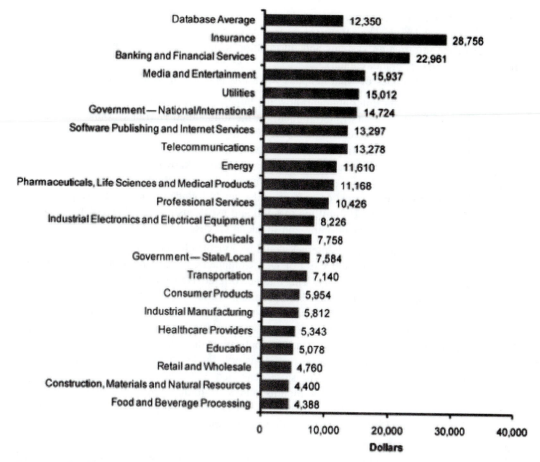

Figure 1.3 IT spending per employee by industry *(Source:* Gartner ITKMD, 2011.)

is no longer exclusively the job of the technology professional, but is now the shared responsibility of all modern general and functional managers. Bill Gates neatly captured this point when he stated: "Information technology and business are becoming inextricably interwoven. I don't think anybody can talk meaningfully about one without the talking about the other." As a consequence, general and functional managers must work in partnership with information systems and technology professionals—those individuals with substantial technical training and education in management information systems, computer science, and engineering—when it comes to carrying out these decisions. Partnership is the key word here; it is no longer acceptable for general and functional managers to claim ignorance of IT and delegate all IT decisions to technologists. As Douglas Merrill put it when he was serving as the CIO of Google, Inc.: "The distinction between technology and the business is antediluvian—it's gone." The notion that the IT function needs to cater to its internal customer—"the business" (as if the IT function was not part of "the business"!)—no longer represents reality. So many managerial and organizational decisions depend heavily on information systems to be successfully implemented, and new information technology constantly opens up new possibilities for innovation in strategy, products, processes, and organizational design. The success of an organization in today's environment depends on the interplay of the information systems and information technology with the other organizational resources (e.g., labor, brand, capital).

Let's look at examples of what happens when this partnership works well:

- Consider Caesars Entertainment, now the largest casino resort operator in the world. In the mid-1990s, Caesars Entertainment (at the time called Harrah's) found itself unable to compete with new resorts that were wowing gamblers with elaborate buildings and attractions (e.g., the Mirage, Treasure Island, the Bellagio). At that time Harrah's chairman and CEO, Philip Sartre, sensed that customer knowledge and customer loyalty could become the firm's core competency and differentiation driver. Working with its IT department, an external consultant, and a newly founded group of decision scientists, Harrah's spent over $100 million to build and use a business intelligence infrastructure that enabled its new positioning and financial success.

- As it became clear that the Internet would be a viable channel for economic transactions, Michael Dell, founder and CEO of Dell Computers, Inc., challenged his team to take advantage of the opportunity. The Internet offered Dell the chance to sell directly to the consumer (not just to business accounts), without having to compromise its direct model. In charge of the efforts was thirty-year-old Scott Eckert, a recent MBA graduate. Working closely with the information systems and technology group, Eckert developed Dell Online, the online store, and an application that allowed customers to configure their machine. As they say, the rest is history. Fueled by the staggering growth rates of the Internet itself, the online store generated $1 million in revenue per day in six months, $2 million/day in nine months, and $3 million/day in a little over a year since opening for business. Dell Computers is now one of the largest computer makers in the world, and the Dell Online initiative was instrumental in helping the firm achieve this result.

- The Hotel Lugano Dante is a four star hotel in Lugano, Switzerland that is part of a small two-property chain. While the Lugano Dante is a nice hotel, there is nothing intrinsically unique about it in terms of location, facilities, or any other structural characteristic. In the "age of the Internet," where competition is "only a click away," Carlo Fontana, the General Manager of the Hotel Lugano Dante, feared that his property could quickly become a commodity—an undifferentiated good that would be dragged into one price war after another. Believing in the power of differentiation through service, Fontana set out to enable his staff to create superior and highly personalized experiences for guests by providing attention to detail and the unique needs of individual customers—far superior to the standard four-star service. Working closely with Davide Bernasconi, the director of IT, Fontana conceptualized and built a comprehensive system that provides accurate, real-time operational and guest data, and disseminates it to each guest-facing employee. Staff members have personal iPads that allow them to produce and receive the necessary information to provide outstanding service. After a year of operation the system has contributed to make the Lugano Dante the number one hotel in its market based on customer reviews on TripAdvisor, with a 99% approval rate by customers that help both differentiate the hotel and ensure above average loyalty.

The preceding examples highlight a few critical lessons for prospective general and functional managers:

- The general and functional managers in the examples, while not IT experts, were making educated decisions about the deployment of information systems in their organizations.

- The objective of IT deployment was business driven. In other words, the new technology was brought in to serve the growing or changing needs of the organization. The people who perceived and understood the need for this new way of doing things were the general and functional managers.

- These general and functional managers were not IT professionals and had no specific training in technology, but they worked in close partnership with the IT professionals in their organizations to ensure the successful deployment of the needed information systems and technology functionalities.

- The general and functional managers did not use the new technologies firsthand once introduced. Rather, other employees, the end users, had direct contact with the hardware and software programs that had been introduced.

The last of the preceding points is important, as there is a clear difference between general and functional managers and the role of end users.

GENERAL AND FUNCTIONAL MANAGERS VERSUS END USERS

End users are those individuals who have direct contact with software applications as they use them to carry out specific tasks. For example, I am an end user as I use word processing software (i.e., Microsoft Word™) to write this book. You, as a student, are an end user as you engage in spreadsheet analyses using Microsoft Excel™ in your statistics, operations, or finance courses.

Most general and functional managers in modern organizations are also end users. They use software programs to improve their own personal productivity—from the very basic, such as e-mail and calendars, to the most advanced, such as mobile management dashboards designed to keep a real-time pulse of the business' performance (Figure 1.4). Although being a sophisticated end user is an important asset for the modern manager, because effective use of software programs can lead to increased productivity, it is far more important for you to have the skills and knowledge to make appropriate information systems decisions at the organizational level.

It should now be clear why this book is not an IT training book and its focus is not on end-user skills. This book is expressly designed for current and future managers, for those individuals who have general management and/or functional management responsibility, and for those who serve, or will one day serve, on the board of directors of an organization. The promise of this book is that to be an effective manager you need not know an inordinate amount of information about IT, or how technology works, even though some of this IT-specific knowledge undoubtedly helps.

Rather, what you really need to have and feel confident with is knowledge of information systems and the role that IT plays in them (see Chapter 2 for definitions). You need to know how to identify opportunities to use information technology to your firm's advantage; how to

Figure 1.4 The Roambi Mobile Dashboard for the iPad and iPhone (Courtesy of Roambi.)

plan for the use of information systems resources; and how to manage the design, development, selection, and implementation of information systems. These are the skills that separate effective modern managers—those who can be productive partners of the information systems function—from ineffective ones—those who delegate critical IT decision making and, more often than not, live to suffer the negative consequences of their decisions. In the words of Rob Solomon, Senior Vice President of Sales and Marketing for Outrigger Hotels and Resorts, "Every manager must have an IT strategy. You can't delegate to technologists and only worry about your allocated cost or what training your employees need. You must understand how to be master of your own destiny and make IT work best for you. Too many managers still don't get that."

THE NEXT WAVE OF CIOs

Another interesting trend that makes this book relevant to management school students is the increasing permeability of the boundaries of the IT function. That is, the chief information officer (CIO) position is increasingly seen not as the endpoint of a career but as a stepping stone to the chief executive officer (CEO) or president posts. The old joke: "CIO stands for Career Is Over"[3] no longer rings true. Examples of CIOs being promoted to the role of CEO or to other executive level positions now abound. For example, David Bernauer, former CIO at the pharmacy chain Walgreens, was promoted to chief operating officer (COO) after four years in the top IT post, and later to CEO and chairman of the board. Maynard Webb, CIO at Gateway Computers, was hired as COO by online auction giant eBay. Kevin Turner, former CIO of Walmart, became CEO at Sam's Club and later COO at Microsoft Corporation. Dawn Lepore, former CIO of the Charles Schwab company, took the CEO position at Drugstore.com in 2004. Philip Clarke made the jump from the head of IT to CEO of Tesco in 2011.

---

[3] There is even a forum for technology leaders jokingly titled *career is over*!

Two primary reasons are fueling this trend:

■ The increasing prevalence of IT and the consequent need for those who serve on the executive teams and the board of directors to have some understanding of how to use this crucial resource. In the words of a British headhunter, "CIOs are the only ones with a helicopter view of the business and they have a great deal of operational experience of the business."[4]

■ The fact that the prevalence of IT and information systems throughout the organization gives CIOs a broad view of operations, business processes, inter-organizational coordination challenges and opportunities, and a broad understanding of how the firm is positioned to execute its strategy. As Tom Murphy, former CIO of Royal Caribbean Cruise Lines and current CIO of pharmaceutical supply chain services provider Amerisource-Bergen, put it, "Information technology is everywhere; we touch almost every process in the firm. We must intimately understand operations to enable them; from my CIO post I have a complete view of the organization and its operations."

On the flip side, forward-looking firms no longer view the IT function as the province of technologists who speak a foreign language that nobody else understands. Individuals with strong technical skills still represent irreplaceable assets, of course, but the information systems function is increasingly staffed with employees with business or humanities training who share an excitement for the potential of technology to solve business problems, and who are relatively well versed in information systems issues and vocabulary. For example, Douglas Merrill, former Google CIO, majored in psychology, while Tom Murphy, who held the CIO post at Royal Caribbean Cruise Lines and AmerisourceBergen has an English Literature degree! The modern IT function increasingly finds in its ranks business analysts, system analysts, project management specialists, and even CIOs that don't have an engineering or computer science background, and yet complement software designers and developers, IT architects, and other professionals with more technical profiles.

Modern CIOs are required to exhibit many of the skills of their executive counterparts while maintaining priorities that are focused on keeping the lights on and IT operations running. They need to be well versed in business while not losing sight of the delivery of information services that enable the organization to operate effectively (Table 1.1).

Consider this as you begin this course: As much as you might not think you will ever be an integral part of the IT group, the truth is that you may soon find yourself becoming involved in information systems selection, development or implementation projects. This is a very common occurrence, as younger members of the workforce often are (or are assumed to be!) tech savvy and comfortable with information technology. It is therefore natural for your more senior colleagues to think of you as the right person to represent your organizational function on the design and implementation of new information systems. Participating in such projects is an opportunity to showcase your talent... and perhaps to discover that a career in information systems is for you. Whether you are trying to position yourself for this career path or just looking to be a successful general or functional manager, this book is written for you.

---

[4]http://www.silicon.com/cxoextra/0,3800005416,39155417,00.htm

Table 1.1   Top 10 Business and Technology Priorities in 2010 according to Gartner Research

Top 10 Business Priorities	Top 10 Technology Priorities
Business process improvement	Virtualization
Reducing enterprise costs	Cloud computing
Increasing the use of information/analytics	Web 2.0
Improving enterprise workforce effectiveness	Networking, voice, and data communications
Attracting and retaining new customers	Business Intelligence
Managing change initiatives	Mobile technologies
Creating new products or services (innovation)	Data/document management and storage
Targeting customers and markets more effectively	Service-oriented applications and architecture
Consolidating business operations	Security technologies
Expanding current customer relationships	IT management

Source: Adapted from Gartner EXP (January 2010)

FUNDAMENTAL IT TRENDS: THE STAYING POWER OF MOORE'S LAW

Information systems (IS)—those organizational systems that enable the processing and management of an institution's information—are the backbone of organizational operations. These information systems are powered by more or less advanced information technologies (IT) at their core in all but the smallest of firms. Understanding the drivers and the trends that shape the evolution of IT is important for you as a general or functional manager because new technologies constantly enable new strategies, new initiatives, and the effective management and use of greater and greater amounts of data and information.

The popularity and growing importance of IT-based information systems is self-evident in the 21st century. For those in need of further convincing, we need to only show statistics that capture the breathtaking rates at which IT has become, and continues to grow into, a critical tool for modern organizations, consumers and individuals alike. For example, in 2011 the number of people with access to the Internet was estimated to exceed the 2 billion mark—over a quarter of the world's actual population.

Another source of evidence is the precision that has characterized Moore's law over the forty years since its announcement by Dr. Gordon Moore. In 1965, Dr. Moore, who three years later cofounded Intel Corp., commented at a conference that if the current rate of improvement in the production process of transistor-based microprocessors continued, the number of transistors that could be etched on an integrated circuit (i.e., a microchip) would double every one to two years. What is remarkable about Moore's law is not so much how Dr. Moore arrived at it, but rather how precisely it has held true over the last 40 years (Figure 1.5), and the fact that it is expected to continue to hold true for a decade or two more.

The unrelenting pace of performance improvement in microchip design and production processes has a number of important managerial implications, which we discuss in detail below. At a more general level, it is this unflagging progress that enables continued innovation and the reinvention of processes, strategies, products, and services. It is critical to recognize, however,

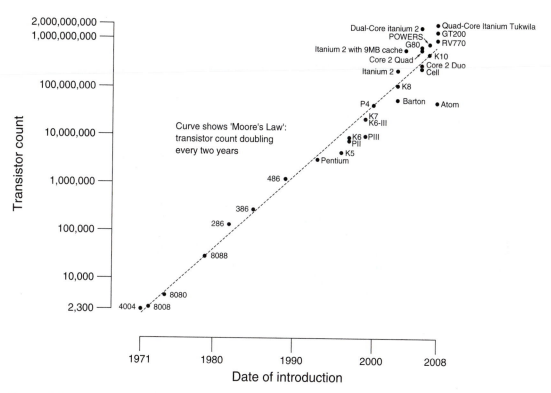

Figure 1.5   Number of transistors in different generations of commercial microprocessors (Created by Wgsimon at the English Wikipedia Project.)

that the responsibility for taking advantage of this continuous technological progress in modern organizations falls squarely on the shoulders of general and functional managers.

PROCESSING POWER AND MEMORY INCREASE

As stated by Moore's Law, the processing power of microprocessors has experienced exponential growth. Because a transistor is the basic unit of computational ability of a microprocessor, more transistors equates to more computational power in any device that uses a microchip—your personal computer, of course, but also your music player, your cellular phone, your digital camera, your car, even your microwave, and your refrigerator. Not only has the programmable computational capacity available to us increased exponentially over the last two decades, but it also has proliferated to a multitude of devices, from game consoles to mobile devices (Figure 1.6).

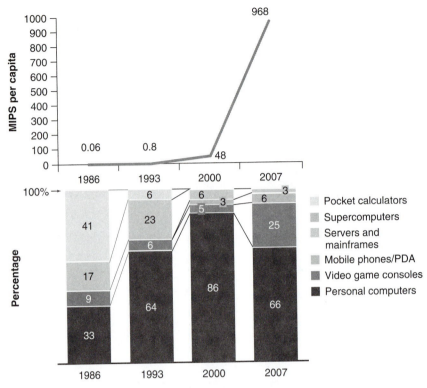

Figure 1.6 Estimated worldwide general-purpose computational capacity (MIPS per capita)[5]

Storage capacity of memory chips has also increased exponentially. With transistors serving as the basic component of memory chips as well, a higher density of transistors makes for increased memory capacity and performance, thus providing the necessary complement to increasing computational ability of microprocessors. A similar pattern of evolution has occurred with respect to secondary storage capacity (i.e., hard disks, tapes), which has grown exponentially shifting decisively to the digital format (Figure 1.7).

COSTS OF COMPUTING POWER DECLINE

The cost of computing power and storage has declined at breathtaking rates as Moore's law has shown its effects. By some estimates, all the power of a mainframe that cost over $10 million in 1965 had been incorporated in a $7 chip by 2002. The cost of that same chip was projected

---

[5] Adapted from McKinsey Report (2011). "Big Data: The next frontier for innovation, competition, and productivity." Estimations and data from Hilbert M. and Lopez P. (2011). "The world's technological capacity to store, communicate and compute information," *Science*.

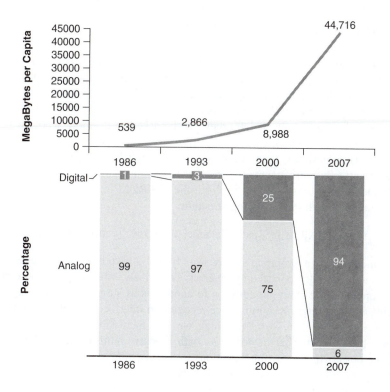

Figure 1.7 Estimated worldwide storage capacity per capita in MB[6]

to drop to about 1 cent in 2017.[7] It is this amazing combination of power and affordability that has led to the spreading of "intelligence"—here defined as computational ability—in products ranging from the more advanced (e.g., smart cameras that can recognize human faces) to the more mundane (e.g., a hotel minibar that can recognize when items are consumed).

While the number of transistors on microchips has steadily increased, chip manufacturers have been able to contain energy requirements through innovative designs. This trend, coupled with continued improvements in battery technology, has enabled the development of countless new portable devices based on the digital computer architecture. Familiar examples are iPods and other mp3 players, Blackberrys and other smartphones, palm-top computers, and ultraportable readers and tablets. In parallel we have seen the computerization of products that exhibited little or no intelligence before, such as cars, appliances, and the transformation of plastic cards and labels into smart cards and radio frequency ID (RFID) tags. This trend, sometimes labeled pervasive computing or the Internet of things, is poised to spur significant innovation in the years to come (see Chapter 12).

---

[6] Adapted from McKinsey Report (2011). "Big Data: The next frontier for innovation, competition, and productivity." Estimations and data from Hilbert M. and Lopez P. (2011). "The world's technological capacity to store, communicate and compute information," *Science*.

[7] McFarlan, F. Warren. *The New Strategic Weapon: Information Technology.* Faculty Seminar Series. Boston: Harvard Business School Publishing, 2003. Cd-rom.

COMPUTERS HAVE BECOME EASIER TO USE

One remarkable characteristic of the evolution of IT is that as computers become more powerful and more internally complex, they become easier to use. This is an interesting side effect of Moore's law and one of the most intriguing characteristics of information technology. Because software is extremely malleable, as computers become more powerful and are able to process more and more operations in a unit of time, they can be asked to do more work on behalf of and for the user. If you had the (sometimes painful) experience of using computers before the arrival of graphical user interfaces, then you know how difficult it can be to have to memorize a command—with perfectly correct syntax!—in order to have the computer perform a task. For example, in MS-DOS, in order to copy a file from the CD-ROM to the hard disk, you would have to issue a command with the following structure:

$$\text{COPY}[/Y| - Y][/A][/B][d:][path]filename[/A][/B][c:][path][filename][/V]$$

Failing to remember the appropriate syntax would yield a cryptic error message and, typically, little hint as to how to go about fixing the error. Conversely, when using modern graphical user interfaces, copying a file from one location to another is as simple as identifying the right icon and dragging it to the target location. Voice recognition interfaces are also becoming more common, and we can envision a world in which we will increasingly issue commands to a computer by simply telling it what to do or, as with modern multi-touch interfaces, we will simply manipulate objects to convey our intentions to the machine.

The simplicity of user interfaces is just one example of how IT, as it becomes more sophisticated and complex, becomes easier to use. Another example is offered by the many software-enhanced objects we come into contact with on a regular basis. Modern cars are quite difficult to service and quite powerful in terms of the number of software instructions that their controllers and control units can process. However, while all this software and hardware makes the car more internally complex, modern automobiles are easier and safer than ever to drive, with features like night vision systems, rear view cameras, automatic brakes that activate if you get too close to the vehicle in front of you, and alert systems that can detect if you fall asleep at the wheel.

As more powerful computers can process more and more sophisticated software code, they are able to interact with humans in ways that are closer and closer to our natural behavior—such as the interpretation of visual cues and the use of vocal commands—and support us in unprecedented ways in an incredibly varied array of tasks. It is not a coincidence that senior citizens represent a sizable, and growing, portion of the online population. Note that these are individuals, age 65 and older, who often claim to be unable to program a VCR. Yet they are connected to the Internet, e-mailing and chatting with their grandkids, sharing pictures, and organizing trips and cruises. Why? Because modern computing devices offer things they want (e.g., keeping in touch with family), are affordable, and shelter them from much of the complexity of the machine's inner workings.

OTHER IT TRENDS OF MANAGERIAL INTEREST

Beyond the lasting effects of Moore's law, there are other IT trends that are critical for general and functional managers to recognize.

Declining Storage Costs

The cost of computer storage has plummeted at ever increasing speeds. It took 35 years from the shipping of the first hard disk by IBM to the introduction of the 1 GigaByte (GB) hard disk. It took 14 years from there to reach 500 GB and only two more (in 2007) for the 1 TeraByte (TB) hard disk to be introduced by Hitachi. By some estimates, one GB of storage cost over 600 USD in 1993, about 5 USD in 2003, 39 cents in 2007, and is projected to cost 2 cents in 2015. While the exact numbers are of secondary relevance, as a manager you should realize that this trend has enabled the emergence of a whole host of strategic initiatives predicated on the collection and analysis of significant amounts of data. Consider the example of Bing, the search engine by Microsoft that has the ability to make suggestions about *future* airline prices. While many sites can tell you what the lowest fare is today for a Paris to New York flight, only Bing (using technology obtained when they acquired a startup called Farecast) can tell you whether you should purchase today or wait for fares to decrease. How do they do it? They use a proprietary forecasting model based on the analysis of years of multiple daily searches for air tickets and hotel reservations to identify patterns of fare and hotel room rate changes. Cheap storage is a critical enabler for the Bing service.

Ubiquitous Network Access

Ubiquitous networks are now a reality. In the early 1990s, the Internet, and its most visible services such as the World Wide Web and electronic mail, took the world by storm. "The Internet changes everything" was the rally cry that spurred the emergence of new business models and sent billions of dollars through the hands of venture capitalists and into those of high-tech entrepreneurs all over the world.

The dot-com era, as it is sometimes called, has now come and gone. What remains is the Internet: a global network of networks relying on distributed ownership and openly available standards and communication protocols. Access to the Internet is increasingly pervasive, with wireless and cellular network access having eliminated the final obstacle to "always on" connections. We can already imagine a world in which we won't wonder whether we'll have access to a high-speed Internet connection when we travel, we will assume so—just like we do today with access to electricity in many parts of the world.

Network access is not only becoming ubiquitous, but the costs of data transmission are becoming negligible. The convergence of these trends is spurring an amazing array of initiatives. Consider the recent trend to enable cell phones to receive a text message when your bus is approaching your stop (no more waiting in the cold!) or to enable payments for small purchases at vending machines via cell phones (no more being thirsty due to lack of correct change!). Some startups, along with innovative established players, are positioning themselves to capitalize on ubiquitous network access. Foursquare, the location-based social networking application, is an apt example as it is predicated on users having constant data connectivity through their portable devices (Figure 1.8).

Ubiquitous Computing and Digital Data Genesis

As IT costs and storage costs have plummeted, and as global data networks have become widely available, more and more devices are now intelligent (i.e., able to store and process data) and connected (i.e., able to communicate with other devices). The smart home is now a reality, with smart refrigerators that can tell you what they have in store, alert you when food is going bad,

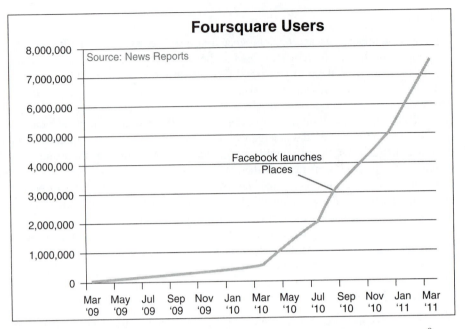

Figure 1.8 Foursquare users growth, based on data from businessinsider.com[8]

suggest recipes that use ingredients you have on hand, and even order food (Figure 1.9); smart heating systems that you can control over the Internet from your office; and bathtubs that will allow you to start running a bath before you get home. For the aging population, the availability of cost-effective sensors enables people to remain independent, in their homes, longer than ever before.

Modern automobiles often pack as much computing power as your personal computer, and, through satellite networks and telemetry technology, some can self-diagnose and e-mail you alerts about preventive maintenance and potential trouble you may experience down the road (Figure 1.10). Moreover, the presence of intelligent devices enabling or monitoring events and human activity implies that data is generated by those activities in digital form. This digital data genesis dramatically reduces the barriers to data collection and analysis. While there are serious implications to be considered, for example privacy, digital data genesis enables further innovation.

The trends discussed in this chapter, summarized in Figure 1.11, have had a few direct and indirect effects. First, computing devices are smaller and increasingly embedded in everyday products (Figure 1.12). As a consequence, digital content and services have increased dramatically and will continue to increase over time, along with the convergence of multiple devices. Chances are you already carry a cell phone that doubles up as a planner, a digital still camera, a digital video camera, an e-mail client, a music player, a GPS, a compass, and who knows what else.

---

[8]http://www.businessinsider.com/chart-of-the-day-foursquare-users-2011-3

Figure 1.9   Smart refrigerator   *Source*: © David Becker/Getty Images, Inc.

Figure 1.10   Internet-connected, self-diagnosing cars   *Source*: © Drive Images/Age Fotostock America, Inc.

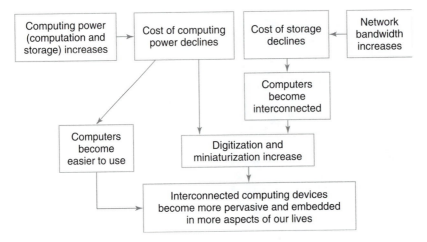

Figure 1.11   Interconnected trends

Figure 1.12   A stark example of miniaturization (Courtesy of Imgur.com.)

Second, the rapid proliferation of easy-to-use computing equipment has spurred more and more digitization—the method by which content and processes become expressed and performed in digital form. Digital data genesis is a clear example of digitization, as is this book if you are reading it on a book reader or listening to it in the form of a podcast. Finally, as computing devices become increasingly easy to use and interconnected, they become pervasive. These trends have important implications for the manager of the future.

HOW DO THESE TRENDS AFFECT TODAY'S MANAGERS?

The discussion in the previous section depicted the world in which you, as a modern general and functional manager, will operate. You will increasingly be challenged to devise strategies and implement processes that enable your organization to take advantage of these trends and better serve your increasingly IT-savvy customers.

Perhaps, though, the most important implication of the pervasiveness of computing for today's management is to be found in the sheer size of organizational investments in IT equipment, software, and services. The ever-increasing amount of money being spent on IT is largely due to one of the most interesting characteristics of software. Software is extremely malleable and can be molded into almost anything. Through the infinite combinations in which software code can be written by talented engineers and programmers, digital devices can morph into an infinite number of applications, many still left to invent! Vinton Cerf, co-inventor of the TCP/IP protocol, said in a 2007 interview: "Specifically for young people pursuing careers, software is an endless frontier. There isn't any limit to what you can do. I can confidently argue that maybe only 1% or 2% of the possible applications have already been implemented or thought of."[9] As a consequence, the number of opportunities for innovation and business success that depend on the appropriate use of IT is literally skyrocketing. If you think for a moment about the different types of software you come in contact with on a daily basis, you'll see that they support a huge variety of tasks.

For example, we use e-mail, Instant Messenger, and Voice over IP (VOIP) applications such as Skype to communicate with our friends, family, and colleagues. With these applications, IT acts as a communication device, replacing our traditional telephone or penned letters. Many of us listen to streaming radio and watch videos on our personal computers or mobile phones; we play video games and organize our pictures using Web sites such as Flickr or Picasa. With these applications, our IT behaves like an entertainment device, replacing our radio, stereo, television, and scrapbooks. We use word processing, spreadsheets, and presentation software to carry out our work. With these applications, our IT takes on the role of a productivity tool for the office, replacing typewriters, calculators, and flipcharts. Finally, and most important for you as a manager, IT can embed intelligence and decision-making capabilities previously required of employees or organizational functions. For example, modern check-in kiosks used by airlines and hotels replace the work of front-line employees; forecasting software and automatic inventory reorder software used in retail embed some of the intelligence and the decision-making ability of skilled inventory managers; and automated sprinkler systems in modern greenhouses monitor and analyze the state of the soil and decide when to turn on or off, and even what and how much fertilizer to add to the water.

---

[9]King, J. (2007). "The Grill: Google's Internet Evangelist Vint Cerf on the Hot Seat," *Computerworld*.

Beyond replacing earlier ways of doing business, new technology creates a constant stream of new possibilities. For example, it is now possible for us to get custom-made apparel by simply typing in some measurements and a few style preferences at the Lands' End Web site. Behind the scenes, far from view, software from Archetype Solutions, Inc. goes to work to create unique patterns that will be automatically fed to cutting machines that will generate your custom-made, perfect-fitting jeans.

WHY CAN'T WE JUST HIRE GOOD IT PEOPLE?

One of the most enduring results of research in information systems has been the degree of discomfort that executives exhibit when it comes to making decisions about information systems and information technology. The great number of acronyms (increasing daily, it seems), the pervasiveness of technical language, and the unique blend of skills that are required to understand computing can be very intimidating. As a consequence, we often hear executives wonder why it isn't enough to hire "good" IT professionals and let them worry about all the IT stuff.

This stance immediately raises the question: "How do you know if an IT professional is indeed good without knowing a minimum amount about what IT professionals do?" More importantly: "How can you establish a good partnership with your firm's IT group if you are not equipped to prove useful in the relationship?" Just as most general and functional managers are not trained in the design and implementation of IT the way computer scientists and engineers are, most computer scientists and engineers are not trained in marketing, management, finance, or accounting.

This diverse training leads to a great deal of communication difficulty. Because the skills and knowledge of general and functional managers are complementary to those of the information systems professionals in the organization, communication, and a good relationship are critical to the firm's success.

As a simple example, imagine being the vice president of marketing for a retail chain (e.g., Ikea) that wants to be able to measure customer spending patterns precisely and rank shoppers based on the customer life-time value[10] they contribute to the firm. Business intelligence technology and techniques (discussed in Chapter 3) will enable this strategy. However, how can your IT group build the appropriate infrastructure, track all the relevant data, perform accurate analyses, and best segment the customer base unless you and your marketing team are intimately involved in the design and development of this technology and analytical infrastructure? The IT professionals in your organizations are not as familiar as you are with the retail operations, and they are certainly not well versed in marketing segmentation and customer valuation techniques.

The only recipe for success in this case is to have a productive partnership. You contribute the marketing-specific knowledge and make decisions about the critical requirements and capabilities of the initiative and the information systems. The information systems and technology

---

[10]Customer life-time value is a metric used to estimate the value of a customer over the complete history of his or her interaction with the firm.

professionals make decisions about platforms, interfaces, programming languages, and hardware performance. Together, you ensure that organizational processes are accurately redesigned and that data models used are coherent with business operations and comprehensive.

While you clearly should not delegate information systems decisions to technologists, there is good news. You need not know an inordinate amount of IT-specific information to be a good user of the information systems and technology resource or a good partner of the IT function. The sheer size of the information technology expenditure, however, commands the attention of today's managers. This ever-increasing budget means that as you join the workforce you will find yourself making decisions that have an increasingly large IT component. Moreover, as IT becomes an increasingly important business tool, you will find that a larger and larger stake of your function's (and your personal) success rides on making good decisions when it comes to investing in and using, or not investing in and not using, information systems and IT.

 SUMMARY

This chapter laid the groundwork for this book by identifying the managerial and technology trends that make it imperative for the modern general and functional manager to get involved in decision making pertaining to information systems and information technology. In this chapter we learned that:

- General and functional managers, those individuals in organizations who have the responsibility to lead a functional area or a business, can no longer abdicate their right, and duty, to be involved in information systems and IT decisions. They should act in partnership with the firm's information systems and technology professionals.
- The information systems skill set required of the modern general and functional manager pertains to decisions about identifying opportunities to use information technologies to the firm's advantage; planning for the use of information systems resources; and managing the design, development, selection, and implementation of information

systems. While end-user skills (i.e., the ability to use computers proficiently) are an important asset for any knowledge worker, the critical skills for modern managers relate to the organizational, not personal, uses of information technology.

- Chief information officers (CIOs), the leading figures in the information systems and technology function, are increasingly being selected from the functional and managerial ranks rather than from the technology ranks.
- The enduring effects of Moore's law have led to increasingly powerful yet cheaper computing strength, declining costs of computer memory, and a dramatic improvement in the ease and breadth of use of digital devices. Moreover, increasingly available network connectivity and storage capacity, improved battery life for portable devices, and the proliferation of intelligent devices have contributed to dramatically change the business and social landscape.

 STUDY QUESTIONS

1. Define the following terms: general manager, functional manager, CIO, end user. Explain how these roles differ and the skill set each role requires.

2. Explain why it is critical to the success of modern firms that general and functional managers be directly involved in information systems and technology decision making.

3. Explain why modern firms are increasingly selecting CIOs from the managerial ranks rather than from the technology ranks.

4. Describe Moore's law and its direct and indirect effects on organizations.

FURTHER READINGS

1. Estimations and data from Hilbert M. and Lopez P. (2011). "The world's technological capacity to store, communicate and compute information," *Science*.

2. Huff, S. L., Maher, P. M., and Munro, M. C. (2006). "Information Technology and the Board of Directors: Is There an IT Attention Deficit?" *MIS Quarterly Executive* (5:2), pp. 1–14.

3. Leavitt, H. J., and Whisler, T. L. (1958). "Management in the 1980s." *Harvard Business Review*, November/December, pp. 41–48.

4. Nolan, Richard, and McFarlan, F. Warren. (2005). "Information Technology and the Board of Directors." *Harvard Business Review* 83, no. 10 (October), pp. 96–106.

5. Ross, J. W., and Weill, P. (2002). "Six IT Decisions Your IT People Shouldn't Make." *Harvard Business Review*, November, pp. 84–92.

6. Hunter R., and Westerman, G. (2009). "Real Business of IT: How CIOs Create and Communicate Value." *Harvard Business Press*.

GLOSSARY

- **Chief information officer:** The individual in charge of the information systems function.

- **Digitization:** The process by which content and processes become expressed and performed in digital form.

- **End user:** Those individuals who have direct contact with software applications as they use them to carry out specific tasks.

- **Information system:** Formal, sociotechnical, organizational system designed to collect, process, store, and distribute information.

- **Information technology:** Hardware, software, and telecommunication equipment.

- **IT professionals:** Those employees of the firm who have significant technical training and are primarily responsible for managing the firm's technology assets.

- **Manager:** A knowledge worker of modern business and not-for-profit organizations who is in charge of a team, a functional area (i.e., a functional manager), or the entire organization or a business unit (i.e., a general manager).

- **Polymediation:** The process of convergence of multiple digital devices into one.

2

Information Systems Defined

What You Will Learn in This Chapter

This is one of the most important chapters of this book because it defines the key concepts that we will use throughout. Specifically, in this chapter you will learn:

1. The definition of *information system (IS)* and *information technology (IT)*, and the difference between the two concepts.

2. The definition of *information system success* and *information system failure*.

3. The principal reasons why modern firms create and deploy information systems.

4. The influence of the firm's context and the external environment in which it is embedded on organizational information systems.

5. The four components that make up an information system and the manner in which they interact.

6. How to design successful information systems and how to troubleshoot problematic information systems implementations.

MINI-CASE: IPAD MENUS AT MCDONALD'S

As you get settled in your office for another day of work at WizConsult, the consulting firm you have recently joined, you sip your morning coffee and start your computer. Surprisingly for this early hour, your boss walks in and asks you to follow him immediately. You take one last sip of your coffee and go. Your boss is on the phone with a large McDonald's franchisee who operates 42 restaurants in the upstate New York area. They quickly bring you up to speed: McDonald's has been quietly evaluating whether to join the iPad bandwagon. The corporate office is investigating the option of rolling out iPad-based menus that would allow patrons to walk in and immediately sit at a table, then order using the device available at the table. They place an order, customize it to their taste, then submit it. When their number is called the guests can then pay for and pick up their order as they normally would.

As iPad menus are becoming popular in restaurants around the world, such as Mundo Global Tapas in Australia, or Stacked in Torrance, CA (USA), the approach that McDonald's is considering is very similar to the one recently introduced by Delta Airlines in its Terminal at JFK airport. There, travelers can use available iPads to surf the Internet and order from two of the terminal's restaurants: Croque Madam for French cuisine and Bar Brace for upscale Italian food. Funny enough, you were there last week! At these restaurants patrons sit down and use one of the 200 devices to order directly from a graphically pleasing and interactive menu. As they wait for their food to be delivered they can play games, check flight information, read the news, and surf the web. As Rick Blatstein, the CEO of OTG, the management company behind the concept put it: "We are giving travelers a one-of-a-kind experience [....] by combining cuisine with innovative seating and ordering technology, we are offering a truly unique airport travel experience."[1]

Your client explains that McDonald's doesn't expect to earn money initially from this service. He quotes a conversation he had with Ron Jonson, president of McDonald's North-East Division: "What we're banking on is that more customers will visit McDonald's. Moreover, your customers may stay longer as they can surf the internet and read the news right on the iPad, and therefore increase their consumption." The program seems to be gaining strong support at corporate, but your client, the franchisee, has heard mixed feedback on the idea from his fellow franchisees attending a recent conference. He does not want to miss out making extra revenue, as every bit helps. However, he does not want to waste money on the latest high-tech gizmo just for the sake of staying on trend.

As a knowledgeable and enthusiastic early adopter of technology, you are now in the hot seat as your boss and the franchisee turn to you for a recommendation.

DISCUSSION QUESTIONS

1. Drawing on your own experience at JFK airport last week, do you think that iPad menus will work well at McDonald's restaurants? Justify your answer.
2. Given your answers to Question 1, can you see exceptions or do you believe your answer applies to all restaurants? What about McDonald's restaurants in other countries?
3. What do you suggest WizConsult's client should do tomorrow?

INTRODUCTION

Despite the well-documented challenges associated with achieving satisfactory return on information technology (IT) investments, modern organizations around the world continue to spend significant amounts of money on IT, lured by its promise to yield efficiencies and improved competitive positioning. With IT spending on the rise, there is little doubt that being able to wring value from these investments is critical for the modern organization. However, a narrow focus on IT investments alone is problematic. Instead you should focus on information systems

---

[1]Robbins, K (2010). "At JFK airport eateries, iPad will be your server," *Delish* (Available online 06/06/2011 http://www.delish.com/food/recalls-reviews/at-jfk-airport-eateries-ipad-will-be-your-server).

(ISs) and their design. To do so, we must first cover some important background information and introduce some key definitions.

 ## INFORMATION SYSTEMS: DEFINITION

In order to refocus our attention from the IT investment perspective to a more comprehensive IS design perspective, we need to first define the concept of information system and separate it from IT.

IS, Not IT

Without a doubt, information technology engenders a plentitude of confusing lingo, technical terms, and acronyms—a problem compounded by the many half-prepared, fast-talking individuals using terminology incorrectly. Of all the potentially confusing terms, none is more insidious than the term *information system*, usually abbreviated IS. In this context, information system is often used as a rough synonym for information technology. But there is a critical difference between IT and IS!

Consider a simple example. The famous Ricasoli winery is the oldest family-owned winery in Italy, producing wine in the heart of the Chianti region since obtaining ownership of the Brolio Castle (Figure 2.1) in the year 1141. It is to one of the members of the Ricasoli family in fact, the Baron Bettino, that we owe the formula of the "sublime wine"—the Chianti. Bettino Ricasoli perfected the blend in 1872 after years of studies and experiments, at a time when his estate was exporting wine all over Italy and beyond. Did the Ricasoli estate have an information system when the Baron perfected the Chianti recipe?

The answer is yes, of course. The Ricasoli Winery's information system allowed the firm to take orders, track payments, organize activities around the farm, manage its inventory of aging wines, and help the Baron collect information about the blends and treatments that enabled the wine to maintain its organoleptic characteristics when shipped far from the Brolio Castle. Using books and ledgers, the technology of the time, the estate was able to keep track of all data and information necessary to its proper operations and longevity.

Yet the first-known implementation of digital computing did not occur until World War II, and digital computers did not begin to enter business organizations until the post-war years. However, all kinds of organizations—from car manufacturers to laundry services, from banks to soft drink makers—had been conducting business for decades (in some cases, as the example of the Ricasoli estate shows, even centuries!). Clearly, while IT is a fundamental component of any *modern* information system, we can see from these examples that IT and IS are separate concepts.

Figure 2.1   The Ricasoli estate (Courtesy of Barone Ricasoli.)

Information Systems as Sociotechnical Systems

Information systems are formal, sociotechnical, organizational systems designed to collect, process, store, and distribute information. Within this book we primarily concern ourselves with formal organizational information systems, those that are sanctioned by a company, not-for-profit endeavor, or government entity. While as students you are likely very familiar with various *informal* information systems, for example the valuable "grapevine" at your school that you tap into for networking contacts and to find out the scoop about a professor or a class, such informal systems are beyond the scope of this book. Facebook.com, the social networking site born on the Harvard University campus as a tool for students to establish connections and exchange information, is another example of such an informal information system (Figure 2.2).

The key aspect of our definition is the notion of sociotechnical system. Sociotechnical theory has a long tradition of research dating back to work done at the Tavistock Institute in London, England. Sociotechnical theory questioned the overly optimistic predictions about the potential benefits of new technology and suggested that the impact of new technologies on work systems was not a direct one but depended on the interplay of technology with other aspects, or components, of the work system.

Figure 2.2   Facebook news feed

The Four Components of an Information System

While sociotechnical theory is general in nature and applicable to any work system, it has been successfully applied to IT-based information systems. Specifically, we can represent any formal organizational IS as having four fundamental components that must work together to deliver the information processing functionalities that the firm requires to fulfill its information needs.

The four components of an IT-based information system are IT, people, process, and structure (see Figure 2.3). They can be grouped into two subsystems: the technical subsystem and the social subsystem. The technical subsystem, composed of technology and processes, is that portion of the information system that does not include human elements. The social subsystem, composed of people and people in relation to one another (i.e., structure), represents the human element of the IS.

As a general and functional manager, you will be called on to make information systems decisions as they impact your sphere of influence (e.g., your department or functional area). In order to make appropriate decisions in this realm, you will need to have a solid understanding of each of the four components and how they interact with one another.

Information Technology Information technology (IT) is defined here as hardware, software, and telecommunication equipment. The IT component is a cornerstone of any modern IS, enabling and constraining action through rules of operation that stem from its design. For example, if you choose to collect and analyze data using spreadsheet software such as Microsoft Excel rather than using a relational database management system such as Microsoft Access (Figure 2.4), you are limited by the design of the spreadsheet software. Microsoft Excel cannot create meaningful associations between separate data elements. The result is substantial duplication of data, leading to redundancy, inconsistencies, and inefficient data management. This is because the design of Microsoft Excel is focused on computations and formulaic calculations, not on efficient data management.

In addition, it is important to remember that software design, still as much an art as a science, is driven in large part by the choices and opinions of the developers and programmers who create it. InfoWorld columnist Bob Lewis put it well when he said, "Every piece of software

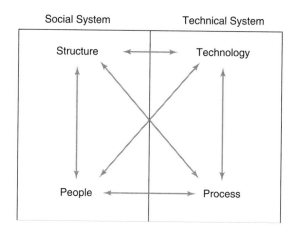

Figure 2.3 Information system components

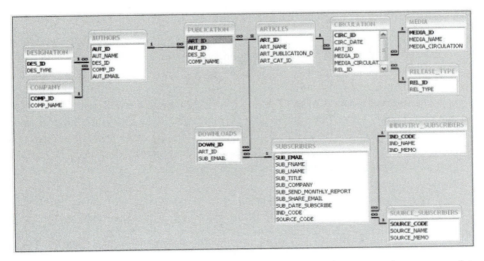

Figure 2.4 A relational database management system enables connections among data elements

is an opinion." Software, particularly custom developed applications, represents the developers' viewpoint on how the data should be represented, organized, and manipulated.

To relate to Lewis's quote, you need to only think about the last time, on the phone with a customer service representative, you heard the phrase, "The system won't allow that." In such a circumstance the software design team did, knowingly or unknowingly, restrict the functionality of the software to enforce a given behavior. Note, however, that this ability to enforce rules through software is a double-edged sword. For example, some car rental companies do not allow a rental contract to print unless the customer provides two distinct phone numbers. The design of the software seeks to ensure that the customer can be easily contacted if needed and that valuable customer contact data can be tracked. However, those customers who do not have (or do not want to provide) more than one number, and rushed employees trying to move quickly through the cue of customers waiting, find it easy to produce "phantom" phone numbers—thus defeating the very purpose for creating the restriction in the software.

Process The process component of an information system is defined here as the series of steps necessary to complete a business activity. Consider the job of a small, family-owned grocery store manager and the process he engages in when restocking inventory. The store manager must (1) check the inventory and identify the needed items; (2) call individual suppliers for quotes and delivery dates; (3) compare the various quotes; (4) select one or more suppliers for each of the needed items based on the terms of the agreement (e.g., availability, quality, delivery); (5) call these suppliers and place the orders; (6) receive the goods upon delivery, checking the accuracy and quality of the shipped items; and (7) pay the suppliers.

Note that the same activity may be performed using a variety of different business processes. Note as well that gaps can exist between the official business process that forms the basis of training programs and customer service protocols, and the informal ways in which these processes are actually performed. This discrepancy is due to the fact that, while many business processes are codified in procedure manuals and training materials, ultimately they are enacted by people. Consider again the case of the rental car company mentioned previously. While the

Figure 2.5 Long line at a counter. *Source*: OJO Images/Image Source

stated business process calls for the collection of two separate customer phone numbers, you can imagine an employee who sees a long line and is attending to a customer who is not willing to provide two numbers, typing in a fictitious number rather than wasting time arguing (Figure 2.5).

This potential discrepancy between the business processes as designed by the organization and the manner in which they are actually enacted is often the root cause of IS failure. When designing a new IS or when confronted with IS failure, it helps to think about what possible obstacles exist that may make it difficult for employees to accurately follow the business process.

People   The people component refers to those individuals or groups directly involved in the information system. These individuals—whether they are end users, managers, or IT professionals—have their own set of skills, attitudes, preconceptions, and personal agendas that determine what they are able to do and what they will elect to do as part of the IS. A genuine understanding of the people involved, including their skills, interests, and motivations, is necessary when designing and implementing a new IS or when troubleshooting an existing IS that is not performing as expected.

Consider the example of a national government intent on rationalizing and improving communication between the local administrations (e.g., school districts) and the central institutions (e.g., ministry of education). As part of this initiative, e-mail addresses are produced for the school district superintendents and each school's principal and assistant principal. You quickly realize that this simple initiative is more likely to be successful today than it was ten or fifteen years ago when computer skills were scarce and computer anxiety was high even among highly educated individuals.

Structure   The organizational structure component (structure for short) refers to the organizational design (hierarchy, decentralized, loose coupling), reporting (functional, divisional, matrix), and relationships (communication and reward mechanisms) within the information system.

Understanding the structure component is crucial because user resistance, incentive systems, and relationships are often silent enemies of IS success that go undetected before, and sometimes even after, IS failure becomes apparent.

Consider the famous case of a large IT consulting firm. The firm, with global operations, recognized the potential for knowledge sharing among its consultants. "If we introduce a knowledge management system," the thinking went, "we can create repositories of knowledge to which our consultants will contribute upon completing a project. This will enable us to surface and share best practices, rather than having to reinvent the wheel with similar projects just because they are in different regions and involve a different team of consultants. Moreover, we will be able to identify subject matter experts to whom we will direct questions on specific topics. The outcome of this IS implementation will be increased turnaround time on projects, better quality results, and more satisfied clients."

A few months after the rollout of the system, it became clear that usage was spotty at best. Upon careful analysis, the firm realized that there was little incentive for consultants to contribute to the knowledge base. In the fast-paced world of IT consulting, the road to success was the "billable hour," which was gained by spending productive time working on client projects. Moreover, the organizational culture was such that individual behavior and superior skills were valued over teamwork and knowledge sharing. The inevitable conclusion was that, in order for the knowledge management systems to reap the expected benefits, the tangible reward structure and the traditional mentality of the organization would need to change.

Systemic Effects

It should be clear from the preceding discussion that all four components are necessary to ensure that the information system is successful and delivers the functionality it was intended to provide. Imagine dropping any one of the four components in any of the preceding examples—the system would not work. More subtly, the four components of an information system don't work in isolation, but instead interact with one another—as noted by the arrows in Figure 2.3. This notion of interdependence of the components goes by the name *systemic effects*, indicating that changes in one component (e.g., the introduction of a new software application, a process redesign, a new organization chart, or turnover among employees) affect all other components of the system and, if not properly managed, its outputs. Mark Hedley, the former CIO of Wyndham International, perfectly captured this notion: "Many companies rush out, buy software solutions, install them quickly, and then can't understand why the system failed. You have to look at what business issues exist, what people and processes pertain to that business issue, and what those people do. Technology won't solve [a problem] by itself—other components have to be part of the solution."

Because of systemic effects, when called upon to design a new IS or to modify an existing one, you should focus not on optimizing the technology (i.e., adopting the most innovative and cutting edge IT) or any other component individually. Rather you should optimize the IS as a whole (i.e., selecting components that create the best chance to deliver the needed information processing functionality when working simultaneously with the other components). This focus on information systems design, rather than IT investment decisions, also suggests that there are multiple ways to achieve the same information systems goal—as demonstrated by the many different ways in which similar organizations meet their information processing needs.

Understanding the importance of systemic effects is critical not only when designing a new system, but also when troubleshooting an existing one that is underperforming, in order to diagnose the root causes of the failure and to devise the appropriate intervention. Consider a restaurant that introduced hand-held ordering devices only to face discontent and rejection by the wait staff, who complain about the fact that the system is not intuitive, is difficult to use, and gets in the way of their interactions with the guests—the source of their tips! How would you solve this problem if you were the restaurant manager? There may be a number of options here:

- You could deem the new system a failure and cut your losses by dropping the use of hand-held technology.

- You could ascribe the failure to the quality of the user interface of the hand-held ordering devices. You could then negotiate with the provider to improve the interface. This solution focuses on IT.

- You could ascribe the failure to the quality of the user interface of the hand-held ordering devices, but choose a different solution. You could work with your staff and convince them that the system is not as awkward as it seems and a bit of training will solve all their issues. This solution focuses on people.

- You could ascribe the failure to the fact that your staff, composed mostly of old-fashioned gum-chewing waiters and waitresses, just does not have the knowledge and skills to adopt computerized devices. You would then turn over your staff, replacing them with iPod-carrying, cell-phone-toting college students. This solution also focuses on people.

- You could ascribe the failure to human inertia and your staff's resistance to change. You could then call a meeting and inform staff that the hand-held devices are going to stay and the next person who complains is going to be fired (you may offer incentives if you are more of the positive-reinforcement management type). This solution focuses on structure.

WHY DO ORGANIZATIONS BUILD INFORMATION SYSTEMS?

Now that we know what an information system actually is, we should step back and question why organizations build them in the first place. Simply put, a firm's objective when introducing IT-enabled information systems is to fulfill its information processing needs. Sometimes external requirements, such as financial reporting, safety, or tax regulations, mandate the introduction of a new IS. More typically, an organization introduces information systems in an effort to improve efficiency[2] and effectiveness.[3]

In order to fulfill its information processing needs, an organization must capture relevant data that are then manipulated, or processed, to produce an output that will be useful to the appropriate users, either internal or external to the firm (e.g., customers). These data and information are typically accumulated, or stored, for future retrieval and use (see Figure 2.6). Thus, while not a component of the information system per se, information itself plays a critical role in modern organizations.

Note that, while the focus of this book is on IT-enabled information systems, the processing of information does not necessarily require IT support in order to happen. Consider the last time you contributed to the in-class discussion of a case study. In order to produce valuable comments

---

[2] *Efficiency* is defined as the ability to limit waste and maximize the ratio of the output produced to the inputs consumed. In other words, a firm is more efficient when it produces more with the same amount of resources, produces the same with less resources, or produces more with less resources.

[3] *Effectiveness* is defined as the ability to achieve stated goals or objectives. Typically, a more effective firm is one that makes better decisions and is able to carry them out successfully.

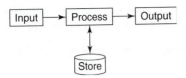

Figure 2.6   Information processing in an IS

for the class, you gathered substantial information (i.e., you read the case, you read assigned articles and other class materials, you actively listened to the professor setting the context for the discussion, and you listened attentively to your classmates' comments). You then processed the information (i.e., during preparation you thought about the case issues in the context of the information presented in the readings, during class discussion you thought about how your classmates' comments supported or contradicted your point of view). Finally, you produced some output—your insightful analysis for the whole class to hear. In other words, you engaged in significant information processing without ever using a computer.

IT is not to be downplayed, as all but the most trivial of today's organizational information processing requirements cannot be fulfilled in a reliable and cost-effective manner without IT. However, IT can only be successfully leveraged as an integral part of an information system, not in isolation. Moreover, while managers often focus on the financial results produced by the design and introduction of a new IS, there are nonfinancial outcomes, both planned and unexpected, that you need to be aware of as well.

Successful Information Systems

Any information system should be built according to an explicit goal (or a set of goals) designed to fulfill the specific information processing needs of the implementing organization.[4] Examples of typical IS goals include the following:

- For a large retail store (e.g., Walmart, Carrefour): To increase the efficiency and speed of customer check-out, perhaps using self-check-out stations.
- For a high-end car manufacturer (e.g., BMW): To improve customer service by allowing individual customers to select finishing and accessories on their car, and quote in real time price changes and delivery date changes.

Consider the choice faced by McDonald's franchisees in 2003 who had to decide whether or not to offer Wi-Fi connectivity in their restaurants—taking a page out of Starbucks' approach. While a cursory examination may suggest that Wi-Fi simply does not fit with McDonald's strategic positioning, a more careful analysis would indicate that for some customers (e.g., busy parents, truck drivers) and in some locations (e.g., tourist areas) connectivity may be highly valued. This lack of clear fit led to McDonald's failing to develop a clear Wi-Fi strategy. After testing the program in 2003 with a $4.95 charge for two hours of use, the firm lowered the charge to $2.95 in 2004, allowing franchisees to decide whether they wanted to join the program. In 2009, Wi-Fi connectivity became a standard, available in every one of the over 32,000 restaurants in the world free of charge.

---

[4]Note that, while the IS goals should fit with the firm's strategic goals, the IS cannot ensure that the correct business objectives have been chosen. In other words, an IS is deemed successful when its information processing goals are achieved—even in the face of business failure due to the pursuit of a flawed strategy.

One of the difficulties that McDonald's executives faced was in clarifying for franchisees what the primary objectives of the program were. While at first they suggested that the program would increase consumption, the benefits weren't very clear. At the very least, if customers felt that McDonald's plastic seats were too uncomfortable to sit on for more than fifteen minutes and that the food was too messy to fumble with their laptops during or after the meal, the systems would be largely unused, hence delivering little benefit to the franchisee that paid for it. When the program became a brand standard, it became clear that the value of Wi-Fi at each McDonald's was in attracting more customers to the stores with the added benefit that they could quickly check their e-mail while on the road. Whichever the best objective is in this particular case, it is important to note that establishing a clear aim for the system is a critical prerequisite.

Information Systems Success: Definition   We can unequivocally deem an information system a failure if it is abandoned (i.e., the design and implementation phase is never concluded) or not used (i.e., the information system is completed only to be rejected by its intended users). In either case, the system is a failure because, due to nonuse, it will yield none of the promised benefits (e.g., efficiency improvements). Table 2.1 highlights some high-profile failures.

Beyond nonuse, discriminating successful information systems from failed ones requires an evaluation of whether, and to what extent, the system has delivered the expected results. This is why it is so important to articulate information system goals during the design and justification phase. Yet for as thorough a job you may do in defining the intended IS goals, there are many situations when unintended results, both positive and negative, will emerge. The best-known case of a strategic information system, the celebrated SABRE reservation systems pioneered by American Airlines (Figure 2.7), was originally introduced simply to enable inventory control in response to a very tangible operational problem: American Airlines found itself unable to manage and sell the increasing number of seats it supplied in response to mounting consumer demand for commercial air flights.

Figure 2.7
SABRE—The first airline reservation system. *Source*: © Underwood & Underwood/CORBIS

Table 2.1 Some Noteworthy Systems Failures in the Recent History of Business Computing

Year	Company	Outcome
2011	Allied Irish Banks (AIB) [Ireland]	AIB sues Oracle Financial Services Software for €84 million, plus damages and lost profits, claiming it wasted the money on a failed implementation of a new retail banking system.
2011	Federal Bureau of Investigation (FBI) [U.S.]	In 2001 the FBI started work on a criminal case management system called Virtual Case File. The project was scrapped four years (and $170 million) later. The project was restarted under the name Sentinel and, as of May 2011, was unfinished after 5 years (and $400 million) in development.
2010 (2007)	AXA Rosenberg, a privately owned investment management company. [U.S.]	"Coding error" leads to under-represented investing risk factors and results in investors losing a total of $217 million.
2010	Electronics retailer Dixons [UK]	Reiterated difficulties with its new e-commerce system are blamed for £15 million in lost revenue.
2009	Government of Victoria [Australia]	Smartcard ticketing system (Myki), contracted for in 2005 with AU$500 million budgeted, is rushed into operations (current cost AU$1.3 billion) with limited functionality but still encounters significant operational problems.
2009	Britain's National Health Service's (NHS)	NHS scales down its "Connecting for Health" program designed to create the national electronics health record system after investing an estimated £12 billion since the project began in 2002.
2008	Centrica, the largest utility supplier of gas to domestic UK customers	Centrica sues Accenture for £182 million in damages stemming from a collapse of customer service levels and loss of over 1 million customers attributed to the failure of a "best of breed" customer billing system.
2008	J. Crew [U.S.]	Shares of the company fell more than 7% after announcement of persisting website performance, order fulfillment, and call center performance problems leading to slowing sales trends, lower gross margins, and $3 million of unanticipated costs.
2007	LA Unified School District (LAUSD) [U.S.]	LAUSD discovers that, due to on-going payroll system's problems, it overpaid 36,000 employees by a total of $53 million.
2007	Palm Beach County [U.S.]	Palm Beach County evaluates scrapping $13.6 million upgrade to its computer systems that took three and a half years in development (six months originally budgeted) due to inability to operate with it.

(continued)

Table 2.1   *(continued)*

Year	Company	Outcome
2006	Child Support Agency (CSA) [UK]	The CSA is shut down in part due to a problem-ridden deployment of a £456 million IT system, built by EDS.
2005	Hudson Bay Co. [Canada]	Problems with inventory system contribute to $33.3 million loss.
2005	UK Inland Revenue	Software errors contribute to $3.45 billion tax-credit overpayment.
2004	Avis Europe PLC [UK]	Enterprise resource planning (ERP) system canceled after $54.5 million is spent.
2004	Ford Motor Co. [U.S.]	Purchasing system abandoned after deployment costing approximately $400 million.
2004	J Sainsbury PLC [UK]	Supply-chain management system abandoned after deployment costing $527 million.
2004	Hewlett-Packard Co. [U.S.]	Problems with ERP system contribute to $160 million loss.
2003-04	AT&T Wireless [U.S.]	Customer relations management (CRM) upgrade problems lead to revenue loss of $100 million.
2002	McDonald's Corp. [U.S.]	The Innovate information-purchasing system canceled after $170 million is spent.
2002	Sydney Water Corp. [Australia]	Billing system canceled after $33.2 million is spent.
2002	CIGNA Corp. [U.S.]	Problems with CRM system contribute to $445 million loss.
2001	Nike Inc. [U.S.]	Problems with supply-chain management system contribute to $100 million loss.
2001	Kmart Corp. [U.S.]	Supply-chain management system canceled after $130 million is spent.
2000	Washington, D.C. [U.S.]	City payroll system abandoned after deployment costing $25 million.
1999	United Way [U.S.]	Administrative processing system canceled after $12 million is spent.
1999	State of Mississippi [U.S.]	Tax system canceled after $11.2 million is spent; state receives $185 million damages.
1999	Hershey Foods Corp. [U.S.]	Problems with ERP system contribute to $151 million loss.
1998	Snap-on Inc. [U.S.]	Problems with order-entry system contribute to revenue loss of $50 million.
1997	U.S. Internal Revenue Service	Tax modernization effort canceled after $4 billion is spent.
1997	State of Washington [U.S.]	Department of Motor Vehicle (DMV) system canceled after $40 million is spent.
1997	Oxford Health Plans Inc. [U.S.]	Billing and claims system problems contribute to quarterly loss; stock plummets, leading to $3.4 billion loss in corporate value.

(continued)

Table 2.1 Some Noteworthy Systems Failures in the Recent History of Business Computing *(continued)*

Year	Company	Outcome
1996	Arianespace [France]	Software specification and design errors cause $350 million Ariane 5 rocket to explode.
1996	FoxMeyer Drug Co. [U.S.]	$40 million ERP system abandoned after deployment, forcing company into bankruptcy.
1995	Toronto Stock Exchange [Canada]	Electronic trading system canceled after $25.5 million is spent.
1994	U.S. Federal Aviation Administration	Advanced Automation System canceled after $2.6 billion is spent.
1994	State of California [U.S.]	DMV system canceled after $44 million is spent.
1994	Chemical Bank [U.S.]	Software error causes a total of $15 million to be deduced from 100,000 customer accounts.
1993	London Stock Exchange [UK]	Taurus stock settlement system canceled after $600 million is spent.
1993	Allstate Insurance Co. [U.S.]	Office automation system abandoned after deployment, costing $130 million.
1993	London Ambulance Service [UK]	Dispatch system canceled in 1990 at $11.25 million; second attempt abandoned after deployment, costing $15 million.
1993	Greyhound Lines Inc. [U.S.]	Bus reservation system crashes repeatedly upon introduction, contributing to revenue loss $61 million.
1992	Budget Rent-A-Car, Hilton Hotels, Marriott International, and American Airlines [U.S.]	Travel reservation system canceled after $165 million is spent.

Source: Adapted from *IEEE, BusinessWeek, CEO Magazine, Computerworld, InfoWeek, Fortune, The New York Times*, and *The Wall Street Journal*.

Information Systems Outcomes

Beyond efficiency and effectiveness improvements and the associated financial considerations, information systems have other direct and indirect effects on people within and outside the firm (e.g., employees, customers, suppliers). These effects can be positive, including employees' empowerment and the widening scope of their responsibility; or negative, including deskilling (i.e., the reduction of the scope of an individual's work to one, or a few, specialized tasks), loss of responsibility, and the creation of a monotonous working environment.

Another important outcome of information systems use pertains to their effect on future opportunities available to the firm. The introduction of a new information system may enable or constrain future information systems and strategic initiatives available to the organization. This is due to the fact that future systems typically rely on, or connect with, preexisting ones. Consider the example of social networking sites like Facebook. As the user base grows larger, and each individual member has more connections within the social network, Facebook and third-party developers have the opportunity to develop applications that leverage this data. Social games like *Farmville* or *Mafia Wars*, and applications such as *Where Have I Been*, could not be easily created without the underlying Facebook social graph.

Beyond an appreciation of their goals and outcomes, successfully designing and implementing information systems requires recognition that any information system that you envision or propose exists in a unique and very specific organizational context.

INFORMATION SYSTEMS IN THE ORGANIZATIONAL CONTEXT[5]

Consider a five-star hotel chain with 62 properties within the United States, and a small Silicon Valley start-up outsourcing part of its software development to high-tech firms in Ireland and India. Imagine that management in each organization heard about the potential for virtual teaming and collaboration at a distance. At the hotel company, executives pushed to have general managers from each of the locations work together as a team to share best practices and help one another respond to emergencies, such as the massive blackouts that affected Brazil in 1999 and North America in 2004, or an approaching hurricane. At the start-up, the objective is to enable programmers in the three locations to share their knowledge and help each other with coding questions. Both firms introduce a groupware solution supporting the following functionalities: shared calendar, contact manager, personal e-mail, discussion forum and chat functions, resources and content management system, file manager, knowledge-base engine, and a shared whiteboard. Will the same system yield comparable results in each of these firms? Where will the "virtual teaming" vision most likely come to bear?

Every Organization is Unique

The simple example just described should clarify that organizations are unique in many respects. This is not only true for companies in different industries, but also of otherwise similar firms that compete head to head. Microsoft and Apple Computers were the two most recognizable names in the software industry throughout the 1990s, vying to establish their respective operating systems as the dominant platform. Yet the two firms had dramatically different images and cultures. Even starker is the difference between two of today's London, UK–based airlines—British Airways and EasyJet.

At the highest level of abstraction, a firm is characterized by its strategy, its culture, and its current infrastructure, stemming from the organization's history, size, product line, location, values, and so on.

Firm Strategy   A firm's strategy represents the manner in which the organization intends to achieve its objectives. In other words, understanding a firm's strategy tells us what the firm is trying to do and what course of action it has charted to get there.

Consider two other head-to-head competitors: Dell Computers and Hewlett-Packard (HP) who, during the late 1990s, battled for supremacy of market share in the personal computer industry. At the time Dell and HP were the number one and number two makers of personal computers, respectively. While the market share rivalry between the two is still going on, the two manufacturers had two drastically different strategies. On the one hand, Dell focused on highly customizable, made-to-order devices that were assembled upon receipt of orders directly from

---

[5]The following discussion is largely influenced by the following article: Silver, Mark S., Markus, M. Lynne, and Beath, Cynthia M. "The Information Technology Interaction Model: A Foundation for the MBA Core Course," *MIS Quarterly*, vol. 19, no. 3 (September 1995), pp. 361–390.

consumers and business clients. Conversely, HP historically focused on producing standardized devices to be sold through a wide channel of distribution (e.g., Best Buy, Media World). Similar examples of direct competitors, in the same industry, with very different strategies abound.

Firm Culture   A firm's culture is defined as the collection of beliefs, expectations, and values shared by the members of an organization. The firm's culture, a broad representation of how the firm does business, is an important characteristic of the organization because it captures the way, often unspoken and informal, in which the organization operates. Practices that are deemed appropriate in one organization may not be in another one.

Consider the 2004 merger between software titans Oracle Corp. and PeopleSoft, Inc. Announcing the merger, the *San Francisco Chronicle* posed the question, "What do you get when you combine a company run by an Armani-clad executive known for take-no-prisoners tactics with a firm led by a fatherly founder who hands out bagels and lets his workers wear flannel to work? ...For the merger to succeed, Oracle faces the tough task of creating a cohesive company out of two firms with distinct, even contradictory, cultures." Quoting a Forrester Research analyst, the article concluded, "Pretty quickly, the PeopleSoft employees are going to divide themselves into those who say 'I think I can work for Oracle' and 'I don't ever want to work at Oracle.'"[6]

Infrastructure   When it comes to making information systems decisions, it is also important to consider the current IT infrastructure of the firm. The existing IT infrastructure, defined as the set of shared IT resources and services of the firm, constrains and enables opportunities for future information systems implementations.

The preceding example of check-out scanners at grocery stores highlights this point. Once the infrastructure is in place, the grocery store can consider future initiatives that rely on it, such as automatic inventory reorder, but also check-out coupons (i.e., the ability to print coupons at check-out based on the items the customer bought), frequency shopper cards, and basket analysis (i.e., the ability to identify correlations among items purchased by the same customer).

The External Environment   Organizations themselves don't exist in a vacuum, but instead are embedded in the external environment that encompasses regulation, the competitive landscape, and general business and social trends (e.g., outsourcing, customer self-service).

Consider three competitors, such as the Sony Corporation, Philips Electronics, and Samsung Group, headquartered in Tokyo, Japan, Amsterdam, Holland and Seoul, South Korea, respectively. While these three firms compete, at least in part, in the world market for consumer electronics, they have to contend with widely different local labor and taxation laws, governmental incentives, and so on. The external environment is fairly removed from day-to-day operations, yet these factors have an influence on the firm and, as a consequence, on the type of information systems the firm will need to introduce.

Bringing It All Together

The previous discussion of the outcomes associated with information systems use and information systems in context is summarized in Figure 2.8.

---

[6]Pimentel, B. (2004). "When firms merge, a clash of cultures/Oracle, PeopleSoft managing styles couldn't be more different," *San Francisco Chronicle*, 12/15/2004.

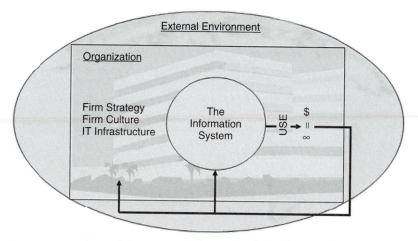

Figure 2.8   Information systems in an organizational context

The model in Figure 2.8 indicates that the immediate effect of information systems is whether they are used or not. If they are used, then intended and unintended outcomes ensue, including financial results, effects on people, and effects on the future opportunities and constraints available to the firm. The model also shows that information systems do not exist in a vacuum, but are embedded in a specific organizational context, defined by the firm strategy, culture, and IT infrastructure. Moreover, the organization itself does not exist in isolation, but is embedded in the external environment, including social and competitive forces. The feedback loops represented by the solid bold line remind us that whatever outcomes are produced by the information system, positive or negative, will affect organizational characteristics and future information systems decision making.

This model is important for you as a general or functional manager because it draws to your attention all of the external influences that will aid or undermine information system success.

INFORMATION SYSTEMS AND ORGANIZATIONAL CHANGE

As a general or functional manager, you must pay close attention to organizational change. With the widespread adoption of IT by modern organizations, increasingly this organizational change is brought on by the introduction of new IT. The definition of information systems as sociotechnical systems is instrumental in helping you better manage organizational change. Specifically, we can identify three levels of organizational change brought about by the introduction of a new IT.

First-Order Change: Automate

The simplest order of change ensuing from the deployment of technology is automation. This level of change involves technology and processes but does not affect the sphere of the social subsystem (Figure 2.9). First-order change occurs when an IT innovation is introduced that modifies how an existing process is performed.

Consider those online banking tasks previously executed through a touch-tone phone interface—such as checking balances or transferring money between accounts. Many of us

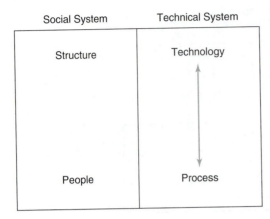

Figure 2.9   First-order change

now perform those same tasks through a Web interface or a smartphone. What has changed with the move to the Web is the manner in which these processes are performed, not the tasks themselves or the individuals involved (e.g., customers). With the introduction of the Web as a customer interface, the process has become simpler and more intuitive.

Managing first-order change   The limited scope of first-order change makes it relatively easy to envision, justify, and manage. General and functional managers understand how the new technology impacts the firm's operations, and the project is straightforward to justify since the financial benefits of the change, in terms of the return on investment, can be estimated with some precision. Thus, first-order change requires little executive sponsorship and involvement.

Second-Order Change: Informate

Second-order change has major implications for the people component of the information systems, as well as IT and processes (Figure 2.10). With second-order change, not only the manner in which the process is performed changes, but also those individuals who perform it are affected by the change—either their role is modified or a different set of people is now involved. Moreover, the manner in which people interact with the technology also undergoes modification. This

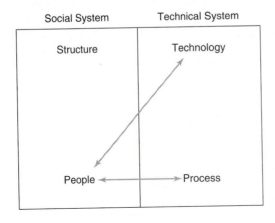

Figure 2.10   Second-order change

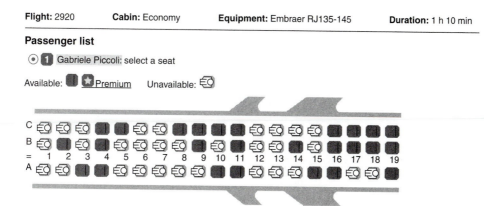

Figure 2.11   Choosing a seat during web check-in

level of change typically occurs when the information intensity of the process being performed changes substantially due to the introduction of new IT. For this reason, this level of change is called *informate*.

A good example of second-order change is IT-enabled customer self-service. Consider airline check-in kiosks. Traditionally, as an airline traveler you'd have to go to the airport, cue up, and interact with an agent, who would authenticate you by checking your ID card and then provide you with a seat and boarding passes. The advent of check-in kiosks, and now online check-in, has dramatically changed this process. First, it is now the machine that authenticates you—using a credit card or frequent flier card. Then you can proceed to select a seat and print the boarding passes (see Figure 2.11).

For anyone who is very tall and used to implore the agent for an exit row seat, the kiosk has opened a wealth of new possibilities. More important, the kiosks have had a dramatic impact on the agents themselves, who now serve in more of a training and troubleshooting role, helping travelers solve any problems they encounter with the system, rather than completing the check-in process on behalf of the travelers.

Managing Second-Order Change   The primary impact of second-order change is on the people dimension of the sociotechnical system. As such, second-order change provides much more of a challenge to managers who seek to implement it than does first-order change. Those affected may include employees as well as customers. Thus, appropriate training and overcoming the human tendency to resist change are key challenges.

The objectives of second-order change are typically far reaching as well. While first-order change is focused on automating existing tasks, informate level change is often seeking to take advantage of available market opportunities. Thus, justifying this level of change is more difficult and requires a more speculative analysis.

Third-Order Change: Transform

Third-order change represents the most pervasive and radical level of change—as such it is often referred to as transform. Third-order change subsumes first- and second-order change

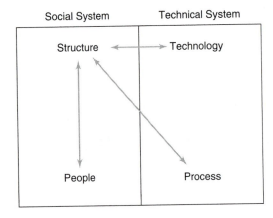

Figure 2.12   Third-order change

while also causing organizational structure disruptions (Figure 2.12). The interaction between structure and technology is substantiated by a change in the way the organization selects, uses, and manages technology. The interaction between the organizational structure and the people generally results in a change in the reporting and authority structure of the organization. A flatter or more permeable organizational structure usually emerges after the technology implementation. The interaction between the organizational structure and tasks manifests itself in a novel way of task accomplishment or a new set of tasks.

Consider a familiar example: Wikipedia. Wikipedia, the free online user-written encyclopedia, transformed the way we access and produce knowledge. Traditional encyclopedias have a strong top-down approach to content creation. Editors commission articles from individual experts who write an entry (e.g., Italy, electricity). Editors then review the entry and might share it with one or two other experts for peer review before finalizing and including it in the next release of the encyclopedia. We then buy the book and read the experts' entries. In contrast to this, thanks to the ability to easily connect any of the two billion people currently online across the globe, and thanks to the capability of Wikis to allow easy, multiple editing of the same document, Wikipedia uses a very different knowledge codification and dissemination process. Anyone can contribute to an article and the quality assurance is performed by the community of readers through a discussion page associated with each entry. As such, the people involved in content generation and the process by which knowledge is produced change dramatically. But also the organizational structure of the online encyclopedia is significantly different than their traditional printed counterparts. In fact, the very notion of an expert on a subject is lost and expertise is instead contributed by the population of readers at large.

Managing Third-Order Change   Third-order change requires significant managerial and executive involvement. Championship by the top management team is necessary both for signaling purposes and to provide the necessary political impetus to complete the transition. Changes in organizational structure are in fact likely to engender political battles and resistance by those whose authority and political influence is diminished. The history of the business process reengineering (BPR) movement (see Chapter 3) provides countless examples of the perils associated with third-order change and the difficulties in managing dramatic IT-enabled change.

CULTURE AND INFORMATION SYSTEMS[7]

Every society possesses an internal logic that enables it to run—if this was not so, that society would no longer exist. This logic is embedded in shared systems of meaning, or "culture." Culture is defined as the unwritten rules of the social game that are shared by the members of some group. This could be a firm, or a family, or a society. Today, there are vast amounts of research confirming that countries tend to have distinct cultures. To be sure there are also regional and ethnic differences within countries, and some countries have similar cultures—for instance, all the Anglo countries: UK, United States, Canada, Australia, and New Zealand. The unwritten rules of culture at the level of society are about basic issues of social life that need to be settled in order to divide scarce societal resources such as possessions, but also social resources such as prerogatives, power, and belongingness. These unwritten rules are sometimes referred to as "deep values." People acquire them in early childhood, and after puberty they are very hard to change. Moreover, cultures have a strong continuity across generations.

National Culture

Culture is pervasive, and anyone working in a multinational environment should have a basic understanding of it, or they might make severe errors. A growing number of cross-nation studies have confirmed that dimensions of culture at the level of countries have bearing on the following issues:

- Collectivism: the degree to which members of the society feel interdependent, bound to their fixed role in society by rules of position, loyalty and relatedness. The opposite of collectivism is individualism, meaning people consider themselves to be independent. Job-hopping, process perspective, working on contracts, and organizational change are much more typical in individualistic societies than in collectivistic ones. What is often called "the West" usually refers to individualistic societies: northwest Europe and Anglo countries worldwide.

- Hierarchy: the degree to which subordinate people accept their position as natural. The opposite of a hierarchical or "large power distance" culture is an egalitarian or "small power distance" one. Civic rights, empowerment and shifting leadership are typical of small power distance countries, such as Anglo, Scandinavian, and Germanic ones. Asymmetric relationships, with paternalistic leadership versus obedience, are typical of large-power-distance societies, such as the BRIC countries (Brazil, Russia, India, China) whose economies are rising to prominence at the moment.

- Aggression: the corresponding dimension is called masculinity versus femininity. Masculinity is the degree to which society is seen as a fighting arena, and there tends to be a "winner takes all" mentality. Its opposite, femininity, corresponds with a consensus-oriented, forgiving society. Masculinity is also associated with very different emotional roles between the sexes. Typical feminine countries are the Scandinavian countries, with

---

[7]This section has been kindly contributed by Gert Jan Hofstede. Further reading after this section could start at http://www. geert-hofstede.com and be pursued in the book *Cultures and Organizations: Software of the Mind* (McGraw-Hill, 2010).

their taste for schooling and for having "welfare states." Masculine countries include Germanic and Anglo countries and China and India.

■ Otherness: this dimension is about anxiety in the face of the unknown. It separates "uncertainty avoiding" societies from "uncertainty tolerant" ones. In the former, there is an emotional need for rules, even though these rules may not be kept. In the latter, rules are deemed unnecessary unless they are kept. Uncertainty tolerant countries include China and the Anglo countries, while Latin and Slav countries are uncertainty avoiding.

■ Context: Short- versus Long-term Orientation. This dimension is about the width of perspective that people take to their life events. People in long-term oriented cultures, of which the southeast Asian countries are prime examples, consider themselves to be small entities in a large and ever-changing world. People in short-term oriented cultures, exemplified by African countries, consider themselves to be proud and living in the here and now in which adherence to rules for good behavior, based on tradition, are important.

■ Happiness: Indulgence versus Restraint. This last dimension concerns the degree to which people feel in control of their lives and free to do as they like, as opposed to bound by duty, fate, or rules and powerless to take action. Indulgent parts of the world include Central America and, to a lesser degree, the Anglo world. Individual freedom is an important concept here. Restrained parts of the world include the Slavic countries and southeast Asia. Duty and fate are important here.

Cross-cultural competence involves the ability to recognize one's own "deep values" and those of others, and to account for the difference when interpreting others' behavior. This is usually a process that takes years of life experience that can be helped, but not replaced, by study. With globalization, and with the rise of non-Western economies, cross-cultural competence is becoming a fundamental skill for managers.

Organizational Culture and National Culture

Firms also have cultures. But the members of a firm do not need to agree on "deep values"; research has shown that firm cultures center on the shared understanding of practices. For instance, what does "empowerment" mean? What is an appropriate dress code? How bad is it to be late for a meeting? Firms like to speak about their values; but this tends to be window dressing or, in the best cases, limited to work-related practices.

Almost all of business literature assumes an organization culture that fits with an individualistic, egalitarian, uncertainty tolerant mindset. But firms are populated by people who live the values of their own cultures. The cultural backgrounds of a firm's leaders, its headquarter location, and of its main workforce, are likely to have a strong influence on its culture. This in turn will strongly affect the working of the organization's information systems. Here we focus on two culture-contingent decisions that are crucial to the operation of a firm: "Who decides what?" and "According to what process are decisions reached?" Information Systems tend to include implicit or explicit assumptions about these questions that may not be in harmony with the organization's culture. For example, if the design of an information systems assumes delegated authority, or if it assumes a process perspective, while employees are acculturated to obedience and managers to non-delegation, then that system will likely fail miserably.

In practice, one dimension of culture tends to change much more readily than the others: individualism, which correlates with national wealth. It is not to be confounded with it though. For instance, east Asian cultures tend to be much more collectivistic than Indo-European ones, even at equal prosperity. France is a case of a country with a culture that is individualistic but has a strong hierarchy.

As discussed before, firm culture contributes to the creation of the context in which the information system is embedded. As a consequence, there has to be a fit between organizational culture, which itself is a child of dominant national cultures in the firm, and the IS design. This requirement is particularly significant and particularly challenging to multinational or transnational organizations that wish to have one unified information systems architecture based on standardized technology (e.g., enterprise systems).

How Culture Impacts Structure

Business terminology changes its meaning when you travel. I once asked a number of European telecommunications managers to define strategy. A German said "bringing order into elements." A Brit smilingly countered "letting ideas bubble up into the organization," upon which a Dane said "yes, but realistic ideas." Two Spaniards had been silent and when prompted said "a sense of direction." And similar variability holds for the social sub-system of any information system.

There is method in this madness, and the above-mentioned six dimensions can help show that method. When it comes to the implicit structure of the social system in a company, plotting two of them against one another has good predictive value. For example, plotting uncertainty avoidance and power distance (Figure 2.13) provides information about how organizations of that country, or business leaders socialized in a particular country, are likely to think about decision-making and organizational structure.

In the upper left "market" quadrant we find egalitarian, uncertainty tolerant countries. Here, organizations resemble markets. Managers, or indeed anyone, can come up with generalistic ideas, others can "buy into" these ideas, ad hoc task forces can be created or consultants hired, and projects started. This quadrant fits with attaching importance to marketing, to change, and to strategic use of IT.

In the lower left "machine" quadrant are countries with organizations that are organized as well-oiled machines. The overall structure is more important than any part, detailed descriptions are preferred, and predictable behavior is important. These countries tend to be good at precision production. When it comes to IT they favor Enterprise Requirements Planning (see Chapter 3) software, and other applications that structure the internal organization of the firm.

In the right-hand side "family" and "pyramid" quadrants we find countries where person-bound power prevails over structural power. Here, bosses can be expected to disregard any rules that might hold, if the fancy—or a good idea—strikes them. The top half is the family quadrant where there are few rules except a great respect for authority. The bottom half is the pyramid quadrant where there is respect for specialism and there tends to be a great deal of red tape.

The upshot of all of this is that no multinational can escape culture, and no leader in a multinational organization can afford to be ignorant of. Consider the fictitious case in the sidebar as an example of all too common discrepancy in the interpretation of the same situation by managers from different cultures.

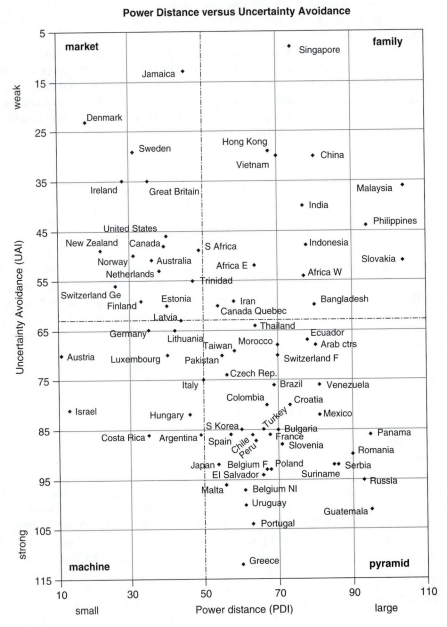

Figure 2.13 Plotting uncertainty avoidance and power distance (*Source*: Hofstede, Hofstede, and Minkov 2010, used with permission.)

IMPLICATIONS

From the preceding definitions of information systems and IS success, and the discussions of the role of systemic effects and organizational context, a number of implications of interest to general and functional managers follow, including:

Don't Put the Cart before the Horse

We often receive inquiries from former students or other managers asking our opinion about one or the other IT solution (e.g., what is the best CRM software?). However, you now recognize that asking such questions is equivalent to putting the proverbial cart before the horse by letting technology drive decision making.

While it is common for strategy to be inspired by the functionalities of a powerful software product, the selection of a specific IT product should not be the point of departure, but rather the point of arrival of your information system design effort. When asked to express an opinion about a software program or other technology, you should always start by asking, Why are you investigating this software program (i.e., what is the firm strategy)? What are you attempting to do with the software (i.e., what is the IS goal)?

SIDEBAR 1: INFORMATION SYSTEMS AND THE NEED TO RECONCILE DIVERSE CULTURAL PERSPECTIVES[8]

Wei Liu was frustrated. It had seemed so nice, a joint venture of his Chengdu glass manufacturing company with a British partner, opening up new sales channels in high-quality markets. But in the ten years that he'd been involved with the British, he had never been able to build up a good relationship with one of them. It was no use; if for once there was a decently behaved manager, that person would be gone the next year. The Brits were creative and good at investing in plants but they had no sensitivity for the needs of Chinese personnel, who usually came from rural areas to feed their families and needed a fixed contract and a company-provided place to sleep. He regularly had to calm down personnel, or local officials. The only sure thing about the Brits was that they had a fetishist reliance on their ERP systems, in particular the quarterly reports. Two years ago they had appointed a Brit to enter data into the ERP in Chengdu—this person was just a dead weight, costing money but not bringing in a yuan. Worse, the English made him harass his Chinese business partners, with whom he had excellent Guanxi, for immediate payment before the end of the quarter. There was no way in which he could convince them that his good Guanxi relationship was worth far more than today's cash flow. Was it time to say goodbye to the Brits?

Meanwhile in London, Chris Westrup was being instructed by his predecessor James Oldman as CIO of the joint venture. James was obviously glad to be rid of the job. "Chris," he said, "I've done this for two years now and I tell you, you just cannot trust these Chinese. They do not care about data, they do not care about transparency. They'll enter any old figures into the ERP, and when you call them to task they just sit there and nod politely, but take no action whatsoever. That's why I appointed our own man in Chengdu, so that we have a decent control of our operations. But the worst thing is they do not care about cash flow; you've got to be at their heels all of the time. It's oral promises all along, all of it in Chinese!" Chris grinned—with a master's in international business and in Chinese, he was game. "Yes, grin, and good luck," said Oldman, "I'll talk to you again in a year, when you have been driven crazy too. You know what it is, they just cannot work according to any plan. All they ever do is improvising, changing, dealing. How they get so much done is still a mystery to me. I sometimes wonder if this whole joint venture is worth the trouble." Chris thought that it was time for Oldman to retire, and for someone like himself to take over and take the collaboration to a new level.

---

[8]This vignette is inspired by the article, "Both Global and Local: ICTs and Joint Ventures in China," by Chris Westrup and Wei Liu, *Information Systems Journal* (2008) 18, pp. 427–443.

In our opening mini-case, the firm's intention was to be able to improve its volumes (i.e., increase the number of customers and their level of consumption). This can be classified as the strategic goal. From this goal the firm should derive a precise set of IS goals that specify what information processing functionalities are needed to achieve the strategic objective (e.g., to create a comfortable space for restaurant patrons to more conveniently place orders at the table and to access the news and other relevant information). Once the goals are set, the IS design team can identify, shape, and deploy the appropriate components of the system, of which IT is one.

The Rock in the Pond

As in any other system, the components of an IS mutually influence one another (systemic effects). Similar to the ripples resulting from the act of throwing a rock into a pond, changes to one or more IS components impact, sooner or later, all other components. This influence may be significant or limited. However, when you are called upon to participate in IS design and implementations, you should try to contribute to your team's successful introduction of a new IS by anticipating these ripple effects and proactively managing them before they become a cause of concern. Let's return to the example of airline check-in kiosks. When kiosks are installed, the business process of identifying travelers and assigning them seats must change for those customers who prefer this method. The role, and the skills required, of check-in agents is modified as a result of the change in the business process—at a minimum they must be able to explain the kiosk operations and provide helpful support as customers learn to use them. In this case, the new technology significantly impacts both process and people, while the effect on structure is negligible. However, the more precise you can be a priori in estimating what the effects will be, the better able your firm will be to proactively manage the changes.

Information Systems Are in Flux

An information system is not designed "once and for all" as if it were a static artifact. Business strategy and the external environment evolve continuously. This evolution calls for a constant reevaluation of IS goals and needed information processing functionalities. In turn, this reevaluation will at times engender the need for changes to the design of an existing information system.

The design and use of an IS should be seen as an iterative process involving the cyclical evaluation of individual IS components and the assessment of how different organizational systems work together to support the business. The synergy among IS components, as well as among discrete organizational IS, can be maintained over time only if there is a willingness to modify aspects of this IS configuration as needed. Any time a major change occurs, the current IS design must be reevaluated and the system must be optimized once again.

Optimize the Whole As mentioned earlier, you should never lose focus of your objective: to optimize the information system rather than any of its constituent parts. Optimizing the system as a whole often requires that one or more components be de-optimized (i.e., they are not as powerful or cutting edge as they could be). This fundamental insight is one that is often forgotten when managers get caught up in the IT investment mentality—the most effective information system need not be comprised of all the best parts.

To the contrary, examples abound of firms that deployed cutting-edge technology where there was no need for it to deliver the desired information processing functionalities. In some cases, the adoption of cutting-edge technology in fact reduces the effectiveness of the IS as a whole, making the achievement of the needed information processing functionalities more difficult.

CONCLUSION

Like all frameworks, those presented in this chapter are valuable because of their ability to support a systematic and disciplined analysis of specific issues (e.g., software selection, IS design, system failure diagnosis). They don't offer cookie cutter answers, but they provide the support necessary for a disciplined and thorough analysis. By using them to guide your thinking, you can be sure to complete a comprehensive analysis rather than being tempted to stop upon identifying the first or second most obvious explanations, perhaps those communicated by the most vocal members of your organization.

Furthermore, working with the models challenges conventional wisdom and management fads and fashions that may lead you to reach simplistic conclusions that, while true, often only reveal part of the story (e.g., "You must train your employees when new software is introduced"). The alternative—being driven by a best practice mentality, benchmarking your organization against the performance of competitors—is a risky strategy, and you should always beware of so many buzzwords in one sentence! You as a manager must always consider how new IT fits within the context of your own company. Does it suit the unique people, processes, and structures of your firm? If not, is it a wise strategy to make changes to these components in order to fit with the IT? Or do you need different IT? All too often when selecting a system, considering change initiatives, or troubleshooting underperforming information systems, the focus is on IT and system functionality. The frameworks presented here challenge you to think in terms of overall IS design instead—perhaps a more difficult task, but certainly a more appropriate and productive one.

SUMMARY

This is a critical chapter in the book because it provides fundamental definitions and sets the stage for the discussion in the next chapters. The chapter defined information systems as sociotechnical systems composed of four components: IT, people, processes, and structure. This definition and its implications provide the basis for this book.

Specifically, in this chapter we learned that:

- Information systems are designed and built with the objective of improving the firm's efficiency and effectiveness by fulfilling its information processing needs. Successful information systems are those that are used and that achieve their intended goals.
- Information systems exist in an organizational context, characterized by the firm strategy, culture, and IT infrastructure. The organization itself is subject to the influences of its external environment,

including regulatory requirements, social and business trends, and competitive pressures.

- Information systems are subject to systemic effects, defined as the notion that the different components of a system are interdependent and that changes in one component affect all other components of the system. Thus, when designing a new information system, or troubleshooting an underperforming one, you can devise multiple ways to achieve the system's goal.
- Increasingly in modern firms, organizational change stems from the introduction of new information technologies. Depending on the objectives and reach of the new system, we identify three levels of change—first-, second-, and third-order change—each requiring different levels of commitment and sponsorship to be successfully managed.

STUDY QUESTIONS

1. Describe the difference between information systems and information technology. Provide an example of each.

2. Provide an example of two organizations in which you think a similar information system would engender two very different outcomes. Explain why.

3. Provide two examples, from your personal experience, of information systems that generate positive and negative unintended results.

4. Define the concept of systemic effects. Explain why it is important for you as a general or functional manager to be aware of this concept.

5. Describe first-, second-, and third-order organizational change induced by the adoption of new IT. Provide an example, real or imagined, for each of these three levels of change.

 ## FURTHER READINGS

1. Glass, Robert L. *Software Runaways: Monumental Software Disasters*. Prentice Hall, 1997.
2. Hofstede, G, Hofstede, GJ and Minkov, M. *Cultures and Organizations: Software of the Mind. Revised and expanded.* New York: McGraw-Hill, 2010.
3. O'Hara, Margaret T., Watson, Richard T., and Kavan, C. Bruce. (1999). "Managing the Three Levels of Change." *Information Systems Management Journal* 16(3), pp. 63–70.
4. Zuboff, S. *In the Age of the Smart Machine: The Future of Work and Power*. New York: Basic Books, 1988.

 ## GLOSSARY

- **Efficiency:** *Efficiency* is defined as the ability to limit waste and maximize the ratio of the output produced to the inputs consumed. In other words, a firm is more efficient when it produces more with the same amount of resources, produces the same with less resources, or produces more with less resources.

- **Effectiveness:** The ability to achieve stated goals or objectives. Typically a more effective firm is one that makes better decisions and is able to carry them out successfully.

- **External environment:** The world outside the firm that creates influences such as regulation, the competitive landscape, and general business and social trends (e.g., outsourcing, customer self-service).

- **Firm culture:** The collection of beliefs, expectations, and values shared by the members of an organization.

- **Firm strategy:** The manner in which the organization intends to achieve its objectives.

- **Information system:** Formal, sociotechnical, organizational system designed to collect, process, store, and distribute information.

- **Information technology:** Hardware, software, and telecommunication equipment.

- **IT infrastructure:** The infrastructure is the set of shared IT resources and services of the firm, and it forms a firm's technological backbone that constrains and enables opportunities for future information systems implementations.

- **Organizational structure:** The organizational design, reporting, and relationships within the information system.

- **Process:** The series of steps necessary to complete an organizational activity.

- **Systemic effects:** The notion that the different components of a system are interdependent and that change in one component affects all other components of the system.

3

Organizational Information Systems and Their Impact

What You Will Learn in This Chapter

This chapter completes our introductory series on the foundations of information systems. In Chapter 1 we made the case for this book's value to general and functional managers. In Chapter 2 we provided important definitions. In this chapter we discuss the vocabulary and concepts that will enable us to categorize different types of information systems and to communicate with other managers and IS professionals.

Specifically, in this chapter you will learn:

1. How to categorize systems according to the hierarchical, functional, and process perspectives. You will also learn the rationale for each perspective and its limitations.

2. Become familiar with the underlying principles, and applications of business process reengineering (BPR), as well as its advantages and disadvantages.

3. Evaluate the integration trend and the role of integration principles in the modern firm. We will explore the pressures toward integration and the challenges integration creates. We will also discuss business and systems integration trends and the relationship between the two.

4. Understand the genesis of the enterprise systems (ES) trend and why so many companies are employing or introducing them. You will also learn to articulate the principal benefits and risks associated with these systems.

5. Understand what is meant by supply chain management and be able to explain the role that supply chain management applications play in modern organizations.

6. Understand what is meant by knowledge management, be able to categorize the different types of knowledge commonly found in organizations, and comprehend why organizations feel the need to employ knowledge management applications.

7. Evaluate the business intelligence (BI) trend and understand the components of the BI infrastructure. You will also learn how to identify and describe the role of the technologies that comprise a modern BI infrastructure.

8. Understand what customer relationship management (CRM) is and be able to articulate both its benefits and limitations. You will also learn how the CRM and BI trends relate to one another.

MINI-CASE: INTEGRATION AT BIGPHARMA, INC.

As you walk out of the board room, still shaking your head in disbelief, you mumble to yourself, "Boy, that was fun! They were really going at it today!" As you get to your desk, though, it hits you—you have to make sense of what just happened in there.

As the executive assistant to the CEO at BigPharma, Inc., the second largest pharmaceutical firm in the United States, you have had the luxury of attending all of the executive team meetings, and sometimes participating in the decision making with your analyses, without any of the responsibility that comes with making those decisions. However, far from what you had imagined the glamour of board room discussions to be, most meetings of the executive team were pretty boring. Not today!

Surprisingly, you had predicted this one to be a real snoozer. A pretty safe bet given the topic: the need to gain efficiencies by better integrating across functional areas. The meeting took a turn toward the exciting right out of the gates when Laura Jean Polly, your boss, announced that at PharmaMed (the premier industry trade event of the year) she had drinks with the senior VP of business development of BigCoSoft, the second largest vendor of enterprise systems.

She said that BigCoSoft was interested in breaking into the pharmaceutical market and was seeking to sign up a high-profile customer. They looked at this contract as a mutually beneficial partnership that would lead to lots of press and advantages for both firms. The client would be a "showcase customer," featured on the Web site and in case studies. BigCoSoft was willing to waive licensing fees for the first three years. "But the biggest advantage," the senior VP had said, "is that with you on board we will attract more customers. With critical mass we can put huge development resources into this product."

At this point you were thinking, "Yep, snoozer! I was right." Two seconds later the first salvo was fired. Jane Pinket, the senior VP of finance, said, "Everyone knows that BigCoSoft's strength is manufacturing. Their financial package stinks. They will surely want to reuse that code and I am going to have to take the hit. We can cut the same deal with LargeCoSoft. They already have an enterprise system for pharmaceutical firms, and their financial module is top notch."

"Another option could be to write a bolt-on," chimed in Erik Dino, the chief operations officer (COO), "that should take care of the missing finance functionalities." "But the Human Resource module of BigCoSoft also leaves much to be desired," interjected Joe Cole, the senior VP of human resources. "Plus, we just spent $12 million on the overhaul of the benefits management system; am I going to get hit with more information systems service charges for an upgrade I don't need?"

This is about the time confusion set in, and the story becomes fuzzy as you got lost in the ping-pong volleys of comments, questions, and responses. With a heated topic on the agenda, it was painfully clear that the people in the room were more used to being listened to than to listening.

You were snapped back to attention when Ms. Polly closed the meeting by calling your name. She said, "Well, it looks like I underestimated how much my staff cared about systems! I will need a report with an investigation of the top three most viable options; the need to integrate is not going away, so we have to do something. I told BigCoSoft I would get back to them in three weeks."

DISCUSSION QUESTIONS

1. Even as the lowly executive assistant to the CEO, it was apparent to you that there was some groupthink going on here. Was buying an enterprise system the only option?
2. You vaguely recall this idea of best-of-breed applications from your information systems class two years ago. Could that approach work here?

INTRODUCTION

In Chapter 2, we formally defined information systems (IS) as those sociotechnical organizational systems designed to collect, process, store, and distribute information. We identified the four components of an IS and introduced the notion of systemic effects to represent the mutually interdependent relationships among the four components. We also discussed how information systems fit within the organization in which they are embedded and within the larger external environment.

In this chapter we rely on those definitions to explore the organizational impacts of information systems. This chapter is important for two main reasons. First, information systems pervade the modern organization, so understanding how they are classified and organized is a prerequisite to becoming a successful manager and being able to navigate the infrastructure of the modern firm. Second, because you are ultimately responsible for the success of your company or the organizational function that you oversee (e.g., finance, marketing), it is critical that you optimally manage organizational change when it occurs. Increasingly today, the impetus behind organizational change comes from the introduction of new IT and the implementation of information systems. Moreover, even when IT is not providing the impulse for change, organizational change calls for information systems adaptation. It is therefore paramount that you have the appropriate vocabulary to join the conversation, and that you have a solid understanding of what classes of software programs underpin information systems in modern organizations.

CATEGORIZING SYSTEMS

Since Leavitt and Whisler popularized the term *information technology* (IT) in the business literature in 1958,[1] researchers have advanced a number of approaches to classify and describe the role that IT plays in organizations. These efforts focus on categorizing the software applications as the point of departure for understanding the function and functionality of the information systems built around them.

Classification models are useful for two reasons. First, they provide you with a vocabulary to interact with your colleagues and with IS professionals—a vocabulary that today is taken for granted in modern organizations and in the business press. Second, the models described below provide the basis for you to develop your own thinking about the role that technology plays in your organization and on how to best manage its impacts.

Hierarchical Perspective

The hierarchical perspective recognizes that decision making and activities in organizations occur at different levels. At each level the individuals involved have different responsibilities, make different types of decisions, and carry out different types of activities (see Table 3.1). As a

Table 3.1   Activities by hierarchical level

Activity	Time Horizon	Hierarchical Level	Characteristics
Strategic	Long term	General management	Externally focused
		Functional management	Ad hoc
			Highly unstructured
Tactical	Mid term	Middle management	Repeatable
			Semi-structured
			Recurrent
Operational	Short term	Front-line employees	Low discretion
			Highly structured
			Transaction focused

[1]Leavitt, H. J., and Whisler, T. L. (1958). "Management in the 1980s," *Harvard Business Review*, November/December, pp. 41–48.

consequence, the type of information systems introduced to support each level must take these differences into account.

Operational Level   The operational level of the organization is mostly concerned with short-term activities, typically those that occur in the immediate term. Operational personnel are focused on performing the day-to-day activities that deliver the firm's value proposition. For example, in a grocery store, operational personnel concentrate on keeping the shelves stocked, keeping the store clean, addressing customer questions and requests in a timely fashion, and ensuring speedy transaction processing at checkout.

Decision making at the operational level is typically highly structured by means of detailed procedures, and, traditionally, front-line employees enjoy little discretion. The objective here is efficient transaction processing under a limited degree of uncertainty. When referring to IT-enabled data management (e.g., in a database structure), the term transaction identifies a single logical operation on the data. To ensure reliable transaction processing by software, the system must respect the ACID properties of every transaction (Table 3.2). A classic example of a transaction is your withdrawal of funds at an ATM, or the change of a passenger's seating assignment by an airline employee.

We refer to the information systems that support this organizational level as transaction processing systems (TPSs). The information technologies underpinning a TPS are typically used to automate recurring activities and to structure day-to-day operations, ensuring that they are performed with speed, accuracy, and as prescribed by the procedures. The scanner checkout system in the aforementioned grocery store represents a classic example of a TPS. Another example, in any retail store, is represented by the inventory management system.

Transaction processing can occur in batch, when transactions are acquired, and stored before being computed all at once (e.g., payroll processing), or online, when transactions are processed as they occur, in real time (e.g., credit card authentication). A typical batch process is the end-of-day reporting done by many TPSs. For example, a restaurant point of sale software will,

Table 3.2   ACID principles for reliable transaction processing

Atomicity	Transactions are atomic. If one part of the transaction fails, the system must cancel the transaction. For example, if while withdrawing money at the ATM the cash dispenser jams, your balance should not be debited.
Consistency	Transactions are consistent. In other words, only valid data is committed to long-term memory and stored in the system. For example, if the airline seat assignment system requires only letters in the first name field, no transaction with numbers in the field is accepted.
Isolation	Transactions are non-concurrent. If the system has yet to store the results of a transaction while writing the results of a second transaction, its database may end up holding invalid data. For example, if you are withdrawing money from an ATM while your sister at home is moving money electronically, the resulting balance may be invalid unless the system maintains isolation of the two transactions.
Durability	Transactions are durable when they can be recovered in the face of system failure. In other words, once the system has successfully processed the transaction, it will no longer lose it. For example, once the agent has changed your seat, the change is recorded in a transaction log. If anything were to go wrong with the database, the current state could be re-created by reprocessing the transactions from the log.

at closing, tally up all sold food and beverage items as well as compute total revenue, number of covers, and the like. While this type of reporting could be done in real-time (i.e., online processing), it is unlikely that busy chef can consult the report while the restaurant is open. Contrast this situation with the wine inventory system at Aureole restaurant where a 42-foot-tall (12 m) glass tower houses the restaurant's 2,300 bottles wine list. Having real-time knowledge of the inventory is necessary for the restaurant's sommeliers to be able to make optimal suggestions.

Managerial Level   The managerial level of the organization is mostly concerned with mid-term decision making and a functional focus. The activities performed tend to be semi structured, having both well-known components and some degree of uncertainty. Returning to our grocery store example, consider the job of the store manager. Store managers in large chains are typically responsible for selecting that portion of the inventory that experiences regional and local demand. The store manager therefore must be able to monitor demand for these products, forecast future demand, and make inventory management decisions. In manufacturing contexts, such as a chemical plant or a factory, middle management is charged with decision making that pertains to optimizing plant operations (e.g., inventory management, production schedules, labor utilization) given the overall production goals.

Decision making at this level is typically semi structured, but characterized by repeatable patterns and established methods. The focus is on tactical decision making characterized by some discretion. The objective is to improve the effectiveness of the organization, or one of its functions, within the broad strategic guidelines set by the executive team.

The information systems that support this organizational level are typically called decision support systems (DSSs).[2] DSSs provide the information needed by functional managers to engage in tactical decision making. The objective is to produce recurring reports (e.g., daily sales reports, monthly customer service reports) and exception reports (e.g., items that are running low and may cause a stockout). DSSs typically focus on internal operations, and the data they use for analysis stems from the firm's TPS (see Figure 3.1).

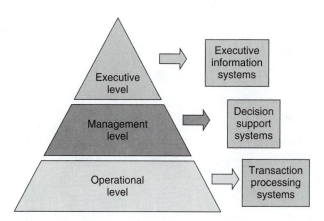

Figure 3.1   Hierarchical perspective

---

[2]There is some confusion about terminology at this level, with some sources referring to information systems in support of middle management as management information systems (MISs). The term MIS can be misleading as it is often used to refer to the collection of all the information systems used by the firm. We therefore use the term DSS.

Executive Level   The executive echelon of the organization is concerned with high-level, long-range decisions. Executives are focused on strategic decision making and on interpreting how the firm should react to trends in the marketplace and the competitive environment. Continuing the example of the grocery store chain, the executive team is focused on judgments such as where to locate new stores, what to do with underperforming stores, what long-term contracts to sign with suppliers, and at what price.

Decision making at this level is highly unstructured, often ad hoc, and reliant on internal as well as external data sources. The objective is, as much as possible, to predict future developments by evaluating trends, using highly aggregated data and scenario analyses. Little structure and formal methodologies exist for activities at this level.

We refer to the information systems that support this organizational level as executive information systems (EISs). A recent development in EIS is offered by the use of software applications known as executive dashboards. These tools enable rapid evaluation of highly aggregated organizational and trend data while still providing drill-down features that enable executives to view detailed information (see Figure 3.2 for an example).

Evolution of the Hierarchical Perspective   The hierarchical perspective proved very useful over the years in enabling managers and IS professionals to easily identify the main characteristics and purpose of information systems and the information technology products designed to support them. However, this perspective is becoming increasingly less representative due to the recent organizational trend toward the adoption of flatter hierarchies with fewer layers between front-line operations and strategic decision making. Moreover, we have recently witnessed a trend toward the empowerment of operational personnel who increasingly enjoy decision-making discretion.

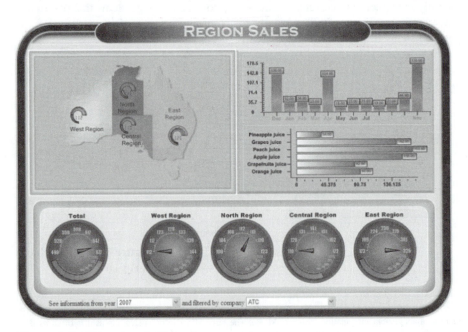

Figure 3.2   Executive dashboard

Another limitation of the hierarchical model stems from the fact that it is difficult to separate information systems into clear-cut categories. For example, the defining characteristic of TPSs is their operational focus on day-to-day transaction processing. However, the software applications that support many modern TPSs provide extensive reporting functionality, increasingly giving these systems the traits and functionality that characterize DSSs.

Functional Perspective

As the post-World War II years created significant impetus for the growth of world businesses, the centralized organizational forms could no longer cope with the increasing managerial complexity brought on by size and diversification. As a consequence, there was a trend toward decentralization, with organizations creating business units and distinct functional areas within them (e.g., accounting, finance, human resources).

This decentralized management structure was very successful because it solved the coordination problems brought on by increasing size. Each unit was able to maintain its operations to a manageable degree of complexity while the corporation as a whole grew larger. The functional organization within business units is typically represented in the form of the organizational chart (see Figure 3.3 for an example).

With every function managing its own budget independently and having unique information processing needs, functional information systems emerged.

Functional Systems   Functional systems are expressly designed to support the specific needs of individuals in the same functional area (see Figure 3.4). Functional systems are based on the principle of local optimization, which suggests that information processing needs are unique and homogeneous within a functional area. Thus, the optimal systems are tailored to those highly

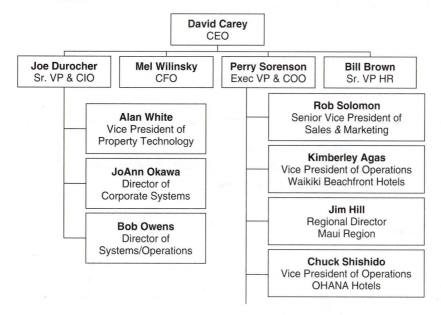

Figure 3.3   Partial organizational chart

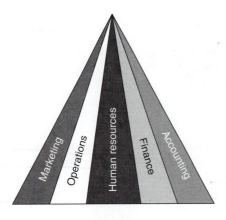

Figure 3.4   Functional perspective

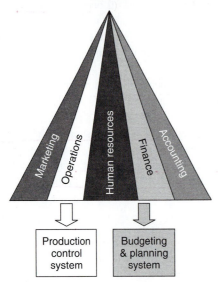

Figure 3.5   Functional systems

specific needs and use a language that is familiar to the professionals in that area. As a result, today there is a vast software industry catering to the information processing needs of every functional area in almost any industry sector.

The functional perspective, in conjunction with the hierarchical approach (see Figure 3.5), worked reasonably well for a number of years, until the recession of the late 1980s put pressure on U.S. firms to both increase efficiency and offer superior customer service.

Process Perspective

The primary limitation of the functional and hierarchical perspectives is their lack of integration among separate systems and the introduction of considerable redundancy. This redundancy often created inefficiency, with duplication of similar efforts in separate business units, and substandard service, with customers often being referred to different representatives of the same organization for support. From a technology perspective, the functional approach led to the development of

Figure 3.6   Silos on a farm (Courtesy of George Kashou at travelthewholeworld.com.)

silo applications. Like silos used in farms to store and keep different grains separate (Figure 3.6), these applications would serve a vertical (i.e., functional) need very well, but made it difficult to enable communication across different functional areas.

Consider the case of Johnson and Johnson (J&J), the highly diversified health care products maker, with product lines ranging from beauty-care goods to medical and diagnostic devices. After engaging in some internal research, J&J found that a number of its customers (e.g., drug stores) would purchase products from up to seven different business units. Customers began to ask why they could not interact once with a single J&J representative for all their needs. This change would make it easier for the customer to do business with J&J, and it would also enable them to negotiate volume discounts, coordinate shipments, and experience superior customer service.

Business Process Reengineering   Business process reengineering (BPR) emerged in the early 1990s as a way to break down organizational silos in recognition of the fact that business processes are inherently cross functional. Since its inception, BPR has evolved under a number of labels (e.g., business process redesign, business transformation), and it has now become a standard approach to efficiency improvement in organizations. A business process is defined here as the series of steps that a firm performs in order to complete an economic activity (see Figure 3.7).

BPR is a managerial approach that employs a process view of organizational activities. BPR was codified as a methodology for achieving internal business integration using a top-down approach to business process redesign, and seeking dramatic performance improvements through

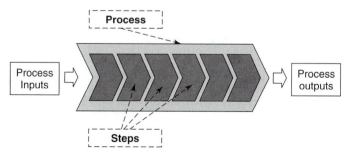

Figure 3.7   Process perspective

rationalization of activities and elimination of duplication of efforts across separate functions and units. As Michael Hammer put it in the article that first popularized the term *BPR*, "We should 'reengineer' our business: use the power of modern information technology to radically redesign our business processes in order to achieve dramatic improvements in their performance."[3] The poster child for BPR was Progressive Insurance, an American car insurance company that, under pressure from larger insurers, conceived a process called Immediate Response claim handling. With this novel approach, Progressive would have claim adjusters who worked out of vans, rather than offices, and were able to inspect a vehicle within nine hours of a customer call. Before the reengineering effort Progressive was much closer to the industry standard of seven to ten days. Moreover, aided by information systems, the adjuster was able to produce an on-site estimate of the damage and even cut a check to the insured driver. By completely re-architecting the claim payment process, the firm dramatically improved its speed of operation and quality of service—resulting in a sales growth from $1.3 billion annually in 1991 to $9.5 billion in 2002.

As the Progressive Insurance example suggests, the BPR methodology focuses on activities internal to the firm and requires that managers in charge of the redesign effort question old assumptions regarding how the business should operate (e.g., claim adjusters have an office). Such redesign should be driven by a process focus—defined as a way of organizing work that centers on the steps necessary to create value for customers (e.g., speed of claim processing), without regard for what functional areas would traditionally be responsible for the process steps (Figure 3.8). Proponents of BPR suggest that it is this process focus that enables the firm to eliminate the redundancy and inefficiency associated with the multiple handoffs of tasks from one

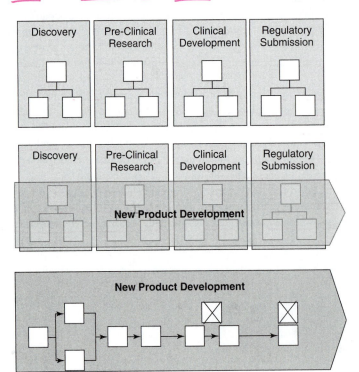

Figure 3.8 Reengineering schematic of a product development process (Created by Kai A. Simon at the English Wikipedia Project.)

---

[3]Hammer, M. (1990). "Reengineering Work: Don't Automate, Obliterate," *Harvard Business Review*, July/August, pp. 104–112.

area to another. The firm should therefore reorganize its work in a series of processes designed around the intended outcomes. In charge of each process is a processes champion, who oversees things from start to finish. Finally, the BPR methodology is radical in nature, requiring total disregard for existing processes to make room for the redesigned ones. Only with this approach could the firm "stop paving the cow paths"[4] and achieve drastic performance improvements.

The Dark Side of Reengineering   As with any far-reaching transformation process, there are significant risks associated with BPR efforts. First, radical third-order change (see Chapter 2), as required by BPR efforts, engenders significant resistance by those involved. Changes in an individuals' scope of work, responsibility, and position within the organizational structure require abundant retraining and careful planning. People tend to be very comfortable with the way they operate, and changes in their job role, scope, or responsibility require the development of new sets of skills and training. This often engenders confusion.

Second, despite its obvious importance, operations (and consequently business processes) are not "glamorous" or highly valued. Consider for example the excitement that surrounds a successful high profile merger and the clout of the executives who conclude it. Compare that with the typical "excitement" surrounding the reduction of claim processing time...

Third, BPR initiatives are very expensive because they often require the firm to retire its legacy systems and develop a costly integrated technology infrastructure. Applications that had been developed to enable a functional perspective rarely can be adapted to support a process perspective. The rise to prominence of BPR was seized by the software industry and spurred the development of a number of integrated applications. New classes of software programs, such as enterprise systems and supply chain management systems (see below), built to support a process focus emerged at this time. However, such complex and expensive initiatives require significant managerial commitment and executive sponsorship. And securing such commitment is often difficult to do, as executives focus on strategic planning, budgeting, capital allocation, and the like.

Finally, the BPR methodology developed a bad reputation after the initial excitement because of its complexity and the fact that for many organizations BPR led to significant downsizing and layoffs.

The Role of IT in Business Process Reengineering Efforts   The main catalyst for BPR efforts is modern information technology; technological innovation typically enables the firm to question old assumptions that constrain current operations. For example, while traditionally firms have waited to receive invoices from a supplier before issuing payment, the advent of affordable and comprehensive networks has enabled the development of secure extranets (see Chapter 5). Such extranets have allowed the redesign of billing processes, with many organizations installing networked computers at receiving docks, where employees can check the accuracy of a shipment as it is received. If the goods are found to be acceptable, payment can be issued immediately, dramatically reducing the number of handoffs required to complete the process, and consequently its cost.

As organizations and technology evolve over time, traditional business processes may become obsolete and need to be reevaluated. The interplay of new technologies, and the opportunities they afford, with the redesign of business processes to take advantage of these technologies,

---

[4]Hammer, M. (1990). "Reengineering Work: Don't Automate, Obliterate," *Harvard Business Review*, July/August, pp. 104–112.

has the potential to yield substantial performance improvements. Note that while BPR was developed as an internal methodology to the organization, the same idea has been extended to interorganizational relationships.[5]

THE INFORMATION SYSTEM CYCLE

When describing the various categories of systems found in modern organizations, we described transaction processing systems as those concerned with automating routine day-to-day activities that happen in the present. Attentive managers though have long recognized that, while the implementation of these systems is typically justified with arguments focused on efficiency improvements, the value of the data that they capture should not be underestimated.

The information systems cycle portrays the progression of business data from their inception in transaction processing systems, to their storage in data repositories, and finally to their use in analytical tools (Figure 3.9). Data are typically produced as a byproduct of daily operations and transactions (e.g., shoppers purchasing items at a retail shop, fans walking through the turnstile at a stadium) that the firm completes as it handles business in the present. Such organizational data, when not disposed of, can be accumulated in data repositories and create a record of past transactions (i.e., the data are used to remember the past). Using analytical tools, the firm can then make sense of the accumulated data to find patterns, test assumptions, and more generally enable decision making in an effort to better prepare for the future.

Often these decisions directly impact the firm's information systems, with the introduction of new systems (i.e., new IT, new people, new processes, new structures) or the modification of existing ones in an effort to position the firm to achieve its future objectives in an ever-changing competitive environment. Consider again the example of a grocery store introduced earlier. As customers come and go, a wealth of transactional data is generated. This information is necessary for the store to manage its daily operations (i.e., to handle the present). Customers need to find shelves stocked with popular items. Managers must optimize inventory in order to minimize working capital and spoilage of perishable items. Correct billing, taking into account promotions and discounts, must be generated at checkout. All these instances describe events

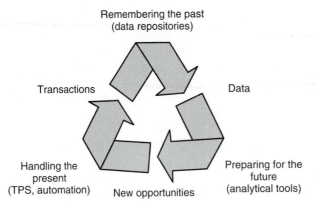

Figure 3.9   The information systems cycle

---

[5]Hammer, M. (2001). "The Superefficient Company," *Harvard Business Review*, September, pp. 82–91.

that happen during the normal course of business in the grocery store. When customers leave, and the present has been handled, all the data generated that are not subject to legal requirements may then be thrown away.

Alternatively, the store can create data repositories that catalog and hold this information—now historical in nature. This act of "remembering the past" is of course only meaningful if the data can be used at a later stage to prepare for the future (e.g., gain beneficial intelligence through analysis of the data). For example, management may commission basket analyses seeking to identify items that sell well together, and, based on the results, change the product mix or the location of some items. Management may also use inventory data to optimize reorder schedules and limit chances of stockouts.

THE INTEGRATION IMPERATIVE

The emergence of the process perspective, and the promise it held for streamlining business operations and thereby creating substantial efficiencies and effectiveness improvements, was at the heart of the impetus behind integration efforts during the last two decades. It was during that time that we saw the popularization of the term *enterprise systems* (see below) and the pro-liferation of large-scale integrated applications designed to answer the call for business process integration.

Defining Integration

The Merriam-Webster online dictionary defines the act of integrating as to "form, coordinate, or blend into a functioning or unified whole" or "unite." Thus, integration is the process that an organization, or a number of organizations, goes through in order to unify, or join together, some of its tangible or intangible assets. Assets here represent physical possessions, like computer networks and applications, or intangible resources, like data, knowledge, or business processes.

The overarching goal of integration is to organize, streamline, and simplify a process or an application. Alternatively, the firm's integration effort seeks to modify processes, applications, or assets so that they better represent the realities of the organization and are more closely aligned with the current business objectives and strategic orientation of the firm. Consider, as an illustration, what may happen the next time you rent a car. Major car rental companies are able to share renter's billing information with the firms that process camera-enforced speeding and traffic light violations. When a camera identifies a rental car violating traffic laws (e.g., speeding) it can immediately query the rental car company's database and identify the driver on record at the time of the violation, charge the person's credit card, and provide a receipt that will be issued to the driver upon return of the car. While it is understandable if you prefer not to experience this situation, you will recognize this as a great example of business process integration across companies!

The Dimensions of Integration

We can categorize integration efforts on two dimensions: their locus and object. The locus of integration can be internal or external. In the first case, the firm is seeking to unify and coordinate owned assets that reside within the boundaries of the firm. For example, a bank may take loan applications at a branch, by phone, or by asking customers to fill out paper-based applications and mail them to the bank. Once an application has been collected, it is checked for accuracy and sent to the bank's administrative office for processing. There, a clerk collects any documentation still needed, such as the applicant's credit score, and passes the application on to a loan officer, who makes a decision.

Using an expert system and networked computers, such a process can be redesigned to achieve dramatic improvements in speed. The application can be completed online or input directly into a computer application by an agent if the applicant prefers to call or visit a branch. Its accuracy can be immediately enforced by rules in the software application that do not allow the process to continue without the needed data. The system, connected to the credit rating agency, can immediately obtain credit scores and any other relevant information. For the majority of loan applications, where decisions are fairly straightforward, this is typically all that is needed to issue a recommendation, and the expert system can do so in real time. More complex applications can be escalated to an experienced loan officer, who, accessing the information through a networked computer, makes a decision.

In the second case, the assets being integrated are not all owned by the firm, and interorganizational integration efforts are involved. Consider the example of General Mills and Land O'Lakes, two companies with different product lines but a similar customer base of grocery stores, and similar needs for refrigerated warehousing and transportation. Realizing the potential for synergies and efficiencies, the two firms now coordinate their logistics efforts. As a consequence, General Mills warehouses Land O'Lakes products and delivers them with fuller trucks that make fewer stops. Integrating their distribution and logistics has proven beneficial to both firms.

The second dimension of interest is the object of integration (i.e., what assets the firm is looking to unify or combine). With respect to the object of integration, we distinguish between business integration and systems integration.

Business Integration   Business integration refers to the unification or the creation of tight linkages among the diverse, but connected, business activities carried out by individuals, groups, and departments within an organization. The outcome of business integration is the introduction of cohesive, streamlined business processes that encompass previously separate activities.

Consider the experience of a large computer manufacturer describing how its financing processes have recently changed: "The last thing we want to do is make customers fill out paperwork and [then] call them at a later date to say, 'you are not qualified' [. . . .] This is no longer a satisfactory way to deal with the customer—we need to qualify the customer on the spot."[6] This degree of responsiveness can only be achieved through an integration of the sales and financing processes.

Business integration is considered critical to the survival of the modern firm. Many observers have suggested that in order to stay competitive today's business ventures must be able to present one face to the customer, provide solutions, and achieve global inventory visibility.

Presenting One Face to the Customer   Increasingly we hear that organizations must organize around their customers' needs, rather than in functional areas or around product lines. With

---

[6]Brohman, M. K., Piccoli, G., Watson, R., and Parasuraman, A. (2005). "NCSS Process Completeness: Construct Development and Preliminary Validation," *Proceedings of the Thirty-Eighth Hawaii International Conference on System Sciences*, Hawaii, HI.

the continuous speeding up of competition, they must be able to react and respond quickly and effectively to customer requests and make it as easy as possible for customers to work with the firm. A request by the firm to call a different department or a different location to have questions addressed is increasingly met with discontent by consumers. Barnes & Noble and other retailers with both online and offline channels are attempting to better integrate their diverse channels of distribution. As customers we have come to expect the ability to shop online, but still check to see if an item of interest is available at the local store. When we have an item to return, we don't understand why we can't simply drop it off at the local store rather than having to fumble with packaging and the postal service. If these are different channels of distribution for the same company, we argue, why can't we work seamlessly with the one that makes it easiest for us at the time?

Providing Solutions   Companies are now expected to provide solutions, not an array of products or services. Hotels, for example, are increasingly defining their business as "travel support" rather than lodging. This redefinition of the firm's value proposition from a product to a solution creates a wealth of opportunity for creating new services, like airline check-in and baggage pickup at the hotel. The sporting goods store Finish Line provides another example for solving a nagging problem: shoes on sale often are missing some of the sizes. At Finish Line, customers who are eyeing a nice pair of sneakers at the right price but find out that their size is missing are not at a loss. Finish Line associates can look up the availability of the same item at other stores affiliated with the chain. If they do find it, they charge the customer and issue a request for direct shipment of the item to the customer's address. This initiative recasts the inventory clearance process from a local store affair to a coordinated chain-wide integrated process. Incidentally, the initiative not only leaves customers more satisfied, but also moves old inventory more quickly by increasing the reach of the sale—a happy note for the company itself.

Global Inventory Visibility   With the increasing rate of speed at which business moves, customers are also progressively coming to expect fast and precise responses to their questions about customization and modification of the firm's products. This trend, perhaps more typical of manufacturing industries and business-to-business relationships, rewards firms that have achieved global inventory visibility. Global inventory visibility represents the knowledge of current inventories and the ability to instantly estimate price and delivery schedule changes in response to requests for customization. At the now famous Dell Online store, you can customize your new computer system and receive a precise estimate of the date you will receive it—such a delivery date will change based on the actual components you request in your machine.

Systems Integration   With the business integration imperative taking center stage, information systems professionals and the software industry have sought ways to enable integration. It is evident that without information systems and technology infrastructure to support them, business integration strategies cannot be feasibly implemented.

The term *system integration* refers to the unification or tight linkage of IT-enabled information systems and databases. The primary focus of systems integration is the technological component of the information systems underpinning business integration strategies. The outcome of system integration is a collection of compatible systems that regularly exchange information, or the development of integrated applications that replace the former discrete ones. More precisely, when the systems integration effort seeks to enable communication between separate software programs, we speak of application integration. When the systems integration effort seeks to enable the merging of data repositories and databases, we speak of data integration.

Internal integration pertains to the unification or linkage of intra-organizational systems, while external integration pertains to interorganizational ones. Internal and external systems integration substantiates itself in custom-developed applications or off-the-shelf commercial products and tools with names that you have probably heard before: enterprise resource planning (ERP), enterprise systems, business intelligence tools, supply chain management software, and the like. Because of their importance and pervasiveness, we discuss some of these systems in detail here.

ENTERPRISE SYSTEMS

Organizations have historically designed and custom developed software applications to support their unique work activities and business processes. This approach was necessary as computers became a staple of operations in large organizations in the 1970s and 1980s, when a stable software industry had yet to emerge. These custom-developed applications were typically designed and implemented at the departmental or functional level, giving rise to what we have termed the functional perspective.

Once organizational computing became prevalent, as software entrepreneurs identified more and more areas where operations of organizations could be automated using standardized software programs, the software industry grew dramatically. Today, the worldwide software industry is a large and diverse one, estimated to net over $300 billion in revenue in 2008 and projected to surpass the $450 billion mark in 2013[7]—a testament to its continuing tremendous growth.

In the late 1980s and early 1990s, the proliferation of stand-alone applications began to highlight the limitations of the functional approach, giving rise to the process perspective, business process reengineering methodologies, and the integration imperative. The missing piece in the quest for integrated operations was a class of standardized software applications that would enable and support integrated business processes. Such applications are now known as enterprise systems (ESs).

The Genesis of Enterprise Systems

While enterprise systems have been a dominant trend in organizational computing over the last decade and a half, and continue to garner significant attention, their roots reach as far back as the 1960s, when computing resources began to be applied to manufacturing problems. At that time, manufacturing organizations employed information technology for the optimization of inventory control, quickly realizing that in order for inventory to be efficiently managed, it would have to be linked to production schedules. Thus, the MRP (material requirement planning) approach was born and manufacturing firms wrote software designed to automatically translate master production schedules into requirements for subassemblies, components, and raw materials.

Under pressure to be increasingly efficient, in the 1980s manufacturing organizations introduced MRP-II (manufacturing resource planning), a concept that extended MRP to encompass

---

[7] DataMonitor—Abstract from Global Software Industry Guide, 2008.

Figure 3.10   Factory shop floor   *Source*: © Bill Backman/Alamy

the entire factory production process (Figure 3.10). At that time, software houses like German-based SAP began to seek integration of activities that had a bearing on manufacturing processes but spanned other functional areas as well, such as human resources, engineering, and project management. So what did they ultimately call the software application that extends the MRP concept to support integrated management beyond the manufacturing function and encompasses other functions across the enterprise? Enterprise resource planning (ERP), of course! Quite a confusing label that only makes sense based on its genesis and its history.

With the relentless pursuit of efficiency by manufacturing firms, the steadily declining cost of information technology assets, and the emergence of the client/server model, which made complex software applications such as ERPs accessible through user-friendly personal computer terminals, the stage was set for ERP (or enterprise systems, as they were later renamed) to become mainstream. The final push for commercial success of enterprise systems came from the fear that twenty- and thirty-year-old legacy applications[8] would suddenly stop running on January 1, 2000 (known as the Y2K bug).

While much early development in this area was focused on functionalities (i.e., what the software applications could do), the parallel development of the business process reengineering (BPR) methodology, which called for a process focus and the use of IT to integrate activities across the organizational functions, led to increasing attention to changing the way activities in the enterprise were performed. At this time ES vendors began focusing on incorporating "best practices" into their applications with the objective of offering a ready-made set of menus of business processes native to the application. Today the label "best practice software" is a pervasive and highly inflationed one.

As enterprise systems have continued to mature, the list of top vendors reads like a who's who of the software industry, and significant consolidation has occurred, with Oracle in particular

---

[8]*Legacy* is a term that does not have a precise definition in information systems. It is typically used to refer to older functional applications based on traditional programming languages (e.g., COBOL) that run on mainframes.

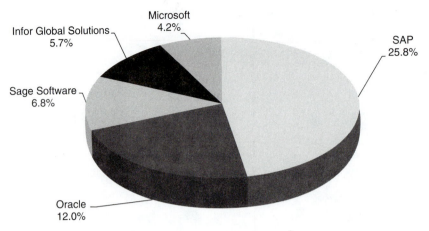

Figure 3.11   Market share of top five ERP vendors[9]

swallowing many former competitors. The top five vendors control almost 55% of the market (Figure 3.11). Competition is now fierce; with the market for larger Fortune 1000 organizations close to saturation, the main vendors have developed enterprise systems aimed at small and medium enterprises (SME).

As a consequence of the commercial success of enterprise systems, as you enter the work-force you will either be managing in an organization that already has an ES or in a smaller firm that is evaluating such a purchase. In either case, you will need to understand the characteristics of these applications—with the advantages and risks they engender—and their impact on the surrounding information system and the organization at large.

Enterprise Systems: Definition

It is clear from the genesis of modern enterprise systems that their defining feature is that of native integration and an effort to support all components of the firm's IT infrastructure. We define an enterprise system as a modular, integrated software application that spans (all) organizational functions and relies on one database at the core (Figure 3.12). An organization can theoretically build its own ES in house. For example, in 2003, Hilton Hotels unveiled OnQ, a custom-made enterprise system estimated to cost over $50 million. Describing it, Tim Harvey, CIO of Hilton at the time, stated, "OnQ is comprised of six major business functions; the idea was to take all the business functions required in a hotel and make them all work together as one system so it's highly integrated."[10]

Some custom development notwithstanding, the great majority of firms will purchase an ES from one of the dominant vendors in an effort to capitalize on the economies of scale associated with off-the-shelf software applications (see Chapter 11). The principal characteristics of enterprise systems are modularity, application and data integration, and configurability.

---

[9]Data from "*Market Share: ERP Software, Worldwide*," Gartner, 2009.

[10]Shein, E. (2003). "Hilton Hotels CIO Talks 'OnQ'," *CIO Magazine*, July 15. http://www.cloupdate.com/insight/article.thp/ 2235231 (Accessed 6/6/07).

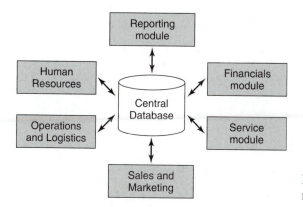

Figure 3.12 Enterprise system's modules

Modularity Enterprise systems are modular in nature, thus enabling the organization that purchases one to decide which functionalities to enable and which ones not to use. The modularity of enterprise systems is a necessity dictated by their size and scope. For as much as ES vendors strive to code comprehensive menus of configuration options and "best practices" into their applications, no single vendor can be the best at each module. For example, PeopleSoft (now owned by Oracle) has historically been known for the strength of its human resource module, while SAP R/3 is known for the strength of its manufacturing module (Table 3.3 for sample ES modules and functionalities).

Modularity enables customers of enterprise systems to exercise some flexibility with respect to the components of the application they intend to purchase and those that they don't need (and should not pay for). In the extreme, modularity also enables a firm to pick and choose individual modules from competing ES vendors, even though this approach defeats the very driver of ES implementations.

Application and Data Integration Native integration is the defining characteristic of enterprise systems. More specifically, ESs enable application integration. With application integration, an event that occurs in one of the modules of the application automatically triggers an event in one or more other separate modules.

Consider the following example:

A Paris-based sales representative for a U.S. computer manufacturer prepares a quote for a customer using an ES. The salesperson enters some basic information about the customer's requirements into his laptop computer, and the ES automatically produces a formal contract, in French, specifying the product's configuration, price, and delivery date. When the customer accepts the quote, the sales rep presses a key; the system, after verifying the customer's credit limit, records the order. The system schedules the shipment; identifies the best routing and then, working backward from the delivery date, reserves the necessary materials from inventory; orders needed parts from suppliers; and schedules assembly in the company's factory in Taiwan.

The sales and production forecasts are immediately updated, and a material-requirements-planning list and bill of materials are created. The sales rep's payroll account is credited with the correct commission, in euros, and his travel account is credited with the expense of the sales call. The actual product cost and profitability are calculated, in U.S. dollars, and the divisional and corporate balance sheets, the accounts-payable and accounts-receivable ledgers, and the

Table 3.3   Sample ES modules and functionalities

Financials

Accounts receivable and payable
Asset accounting
Cash management and forecasting
Financial consolidation
General ledger
Product-cost accounting
Profit-center accounting

Human Resources

Payroll
Personnel planning
Travel expenses

Operations and Logistics

Inventory management
Material requirements planning
Materials management
Plant maintenance
Production planning
Routing management
Shipping

Sales and Marketing

Order management
Pricing
Sales management
Sales planning

---

cost-center accounts are all automatically updated. The system performs nearly every information transaction resulting from the sale.[11]

The above example, a sort of sales-pitch for the perfect world of ES, neatly highlights the notion of application integration. A number of modules—inventory, production, logistics, human resources, and financials—are all engaged by one simple event: the sales-rep presses the enter key to confirm the order.

Data integration focuses on the information that is stored by the ES, instead of the processes it supports. ESs rely on one logical database at the core. That is, while there may be multiple physical data stores and locations where information resides, they will be treated as one, thus ensuring data integration. This feature is a critical selling point of ESs because one logical database ensures a high degree of data integrity (i.e., data are accurate), a limitation of data

---

[11]Davenport, T. H. (1998). "Putting the Enterprise into Enterprise System," *Harvard Business Review*, July/August, pp. 121–131.

redundancy (i.e., data are not repeated unnecessarily), and the enforcement of one data schema (i.e., all modules define the same piece of data, say customer, in the same way).

Configurable   Enterprise systems are parameterized. That is, because they are intended to serve the needs of a wide range of different organizations in an industry, ESs come with configuration tables that enable the adopting firm to choose among a predefined set of options during the implementation of the application. For instance, your firm may prefer to account for inventory on a last-in first-out (LIFO) basis, while another firm that purchased the same ES needs to use the first-in first-out (FIFO) method. During the implementation, you and your competitor will simply configure the application differently by choosing different options.

Enterprise systems also allow the firm to extend the capabilities of the standard application by creating "bolt-on modules." Bolt-on modules, typically written using a programming language that is native to the ES (e.g., ABAP in SAP), are used to further tailor the ES to the specific needs of the organization. While this tailoring of a standardized application may seem counterintuitive, a recent Cutter Consortium survey shows that it is a fairly common occurrence, with 48% of the respondents reporting the development of add-ons to supplement the functionality of the package.[12]

The Advantages of Enterprise Systems

At this point there is considerable literature describing the advantages of adopting enterprise systems, including efficiency improvements through direct and indirect cost savings, responsiveness, knowledge infusion, and adaptability.

Efficiency   Perhaps the biggest selling point of enterprise systems to an executive audience is their promise to rein in complex, generally hard-to-manage legacy IT infrastructures. Because of their support for business and data integration, ESs have the potential to dramatically reduce direct costs, such as those associated with the need for entering the same data in multiple applications. ESs also promise improved efficiency through the reduction of indirect costs achieved by streamlining business processes and operations.

Responsiveness   As the scenario presented earlier shows, one of the advantages of application integration is a dramatic improvement in the firm's ability to respond to customers and market demands. With up-to-date information available in the field, the sales representative in the example was able to quote a delivery date and price on the fly. Moreover, application integration confirmed the order seamlessly and immediately engaged all processes necessary to fulfill the contract.

Knowledge Infusion   As with most off-the-shelf applications, enterprise systems enable the infusion of knowledge into the adopting firm. That is, the application is thought to embed the state of the art in industry practice so that it can be used as a vehicle for updating business processes and operations within the firm. The appeal of knowledge infusion has traditionally been one of the primary selling points of enterprise systems because ES vendors have made it a cornerstone of their strategy to embed "best practices" in their software releases by vetting and selecting the parameters of the application.

---

[12]Ulrich, W. (2006). "Application Package Survey: The Promise versus Reality," *Cutter Benchmark Review*, (6:9), pp. 13–20.

ES vendors have been largely successful in these efforts, and the major vendors now commercialize ES geared for specific verticals that make industry best practices a key value proposition. In fact, many enterprise systems implementations have been justified on the basis of senior executives' frustration with the current state of operations. In these organizations the ES project became a means to drastically reorganize the firm's operations using business process reengineering techniques and the software to enforce the new business processes.

Adaptability   A final advantage offered by enterprise systems is their high degree of adaptability to each unique organizational context. While certainly not comparable to the adaptability of tailor-made applications, enterprise systems offer a degree of customizability rarely provided by off-the-shelf applications. The adaptability of ES is achieved through the use of configuration tables and bolt-on functionality.

Because of the size, scope, and complexity of ES, implementation and configuration processes are very complicated. For example, SAP R/3 has over 3000 configuration tables. Beyond configuration and the development of bolt-on functionalities, an ES implementation requires migration and consolidation of data repositories. For this reason every major vendor has a network of partners, called integrators, who have developed specific expertise in implementing the applications. Large integrators, such as IBM Global Services, Accenture, Deloitte, Infosys, and Wipro, take ownership of the installation, implementation, and adaptation processes, and their fees (rather than software licenses) make up the bulk of the cost of an ES implementation.

The Limitations of Enterprise Systems

A massive undertaking of the kind that enterprise systems implementations bring about is bound to have significant drawbacks, and the potential for project failure and ensuing litigation (Table 3.4). To help managers limit some of the risks associated with such sweeping projects, there is now a comprehensive literature on the limitations of enterprise systems. The critical issues to consider are the trade-off between standardization and flexibility, the limitations of best practice software, the potential for strategic clash, and the high costs and risks of the implementation process.

Standardization and Flexibility   Despite the potential for adaptability and the support for the development of bolt-on modules, when implementing enterprise systems organizations are highly encouraged to implement as close to a standard version of the software as possible. This "vanilla" implementation ensures that the organization capitalizes on the development economies of scale of the vendor, and that implementation time and effort are kept to a minimum. Moreover, if the firm limits itself to configurations and adaptations that are native to the ES, it will find it easiest to transition when upgrading its current software during marketplace migrations.[13]

This approach is diametrically opposite to the custom development approach, where the technology is shaped to fit the unique needs of the organization. With "vanilla" enterprise systems implementations, it is the firm and its business processes that need to accommodate the characteristics of the packaged enterprise system—often requiring significant business process reengineering and change management.

---

[13]The term *marketplace migration* refers to the cyclical upgrades associated with new versions of the software.

Table 3.4 A sample of high-profile ERP failures and litigation cases

Year	ERP Vendor/ Integrator	ERP Customer	Reason for ERP Failure and/or Lawsuit
2010	JDA Software (i2)	Dillard's, Inc.	Dillard's had alleged i2 failed to meet obligations regarding two software-license agreements for which the department-store operator had paid $8 million.
2010	SAP and Deloitte Consulting	Marin County, California	The lawsuit alleges that Deloitte committed fraud and "misrepresented its skills and experience."
2010	Capgemini and SAP	Dorset County in the UK	A job that previously only took a minute is now alleged to take an hour. The system has to shut down a few days each month to allow data to be processed.
2009	Epicor Software Corporation	Ferazzoli Imports of New England	Epicor's system never worked as intended or promised. Initial budget: $184,443, Cost to date: $224,656.
2009	SAP and Axon	City of San Diego	The city of San Diego, CA terminated its software implementation contract with services provider, Axon. The project was $11 million over budget.
2009	Lawson Software	Public Health Foundation Enterprises	Failed ERP implementation.
2008	SAP	Levi Strauss	The company was forced to take shipping systems at its three massive U.S. distribution centers off line for a full week with ensuing loss of business.
2008	Oracle	Overstock.com	ERP implementation problems blamed for losses during the 2005 Christmas season and extending into 2006.
2008	SAP	City of Portland	Portland's SAP project, budgeted at $31 million in 2006 for a 2007 go-live date, is now estimated to be nearly $50 million.
2004	PeopleSoft	Cleveland State University	A faulty installation of the company's ERP applications. The lawsuit charges PeopleSoft with breach of contract and negligent misrepresentation.
2003	EDS	British Sky Broadcasting	Late delivery of the project and lost benefits that amount to estimated £709m.
2001	Oracle Corporation and KPMG	University of Cambridge	ERP project considered "faulty" after spending $13 million in the implementation.
2001	SAP (R/3) and Accenture	FoxMeyer Corp.	The company claimed that a botched SAP R/3 implementation in the mid-1990s ruined them, driving them to bankruptcy.
2000	J.D. Edwards and IBM	Evans Industries Inc.	The suit alleged that OneWorld was "defective and failed to operate and function as promised by the defendants."

Source: Adapted from http://www.backbonemag.com/Backblog/erp-failures-and-lawsuits-its-not-just-for-the-tier-i-erp-vendors.aspx

Figure 3.13 Statue made of concrete *Source*: © Wally Stemberger-Fotolia.com

The trade-off between standardization and flexibility is further amplified by the fact that there is a significant premium associated with the consolidation of a firm's IT infrastructure around one enterprise system. The high degree of application and data integration promised by enterprise systems can only be delivered if the firm is willing to standardize on one vendor and install a sufficient number of modules. Yet as the reach of the application within the organization extends (i.e., more modules are implemented), so do the limitations to the flexibility of individual units. The high degree of integration of ESs requires that the separate units learn to coordinate their efforts and negotiate their preferences.

Finally, enterprise systems are often referred to as software concrete. Concrete is very adaptable and moldable while being poured, yet very inflexible and difficult to modify after it has set (Figure 3.13). In other words, while it is true that enterprise systems offer degrees of adaptability that are not typical of off-the-shelf applications, it is important to note that much of the adaptability comes from configuration tables that can only be used during the implementation process.

Is the Best Practice Embedded in the ES Really Best? One of the critical selling points of enterprise systems is the fact that they are thought to embed industry best practices. The notion of best practice software is predicated on the idea that it is possible to identify the technique or techniques that are optimal to delivering a given outcome, and that these techniques or methods can be codified in a software program. When the application is implemented in an organization, it will "force" the firm to adapt, thus putting into practice the optimal technique.

While the notion of best practice software is intuitively appealing, it is critical that you recognize some of its limitations. First, it is unclear how best practices are identified. In the case of enterprise systems, the best practice may simply be what the software design team deemed as the optimal set of processes necessary to complete the activity. Second, as we discussed in Chapter 2, it is not enough to implement a software program to enact a new practice. Third, and most important, the unique approach your organization has developed to carry out a given activity, your own best practice if you will, may not be supported by the ES. This limitation of the best practice approach can have dramatic impacts when it leads to a strategic clash.

Strategic Clash When a firm adopts an enterprise system, it will have to choose among the set of business processes supported by the software—the best practices. Often they will be readily available within the existing set of configuration tables provided by the application (e.g., FIFO inventory management). In other cases, the established business processes of the firm may not be supported. This is not a problem when the traditional organizational processes are considered substandard. Indeed, as mentioned above, the case for ES implementation often stems from the need to update the firm's operations. But what if one of your unique practices, one that you think gives you a competitive edge, is not supported by the ES?

Consider the case of a spare parts manufacturer. The firm made customer service a cornerstone of its strategic positioning and was willing to "shuffle the cue" of orders when one of its best customers required a rushed order. The firm did not advertise this "best practice" and such practice was not coded into the ES the firm was considering implementing. Yet management thought that such a differentiating process was a source of competitive advantage. What would you do in this case?

As the example above illustrates, as a general or functional manager you must be extremely careful with enterprise systems installations. You need to be able to identify those highly unique business processes that differentiate your organization from the competition. Such processes will likely not be codified in the ES inventory of best practices. Thus, you will have to weigh each of the following options:

- Forgo the ES implementation.
- Implement the ES but build bolt-on modules to maintain support for your unique processes.
- Implement the ES without the modules that impact the unique processes and maintain the associated legacy systems.
- Implement the ES in standard fashion (i.e., vanilla installation) and sacrifice your unique processes to seek improved efficiency and preserve integration.

The appropriate course of action will depend on the number of unique business processes you identify and their impact on the firm's performance. The important consideration here is to evaluate the decision beforehand rather than during implementation or, even worse, afterward.

High Costs and Risks   Enterprise systems have achieved a high degree of maturity, and the ES industry has consolidated around a few major vendors. Yet over the years ESs have had plenty of casualties. This is because enterprise systems, like most large-scale systems implementations, are costly in terms of time and money, and are risky endeavors overall.

Consider the following well-documented case: "FoxMeyer Drugs was a $5 billion company and the nation's fourth largest distributor of pharmaceuticals before the fiasco. With the goal of using technology to increase efficiency, the Delta III project began in 1993. FoxMeyer conducted market research and product evaluation and purchased SAP R/3 in December of that year. FoxMeyer also purchased warehouse-automation from a vendor called Pinnacle, and chose Andersen Consulting [now Accenture] to integrate and implement the two systems. [....] FoxMeyer was driven to bankruptcy in 1996, and the trustee of FoxMeyer announced in 1998 that he was suing SAP, the ERP vendor, as well as Andersen Consulting, its SAP integrator, for $500 million each."[14]

An enterprise system engenders a number of technical (e.g., migrating and integrating existing databases) and behavioral (e.g., significant degree of business process change) challenges that must be actively managed by the adopting firm with the help of a skilled integrator. While ERP have matured as a product, and there is significant expertise now available to manage ERP implementation projects, a recent survey by Panorama Consulting suggests that ERP implementations remain complex and costly projects (Table 3.5) characterized by a significant degree of risk in the outcome (Figure 3.14).

---

[14]Scott, J. (1999). "The FoxMeyer Drugs' Bankruptcy: Was It a Failure of ERP?" *Proceedings of The Association for Information Systems Fifth Americas Conference on Information Systems*, Computer Society Press, Milwaukee, WI, August 1999.

Table 3.5   Sample project metrics for recent ERP implementations (Courtesy of Panorama Consulting Solutions www.panorama-consulting.com.)

	2010	*2009*
Average project cost	$5.48 million	$6.2 million
Project Duration	14.3 months	18.4 months
Late projects	61.1%	35.5%
Projects over budget	74.1%	51.4%

Source: Adapted from Panorama Consulting 2011 ERP Report (2011).

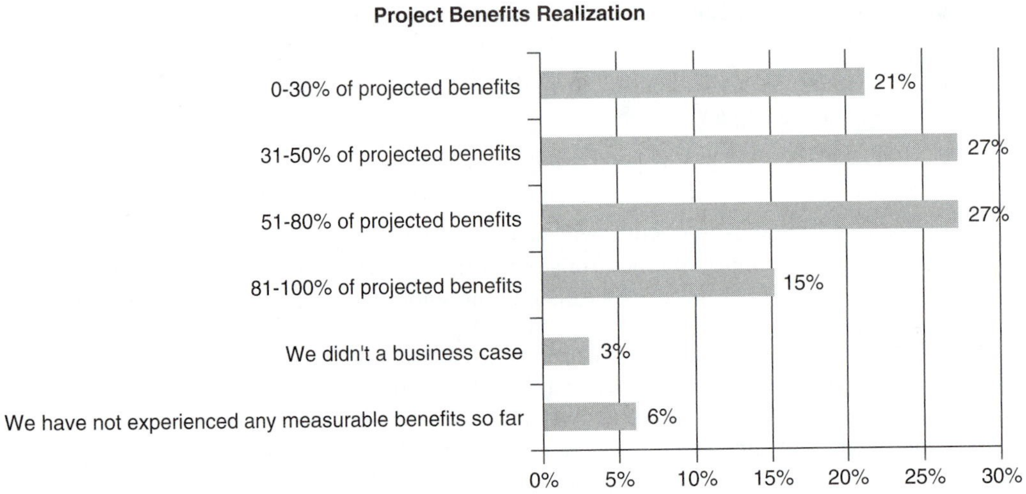

Project Benefits Realization

Figure 3.14   Estimated percentage of benefits actually realized (Courtesy of Panorama Consulting Solutions www.panorama-consulting.com.)

SUPPLY CHAIN MANAGEMENT

In its most general terms, a supply chain is the set of coordinated entities that contribute to move a product from its production to its consumption. From the standpoint of a given firm, the upstream supply chain is concerned with gathering and providing the organization with the resources it needs to perform its transformation process (e.g., raw materials, energy, and equipment). The downstream supply chain is concerned with moving the outputs of the firm's production process to its intended consumers.

For instance, the supply chain of a grocery store is the complex network of firms that produce the groceries consumers purchase at the individual stores (Figure 3.15). Supply chain management (SCM) is the set of logistical and financial processes associated with the planning, executing, and monitoring of supply chain operations.

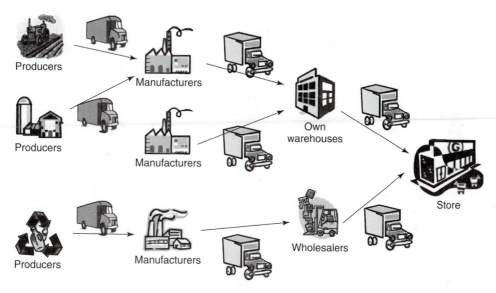

Figure 3.15   Supply chain of a grocery store

A Brief History of Supply Chain Management

The use of information technology to enable supply chain management has a long tradition, following a pattern of increasing integration of separate processes similar to that of enterprise systems. Software support for supply chain management emerged to capture the strong linkages between the warehousing and transportation functions of the organization (Figure 3.16).

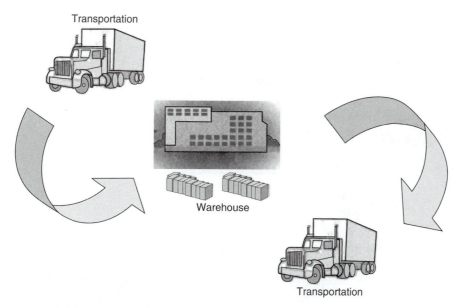

Figure 3.16   First-generation supply chain

Integrated warehousing and transportation allowed firms to create efficiencies due to the joint optimization of warehouse locations, layouts, transportation routes, and related processes. Something as simple as ensuring that delivery trucks leave the warehouse full, rather than half-empty, can have dramatic impacts on a firm's profitability because of the high fixed costs of this activity.

The next step in the evolution of integrated supply chain management was marked by the recognition that further efficiencies could be created by integrating the logistics processes (i.e., transportation and warehousing) with manufacturing schedules and activities (Figure 3.17). At this stage, the financial and information flows associated with the management of the supply chain (i.e., procurement and order management processes) were also integrated.

This increasing degree of integration was enabled by the continued improvements in the power of IT and supply chain management software functionalities. Those firms able to manage these activities in concert could minimize slack resources (e.g., costly slow-downs or stoppage in manufacturing due to lack of the needed raw materials), improve logistics, and make better purchasing decisions.

Modern Supply Chain Management

The last step in the evolution of supply chains consisted in the realization that tight linkages could be established with upstream (i.e., suppliers) and downstream firms (i.e., customers). Modern supply chain management systems are therefore interorganizational systems (Chapter 2) increasingly supported by the use of the Internet (Figure 3.18). Typically a firm will establish an extranet in order to coordinate activities with its supply chain management partners. An extranet is a private network that uses the public Internet infrastructure and Internet technologies, but spans the boundaries of the organization and enables secure transactions between a firm and its suppliers, vendors, customers, or any other partner.

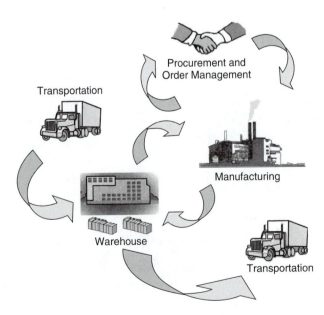

Figure 3.17 Second-generation supply chain

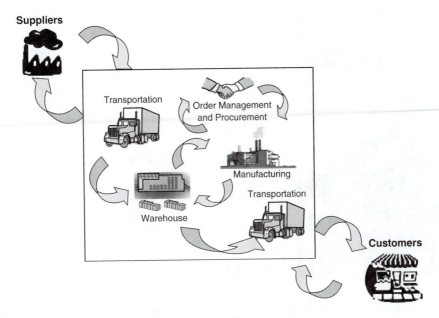

Figure 3.18 Third-generation supply chain

The last stage in the evolution of supply chain management has been its integration with enterprise systems. As ERP applications have traditionally been focused on internal operations, merging with boundary-spanning supply chain management systems has been a natural evolution. Moreover, as the ES market is maturing and the majority of large organizations have deployed them, linking firms in the supply chain has become simpler.

The increasing attention to IT-enabled supply chain management has also given rise to focused intermediaries whose value proposition is providing the tools to enable integrated supply chain management in specific industry "verticals" (i.e., industry segments). Such B2B intermediaries (see Chapter 5) facilitate coordination of the material, financial, and information flows in the supply chain.

More recently the emergence of cost-effective radiofrequency identification (RFID) chips has opened a new frontier for supply chain management. RFID relies on a set of tag readers that detect and decode information contained in RFID tags using radio frequencies. RFID has a number of advantages:

- *No line of sight requirements.* Because RFID tags use radiofrequencies, they do not require that a tag be directly in contact or have an unimpeded path to the transponders, as is the case with bar code scanners, for example.

- *Embedding.* Because RFID tags need no line of sight to communicate with tag readers, RFID tags can be embedded in the products they are to identify. Moreover, tags can be embedded in livestock and even humans (e.g., patients in a hospital).

- *Writing capability.* The content of RFID tags, unlike that of bar codes, can be changed over time by erasing and rewriting to the tag.

Figure 3.19   RFID tag   *Source*: John Nordell/Getty Images, Inc.

- *Storage capacity.* RFID tags are an evolving technology (Figure 3.19), but they can already contain significant descriptive information. For example, a tag may tell us when the product was manufactured, where, its expiration date, and so on.

RFID tags are not new. For instance, they have been used in highway toll-booth payments for over a decade. Their price point is rapidly falling to the point where it is feasible to incorporate RFID tags in a myriad of products, including consumer goods. RFID tags promise substantial efficiency improvements in the supply chain, from speeding the process of receiving and warehousing products to improving the monitoring and control of inventories. However, the true potential for RFID tags, as it is for most new information technologies, may be in their ability to enable new processes and new applications. Imagine a day when cartons of milk will come equipped with RFID tags and signal to your fridge that this milk is nearing the spoil date.

KNOWLEDGE MANAGEMENT

Recognizing the importance of knowledge as an organizational asset, Thomas Watson, the legendary CEO of IBM, once stated, "All the value of this company is in its people. If you burned down all our plants, and we just kept our people and our information files, we should soon be as strong as ever."

Knowledge: Definition

Knowledge can be thought of as a blend of actionable information built over time based on accumulated experiences and the understanding of a phenomenon. We can categorize knowledge with respect to its object as follows:

- *Knowing what.* This type of knowledge is based on the ability to collect, categorize, and assimilate information. An example is the ability of a financial intermediary to articulate and explain what type of investment is best suited to the goals expressed by a given client.

- *Knowing how.* This type of knowledge is predicated on the ability to recognize or create the sequence of steps that are needed to complete a task or carry out an activity. An example is the ability of the financial intermediary mentioned above to create the portfolio of investments by completing the appropriate forms and purchasing the appropriate securities.

- *Knowing why.* This type of knowledge is based on an understanding of cause-effect relationships and the laws that govern a given phenomenon. An example is the ability of the same financial intermediary to recognize why some investments are best suited for her various clients as they progress through life and conditions change. This understanding will allow her to identify relevant changes and suggest the appropriate adjustments to each of them.

Knowledge has also been categorized with respect to its type, in explicit and tacit knowledge.

- *Explicit knowledge.* Explicit knowledge can be articulated, codified, and transferred with relative ease. An example is provided by the training manual that the financial intermediary described above used to learn how to purchase securities for her clients. The manual enables the intermediary to know how to perform the transaction. She can then pass this knowledge on to her associates if necessary.

- *Tacit knowledge.* Tacit knowledge is the type of knowledge that individuals possess but find difficult to articulate, codify, and transfer. A classic example is offered by athletes who, when asked about the reasons for a specific decision during the game, often refer to instinct—an instinct developed through years of practice and handling of similar game situations, but, as such, hard to express in words and convey to others (Figure 3.20).

Figure 3.20   It is hard to codify when to use the "no look pass" in a game situation

The above distinction is important because a firm that engages in knowledge management will find it easier to handle explicit rather than tacit knowledge. Whether explicit or tacit, however, knowledge is increasingly considered a critical asset for modern organizations and, as such, it needs to be protected and proactively managed. Knowledge enables a firm to interpret environmental signals, process these inputs, and identify and implement appropriate responses.

Knowledge Management: Definition

Given the increasing importance assigned to knowledge assets, the last decade has seen growing attention to their active management. It is perhaps no coincidence that knowledge management became a full-fledged business trend in the mid-1990s, seemingly in response to the realization that the downsizing and "de-layering" that followed the rise to prominence of business process reengineering engendered significant loss of organizational knowledge. As a consequence, business leaders—aided by consulting firms—concluded that institutional systems needed to be developed to preserve and communicate organizational knowledge in the face of change and over time.

The term *knowledge management* refers to the set of activities and processes used to create, codify, gather, and disseminate knowledge within the organization. The challenge is best articulated by the chief knowledge officer of a large, multinational consulting organization: "We have 80,000 people scattered around the world that need information to do their jobs effectively. The information they need is too difficult to find and, even if they do find it, it is often inaccurate."[15] Thus, knowledge management is the set of activities and processes that an organization like this enacts to manage the wealth of knowledge it possesses, and to ensure that it is properly safeguarded and put to use to help the firm achieve its objectives.

Information technology has featured prominently in knowledge management initiatives since the inception of this trend, giving rise to a class of applications known as knowledge management systems. However, no single software application can enable a firm to successfully implement a knowledge management initiative. Rather, a number of technologies are used in concert to enable the various aspects of a knowledge management initiative: creating, capturing and storing, and disseminating knowledge.

Creating Knowledge Knowledge creation is the first phase in any knowledge management initiative. In this phase the organization's employees generate new information, devise novel solutions to handle existing problems, and identify new explanations for recurrent events. Such new knowledge is potentially very valuable to others in the organization who may be facing similar problems.

Consider, for example, the genesis of the now ubiquitous "to go" service at your local casual dining chain (e.g., Chili's Bar and Grill). A restaurant manager at Outback Steakhouse noticed a group of his customers opting not to wait for a table in the long line of people ahead of them. Rather, they would order their food from the bar and then set up a makeshift dining table in the bed of their pick-up truck. Identifying an opportunity for increased sales to customers willing to trade off eating on the premises for speed, he set up a separate pick-up area and began to promote the take-out service. When corporate saw what he was doing, it formalized

---

[15]Leidner, D. E. (2006). "The Ongoing Challenges of Knowledge Management Initiatives," *Cutter Benchmark Review*, (6:3), pp. 5–12.

the program and encouraged all restaurant managers to establish separate take-out operations. In many franchises now the take-out area is a brand standard. This case exemplifies the potential far-reaching impact of locally developed knowledge.

Capturing and Storing Knowledge   The main objective of a knowledge management initiative is to consciously compile and use knowledge. The process of capturing and storing knowledge enables the organization to codify new knowledge and maintain an organizational memory. While this process may sound trivial at first glance, you need only to imagine the multiple forms that organizational knowledge can take (e.g., paper documents, computer files, hallway conversations, interactions with customers, images, videos) to realize the complexity of the challenge. More insidiously, it is critical that the firm be able to create a culture that values knowledge and knowledge sharing in order to ensure that the firm's employees are willing to engage in knowledge management activities—activities that often do not have immediate and measurable impacts on the firm or individual performance.

Knowledge repositories and content management systems (CMSs) feature prominently among the technologies used to capture and store knowledge. A knowledge repository is a central location and search point for relevant knowledge. However, as the popularity of such repositories increases, so too does the volume of knowledge. And as the volume of knowledge increases, so too does the difficulty of finding high-quality, relevant information to address a specific problem. A CMS offers a partial solution to this. A CMS is a software program designed to organize and facilitate access to digital content such as text, pictures, and video.

Disseminating Knowledge   Knowledge dissemination is the last phase in a knowledge management initiative. It is at this stage that the investments made in knowledge creation and storage pay off. When knowledge is available in a format that is quickly searchable and readily usable for those employees confronted with a new problem, dramatic improvements in effectiveness and efficiency can be achieved.

BUSINESS INTELLIGENCE

Organizations have been managing data and information since the beginning of organized social life. You can imagine traders in Asia Minor keeping records of inventory and sales in 3,000 B.C. and even before. Consider ancient Rome as a more recent example. The provinces would have to keep detailed records to account for taxes to be paid to the Emperor. With the emergence of computerized information systems, databases took center stage. In technical parlance, a database is a self-describing collection of related records. Modern organizations manage their databases using a database management systems (DBMS)—the software program (or collection of programs) that enables and controls access to the database. A DBMS equips a database administrator with the tools to manage the data (e.g., protect it through authentication, schedule backups) and enables application/data independence. That is, when using a DBMS, applications need not store the data themselves, but rather issue requests to the DBMS. The database can therefore be shared among multiple applications, and upgrades to one of the applications or the database itself can be made independently.

You are perhaps most familiar with personal DBMSs, such as Microsoft Access, that allow individuals or small groups to create and manage relatively small databases (Figure 3.21). Such

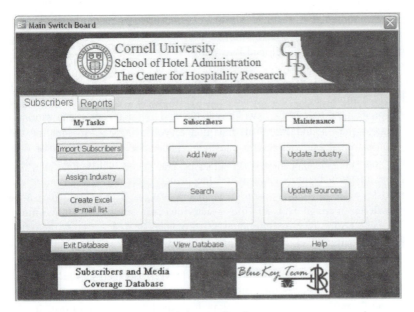

Figure 3.21   MS Access database application

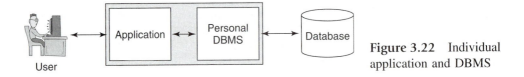

Figure 3.22   Individual application and DBMS

a system can be confusing because typically it embeds both the DBMS and the database applications (Figure 3.22).

Now consider a large organization, say Sabre Holdings Corporation, the parent company of Travelocity, Sabre Travel Network, and Sabre Airline Solutions. Sabre manages what at one point in time was the second-largest computer system in the United States. The Sabre systems are anchored by a database that supports a huge number of users, ranging from travel agents and individuals seeking to make airline and hotel reservations, to airline check-in agents issuing boarding passes and seat assignments, to airline employees routing planes and managing their maintenance schedules. The Sabre database was once estimated to perform 8,000 transactions per second! For such large operations, and for much smaller ones like grocery stores, eCommerce Web sites, and the like, you will need a multiuser industrial-strength DBMS (e.g., Oracle Database 11g). Making requests to the DBMS are a set of separate database applications (Figure 3.23).

While databases have been a staple of organizations' operations since their inception, data has only recently gained widespread popularity as a critical organizational resource. Referring back to the IS cycle discussed earlier, you will note that each of the examples described up to this point focuses on the first stage: handling the present. In other words, up to this point we have only described transactional database applications.

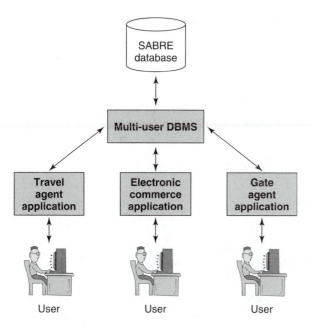

Figure 3.23   Multi-user database structure

As we described in Chapter 1, the declining cost of computing and storage, along with the increasing interconnectivity of computing devices, has given modern organizations access to more data and information than ever before. The business opportunities associated with this wealth of available information have spurred the emergence of the business intelligence (BI) phenomenon.

Business Intelligence: Definition

Business intelligence (BI) is one of the most recent buzzwords in a long tradition of confusing lingo associated with business computing. Yet as with many of the acronyms and jargon in business computing, it is intuitively simple when stripped to its core. Intelligence, in the connotation used, for example in the term *Central Intelligence Agency,* represents the ability to gather and make sense of information in a given area of interest—in the case of the CIA, it is enemies and their behavior. Business intelligence is therefore the ability to gather and make sense of information about your business. It encompasses the set of techniques, processes, and technologies designed to enable managers to gain superior insight and understanding of their business and thus make better decisions (Figure 3.24).

Consider the example of Anheuser Busch, Inc., the parent company of beer brands such as Budweiser and Michelob. Anheuser Busch's distributors carry hand-held devices, rather than the traditional clipboard, when they visit the stores they supply. They use the device to take orders, but also to gather data about competitors' products and strategy (e.g., pricing, placement, promotions). The data is immediately uploaded to Anheuser Busch's data warehouse, where it is joined with demographic, marketing, and other external data to become available for analyses using an application called BudNet. Mapped to the IS cycle, this application shows how data progresses through it, from collection as orders are taken (handling the present), to long-term

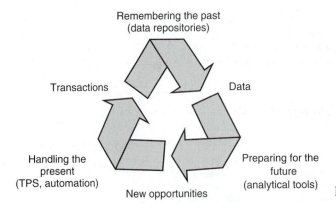

Figure 3.24   The IS cycle

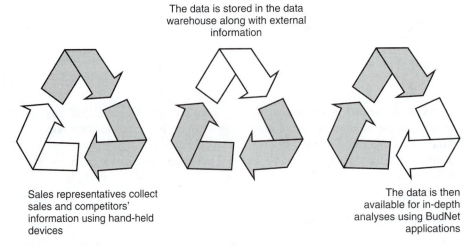

Figure 3.25   Business intelligence at Anheuser Busch, Inc.

storage in the data warehouse (remembering the past), to its employment for analytical purposes (preparing for the future) (Figure 3.25).

As the example above shows, business intelligence encompasses transaction processing, since these transaction processing systems generate the data. However, the defining characteristic of business intelligence is a conscious focus on the analysis of the data generated.

Components of the Business Intelligence Infrastructure

From our definition of business intelligence, it is clear that BI is not a technology or set of technologies. In fact, as was the case in the Anheuser Busch example, in order to engage in business intelligence, the firm must develop an information system paying particular attention to each of the four components (see Chapter 2). Yet given the sheer volume of data and information that a firm needs to manage as part of its BI initiatives, IT is a critical component. As a consequence, business intelligence applications now represent a thriving segment of the software industry.

We use the term *business intelligence infrastructure* to refer to the set of applications and technologies designed to create, manage, and analyze large repositories of data in an effort to extract value from them. Beyond the transaction processing systems that generate the needed data, the main components of a BI infrastructure are data warehouses, data marts, query and reporting tools, online analytical processing (OLAP), and data mining.

Data Warehouse   A data warehouse, or, more precisely, an enterprise data warehouse, is a data repository that collects and consolidates data from multiple source systems, both internal to the organization and external, with the purpose of enabling analysis. A data warehouses typically has the following characteristics:

- *Large in size.* Data warehouses easily span into the terabytes scale—the rough equivalent of all the content of an academic library.

- *Large in scope.* Data warehouses draw information from a wide variety of source systems.

- *Enabling data integration*. Data warehouses compile and collect data from multiple source systems, ensuring that data is accurate and current.

- *Designed for analytics.* The defining characteristic of a data warehouse, what makes it different from a large transactional database, is its focus on analysis and analytics.

A data warehouse is typically the cornerstone of a BI infrastructure, but the repository is only valuable insomuch as the data it contains is accurate—a condition that IT professionals like to call GIGO—garbage in, garbage out. Thus, the primary driver of the complexity and cost of building a data warehouse is associated with the need to gather and clean the data to be compiled—the extracting, transforming, loading (ETL) process, as it is known. What may appear to be a trivial process at first glance is in fact a lengthy and complex undertaking designed to ensure that redundancy, data integrity violations, and inconsistencies are kept to a minimum.

As mentioned above, a data warehouse is optimized for analysis. While traditional transactional databases enable analysis and reporting, their structure is optimized for fast data retrieval at the atomic level. For example, if you asked a gate agent to change your seat assignment as you get ready to board an American Airlines flight, she will have to retrieve your individual record, make the change, and store it before issuing the new boarding pass. Such a transaction is focused on the present, accesses one record, and addresses a specific item in the recordbreak (Table 3.6).

Now consider the example of Anheuser Busch. The firm is not interested in any one of its target customers individually (i.e., how much beer you purchase). Rather, it focuses on large

Table 3.6   Transactional versus analytical databases

Transactional Database	Analytic Database
Atomic level	Aggregate level
Current data	Historical data
Individual record access	Multiple record access

groups of individuals who share some characteristics, in an effort to identify patterns and draw conclusions about their collective behavior (i.e., how much, when, and how people in your neighborhood purchase a given brand of beer). Such transactions seek to access multiple (i.e., thousands of) historical records and aggregate them on several dimensions of interest (Table 3.6).

While such aggregation is possible with transactional databases, and indeed it is performed every day in organizations to extract reports, as the size of the database grows, aggregating data in transactional databases can put a lot of strain on the system. There are situations where, beyond a certain size, the database will require more than twenty-four hours to create a report—clearly negating the possibility of daily analysis.

Using techniques such as multidimensional representations and pre-aggregation, an analytical database is optimized for enabling complex querying and the analysis of large amounts of data with a response time of a few seconds. For example, using OLAP tools (described below) and an analytical database, a bank analyst would be able to identify which accounts are currently overdue, organizing the results by branch, type of loan, customer type, and so on. What's more, the analyst can expect the results within a few seconds of issuing the query.

Data Mart   A data mart is a scaled-down version of a data warehouse that focuses on the needs of a specific audience. Like a data warehouse, a data mart is a repository built explicitly to enable analysis. Unlike a data warehouse, though, a data mart is designed for the specific needs of a narrowly defined community of knowledge workers (e.g., marketing group, accounting). The advantages of a data mart over a data warehouse are that the data mart is smaller in scope, thus easier to build, and uses audience-specific data classifications and language. In very large organizations that have already created an enterprise data warehouse, data marts may be introduced to simplify and focus analysis by a department or function.

In many cases, a firm will develop data marts in order to take an incremental approach to its BI strategy. In this case the firm will introduce one or more data marts before creating a data warehouse. The early data marts focus on areas that offer the highest potential return on the investment in data analysis. This incremental strategy can help generate buy-in from senior executives and momentum behind business intelligence initiatives. The drawback of this approach is that a proliferation of data marts creates the potential for replicating the problem that centralized data storage was designed to eliminate—data redundancy and lack of data consolidation.

Online Analytical Processing   The term *online analytical processing* (OLAP) refers to a class of software programs that enable a knowledge worker to easily and selectively extract and view data from analytical databases. The defining characteristic of OLAP tools is that they are user driven. In other words, an analyst must issue a query that specifies what data items the user is interested in. Note that OLAP users need not be IT specialists; in fact, if you elect to become an analyst for a financial institution or a marketing organization, you stand a very good chance of using OLAP tools yourself.

For instance, as an analyst for Spalding, the sports equipment maker, you may be interested in viewing all of the beach ball products sold in southern Spain in the month of July and comparing revenue figures from these items with those for the same products in September in the same location and/or in the south of France during the same period. The revolutionary aspect of OLAP is that you would no longer need to request such data from the IT department and wait for them to design ad hoc queries for you. Rather, you can perform the analysis on your own and receive an immediate response employing a user-friendly application.

Data Mining   Data mining is the process of automatically discovering non-obvious relationships in large databases. The recent popularity of data mining is due to the availability of powerful computer systems that can quickly search through large volumes of data contained in data warehouses. A recent example of the power of data mining is offered by Walmart, a company that built its data warehouse in the early 1990s. Using years of compiled data, Walmart analysts recently sought to identify what the best-selling items were in areas under threat of an approaching hurricane. Much to everyone's surprise, the most important item needed to prepare for a hurricane was not water, wood, or nails. It wasn't even beer, a perennial favorite in audiences confronted with this question. In fact, Walmart found that strawberry pop-tarts sold most! While it is relatively easy to make sense of this finding once we are told about it (i.e., pop-tarts have a long shelf life, they need not be cooked, kids like them), it is a non-obvious and largely unexpected finding beforehand.

Like OLAP tools, data mining is used to analyze historical information. Unlike OLAP, though, data mining is more akin to a brute force approach enabling the software to identify significant patterns by analyzing all possible combinations rather than relying on an analyst to structure a specific query. Of course, analysts are still heavily involved in data mining as they must interpret the results. Yet, as in the Walmart example, data mining is used to seek unexpected (i.e., nonobvious) relationships among data items. The following is a list of possible patterns a data mining application may identify:

- *Associations*. Associations occur when one event can be correlated to another event (e.g., beer purchases are highly associated with chips purchases in the week leading up to the Superbowl).
- *Sequences*. Sequences occur when one event leads to another subsequent event (e.g., a rug purchase followed by a purchase of curtains).
- *Classification*. Classification occurs when categories are generated from the data (e.g., customer profiles based on historical spending).
- *Forecasting*. Forecasting occurs when patterns in the data can be extrapolated to predict future events.

The Evolution of Business Intelligence

At its core, business intelligence is about decision making and managing change. As such, organizations (and the vendors serving their needs) are constantly seeking ways to improve the timeliness of decision-making support and its capillarity. For this reason, business intelligence trends include:

- *Real-time BI*: Real-time BI, also called business activity monitoring, is a business intelligence approach focused on real-time situation awareness through the constant monitoring of critical business performance indicators, based on event-driven sources of data.
- *Mobile BI*: With the rapidly increasing mobility of the workforce and the increasing widespread use of mobile devices in the organization, BI vendors have been trying to bring decision analysis tools to the user anywhere they may need it. Renewing the interest in mobile BI have been the new form factors, such as powerful smartphones and tablets (Figure 3.26).

Figure 3.26   Analytics on the iPhone and iPod (Courtesy of Roambi.)

CUSTOMER RELATIONSHIP MANAGEMENT

Customer relationship management (CRM) has been a dominant business trend over the last decade and a half and, like enterprise systems, is still receiving substantial attention. CRM finds its roots in the proliferation of customer data and the efforts of modern business organizations to differentiate themselves through customer service.

As with many of the business technology trends that preceded it, CRM has been co-opted by vendors, consulting firms, and various other pundits, and the term has increasingly lost a precise meaning. We define customer relationship management as a strategic orientation that calls for iterative processes designed to turn customer data into customer relationships through active use of, and learning from, the information collected. Thus, the defining characteristics of CRM are the following:

- CRM is a strategic initiative, not a technology. Information technology is an essential enabler of all but the smallest CRM initiatives.

- CRM relies on customer personal and transactional data, and is designed to help the firm learn about them.

- The ultimate objective of a CRM initiative is to help the firm use customer data to make inferences about customer behaviors, needs, and value to the firm so as to increase its profitability.

Aspects of CRM

A CRM strategy needs to encompass front-office functionalities—termed *operational CRM*—which determine how the firm interacts with customers to create and maintain the relationship. Today customers in most industries expect to be able to interact with firms through a multiplicity of touchpoints, such as a firm's Web site, stores, call center, and so on. Moreover, modern firms are increasingly expected to be able to provide consistency across these proliferating touchpoints and channels of communication. As a consequence, integration

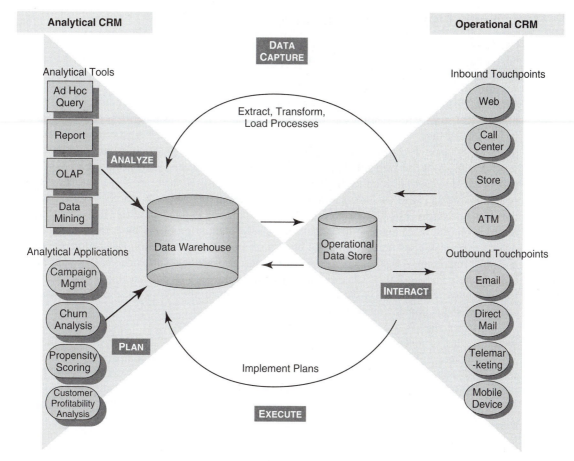

Figure 3.27   Example of CRM infrastructure[16]

of the transactional databases that have historically supported the different channels into one operational data store is a priority for organizations today (Figure 3.27).

A CRM strategy requires that the organization be able to actively manage and strengthen their relationships with profitable customers, while achieving efficiencies with (and sometimes firing!) less profitable ones. This level of precision and granularity of interactions with customers requires substantial data analysis—analytical CRM.

It should be clear at this point why it is nonsensical to be talking about a CRM system as a technology product that, once installed, allegedly enables the firm to establish and maintain relationships with customers. CRM is a highly customizable strategic initiative that will differ dramatically between companies. Thus, as with business intelligence, we need to talk about a CRM infrastructure as the collection of applications that support and enable the specific aspects of the firm's CRM strategy.

---

[16]*Source*: Goodhue, D. L., Wixom, B. H., and Watson, H. J. (2002). "Realizing business benefits through CRM: Hitting the right target in the right way," *MIS Quarterly Executive*, pp. 79–94.

The Limitations of CRM

CRM is an intuitively appealing concept, but it may engender the very seed of its demise. If this is the case, companies that make it a cornerstone of their strategy may in turn be setting themselves up for failure.

CRM Is Firm Centric   One of the main limitations of current CRM approaches is that a firm's CRM strategy only relies on transactional and behavioral customer data pertaining to the interactions of the customer with the firm. Consider what is probably the most celebrated example of CRM strategy: Amazon.com's collaborative filtering initiative. When a returning customer logs on to the Amazon Web site, he is personally greeted and receives suggestions based on prior purchases. However, as good as the Amazon CRM initiative is, there are some problems. First, not all the products that customers purchase are for themselves; they also purchase gifts. Second, not all the products customers buy are for the same purpose; we may purchase items for work or leisure. Amazon has attempted to account for these potential problems by asking customers to qualify their purchases (i.e., shifting the burden of precise data collection to customers). Third, and most important, Amazon only knows customers' transactions with Amazon. Yet your music library surely includes gifted CDs, and it may include old vinyl records and tape cassettes, items you purchased from Amazon's competitors—online and in physical stores—and, increasingly, individual songs you download from iTunes.

This limitation is rooted in the fact that the firm has access only to transactions and behavioral data that is generated in the interaction between its customers and itself. Indeed, the firm can buy demographic and other personal data about customers from companies such as Acxiom and ChoicePoint, but it can't obtain customers' transactional data from competitors. Under these circumstances, the picture that the firm creates about each customer is irremediably partial, and drawing accurate inferences or producing good advice based on it is difficult at best and impossible at worst.

CRM Has Limited Predictive Ability   Even those organizations that have exclusive relationships with their customers (i.e., 100% share of wallet) still face a challenge. Some events are unforeseeable and only the customer knows about their occurrence or future plans about them. Think of customers who have just had a baby, purchased a house, or those who just gotten divorced or were involved in a big accident. As good as the firm's inference systems may be, they rely on historical data and patterns and, unless the customer volunteers information about life-changing events, it will typically fall short on accuracy. While there are many areas, industries, and organizations that have benefited and will continue to benefit greatly from their CRM strategy, the example above highlights an endemic problem. To the extent that the objective of a CRM strategy is personalization, inference, consultation, and advice, the battle may be an uphill one and the end result not as comprehensive as hoped.

BEST-OF-BREED INTEGRATION

Organizations have implemented enterprise systems and integrated supply chain management applications in response to the recent emergence of the integration imperative. Both of these solutions rely on the use of a single-vendor, highly integrated, modular software program that limits the firm's flexibility. While a firm can install a subset of ES modules and use multiple vendors, this approach reduces the advantages offered by the package. Thus, the firm typically will install modules that are not considered the best for the firm's needs in order to preserve integration.

Recognizing these limitations, a competing approach, known as best-of-breed, emerged over time. The best-of-breed approach is designed to enable the firm to retain a high degree of flexibility with respect to the applications it decides to adopt, while still being able to achieve tight integration among them. As the term suggests, best-of-breed allows the firm to choose the module or application that best suits its information processing needs. As such, the best-of-breed approach enables a firm to achieve integration using applications from different vendors.

Enterprise Application Integration (EAI)

The best-of-breed approach is enabled by a new integration paradigm that focuses not on applications to be integrated, but on the linkages among them. Integration of separate systems has been traditionally achieved with point-to-point connections called interfaces. This approach engenders significant limitations as the number of interfaces grows dramatically with the number of applications that need to be connected. That is, the number of bilateral interfaces needed to connect n systems is $n(n-1)/2$ (i.e., 3 systems, 3 interfaces; 5 systems, 10 interfaces; 10 systems, 45 interfaces, and so on). Such an approach can quickly result in a messy infrastructure that is difficult and costly to maintain (Figure 3.28). Note that any time a change is made to one system, all interfaces that connect to it will need to be modified.

In order to achieve the promise of best of breed integration without the limitations of bilateral interfaces, the enterprise application integration (EAI) approach has recently emerged. EAI consists of "re-architecting" existing programs so that an intermediate layer, termed *middleware,* is developed between the applications and databases (Figure 3.29). The existing applications are designed to make calls to the middleware layer rather than to one another, as with bilateral interfaces. Integrating applications and databases in this fashion provides the firm with the highest degree of flexibility when selecting applications, and the ability to swap them independently when upgrades are needed.

The EAI approach also streamlines the maintenance process because changes to an application will not affect all the interfaces connected to it. Rather, as long as each application is able to make requests to, and receive requests from, the middleware layer, no other application needs to be modified.

Ultimate Flexibility: Service-Oriented Architecture

Business organizations are under constant pressure to become increasingly flexible and agile in order to respond to rapidly evolving customer needs and accelerating competition. IT professionals and the software industry have seized the opportunity to enable such increasing levels of agility and flexibility. The dominant solution goes under the broad label of service-oriented architecture (SOA).

SOA is a software design perspective focused on reusability of software components, interoperability, and ongoing optimization of business processes. SOA works by using standards to make independent services available on a network. These services, sometimes referred to as

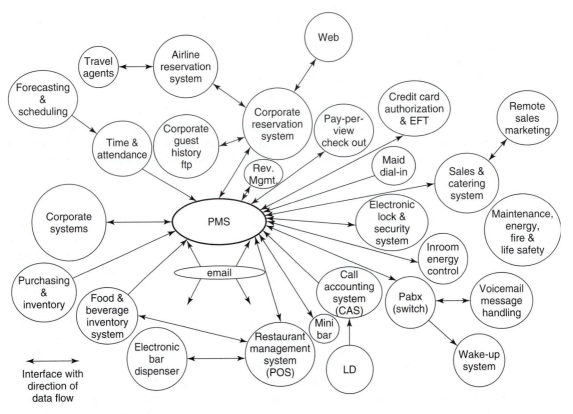

Figure 3.28   Best-of-breed infrastructure of a hotel

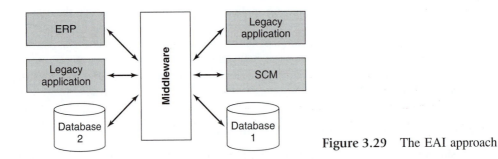

Figure 3.29   The EAI approach

Web services, are made available as components to be accessed and used by applications without knowledge of their underlying design or structure. In other words, SOA enables the rapid creation of applications by the combination of pre-built services.

The SOA approach is different from EAI, even though it conceptually builds on the same ideas. EAI calls for the integration of separate best-of-breed applications through middleware.

With SOA the applications themselves, as well as the manner in which they communicate, are built using separate but interoperable components that can be modified and combined depending on the characteristics of the business process they are designed to support.

INTEGRATION: CONCLUDING REMARKS

Like many business and organizational trends that you will find yourself assessing in your position as a general or functional manager, the integration imperative has created its share of hype and buzz. As you have learned there are a number of approaches to achieving integration, either through one solution or a blend of solutions, and the scope of the integration effort can vary significantly. While integration remains one of the most often cited business imperatives, it is, of course, no panacea; more integration is not necessarily better or advisable. Rather the integration trend engenders trade-offs that need to be evaluated.

Benefits of Integration   An organization undertakes integration efforts because they offer a number of benefits. First and foremost, integration promises a drastic reduction in duplication of efforts and redundancy of operations. For example, once a firm integrates its receiving and inventory applications, it no longer needs data to be keyed into separate databases multiple times. This reduces not only direct costs, but also the potential for errors and inconsistencies leading to further expenditures of time and money. Second, integration offers advantages in terms of access to information, speed, and response time. It also serves to increase coordination across organizational units and to enforce standardization.

Drawbacks of Integration   The advantages mentioned above come at a cost, however. Aside from the actual expense of achieving integration itself, successful integration requires that organizations bear a number of coordination costs that the decentralization movement was designed to eliminate in the first place. While modern information technologies have helped reduce such costs, many of them are still significant. Let's return to the General Mills and Land O'Lakes example. Both firms clearly benefited from the integration of their logistics and distribution processes. Now, however, each firm has to coordinate with the other to ensure that the right products are warehoused and ready to go according to the agreed upon schedule.

Moreover, the standardization advantages mentioned above also bring about limitations of flexibility that are all the more relevant for larger firms with unique local operations. With highly integrated operations, the need for change in a business unit or function must be weighed against the needs of the other units and the costs that they will have to bear to accommodate the change.

Consider the example of Barnes & Noble, which originally established its online retail unit as a separate organization. While customers may demand cross-channel integration between the physical stores and the Web, this level of integration requires compromises between the units involved, a level of coordination that is harder to muster the more independently the units are run (e.g., separate profit and loss statements). For example, ensuring that a book purchased online can be returned to a store requires that stores be willing to collect and resell books that they otherwise may not carry due to a lack of sufficient local demand.

 **SUMMARY**

This chapter completed our introduction to the foundations of information systems, by explaining the vocabulary and concepts you need in order to categorize different types of information systems and to communicate with other managers and IS professionals. Specifically, in this chapter we learned the following:

- Different organizational information systems can be characterized through a hierarchical perspective. This perspective identifies three types of systems: transaction processing systems, decision support systems, and executive information systems. These systems are designed and built to support different activities—operational, tactical, and strategic, respectively.

- Different organizational information systems can be characterized through a functional perspective. This perspective identifies vertical organizational systems focused on the specific needs of each unit (e.g., accounting, marketing, finance, receiving).

- More recently a process perspective has emerged. According to the process perspective, the firm and its operations are seen as a set of processes, rather than functional areas. The functional perspective underpins many of the most recent managerial trends, including business process reengineering (BPR) and business systems integration efforts, as well as information systems trends, such as systems integration initiatives.

- BPR, defined as a managerial approach calling for a process view of organizational activities, was one of the principal management trends of the mid-1990s. While its popularity has faded somewhat, you should not forget the key lessons of BPR: firms evolve over time, as do technologies; old assumptions may no longer be valid today; and you have an opportunity to use IT to dramatically improve the efficiency and effectiveness of the firm's business processes.

- Enterprise systems (ESs), also known as ERP, are modular, integrated software applications that span (all) organizational functions and rely on one database at the core. The defining characteristics of ESs are their large scope (seeking to support all aspects of an organization's IT infrastructure in an integrated fashion), their modularity (enabling adopting firms to select what components they need), and their configurability (allowing adopting organizations to choose among a predefined set of options during the implementation of the application).

- While enterprise systems offer much promise in terms of efficiency improvements, increased responsiveness, knowledge infusion, and adaptability, they have some significant limitations as well, including: the trade-off between standardization and flexibility, the limitations of best practice software, the potential for strategic clash, and the high costs and risks of the implementation process.

- Enterprise systems have traditionally focused on internal organizational processes. Conversely, supply chain management applications have been introduced to enable interorganizational business processes across the supply chain. Supply chain management applications have become increasingly integrated in an effort to create efficiencies through tight relationships between suppliers and customers.

- Best-of-breed integration approaches have emerged in response to the limitations of enterprise systems. Specifically, enterprise systems limit the adopting firm's ability to maintain a flexible IT infrastructure by restricting available options. In contrast, best-of-breed, enabled by the enterprise application integration (EAI) approach, allows an organization to purchase applications from multiple vendors and integrate them with its existing legacy systems using middleware.

- Knowledge management is the set of activities and processes that an organization enacts to manage the wealth of knowledge it possesses and ensure that such knowledge is properly safeguarded and put to use to help the firm achieve its objectives. A knowledge management initiative evolves over three phases: knowledge creation, capture and storage, and distribution. While knowledge management has intuitive appeal, knowledge management initiatives are deceptively complex and prone to failure. This is due to the sheer quantity and variety of organizational knowledge, and to the fact that most organizations lack a culture of knowledge sharing and management.

- Business intelligence has been one of the dominant trends in organizational computing over the last decade. It encompasses the set of techniques, processes, and technologies designed to enable managers to gain superior insight and understanding of their business and thus make better decisions. A firm that intends to engage in business intelligence needs to create a business intelligence infrastructure that typically is centered on a data warehouse. Feeding the data warehouse are internal transaction processing systems and external sources. Once the data has been structured for analysis in the data warehouse, or a data mart, it can be examined using analytical tools such as OLAP and data mining.

- Customer relationship management (CRM) represents another enduring business trend of the last decade. We have defined CRM as a strategic orientation that calls for iterative processes designed to turn customer data into customer relationships through an active use of, and learning from, the information collected. While the term *CRM* has lost much of its original meaning as of late, it is critical that you realize that CRM initiatives are unique to the characteristics and objectives of the implementing organization. Thus, the set of technologies and applications the firm will use (i.e., the CRM infrastructure) to enable both the operational and analytical aspects of its CRM strategy will vary dramatically.

STUDY QUESTIONS

1. Describe the principal differences among transaction processing systems, management information systems, and executive information systems.

2. Identify the three types of organizational activities. For each one, describe its typical time horizon, hierarchical level, and principal characteristics. Provide an example for each type.

3. Provide an example of functional systems. What is the defining characteristic of these systems?

4. Define the concept of BPR. Can you provide an example, real or imaginary, of a company operating under old assumptions that are no longer valid? How would you propose to redesign the firm's business processes? What information technology would you expect the firm to adopt to enable the redesigned process?

5. What are the principal limitations and drawbacks of BPR?

6. How have we defined the concepts of business and systems integration? What is the relationship between the two? Can you provide examples of each?

7. What is an enterprise system (ES)? Can you describe its genesis? Identify the principal advantages and risks that a firm considering the installation of an ES should consider.

8. What is a supply chain? Why is it important to actively manage the supply chain? If you were the CEO of a hospital, would you consider using RFID technology? If not, why? If yes, for what applications?

9. Define the term best-of-breed integration. Why has best-of-breed integration recently emerged as a business trend? Explain how enterprise application integration (EAI) works. What are its primary advantages over competing integration approaches?

10. Define the following terms: knowledge, explicit and tacit knowledge, knowledge management. What are the principal phases of a knowledge management initiative? Describe the essential benefits of knowledge management for modern organizations. Why are so many organizations struggling with their knowledge management initiatives?

11. Define the following terms: business intelligence, business intelligence infrastructure, data warehouse, data mart, OLAP, data mining. What is the relationship among the various elements of BI infrastructure?

FURTHER READINGS

1. Davenport, T. H. (1992). *Process Innovation: Reengineering Work through Information Technology*. Boston, MA: Harvard Business School Press.

2. Davenport, T. H. (1998). "Putting the Enterprise into Enterprise System." *Harvard Business Review,* July/August, pp. 121–131.

3. Davenport, T. H. (2006). "Competing on Analytics." *Harvard Business Review,* January, pp. 98–107.

4. Hammer, M. (1990). "Reengineering Work: Don't Automate, Obliterate." *Harvard Business Review,* July/August, pp. 104–112.

5. Hammer, M. and Champy, J. A. (1993). *Reengineering the Corporation: A Manifesto for Business Revolution,* Harper Business Books, New York, 1993.

6. Hammer, M. (1996). *Beyond Reengineering: How the Process-Centered Organization Is Changing Our Work and Our Lives,* HarperBusiness.

7. Hammer, M. (2001). "The Superefficient Company." *Harvard Business Review,* September, pp. 82–91.

8. Hammer, M. (2004). "Deep Change: How Operational Innovation Can Transform Your Company." *Harvard Business Review,* April, pp. 84–93.

9. Hammer, M. (2007). "Process Audit." *Harvard Business Review,* July/August, pp. 104–112.

10. Leavitt, H. J., Whisler, T. L. (1958). "Management in the 1980s." *Harvard Business Review,* November/December, pp. 41–48.

11. Markus, M. Lynne (2000). "Paradigm Shifts—E-Business and Business/Systems Integration." *Communications of the AIS,* (4:10).

12. Senge, P. (1990). *The Fifth Discipline: The Art and Practice of the Learning Organization,* Currency.

GLOSSARY

■ **Business integration:** Unification or the creation of tight linkages among the diverse, but connected, business activities carried out by individuals, groups, and departments within an organization.

■ **Business intelligence:** The ability to gather and make sense of information about your business. It encompasses the set of techniques, processes, and technologies designed to enable managers to gain superior insight and understanding of their business and thus make better decisions.

■ **Business intelligence infrastructure:** The set of applications and technologies designed to create, manage, and analyze large repositories of data in an effort to extract value from them.

■ **Business process:** The series of steps that a firm performs in order to complete an economic activity.

■ **Business process reengineering (BPR):** A managerial approach calling for a process view of organizational activities. The BPR methodology calls for internal business integration and seeks dramatic performance improvements through rationalization of activities and the elimination of duplication of efforts across separate functions and units.

■ **Customer relationship management (CRM):** A strategic orientation that calls for iterative processes designed to turn customer data into customer relationships through active use of, and learning from, the information collected.

■ **Database:** A self-describing collection of related records.

■ **Database management system:** A software program (or collection of programs) that enables and controls access to a database.

■ **Data mart:** A scaled-down version of a data warehouse that focuses on the needs of a specific audience.

■ **Data mining:** The process of automatically discovering nonobvious relationships in large databases.

■ **Data warehouse:** A software program that collects and consolidates data from multiple source systems, both internal to the organization and external, with the purpose of enabling analysis.

■ **Decision support systems (DSS):** Systems designed to provide information needed by functional managers engaged in tactical decision making in the form of regular reports and exception reports.

■ **Enterprise system (ES):** Enterprise systems, also known as ERP, are modular, integrated software applications that span (all) organizational functions and rely on one database at the core.

■ **Executive information systems (EIS):** Systems designed to serve the long-range planning and decision-making needs of senior managers.

■ **Explicit knowledge:** The type of knowledge that can be articulated, codified, and transferred with relative ease.

■ **Extranet:** A private network that uses the public Internet infrastructure and Internet technologies but spans the boundaries of an organization and enables secure transactions between a firm and its suppliers, vendors, customers, and any other partner.

■ **Functional systems:** Systems expressly designed to support the specific needs of individuals in the same functional area.

■ **Information systems cycle:** An analytical model that portrays the progression of business data from its inception in transaction processing systems, to its storage in data repositories, and finally to its use in analytical tools.

■ **Integration:** The process that an organization, or a number of related organizations, uses to unify, or join together, some tangible or intangible assets.

■ **Integrator:** A consulting firm that partners with an enterprise systems vendor and becomes a specialist in the implementation of the ES vendor's products.

■ **Knowledge management:** The set of activities and processes that an organization enacts to manage the wealth of knowledge it possesses and ensure that such knowledge is properly safeguarded and put to use to help the firm achieve its objectives.

■ **Online analytical processing (OLAP):** A class of software programs that enable a knowledge worker to easily and selectively extract and view data from an analytical database.

■ **Supply chain:** The set of upstream firms that produce and sell the resources that an organization needs to perform its transformation process (e.g., raw materials, energy, and equipment).

- **Supply chain management (SCM):** The set of logistic and financial processes associated with the planning, execution, and monitoring of supply chain operations.

- **System integration:** The unification or tight linkage of IT-enabled information systems and databases.

- **Tacit knowledge:** The type of knowledge that individuals possess but find difficult to articulate, codify, and transfer.

- **Transaction processing systems:** Systems mainly concerned with automating recurring activities and structuring day-to-day activities to ensure that they are performed with speed and accuracy.

Competing in the Internet Age

The rallying cry of enthusiastic engineers, entrepreneurs, venture capitalists, investors, and just about everyone else during the late 1990s, or, as it became known, the dot-com era, was, "The Internet changes everything."

In such a statement there was certainly quite a bit of "the emperor has no clothes" syndrome, as Netscape Corp. cofounder Marc Andressen described it. In other words, while most people were unsure as to how exactly the Internet was going to change everything, they did not want to miss out on it... in case it did. The frenzy took the NASDAQ—the tech-focused electronic equity security market—past 5,000 points in March 2000, before seeing it tumble down to a 1,400-point low. The market crash notwithstanding, the dot-com era ushered in what some have named the "network economy." It is evident now, a decade after the crash, that the Internet, and the many related information technologies and innovations that are built on the Internet infrastructure, dramatically changed the competitive landscape for almost every company. Today we see a resurgence of the positive mentality that drove the growth of the Internet. The driving force is the phenomenon called Web 2.0, as well as the now viable mobile platform and, increasingly, three-dimensional immersive environments (see Chapter 5). The first of the Web 2.0 darlings to go public, business-oriented social network LinkedIn, had a very successful initial public offer (IPO) on May 19, 2011 when its stock was offered at $42 but rocketed to $115 in intraday trading to settle at around $93 at closing on the second day of trading. The IPO was so successful that many observed cheered (other feared) the return of dot-com era thinking.

What is the network economy? Simply put, a network economy is one where ubiquitous global networks drastically reduce geographic and time constraints, enabling organizations to truly compete on a global basis. This notion is at the center of a recent book by *New York Times* columnist Thomas Friedman. The main thesis of the book, titled *The World Is Flat*, is that the technology revolution that took place during the dot-com era has changed modern business and has enabled work to move seamlessly around the globe. The consequence is that the global competitive playing field has been leveled, leading to an unprecedented degree of globalization.

The most apparent changes brought about by the network economy took place at the front end of company interaction with their clients, in what is called the business-to-consumer space. You could not imagine running an airline or a hotel today without a professional and functional Web site that your customers could use to learn about your offer, book reservations, and even check in. The same goes for banks, retailers in the widest variety of sectors, publishers, newly released movies, and even celebrities, for whom a Web site seems to be a must! However, while the front end grabbed all the headlines, the bulk of the "Internet revolution" took place behind the scenes, within company walls, and in what is termed the "business-to-business" space. This trend is captured by a quote attributed to Jack Welch, the iconic former CEO of General Electric. Welch, referring to the potential for efficiencies ushered in by the Internet, is rumored to have said, "Where does the Internet rank on my priority list? It is number one, two, three, and four. I don't think there's been anything as important or more widespread in all my years at GE."[1]

Whether or not the Internet does indeed "change everything" is really not the issue. There is no doubt that a global, affordable, digital network infrastructure for communication is a critical business enabler. Thus, you as a modern general or functional manager must be able to appropriately use it to benefit your organization. In order to do so, you must be able to answer two broad questions:

1.   What impacts do Internet technologies have on the competitive landscape? How do they change the environment your firm is, and will be, competing in?

2.   How have the Internet and related technologies been used by organizations before? How can they be used by your firm to improve the business efficiency and effectiveness?

Part II of this book is devoted to answering these two questions. Specifically,

■   *Chapter 4: The Changing Competitive Environment.* This chapter focuses on the first question, and discusses how networks and information differ as economic entities from traditional and physical goods. With this backdrop, the chapter discusses how Internet technologies have changed the modern competitive landscape and the implications this has for strategy in the modern firm.

■   *Chapter 5: Electronic Commerce: New Ways of Doing Business.* This chapter tackles the second question and provides you with a background on the Internet and related technologies. It then introduces a vocabulary with which to understand electronic commerce and electronic business trends, past, present, and future. The chapter also discusses the role of the Internet, and related technologies, both within and outside the modern firm.

---

[1]Fingar, P., and Aronica, R.C. (2001). *The Death of "e" and the Birth of the Real New Economy: Business Models, Technologies and Strategies for the 21st Century*, Tampa, FL: Meghan-Kiffer Press.

4

The Changing Competitive Environment

What You Will Learn in This Chapter

This chapter focuses on the revolutionary changes that have occurred in the global economy since the advent of the commercial Internet in the mid-1990s. The networked world is widely different from the pre-networked one because networks have peculiar economic characteristics. Moreover, in the presence of pervasive networks, the amount of data and information that can be generated and transferred in real time is dramatically increasing. The successful firm, and the successful manager, must be able to design and implement strategies to take advantage of, rather than suffer from, these changes. The concepts and examples discussed in this chapter will help you do so.

Specifically, in this chapter you will become well versed in the language of network economics, information economics, and disruptive technologies. You will:

1. Comprehend the basic principles of network economics, including the sources of value in networks, and the definitions of physical and virtual networks. You will also learn to apply these concepts to strategy and managerial decision making.

2. Understand the concepts and vocabulary of network economics, including positive feedback, network externalities, and tippy markets. Be able to recognize when network effects occur and what makes a market tip, as well as what market will not tip toward a dominant player.

3. Comprehend the basic principles of information economics and the role that information plays in the modern competitive environment. Understand the concepts and vocabulary of information economics, including the ability to define classic information goods and information-intensive goods.

4. Be able to explain how the advent of pervasive networks has enabled information to break the constraints imposed by traditional information carriers. You will also be able to explain what the richness/reach trade-off is and its implications for modern organizations.

5. Be able to distinguish between disruptive and sustaining technologies. Be able to identify each kind and draw implications for decision making in organizations faced with the emergence of disruptive technologies.

MINI-CASE: GROUPON AND THE GHOST OF STARTUPS PAST

"You always had an entrepreneurial streak," you tell yourself with a chuckle as you reflect over a hot cappuccino at your favorite coffee shop. With an undergraduate degree in computer engineering and a soon-to-be-granted Master's of Management degree, a startup sounds like a perfect way to jump back into the real world. While the global crisis during the last few years has put the squeeze on venture funding, potentially good ideas still get attention. Color.com got $41 million from heavy hitters like Sequoia Capital and Bain Capital before it even had launched, and the payoff could be handsome—just a few months back, Groupon had received a buyout offer of $6 billion from Google after a little more than two years in operation... and turned it down!!

As you ponder the issue, you reflect on lessons from tech ventures of the past. One that you know quite well was eBay, having been an avid buyer and a successful seller as a teen, and having followed the company over the years. In fact, you remember an interesting article from back in 2004 drawing a parallel between eBay, Inc. and Amazon.com. At the time, the two firms were respectively 60th and 66th in BusinessWeek's Top 100 Brands[1] and were considered the poster-children of eCommerce, having helped to create the category. "EBay and Amazon.com, the Internet's top two e-commerce sites, are taking opposite approaches to growth. EBay raised its prices this month for the fourth year in a row, while Amazon renewed its pledge to keep cutting prices even if it means lower profits."[2] You recall Meg Whitman, at the time the eBay chief executive officer, saying: "The eBay marketplace is a powerhouse [....] We continue to enjoy ever-bigger, ever-faster cycles of success, fueled by the unlimited opportunity of our huge addressable market." At the time, eBay was reaching the peak of its financial achievement and growth. You recall in the same article, Amazon's founder and CEO Jeff Bezos was quoted saying: "We will, for years and years and years, consistently give back the gains we get in lower operating costs to our customers in the form of lower prices." You also recall the numbers quoted in the article: "EBay's gross profit margin—its revenue minus the cost of sales—was 82 percent. That's after subtracting the cost of running its Web site, customer support and payment processing operations. And eBay's bottom-line profit stood at 22 percent of its revenue after subtracting all other expenses, including the hefty $172 million that eBay forked over for marketing and sales expenses. Amazon's gross profit for the same quarter, by contrast, was 22 percent, and its bottom-line profit was under 4 percent."

Was Groupon applying some of eBay's lessons? Was Color.com? As you ponder your next move, you cannot help but think that replicating eBay's early and sustained success is predicated on understanding these dynamics.

DISCUSSION QUESTIONS

1. As you reflect on what you have read and your knowledge of the impact of new technology on the competitive landscape, why would Amazon and eBay act so differently?
2. What would you say are the key lessons you should draw from the eBay vs. Amazon experience?
3. Would you argue that Groupon and Color.com are indeed applying some of the same lessons?

INTRODUCTION

Whether you believe that "the Internet changes everything," as dot-com enthusiasts vigorously maintained during the late 1990s rally of the NASDAQ, or you take a much more conservative stance, it is undeniable that the Internet and the many information technologies that the global network has spawned are important tools in the strategic arsenal of the modern firm. We discuss the Internet itself as well as the many innovations it has enabled in the next chapter, while devoting the present one to some critical concepts underpinning those innovations.

---

[1] BusinessWeek (2004). "The Global Brand Scorecard," *BusinessWeek* (vol. 72), August, p. 2.

[2] Walker, L. (2004). "A Study In E-Commerce Opposites," *The Washington Post Company*, January 29.

Understanding how to appropriately deploy the information technology now that the Internet is a cornerstone of business infrastructure requires a basic appreciation of what the Internet is and how it works (see Chapter 5). More importantly for general and functional managers, being able to use the Internet and related technology requires an understanding of the economic characteristics of networks and of information, as well as their impact on the competitive landscape and the strategy of the firm. In the remainder of this chapter we discuss each of these issues in turn.

NETWORK ECONOMICS

Consider this question: How can a little piece of software like Skype, as useful and brilliantly coded as it may be, enable the firm that owns it to fetch billions of dollars in only three years (Skype, released in mid-2003, was purchased by eBay in October 2005 for $2.6 billion, then sold back to the original owners and bought again by Microsoft in 2011 for $8.5 billion)?! How could a company create so much value so quickly? Much of the answer is to be found in the economics of networks.

Anyone who has recently gotten engaged can easily rattle off key statistics about diamonds. The value of a diamond depends on its physical attributes: Color, clarity, cut, shape, and, of course, size (measured by its weight in carats). Interestingly, while jewelers may try to convince you that a diamond has a soul, spirit, and personality (!?!), diamonds are cataloged and measured quite precisely by national organizations such as the Gemological Institute of America (GIA) in the United States. The price of a diamond is a fairly precise function of its physical characteristics. A quick online search reveals that as diamonds become harder to find, their value increases. For example, a superior round diamond, of ideal cut, D color, and IF clarity, will cost you about $3,800 for half a carat, $16,000 for one carat, $56,000 for two carats, and a cool $150,000 for three carats.

The lesson is clear: The value of diamonds is proportional to their rarity. In fact, diamonds are a great example because they have little use outside the jewelry domain. What you are paying for is indeed scarcity, which is a function of the physical characteristics that determine its beauty, brilliance, and fire. Ironically, oxygen and water are much more valuable than diamonds. After all, if you couldn't breathe or were severely dehydrated, you would hardly notice the beauty or personality of that diamond you bought! However, water is cheap and oxygen is free because they are plentiful.

To be sure, the relationship between scarcity and value of a resource is the rule, not the exception. Skilled labor and managerial talent, the resource you sell to your employer, is no different. While we can debate the morality of sky-high executive compensations, it is clear that they are justified with the argument that few people in the world have the talent and experience to run large, complex business operations. The same argument is used for professional athletes in popular sports—there was only one Michael Jordan, who could fill seats in an arena, make people tune into the games he played, and have kids clamoring for his shoes and jerseys. Today, the likes of Cristiano Ronaldo, Zlatan Ibrahimovic, and Lionel Messi fill soccer stadiums and help earn lucrative television contracts for their teams. Like scarce diamonds, these people command a premium price for their services. In his last year with the Chicago Bulls, as the scarcest attraction in basketball, Jordan fetched the highest one-year contract in the sport—$34 million for the single 1997–1998 season.

The above examples represent the norm rather than the exception. Value is typically found in scarcity, and the heart of strategy is about being unique in a positive way (see Chapter 7).

Networks Are Different: Value in Plentitude

While fax technology has been around in one form or another since the early 1900s, fax machines did not become a common sight in organizations until the 1970s. How much would you have been willing to pay for the very first fax machine rolling off the assembly line then? If value is found in scarcity... would you have paid hundreds of thousands of dollars? Probably not!

In fact, you probably would take a pass and pay nothing for it. The very first fax machine is valueless. On the other hand, if a business associate of yours had a fax machine too, you might consider purchasing one if the price were low enough given the amount of real-time document exchange you had to engage in with this associate. If many of your business associates had fax machines and were already communicating back and forth, you would see significant value in it and you would consider paying a considerable amount for it. And how much would you pay for the very first copy of Skype, the Voice over IP software? Nothing we'd guess.

Where do fax machines and Skype software draw their value from then? Not scarcity, but rather plentitude (Figure 4.1). In fact, the value of a network is proportional to the number of connected nodes. Similar arguments can be made for network technologies, like the telephone, instant messengers, railroads, and the telegraph. The insight underlying these examples is that networks differ dramatically from most other goods, as their value is tied to how many other nodes are in the network (plentitude) rather than how few (scarcity).

Physical and Virtual Networks

In the previous section, we talked about computer networks and the Internet. There are, of course, other types of networks, like the telephone network or the railroad network. We call these physical networks, where the nodes of the network are connected by physical links (i.e., railroad tracks, telephone wires). However, network economics apply also to "virtual" networks.[3]

Figure 4.1 Networks find value in plentitude

---

[3]We adopt the term virtual networks following the definition used in Shapiro, C., and Varian, H. R. (1999). *Information Rules*, Boston, MA: Harvard Business School Press.

The defining characteristic of a virtual network is that connections between network nodes are not physical, but intangible and invisible. The nodes of a virtual network are typically people rather than devices.

Whether tangible or intangible, network connections enable network nodes to share and communicate. In a virtual network the people in the network can share information (i.e., share files of the same format) with other members of the same user network (e.g., BitTorrent file-sharing users), or they can share expertise (e.g., information on how to use a given software program is the reason why you would join a certain community of practice). Note that a virtual network is generally sponsored by an organization or technology that enables it, controls access to it, and manages its evolution. Apple Computer, Inc., for instance, sponsors the iTunes network, while Skype controls the Skype network of VoIP users. Maintaining control of the network puts the sponsor in a position of advantage.

Consider the writing of this book as an example. We are writing this book using Microsoft Word on a Wintel platform.[4] If you were also a Microsoft Word user, it would be easy for you to become a coauthor on our next edition. This is because we could easily exchange versions of the chapters for comments and editing. Conversely, if you used the Linux operating system and the Scribes Writer text editor it would be much harder for us to work together (Figure 4.2). Documents may not convert correctly, images may be rendered differently, we may lose special

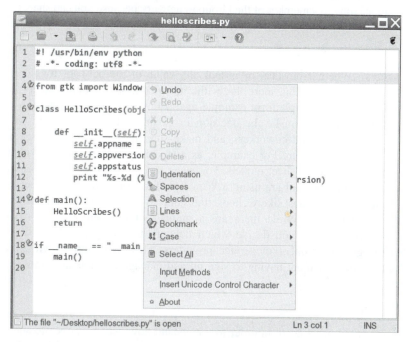

Figure 4.2   Scribes text editor (Courtesy of LinuxLinks.)

---

[4]In a strict sense, a platform is a combination of a hardware architecture and operating system. The Wintel platform refers to the dominant personal computer platform using Microsoft Windows running on machines using the Intel microprocessor.

Figure 4.3   Daily deal on LivingSocial.com

formatting in the exchange, we would not be able to easily track, approve, or reject each other's changes, and so on.

Another example of a virtual network is provided in the opening mini-case: the Groupon network of users—customers and service providers. If you subscribe to Groupon or send your offers via Groupon, you are a member of the Groupon network because you can share information and transact with other users. The Groupon network is sponsored (i.e., created and controlled) by Groupon itself.

Size Still Matters   Whether physical or virtual, the value of the network for its members is a function of its size. That is, the more nodes the network has, the more valuable it is to its members. Consider the Wintel platform example again. If you are getting ready to buy a new computer, you will likely not make the decision in isolation. Rather, you will look at your immediate circle of friends and coworkers, and make sure that you purchase a computer that allows you to interact with them. For example, as a student you write papers with your team members, you exchange spreadsheet models, you swap notes, and so on. As a consequence, if most other people at your school are using a Wintel platform or a compatible one (e.g., Apple Macintosh), then you would most likely choose the same so as not to be left out of the network.

Now consider Groupon. While there are a number of competitors, like Living Social (Figure 4.3) or Groupalia, as you decide which network to join you will be drawn toward the one with the greatest number of service providers. This is because it will give you the greatest access to offers, without having to sign up and manage multiple accounts.

Key Concepts and Vocabulary

To move beyond an intuitive level, in order to understand how networks operate and to explore their potential for firm strategy, we need to introduce some vocabulary and some fundamental concepts.

Positive Feedback   Adoption of a new technology product or service typically follows the pattern represented by the S-curve (see Figure 4.4). Positive feedback is simply defined as that

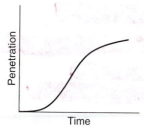

Figure 4.4   Classic technology adoption curve

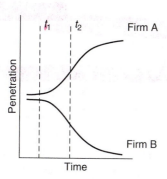

Figure 4.5   The dynamics of positive feedback

self-reinforcing mechanism by which the strong gets stronger and the weak gets weaker. It is very similar to the process by which return in a microphone quickly becomes louder and louder until it reaches a deafening volume (i.e., a high-pitched sound due to interference is picked up by a microphone and amplified, the now louder sound is picked up again by the microphone and amplified some more).

Positive feedback is a well-known economic phenomenon at the heart, for example, of economies of scale. In industries with strong economies of scale, say automobile manufacturing, there is a significant advantage stemming from size. Imagine two car makers, one larger than the other. The larger maker can spread its fixed cost across a larger volume of cars, thus being able to reduce its prices—assuming everything else is the same, including expected profit margins. With lower prices, the larger manufacturer will sell more cars, thus being able to further spread its fixed costs. With even lower prices the cycle begins again, allowing the dominant manufacturer to further reduce unit cost and increase volumes (see Figure 4.5). Note that the smaller manufacturer, losing market share to the larger one, will see its unit cost increase as it loses market share, thus having to raise prices and seeing even lower sales. While the losing firm may still have a chance at time t_1, things look compromised at time t_2.

Positive feedback sets in motion a virtuous cycle, benefiting the larger firm, and a vicious cycle, penalizing the smaller one. Thus, the stronger firm gets stronger and continues to grow while the weaker firm gets increasingly weaker still. Unless the smaller firm is able to identify a profitable niche or somehow differentiate its product, it will likely fade into oblivion, unable to sustain itself as a viable business.

Negative Feedback   The above discussion should clarify that there is nothing inherently positive (i.e., good) about positive feedback—particularly for the firms on the losing side of it! In other words, positive feedback simply means that the process is self-reinforcing, not that it is beneficial.

Negative feedback is the term used to refer to the opposite dynamic. If negative feedback is at play, the stronger gets weaker and the weaker gets stronger. Negative feedback typically characterizes economies of scale and takes effect when the dominant firm has reached a significant size. After a certain size, economies of scale no longer reduce unit cost and, due to coordination costs and increasing overhead, further growth is hampered. In other words, past a certain size, the dominant firm encounters difficulties that limit further growth.

Network Effects   Positive and negative feedback play a crucial role in physical and virtual networks because the value of a network to its members is a function of the number of nodes in the same network. Positive feedback dynamics that occur in networks go under the name of network effects, network externalities, or demand-side economies of scale.

Network effects occur when a new node (e.g., a new Skype user), while pursuing his or her own economic motives, creates value for all the other members of the network by making the network larger, and thus more valuable. Network effects have the characteristic of economic externalities[5]—hence the name network externalities. That is, they create spillover effects that have an impact on other individuals, positive for those members of the growing network and negative for the members of the other ones.

Consider once again the example of Skype, and ask yourself the question of how the firm reached 100 million users before its third year of existence, and today has almost 700 million registered accounts and over 24 million users logged in as I write this line. Skype software enables those who download it to call, chat, and exchange files with other Skype users. If you are a Skype user, you were probably alerted to its existence by a friend or colleague who had already downloaded it. Once you downloaded the application and started using it, you probably began to recruit your own friends and colleagues. The reason is that any one of them who downloads Skype makes your using the application more valuable. In other words, since you can now interact with more people, Skype is more useful to you. The term *evangelist effect* describes this dynamic and the incentive that current members of the network have to "spread the word" and convince others to join it. A similar dynamic has fueled the growth of many other applications you may use today: Facebook, Foursquare, and the like.

Note as well that the more people join the Skype network, the less valuable competing applications such as Yahoo! messenger become, in relative terms. You would rather try and convince your friends to join the Skype network with you rather than install multiple applications to connect with different individuals.

Perhaps the easiest way to understand network effects is to look at the services offered by those organizations that have sought to build an explicit business model around it. Mercata, a firm backed by Microsoft cofounder Paul Allen, pioneered the "group-shopping" business model along with MobShop. Groups of strangers seeking to purchase the same product (e.g., Palm Treo 750) would come together via the Internet to form a Mercata-enabled buying group. As the number of new customers joined the buying group, the price for the item would drop *for each member of the group*.

---

[5]As you may recall from your introductory economics courses, an externality occurs when an economic actor, pursuing his or her own economic motives, affects other actors' economic position. Consider the example of a large resort able to charge $500 a night. If a pig farm is opened upwind of the resort, with no intention to hurt the resort but simply to pursue a business opportunity, the resort will no longer be able to charge premium prices. . . or any price at all! This spillover effect is called an externality—a negative externality in this case.

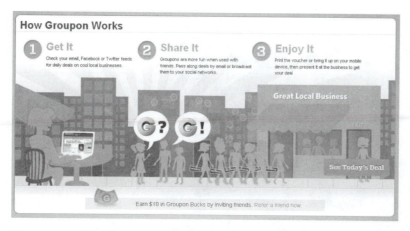

Figure 4.6   The Groupon model

The Mercata Web site showed the current price and future prices available to all once targets in the number of customers were hit (e.g., $550 per item once the size of the group reaches 10, $540 at 15). The network effect at play here is clear. Every new customer who joins the buying group, while seeking his or her own economic benefit, lowers the price for all. While both Mercata and MobShop were casualties of the dot-com bust, their business model offers a great example of network effects at play and new organizations, such as Groupon (Figure 4.6), GroupSwoop, and Living Social have recently tried to build businesses around the same core idea.

Positive feedback associated with traditional economies of scale typically exhausts itself well before one firm can achieve market dominance, but this is not the case for network effects. Positive feedback associated with network effects can play out, without limit, until one firm dominates the network and all others disappear, a situation typically referred to as a "winner-take-all" dynamic (see Figure 4.5).

A firm that finds itself on the losing side of network effects can survive under two conditions:

- Become compatible with the dominant player, thus being able to connect to the dominant network and tap into its value. When Apple Computers found itself on the losing side of the battle for dominance of the personal computer platform, it was forced to seek compatibility with Wintel products—sponsor of the dominant network. However, the sponsors of the dominant network will often resist this move to compatibility. Recently for example, the dominant social network—Facebook—moved to protect its dominant position and sued Brazilian startup Power.com, which enables individuals to "single sign-on" and aggregate information from multiple social networks they are members of.

- Find a niche that is different enough from the broader market and big enough to sustain the firm. Before Apple became compatible with the dominant Wintel platform, it was able to survive by offering a far superior product for designers and publishers, who found the Macintosh computer and software much better than Windows machines for their needs (Figure 4.7).

The dominant network sponsor may react by trying to either block or limit compatibility. It may also try to take over the available market niches. Being able to do so will depend on the characteristics of the market it competes in and the demand for product variety that characterizes it.

Figure 4.7 The original Macintosh (Courtesy of http://www.allaboutapple.com/.)

Tipping Point and Tippy Markets   A tippy market is defined as one that is subject to strong positive feedback, such that the market will "tip" in favor of the firm that is able to reach critical mass and dominate it. A tippy market is therefore a market with "winner-take-all" tendencies.

We define a tipping point as the watershed of dominance. In other words, the tipping point is that moment in the evolution of a market where one organization or technology reaches critical mass and goes on to dominate it—the point of no return where winners and losers are defined. In Figure 4.5, the tipping point occurred sometime between times t_1 and t_2.

The lower the cost of production and distribution of a product, the quicker the onset of the tipping point (Figure 4.8). Software programs such as Skype represent a good example. A random check of your Skype application at any one time may reveal that there are over 25 million users currently connected—not bad for a company with only an eight-year-old product.

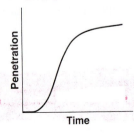

Figure 4.8   A fast tipping point

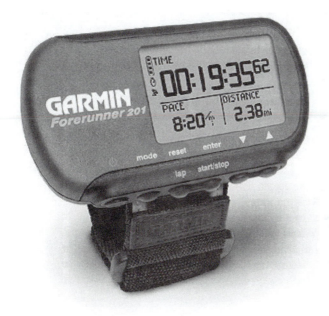

Figure 4.9   A GPS receiver for runners (Courtesy of Garmin International.)

Not All Markets Tip   During the dot-com days, there was a prevalent misguided perception that any business that used the Internet would be able to harness strong network effects. As a consequence, many firms focused on ramping up their user base at any cost, trusting that, once they reached critical mass, they would be able to dominate the market and figure out how to turn a profit.

Not all markets tip, and winner-take-all dynamics are more the exception than the rule. Consider Garmin, the maker of navigation and communication equipment (Figure 4.9). Garmin is a vertically integrated company that directly controls the design, manufacture, marketing, and sales of its products. Its automotive GPS navigators help customers plot their course, identify points of interest along the road, and receive real-time driving directions. Is Garmin in a tippy market?

No, the automotive GPS navigation market is not a tippy market. If you own a Garmin device to help you find your way (i.e., you are in the Garmin network), and I purchase my own GPS navigation device, you don't stand to benefit in any way from my purchase. We both use the receiver independently to find our way. Now, imagine if the navigation device automatically uploaded the location and speed of each user to a database that computed the average speed of cars on different routes. Now, when I seek to find the quickest way home during rush hour, the more people that are in the Garmin network uploading their speed and position, the more accurate directions I would get—thus creating strong network effects and a tippy market.

Contrast the above example with that of Resort Condominiums International, LLC (RCI). RCI is a well-established timeshare company founded in 1974 to enable "exchange vacations." In the timeshare model, customers buy the right to one or more vacation weeks in a condominium unit in a specific property and a specific location (e.g., Unit 235 at The Outrigger Palms at Wailea, on the isle of Maui, Hawaii). Those who own a timeshare can enjoy it during their allotted time. Alternatively, when seeking variation in their vacation, timeshare owners can exchange the right to use their unit with others. RCI, and other companies that support exchange vacations, create

Figure 4.10   RCI's website

the market and facilitate the process of finding suitable trading partners, managing credits (e.g., a week in a high-end Maui resort may be worth two weeks in a midscale Florida property), and providing the many other services necessary to enable the exchange.

RCI has a membership base of over 3 million timeshare owners, with more than 3,700 affiliated resorts in over one hundred countries. RCI now has a Web site that supports many of its interactions with its members and prospective timeshare owners (Figure 4.10), but it is certainly not a "network business." Is RCI's industry characterized by strong network effects?

The answer here is yes. Every new member that joins the RCI network increases the network's value for the entire current (and prospective) membership because the new member's unit increases the pool of available options. Moreover, it increases the potential pool of people interested in current members' own units—thus making current RCI member's units more likely to be requested for exchange. It follows that for prospective timeshare buyers, joining the largest timeshare exchange network offers the highest value.

How to Recognize a Tippy Market   The two examples above show that "being on the Internet" is no guarantee of being able to harness network effects, and that even non-Internet businesses can benefit from network effects. How can we recognize a tippy market a priori? How can you tell if your firm has the potential to harness positive feedback?

Whether a market will tip toward a dominant technology or a dominant player depends on two factors (Figure 4.11):

■ *The presence and strength of economies of scale.* Strong economies of scale, whether traditional economies of scale or network effects, provide an advantage to larger firms.

■ *The variety of the customer needs.* Customer demand for variety creates the potential for the development of distinct market niches that the dominant player may be unable to fulfill.

Network Effects

		Low	High
Demand for variety	Low	Unlikely	High
	High	Low	Depends

Figure 4.11 Likelihood of market tippiness

When economies of scale are significant and customer needs are fairly standard, then the conditions for market tippiness are strongest. Consider our first example, the fax machine. As we discussed, there are strong network effects in the faxing industry. Moreover, the need for fax machines is a very standardized one—customers don't need much variety in the service. It follows, then, that one dominant fax network would emerge. While more than one fax standard may have been vying for dominance in the early days, the market eventually tipped toward one. The others disappeared. A similar dynamic has played out for modems, videocassette recorders, and more recently in the high-definition DVD market.

When economies of scale are limited and the market has a wide range of different needs, the potential for market tippiness is the weakest. This is because not only is there a small advantage associated with increasing size, but there are also a number of smaller niches that can support multiple smaller focused players. Consider sports cars, for instance. Typically the top manufacturers, such as Ferrari, Lamborghini (Figure 4.12), Maserati, and the like, make a limited number of cars. Thus, economies of scale are small. Moreover, those who seek to purchase high-end sports cars do so partly to differentiate themselves from the crowd. Those who purchase exclusive goods seek variety—at times even uniqueness. This is therefore a market that is likely to sustain a number of relatively small players.

When economies of scale are significant and demand for variety is high, the potential for market tippiness depends on the number and size of the available market niches. The ability to tap into a sizeable market niche seeking a product with unique specifications (e.g., graphic designers) is what allowed Apple Computers to survive prior to ensuring compatibility with the dominant Microsoft-sponsored network.

Figure 4.12 The Lamborghini Murcielago (Created by Ian Hughes at the English Wikipedia Project.)

When economies of scale are limited, even if the demand for variety is low, the potential to create positive feedback is small and the market is unlikely to tip.

Two-Sided Networks

Now that we have discussed the dynamics of networks in their purest sense, we can complicate the picture a bit. When network effects are present, the addition of one node to the network directly creates value for all the existing members. However, positive feedback can also occur in what we term two-sided networks—that is, networks that have two types of members, each creating value for the other.

Consider, for example, Adobe, the firm that in 1990 invented the now ubiquitous Portable Document Format (PDF) standard. Documents that are converted to PDF are guaranteed to look exactly the same on any platform. Chances are that you are a heavy user of PDF documents, reading them with Adobe's Acrobat Reader, for which you paid exactly nothing—not because you are a user of pirated software, but because Adobe gives the software away for free. In similar fashion, Microsoft gives away its Windows Media Player, as do all other streaming audio/video makers. Why is this so? Does it make sense for a company to give away its product?

The strategy described above is sensible, particularly as the firm tries to establish its product as the standard. As you realize when you move from wanting to read PDF files to wanting to create them, Adobe Acrobat is not free. In other words, Adobe created a market for software programs that would ensure documents' cross-platform accuracy of display. Then it proceeded to establish its technology as the standard by creating a market of users, all those who downloaded and used the free reader. As the number of users grew, fueled by some early adopters of the authoring software (i.e., PDF document makers), organizations that produce and publish documents (e.g., companies publishing manuals for their products online) decided to adopt Adobe Acrobat. In turn, the increasing number of PDF documents available for download created even more demand for the reader software, aided by the "Free: Download Acrobat Reader" link that would be placed next to it.

You immediately recognize this process as an example of positive feedback. If you tried to break into the cross-platform document maker market as of today, you would be taking on a next-to-impossible feat. On the other hand, Adobe today provides a whole family of "ePaper solutions," including, of course, the ubiquitous (and free) Acrobat Reader. Adobe also offers various versions of the PDF maker, such as Acrobat Elements, Acrobat Standard, Acrobat Professional, and Acrobat 3D, each with different functionalities and price points.

More generally, in a two-sided network, the value of the network to one type of member depends on the number of members from the other side that take part in the network. An example is offered by electronic procurement exchanges (see Chapter 5). In these marketplaces, whether catering to consumers or businesses, buyers are interested in the number of suppliers they will be able to reach (i.e., selection) while sellers are interested in the number of buyers they will be able to reach (i.e., potential sales volume). In this case as well, the firm that enables the marketplace (i.e., the sponsor of the network) and is first to reach critical mass (i.e., passes the tipping point) will dominate the industry, leaving little room for any competitor (i.e., any competing marketplace).

Implications for General and Functional Managers

Network economics have substantial implications of managerial interest. As networks become more ubiquitous, you must take these implications into account.

Figure 4.13   Monster.com—a two-sided network

Network Effects, Not Just Networks   As we have seen in the many examples provided above, network effects, and, more generally, positive feedback, create the precondition for winner-takes-all dynamics. Network effects occur in the presence of technology standards, like the fax machine or a computer platform, but are not restricted to the technology arena. They also occur in the presence of virtual networks and communities of interest.

Consider, for example, the great success enjoyed by dating communities, such as Match.com, or employment search sites, such as Monster.com (Figure 4.13). While these communities do not use or require their members to purchase any specific technology or buy into any technical standard, their value is directly proportional to the number of users they can attract and, as a consequence, enjoy strong network effects.

The Threshold of Significance   We defined the tipping point as the watershed of dominance, that moment in the evolution of a market where one organization or technology reaches critical mass and goes on to dominate it. Traditionally, the onset of the tipping point would take some time, as the dominant technology slowly gained acceptance and became adopted by more and more users. For example, in the classic battle for dominance of the videocassette recorder (VCR) market, Sony and JVC struggled to establish their standard, Betamax and VHS, respectively (Figure 4.14). The battle between these competing standards lasted over a decade and, as we know today, was won by JVC's VHS technology.

The new generation of general and functional managers will not have a decade to monitor competitors before the onset of the tipping point. Case in point, the recent battle in the DVD market between two technologies vying for dominance—Sony's Blu-Ray and Toshiba's High Definition DVD (HD-DVD)—played out much more quickly... and Sony came out on top this time (Figure 4.15). Particularly for digital products delivered over the Internet, the market can tip very rapidly. In some cases, by the time a competitor realizes that a technology is emerging (i.e., the new technology reaches the threshold of significance), it is too late to react. In these markets, being the innovator and the first mover may be critical. ICQ, the firm that popularized

Figure 4.14 Betamax and VHS tapes

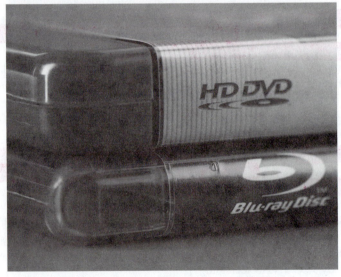

Figure 4.15 Blu-ray and HD DVDs *Source*: © Oliver Leedham/Alamy

Instant Messaging and went on to dominate that industry, reached critical mass before there was even one competitor. While formidable competitors have since emerged, such as Yahoo! and Microsoft, ICQ remains the dominant platform.

Users Select a Network   One of the most important implications of the above discussion is that customers will pick a network, not a product or a service provider. Let's return to your decision to buy a personal computer. If all of your friends are in the Microsoft Windows network, you are most likely to join them in that network. Yet, while many of your friends may be using Dell laptops, you could choose a Compaq machine or even a Mac—which now enables you to be a member of the dominant network. In other words, you will not care about what hardware or software you use, as long as it enables you to tap into the resources of your network of interest.

Controlling the Network Provides Competitive Advantage   Firms are willing to engage in standards battles and invest significant resources to achieve critical mass because sponsoring a dominant network provides the firm with a position of competitive advantage. Consider the recent court battle involving America Online (AOL), sponsor of the dominant Instant Messenger (IM) network after having bought ICQ, and rival IM software providers. AOL found itself having to defend why it resisted making its IM network compatible with Yahoo! Messenger and Microsoft MSN. While the firm claimed that it wanted to be able to control its network to offer the best possible experience to its users and to limit security and privacy concerns (a common line of defense!), it was clear that AOL's decision was a business decision designed to maintain and strengthen its advantage as the sponsor of the largest network. A similar intent seems to be the basis of Facebook's reluctance to join the OpenSocial community and instead develop its proprietary *Facebook Platform* service.

The Importance of Mutual Exclusivity   Up to this point, we have treated competing networks as mutually exclusive. This is true for many of them. Consider the high-definition standards battle once again. Very few individuals would be willing to purchase two DVD players, one using the Blu-Ray standard and the other one using the Toshiba HD DVD standard. This is because not only would they need to purchase two devices that cost money and take up space, but they would also have to maintain separate movie collections with some titles in one format and some in the other.

Simply put, there are costs associated with being a member of both networks. The steeper these costs, the more valuable it is to be able to control and retain ownership of the network. Consider Skype and the Voice over IP (VoIP) market. Skype is a small piece of software that can be installed quickly and requires little configuration. Once installed, Skype runs as a service in the background until the user decides to make a call. If a competitor with very similar characteristics were to emerge, it would not cost users much to run both applications simultaneously. It is a bit of a nuisance to have to install and run two VoIP applications, but the two networks would not be mutually exclusive and the power associated with controlling the dominant network (i.e., Skype) would be largely diminished.

THE ECONOMICS OF INFORMATION

As networks of interoperable digital devices have continued to expand, one of the most important results of managerial interest has been the unprecedented amounts of data and information that are being captured, stored, processed, and distributed by modern organizations. Andy Cohen, former senior vice president of sales and marketing at supply chain operator iTradeNetwork, said it best a few years back: "The information you can derive from e-commerce is as interesting as the commerce itself."

However, in order to be able to wring value from data and information, you must understand its economic characteristics. Information, like networks, has some interesting traits that differentiate it from physical goods. These unique characteristics of data and information have significant implications for firm strategy and competition.

Data and Information

Information systems researchers typically draw a distinction between the terms *data* and *information*. Data is defined as codified raw facts—things that have happened (e.g., a customer has lodged a complaint) coded as letters and numbers and stored, increasingly, by way of digital devices (Figure 4.16).

Information is defined as data in context (Figure 4.17). In other words, data become information when they have been given meaning and can therefore be interpreted by individual users or machines. It follows, then, that information is audience dependent; one person's data is another person's information.

Classic Information Goods

The unique characteristics of information are best understood by first looking at products where information is the heart of the value proposition. We define classic information goods as those products that a customer purchases for the sole purpose of gaining access to the information they contain.

For example, this book (and any other book) is a classic information good. The only reason you purchased it was to be able to gain access to its content.[6] The same goes for movies. The only reason you go to the theater or rent a movie is to gain access to the experience that a film provides. The news represents yet another example. Whether you read the newspaper, watch television, or visit a news agency Web site, the only reason to do so is to acquire the information provided. Other classic information goods are music, stock quotes, class lectures, software programs, and the like (Figure 4.18).

A simple test for recognizing information goods is to verify whether the product can be digitized (i.e., can be encoded into bits and stored in digital format). If so, the product is an information good. You are probably holding a paper copy of this book, but the same content could be delivered online, as an eBook, or as sound if we decided to publish an audio book version. I have a version of this same book on my computer in Microsoft Word format, while the publisher has a version on their computers in Adobe FrameMaker.

7975593065 HAKE4H Th, Dec 30, 2010 6:45 Th, Dec 30, 2010 18:38 DL1072 ATL MSY DR. GABRIELE PICCOLI

Figure 4.16   A string of data

Ticket number	Record Locator	Departure	Arrival	Flight #	Departure	Arrival	Passenger
7975593065	HAKE4H	Th, Dec 30,2010 6:45	Th, Dec 30,2010 18:38	DL1072	ATL	MSY	DR. GABRIELE PICCOLI

Figure 4.17   Contextualized data becomes information

---

[6]While it can convincingly be argued that we can use a book in many other ways (e.g., as a status symbol) we are focusing here in the use of books, and other information goods, in their primary function—that of conveying the author's message.

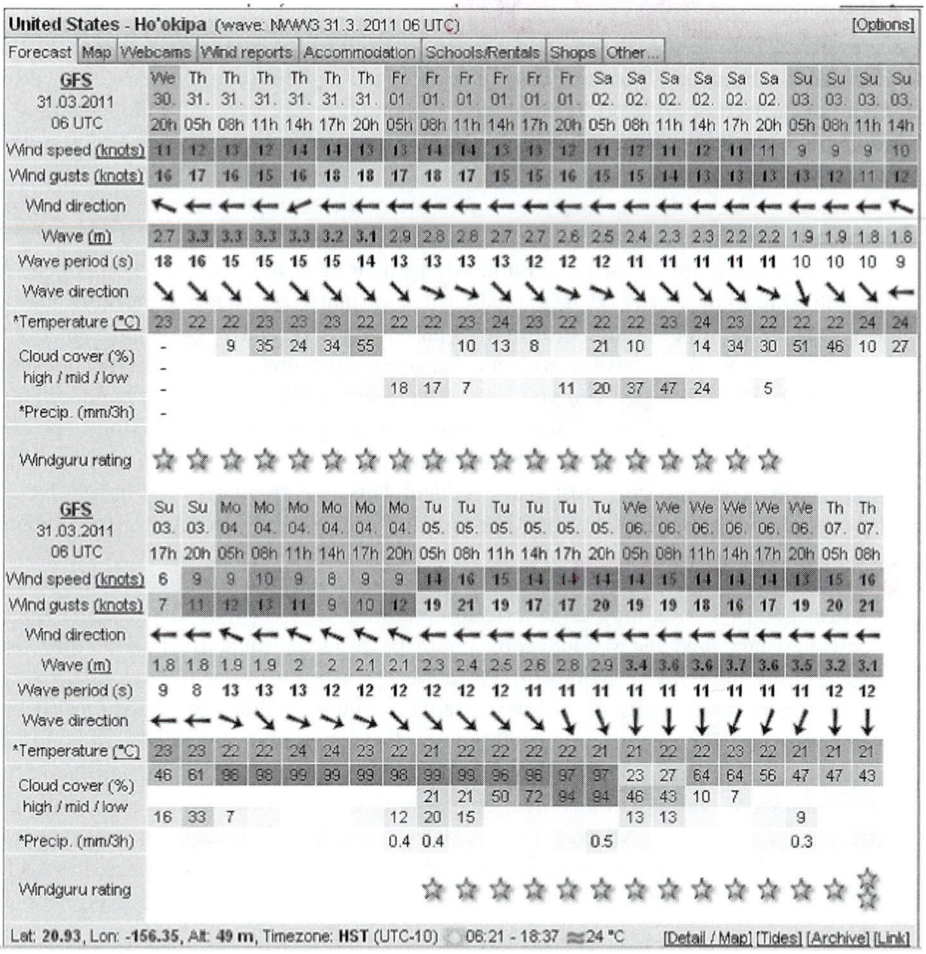

United States - Ho'okipa (wave: NWW3 31.3. 2011 06 UTC)   [Options]

Forecast | Map | Webcams | Wind reports | Accommodation | Schools/Rentals | Shops | Other...

GFS 31.03.2011 06 UTC	We 30. 20h	Th 31. 05h	Th 31. 08h	Th 31. 11h	Th 31. 14h	Th 31. 17h	Th 31. 20h	Fr 01. 05h	Fr 01. 08h	Fr 01. 11h	Fr 01. 14h	Fr 01. 17h	Fr 01. 20h	Sa 02. 05h	Sa 02. 08h	Sa 02. 11h	Sa 02. 14h	Sa 02. 17h	Sa 02. 20h	Su 03. 05h	Su 03. 08h	Su 03. 11h	Su 03. 14h
Wind speed (knots)	11	12	13	12	14	14	13	13	14	14	13	13	12	11	12	11	12	11	11	9	9	9	10
Wind gusts (knots)	16	17	16	15	16	18	18	17	18	17	15	15	16	15	15	14	13	13	13	13	12	11	12
Wind direction	←	←	←	←	↙	←	←	←	←	←	←	←	←	←	←	←	←	←	←	←	←	←	←
Wave (m)	2.7	3.3	3.3	3.3	3.3	3.2	3.1	2.9	2.8	2.8	2.7	2.7	2.6	2.5	2.4	2.3	2.3	2.2	2.2	1.9	1.9	1.8	1.8
Wave period (s)	18	16	15	15	15	15	14	13	13	13	13	12	12	12	11	11	11	11	11	10	10	10	9
Wave direction	↘	↘	↘	↘	↘	↘	↘	↘	→	→	↘	→	→	↘	↘	↘	↘	↘	→	↓	↘	↘	←
*Temperature (°C)	23	22	22	23	23	23	22	22	22	23	24	23	22	22	22	23	24	23	22	22	22	24	24
Cloud cover (%) high / mid / low	-	9	35	24	34	55		10	13	8		21	10		14	34	30	51	46	10	27		
	-						18	17	7		11	20	37	47	24		5						
	-																						
*Precip. (mm/3h)	-																						
Windguru rating	☆	☆	☆	☆	☆	☆	☆	☆	☆	☆	☆	☆	☆	☆	☆	☆	☆	☆	☆	☆	☆	☆	☆

GFS 31.03.2011 06 UTC	Su 03. 17h	Su 03. 20h	Mo 04. 05h	Mo 04. 08h	Mo 04. 11h	Mo 04. 14h	Mo 04. 17h	Mo 04. 20h	Tu 05. 05h	Tu 05. 08h	Tu 05. 11h	Tu 05. 14h	Tu 05. 17h	Tu 05. 20h	We 06. 05h	We 06. 08h	We 06. 11h	We 06. 14h	We 06. 17h	We 06. 20h	Th 07. 05h	Th 07. 08h
Wind speed (knots)	6	9	9	10	9	8	9	9	14	16	15	14	14	14	14	15	14	14	14	13	15	16
Wind gusts (knots)	7	11	12	13	11	9	10	12	19	21	19	17	17	20	19	19	18	16	17	19	20	21
Wind direction	←	←	↖	←	↖	↖	↖	←	←	←	←	←	←	←	←	←	←	←	←	←	←	←
Wave (m)	1.8	1.8	1.9	1.9	2	2	2.1	2.1	2.3	2.4	2.5	2.6	2.8	2.9	3.4	3.6	3.6	3.7	3.6	3.5	3.2	3.1
Wave period (s)	9	8	13	13	13	12	12	12	12	12	12	11	11	11	11	11	11	11	11	11	12	12
Wave direction	←	←	↘	↘	↘	↘	↘	↘	↘	↘	↘	↘	↓	↓	↓	↓	↓	↙	↙	↓	↓	↓
*Temperature (°C)	23	23	22	22	24	24	23	22	21	22	22	22	22	21	21	22	22	23	22	21	21	21
Cloud cover (%) high / mid / low	46	81	98	98	99	99	99	98	99	99	96	96	97	97	23	27	64	64	56	47	47	43
									21	21	50	72	94	94	46	43	10	7				
	16	33	7						12	20	15				13	13				9		
*Precip. (mm/3h)									0.4	0.4					0.5						0.3	
Windguru rating									☆	☆	☆	☆	☆	☆	☆	☆	☆	☆	☆	☆	☆	☆

Lat: **20.93**, Lon: **-156.35**, Alt: **49 m**, Timezone: **HST** (UTC-10)   06:21 - 18:37 ≈24 °C   [Detail / Map] [Tides] [Archive] [Link]

Figure 4.18   Wind and waves forecast—a classic information good

Now consider the chair on which you are sitting as you read this book. Could that be digitized? The answer is no, of course. The plans and drawings for making the chair could be digitized (another example of an information good), but the chair itself is a physical product that you purchased not for its information content, but for its ability to support you in a comfortable reading position.

The Economic Characteristics of Information

The fairly specific definition of classic information goods provided above is important because information has some unique and interesting characteristics.

Information Has High Production Costs The first copy of an information good is very expensive to create in terms of time and money. Consider this book once again. Writing this text required a substantial amount of time in front of a computer typing a first draft, editing it multiple times, selecting appropriate examples, responding to reviewers' comments, and performing further editing as necessary. More subtly, before the writing process even began, substantial time was invested in studying these ideas, learning frameworks proposed by other authors, developing the unique frameworks and analytical models that are original to this text, doing the interviews and writing up the case studies, teaching the material, and taking notes on what seemed to work well in the classroom and what did not. After the draft of the book was completed, editors from the publishing house revised it, paginated it, assistants fact-checked the information, obtained required copyright permissions for images and quotations, and so on. While this book was a big undertaking, you can envision projects that are even more costly and time consuming. Think about the latest big-budget film you have seen, a project that easily cost hundreds of millions of dollars and involved a large number of people who spent years developing their craft. All that work went into creating a less than two-hour-long experience for you to enjoy. In summary, information goods are very costly to produce. This is particularly true in relative terms, when the cost of producing the first copy is compared to the cost of producing the second one.

Negligible Replication Costs This is where information goods begin to differ drastically from physical goods. For as long as it took to create the first copy of this book or the blockbuster movie you last saw, the second copy could be produced at a fraction of the cost. Consider software, say the copy of Microsoft Word we are using to write this book. By some accounts Word is made up of millions of lines of code, written by hundreds of Microsoft programmers over the years. The first copy of such a complex software program takes a significant amount of time and money to produce, but what about the second copy? Producing the second copy of Microsoft Word was essentially free. It simply took up a few megabytes of storage space on a hard disk somewhere at Microsoft Corp. or on a compact disk (CD).

For many information goods, the second copy, and all subsequent ones, has such a low cost of production that it is essentially free. This is not true of physical goods, such as the chair discussed above, or a car, or a meal. In a restaurant, for example, food is the second largest component of cost, second only to labor. Thus, no matter how many steaks the restaurant cooks that evening, each one will consume roughly the same amount of ingredients. The second copy of a steak (i.e., a physical good) is not free.

The Information Is Not the Carrier Note that the cost of the CD that is used to hold the second (or third or hundredth) copy of a software program is not, strictly speaking, to be considered a cost of the copy. The CD is simply the "carrier" of the information, not the information itself. In other words, when you purchase a new software program, you purchase the CD because it allows you to get to what you are actually buying, the information. When the Internet became a viable channel of distribution for digital goods, shrink-wrapped software programs on CD became less and less popular. Today, in the post-pc era (as Steve Jobs was fond of calling it),[7] apps are automatically downloaded on your cell phone through wireless channels and the CD is quickly going the way of the floppy disk (Figure 4.19) and the tape cassette.

---

[7]"Steve Jobs Ushers in Post-PC Era," *PC Magazine*, June 2, 2010 (Available on 03/30/2011 http://www.pcmag.com/article2/0,2817,2364545,00.asp).

Figure 4.19   8″, 5.25″, and 3.5″ floppy disks

The same holds true for all classic information goods, such as the DVDs that you rent at the store so that you can access the movie experience, and paper books that you carry so you can access the content of the book. This is an important point because sometimes the economics of the carrier constrain the economics of the information.

Consider, for example, the service of CinemaNow, Inc., which allows movie buffs to download a copy of their favorite movie to be burned onto a blank DVD and added to their library. While the DVD has not been eliminated in the process, as in the case of movies on demand offered by cable companies or by Netflix, Inc., this service separates the movie being bought and paid for and the carrier of the information. Aside from speed and convenience, the cost structure for CinemaNow more accurately reflects that of distributing an information good, and is reflected in its proposed pricing scheme (from $8.99 to $14.99 depending on how new the title is).

Negligible Distribution Cost   As with replication costs, the distribution costs associated with information goods are very low. Distribution costs are defined here as the expenditures associated with delivering the information good to the customers so that they can access its content.[8]

Consider once again the example of a big-budget movie. How does the movie get to the theater for your enjoyment? Traditionally, the studios copied films onto reels (Figure 4.20)—a typical movie fits on five or six reels—and shipped them in film cans to the theaters. However, strictly speaking, the cost of distributing the cans is the cost of distributing the carrier of the information, not the information itself. In fact, modern delivery systems for in-room entertainment in hotels, for example, rely on digitized movies that are downloaded onto servers that in turn stream them to the TV sets in the rooms. High-definition movie theaters also have done away with the reels.

Where the infrastructure for digital distribution has been created (for example, for digital music sales through the iTunes store), the distribution cost of the information goods is indeed

---

[8]A point of confusion here is that the term distribution cost, for information goods like movies and music, often refers to marketing expenditure (which can be significant for information goods). In this book, the term distribution cost is used in its strict sense and does not include marketing expenditures.

Figure 4.20   Movie reels carry movies to theaters
Source: © Claudia Dewald/ iStockphoto

negligible—free in practice. The same happens for software programs and audio books you can play on your iPod (e.g., audible.com). Information goods are therefore characterized by high fixed costs and very low marginal costs. The cost of producing the first copy is steep while making and delivering incremental copies is almost free.

Costs Are Sunk   Unrecoverable costs, those expenses that the firm has incurred to create its product or service but cannot be recuperated, are termed sunk costs. For example, if you are remodeling your kitchen and purchase some new flooring, only to find out that your significant other hates it and vetoes your installing it, you can return the material and recover the expense, but you can't recuperate the costs (in terms of time, effort, and gasoline in this case) you spent in selecting and transporting the flooring. Your time and the gas you wasted are sunk costs. Information goods are unforgiving. If nobody is interested in reading our book, once available for sale, we will be unable to recover all the expenses associated with writing and publishing it. If you have dreams of making it big in the music industry, all the time and money you invested in making your first CD is lost if nobody cares for your form of artistic expression.

The costs of information goods are mostly sunk costs. It follows, therefore, that there is significant risk involved in producing information goods, and consequently a good deal of attention and research needs to be devoted to gauging and creating demand for them. The reason why movie studios spend so much money on marketing is to create demand for a product; the cost of which is mostly unrecoverable (i.e., sunk cost) once the film is released.

No Natural Capacity Limits   While the creation of new information goods entails the significant risk that the investment will not be recovered, the upside is also significant. Information goods face almost no constraints to reproduction. Let's return to the example above and imagine that your songs struck a chord with the executives at Shady Records, who see in you the next big hip-hop star. When your songs make it into the iTunes music store, there is no limit to how many times they can be downloaded (i.e., how many digital copies can be generated for next to zero cost).

Not Consumed by Use   Perhaps the most intriguing characteristic of information is that it can be reused multiple times. Physical goods, like an apple or one night in a hotel room, are destroyed through their use. That is, if you eat the last apple in the room, there is nothing left for anyone else. If you occupy room 235 at the Ritz in Paris on March 19, 2013, that room, that

Figure 4.21   Acqua di Gió by Armani   *Source*: AP Photo/Acqua di Giola

night, will not be available for others to enjoy. Conversely, information goods are not consumed by use. All the people in the theater with you can enjoy the movie alongside you. The fact that you read the news this morning does not preclude me from learning the same facts from the nightly news... or even from the very same newspaper you left on the subway on your way to work. This characteristic of information is at the heart of the widespread music pirating phenomenon—or sharing, as those who engage in it like to call it. While two thirsty people will think twice before sharing their water, music lovers don't think twice about sharing their music. That's because after you upload your MP3 collection to a peer-to-peer file-sharing network and others start downloading your tunes, the songs are not consumed, instead they multiply! Making this very point in a fairly funny way was rapper Kid Rock who, in a YouTube "public service announcement" aptly titled "Steal Everything", encouraged viewers to "level the playing field" by stealing not just music, but any other good they could put their hands on... from clothes, to computers, to MP3 players and gasoline.

Experience Goods   Information goods are experience goods, defined as those products or services that need to be tried (i.e., experienced) before their quality can be assessed. All new products and services are experience goods; in fact, perfume trials and samples of shampoo have been used for decades to entice people to buy. However, information goods are experience goods every time. If you are happy with the scent of the Acqua di Gió by Giorgio Armani perfume (Figure 4.21) you sampled, you can make it your perfume of choice and purchase it over and over with confidence (or at least until the manufacturer changes the formula).

But how do you know if tomorrow's copy of the *Wall Street Journal* will be as good as today's? Can you be sure that the next book by Dan Brown is worth reading (assuming the first one was!), or that the BBC international newscast is worth watching tonight?

Implications

The unique economic characteristics of information and classic information goods described above have some important implications for you as a general or functional manager:

- *Information is customizable*. Information goods can often be modified with relative ease. For example, movies are typically edited for different showings or different audiences.

Bonus cuts and extra material are often included in DVD releases. This book partly draws from original material that has been published before in different venues in the form of reports, case studies, or lecture slides. Physical goods are typically much more difficult to customize before or after they are produced. Imagine realizing that your kitchen is too small after purchasing a new house—good luck customizing that!!

- *Information is reusable*. Because information is not consumed by use, it is reusable multiple times and, because it is customizable, in multiple forms.

- *Information is often time valued*. The value of information is tied to the user's ability to employ it. Often timely use of the information is necessary to reap the potential value. Stock quotes represent a perfect example of this. Stock quotes on a fifteen-minute delay are useless information to a stock trader. Another example is represented by book publishers, who often release hard cover versions of popular novels and business books before releasing paperbacks that sell for much less. The cost of production of hard covers is not the reason for the price difference. Publishers are simply "versioning" their product to capitalize on the fact that some customers are willing to pay a premium to read the book as soon as it is released.

- *Information goods can achieve significant gross profit margins*. Because of their economic characteristics—high production costs, and low replication and distribution—firms that produce successful information goods can enjoy vast profit margins. Microsoft Corporation has enjoyed legendary profits over the years thanks in large part to its two cash cows: Microsoft Windows, the dominant operating system software for personal computers, and Microsoft Office, the dominant suite of productivity tools.

Information-Intensive Goods

As you followed the above discussion about classic information goods, you may have wondered what applicability it has to industries that don't deal directly with these goods. That is, how useful is the above discussion to executives in industries such as restaurant franchising, car manufacturing, cruise ship operations, or health care? In each of these industries, you may reason, the value proposition customers seek is a tangible product or service, not information. While this is true, a quick look "under the hood" will reveal that information plays a critical role in these businesses as well.

Authors Evans and Wurster, from their vantage point at the Media and Convergence practice of the Boston Consulting Group, claimed back in 1997 that "every business is an information business."[9] As an example they cited health care, an industry that offers a very "physical" service, but where one-third of its cost is "the cost of capturing, storing and processing such information as patient's records, physicians' notes, test results, and insurance claims." Most industries, while not dealing directly with information goods, rely on information to create and bring to market their product or service; from research and development, to logistics, to distribution, to sales and marketing, information is the "glue" that holds together business operations. What this means is that, most products and services are information-intensive goods. For

---

[9]Evans, P. B., and Wurster, T. S. (1997). "Strategy and the New Economics of Information," *Harvard Business Review*, September/October, pp. 70–82.

information-intensive goods, while information is not exclusively what the customer seeks when purchasing the products or service, information is either one of their critical components or a necessary resource during their production process.

The role that information plays could be at the periphery of the product or service (e.g., informational material about the features of a product, the brand) or could be embedded in the product itself as knowledge (e.g., R&D and product development research). Consider, for instance, McDonald's Corporation, the franchiser of the popular fast-food restaurants. Is McDonald's in the "restaurant business" or is it in the "information business"? While you may opt for the first answer, a careful analysis reveals that the second is a more accurate label. What McDonald's Corp. sells to its franchisees around the world is sales volume through customer traffic due to its strong brand (i.e., information in the consumer mind), management know-how (i.e., information about optimal practices ranging from pricing, to purchasing, to human resource management), and various other support services (e.g., training, bulk purchasing contracts). Thus, much of what the franchisor offers is in the form of information and knowledge.

Information is also embedded in the production and organizational processes that enable the transformation of inputs into products and services to be sold. Moreover, products and services in today's economy are increasingly "augmented" by information services. Recall the example discussed in Chapter 1 of car manufacturers embedding self-monitoring and self-diagnosing components on automobiles that can then proactively communicate with their owners via e-mail. Or think about the near future of car windshields that will be able to overlay digital content over the real objects the driver sees through the glass—a technology called augmented reality (Figure 4.22).

Because of its pervasiveness, information has become a clear source of competitive advantage. Many of the most admired modern organizations draw their advantage from a superior

Figure 4.22   Use of augmented reality to digitally capture the floor plan of a house (Created by FMalka at the English Wikipedia Project.)

ability to capture, manage, and distribute (or use) information. We will discuss ways to think about how to create value using organizational data and information in Chapter 8.

INFORMATION IN NETWORKS

As we have seen, information has unique economic characteristics. However, it has traditionally had to rely on physical carriers in order to be delivered. Film reels carry movies to the theater, books carry text and images to readers, professors carry lecture content to a class of students. The fact that information has had to rely on a physical carrier has acted as a constraint, limiting its ability to behave according to its inherent characteristics.

Consider the process of organizing your honeymoon prior to 1993, the date of the commercialization of the Internet. Back then you would likely visit a travel agency with your spouse and, after waiting in line for your turn to speak with an agent (the carrier of the information you were seeking), you would tell the agent your likes and dislikes and receive some suggestions. Based on these suggestions and your reaction to them, a skilled travel planner would narrow his or her suggestions, asking increasingly specific questions and offering advice based on his or her superior knowledge of destinations and even individual resorts.

This example suggests that, when information is constrained by a carrier, such as the travel agent, it is not allowed to behave like information. That is, while information is not consumed by use and is cheap to reproduce and distribute, since it has to be delivered by a person, it has to follow the economics of the carrier—only one person can speak with the agent at a time. The travel agency could hire and train new agents to reduce the lines, but this would be a costly proposition.

Even in 1993, you could have organized your honeymoon independently. You could have collected brochures and publications (Figure 4.23), telephoned individual resorts for pricing and

Figure 4.23   Traditional travel brochures

suggestions, called multiple airlines, and put all the information together—quite a risk for a newlywed, since independent planning would leave you unable to blame the travel agent if your spouse were to have a bad experience! More importantly, this would have been a time-consuming (i.e., costly) proposition on your part.

The travel agency could also reach a larger audience—for example, by creating brochures with suggestions and sample packages and distributing them by mail. Or it could purchase TV time and run some infomercials. However, such brochures and infomercials provide only limited content when compared with the personalized, interactive exchange that an experienced travel planner could offer.

The Richness and Reach Trade-Off

The travel agency example above is representative of a phenomenon known as the trade-off between richness and reach. Richness represents the amount of information that can be transmitted, the degree to which the information can be tailored to individual needs, and the level of interactivity of the message. Reach represents the number of possible recipients of the message. Traditionally, as information has been constrained by its physical carrier, a firm would have to make a trade-off decision between the number of people it wanted to communicate a message to (i.e., reach) and the depth of the message (i.e., richness).

Before the advent of widespread information networks, a firm with a fixed budget would have to decide whether it was willing to reach a smaller audience with a richer message (e.g., individual consultations with a travel agent) or use a leaner message to reach a larger audience (e.g., create a brochure and mail it to perspective travelers). This trade-off, a "compromise" that constrains information to behave like its physical carrier, is represented by the line in Figure 4.24. The line on the graph represents the frontier of optimal decisions. That is, the firm will be able to choose any point below the frontier, but the optimal decisions, those that offer the highest return in terms of simultaneous reach and richness, are those on the frontier. Because of the constraints identified above, the firm cannot go beyond this frontier.

With the advent and widespread adoption of a cheaply and easily accessible information infrastructure, such as the Internet and the services it makes available, these constraints are increasingly being lifted. Ubiquitous communication networks and powerful computers are quickly enabling firms to decouple information from the physical objects that traditionally carried it.

For example, digital music no longer needs a CD, novels and stories no longer need books, lectures and meetings carried out on a platform like WebEx or CISCO's Telepresence no longer need the physical co-presence of participants. The Internet and the technologies that leverage it

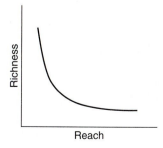

Figure 4.24   The richness/reach trade-off

have mitigated the trade-off between rich information and the reach of the message. Note that the trade-off between reach and richness has not been eliminated. There are still compromises to be made between reaching a large audience and offering a very rich exchange. However, new technology is making it increasingly possible to reach many people with more information-intensive, interactive, and personalized messages (Figure 4.25).

Consider the travel agency example once more. As travel products have moved aggressively to the Internet platform, you now have increasing access to 360-degree views of resorts, live chats with agents, travel blogs, communities of interest where people share their cumulative experiences (Figure 4.26), and travel products packaged by an online agency.

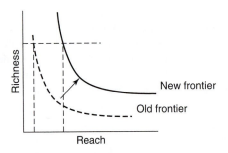

Figure 4.25   Technology pushing the richness/reach frontier

Filter traveler reviews		Write a Review

Trip type

- All reviews (93)
- Business reviews (11)
- Couples reviews (43)
- Family reviews (3)
- Friends reviews (4)
- Solo travel reviews (7)

Traveler rating

- All (93)
- Excellent (61)
- Very good (17)
- Average (4)
- Poor (6)
- Terrible (5)

1-10 of 93 reviews   « 1 2 ... 10 »

Sort by [Date ▼] [Rating]   English first ▼

Ireland

"The Emerald Isle"

⦿⦿⦿⦿⦿

Date of review: June 7, 2011

the emer... ▼
Ireland
1 contribution

Yesterday, as the setting sun glowed over the patchwork fields of The Emerald Isle, my plane touched ground at Cork International Airport in southern Ireland. Just a short flight from Heathrow…
more ▾

Figure 4.26   Online travel review

Yet while these technologies are increasingly pushing the reach/richness frontier and encroaching on travel agents' territory, they have yet to be able to fully replicate the face-to-face interaction and high degree of personalization that a knowledgeable, skilled travel agent can offer.

Implications

As the emergence of new technology eases the trade-off between richness and reach, a number of implications for you as a general or functional manager emerge.

Traditional Business Models Continue to Be Questioned   A number of "traditional" business models were predicated on the fact that information was constrained by its carrier. Such business models have been facing, and will continue to face, challenges from focused organizations that exploit emerging information technologies. Consider the traditional travel agent business model one final time. Many travel agents do an outstanding job of providing valuable consultation and advice to prospective travelers. Others base their value proposition on the fact that most travelers don't have the ability to book their own travel. As airlines, hotels, and car rentals created their own bookable Web sites, and travel intermediaries such as Kayak.com and Skyscanner made it easy to quickly query multiple providers, the latter kind of travel agents faced significant pressure and many closed up shop (Figure 4.27). With technology advancing relentlessly, even those travel agents who offer valuable information and expertise will come under increasing pressure.

The effect of widespread adoption of computer networks is particularly threatening to organizations that historically bundled services, using one to subsidize the other. Consider the daily newspaper industry. By some accounts, a typical newspaper collects 20% to 25% of its revenue from the classified section. Yet the classifieds account for only 5% of the cost of operating a newspaper. As a consequence, the classifieds are subsidizing many other aspects of the newspaper business, such as reporting and editing.

With the advent of the Internet and Web sites such as eBay and Craigslist, newspapers have seen and continue to see a loss of revenue from the classifieds—after all, what is eBay if not

Figure 4.27   A travel agency gone out of business

a global classified ads section with an auction twist? While newspapers are unlikely to become extinct anytime soon, this example shows that the unbundling of information from the physical carrier can have far-reaching consequences—particularly for those firms where the current business model is predicated on the need to bundle information with a physical carrier.

Consider another example, the movie rental business. With high-capacity broadband networks coming to the home in the form of digital cables, we are now able to order movies on demand and start, pause, and restart them at will—just like rentals, but without the late fees. Unbundling the information customers want (the movie) from the carrier (the tape cassette or DVD) has enabled superior convenience, in the form of easy billing in a monthly statement, no late fees, and no need to leave the home, stand in line, or find that the movie we want is sold out.

The Importance of the Customer Interface If information is increasingly allowed to travel independently of its carriers, it becomes feasible to unbundle traditional products and services (as described above), and bundle products that could never be brought together before. Consider the retail banking industry. Traditionally a customer would purchase a bundle of services from her retail bank, say a checking account, a savings account, certificates of deposit, mutual funds, a car loan, and a mortgage. An important value driver of this bundle would be the convenience of one-stop shopping (i.e., being able to visit one branch to address a number of financial needs).

Today that same customer may use Quicken or Mint.com to manage her finances, thus being able to interact directly with individual providers of each of the services she needs—even through a cell phone (Figure 4.28). She may have checking and savings accounts with the local bank, a car loan with another local provider, a mortgage through LendingTree.com, mutual

Figure 4.28 Mint on the iPhone

funds and retirement planning with Schwab.com, and some stocks with Ameritrade. Being able to easily download monthly statements to Mint, she can keep the pulse of her financial standings and easily switch providers, as long as the new one also enables downloads to Mint. The old adage about the importance of, "location, location, location" is in many industries based on information friction and is being challenged by technologies that mitigate the trade-off between reach and richness.

In the environment described by the above example, having a direct relationship with the customer, or owning the customer interface, may become critical. In the banking case it is Mint, a software company, which is in the strongest position. Customers may become more loyal to Mint than to any of the providers of financial services in the background.

The example seems a bit futuristic still, and significant obstacles remain to the widespread adoption of these arrangements (see below), but we are beginning to see a number of organizations vying to control the customer interface. Consider Progressive insurance, for instance. In its advertisements, the firm promises that its agents will seek to find you the best insurance plan, even shopping and suggesting competitors for you. The objective of this approach is to ensure that you think about them when seeking to purchase insurance, thus allowing them to preserve control of the customer interface.

The Decreasing Value of Asymmetric Information   Perhaps the most evident implication of the emergence of technologies that ease the trade-off between reach and richness is the amount of information modern customers have available to them. This has put significant pressure on organizations that benefit from asymmetry of information.[10] If an organization bases its value proposition on the inability of individuals to obtain and use information at low costs, that position is increasingly untenable as the richness/reach frontier is progressively pushed outward. Today, for example, within a few minutes you can shop for a car online, find out the factory price from Edmunds.com, research various dealer packages, find out the value of your used car trade-in, and walk into a dealership ready to negotiate.

Obstacles

While there are many examples of industries where the effects of the easing trade-off between reach and richness are being felt, there are a number of obstacles that have been slowing and will continue to slow down this process.

New Technology Must Replace All Characteristics of the Old One   Consider again the example of newspapers. Newspapers do not offer the best platform for consuming the news; they are not as timely as the television news or the Internet, they support neither video nor high-quality images, they offer limited space, and they have many other drawbacks. Why do we still buy them and read them (albeit in lesser and lesser numbers)? Why don't we all read the news online? Most newspapers have websites anyway.

The answer is simple: With all of the drawbacks newspapers have due to the constraints of printed paper, the broadsheet is still the most portable, most convenient, and easiest to read device

---

[10]Asymmetry of information is the condition where one party to a transaction has more information than the other party. Purchasing a used car is a classic example, where the seller knows the history of the car while the buyer has to rely on the seller or use other imprecise means to gauge the quality of the car (e.g., take it to a mechanic).

for accessing the news. While ebooks and tables are increasingly challenging the dominance of paper, it will not be until new technology is able to supplant these advantages that the newspaper will disappear, its limitations notwithstanding. The lesson is clear: Old technology goes away only when the new one has replaced all of its relevant characteristics. Until then, the new and old technologies tend to coexist—as do newspapers and online news today.

Retaliation from Incumbents   As we attempt to envision how new technology changes society and the competitive environment, seeking ways to create value in the new environment, it is easy to commit a critical fallacy: ignoring incumbent's retaliation. This was one of the main mistakes many observers made during the dot-com days. Retaliation can come in a number of forms:

- Legal means, such as those used by the music industry in reaction to the advent of digital music and the mp3 compression standard.

- Legislative means, such as the lobbying efforts of car dealership networks to stave off direct sales by car manufacturers.

- Hybrid offers, such as those provided by retailers with physical stores and online operations so as to leverage their existing infrastructure.

- Heightened competition, such as that started by telecommunications companies in reaction to the offering of Voice over IP solutions.

While it is enticing to think about the promise of the new technology and the opportunities it offers, you need to always remember that the road from today's landscape to the future reality is paved with competitive battles.

Human Resistance to Change   Perhaps the most powerful bottleneck to some of the changes discussed above is human inertia. New technologies and new ways of doing business, while offering advantages, entail costs in the form of learning to use the new technology or simply stopping the old routine. While easily dismissed, these considerations can spell the difference between success and failure in a fledgling business. The history of IT is full of great ideas that fell prey to the "if we build it they will come" mentality, and failed to address and manage human resistance to change.

Attention Challenges   A byproduct of the unprecedented availability of information is the increasing difficulty people encounter in keeping up with it. Customers' attention is not only required for your product or service to be considered, but it is also required to educate customers about its advantages and how they can best use it. People's time and attention is perhaps the scarcest resource an organization has to deal with. The scarcity of attention leads to slow adoption rates for all but the most revolutionary of innovations.

Consider, for instance, online grocery shopping, an industry mostly remembered for having produced the largest failure of the dot-com era. Webvan, the poster child for online grocery shopping, burned through $1.2 billion in funding before it closed up shop, much to the dismay of its few but enthusiastic customers (Figure 4.29). Yet online grocery shopping is alive and well in many locales, the torch being carried by traditional brick and mortar grocery chains.[11] The

---

[11] http://www.internetretailer.com/internet/marketing-conference/27475-online-grocery-showing-fortified-strength-study-says.html (Accessed 01/10/2011).

Figure 4.29   Webvan stock certificate *Source:* scripophily.com

lesson of the Webvan story is not so much that online grocery shopping was an ill-conceived idea, but rather that the consumer adoption rate of this radically new way of performing a task that is thousands of years old was much slower than the adoption rates Webvan needed to survive as an online-only grocery operation.

THE INTERNET CHANGES EVERYTHING?

Considerable debate still remains with respect to what the impact of the Internet and the technology that are built on it has been, and will continue to be, on organizations and the competitive environment. On the one hand are those who claim that "for all its power, the Internet does not represent a break from the past; rather it is the last stage in the ongoing evolution of information technology."[12] On the other hand are those that consider the Internet a force that goes far beyond technology, such that "no facet of human activity is untouched. The Net is a force of social change penetrating homes, schools, offices, factories, hospitals, and governments."[13] As time goes on, the latter camp seems to have been correct.

Where you choose to fall on this debate is largely up to you. It is clear, however, that the network economy has ushered in a new wave of opportunity for firms that are able to take advantage of, rather than resist, the changes. While the boundaries of a firm have historically been fairly

---

[12]Porter, M. (2001). "Strategy and the Internet," *Harvard Business Review*, March, pp. 62–78.

[13]Tapscott, D. (2001). "Rethinking Strategy in a Networked World," *Strategy and Competition*, Third Quarter, pp. 1–8.

fixed, the adoption of global networks has enabled these boundaries to become increasingly permeable under the guise of outsourcing arrangements and partnerships.

Consider, for instance, the relationship between HEB, the tenth largest grocery chain in the United States, and Procter & Gamble (P & G), the multinational consumer goods giant. While traditionally P & G sold its goods to HEB, who then would resell them to consumers, the two firms have now moved to a consignment model whereby P & G places its goods on HEB's shelves and, once they are sold, receives payment from HEB. HEB benefits from reduced working capital requirements and risk, while P & G benefits by having real-time consumption data that allows it to streamline both production and logistic processes.

A NOTE ABOUT DISRUPTIVE TECHNOLOGY

Beyond the role of the Internet in changing the competitive landscape and the role of information and network economics, it is important that, as a general or functional manager, you are aware of the potential disruptive impact of new technologies. Specifically, you should be able to identify and, to the extent possible, manage the impact of emerging disruptive technologies.

Sustaining Technology

The innovation literature has investigated for decades the characteristics of new technology. Recently, though, Clayton Christiansen's[14] work has identified a classification that has important implications for strategy: the differentiation between sustaining and disruptive technologies.

The defining characteristic of sustaining technologies is that they maintain or rejuvenate the current rate of performance improvement of the products and services that use them. The performance trajectory of a new product (e.g., electric cars) is typically captured visually by the use of the S-curve (Figure 4.30). The S-curve suggests that, as the product is first introduced its performance is limited. With design refinements comes a growth period where substantial improvements in performance are achieved, until the technology underpinning product performance plateaus and further performance improvements become marginal.

Sustaining technologies are those new technologies that enable a product's performance to continue to grow—in other words, sustaining technologies extend the useful life of the product as the market demands further and further improvements (Figure 4.31). A sustaining technology

Figure 4.30   Product performance improvements over time

---

[14]Christiansen, C. (1997). *The Innovator's Dilemma: When New Technologies Cause Great Firms To Fail*, Boston, MA: Harvard Business School Press.

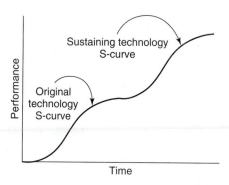

Figure 4.31   Performance improvements over time

will therefore be a good candidate to replace a previous generation because it offers the same set of attributes, but it yields superior performance. Thus, firms that are using the existing technology in their product will find it appealing to switch to the sustaining technology as they seek to improve their products along the established performance trajectory.

Consider, for instance, the mechanical excavation industry. The tool of choice in this industry at the turn of the century was the steam shovel. Steam shovels used a steam engine to generate the required power to pull the cables that would lift buckets full of dirt to be moved. In the early 1920s, the steam shovel began to be replaced by gasoline-powered shovels that offered superior performance on the critical performance dimension: the ability to move dirt in a fast, reliable, and cost-effective manner. This is an example of sustaining technology, since the new technology (i.e., gasoline engines) enabled manufacturers of dirt-moving equipment to improve the performance of their product on critical performance dimensions.

Disruptive Technology

Disruptive technologies are defined by the following two characteristics:

- The technology offers a different set of attributes than the technology the firm currently uses in its products.

- The performance improvement rate of the technology is higher than the rate of improvement demanded by the market (Figure 4.32).

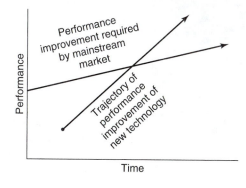

Figure 4.32   Market expectations for performance and new technology performance improvement over time

While a disruptive technology has an inferior performance with respect to current market demands and what is delivered by existing technology, it offers two advantages: a different set of performance characteristics, and a high rate of performance improvement on the critical performance dimensions.

Consider the example of the hard disk industry. The critical performance dimension for customers of hard disk drives (i.e., computer manufacturers) is the storage capacity of the disk. With remarkable precision, hard disk drive manufacturers have been blindsided by the emergence of architecture design that enabled smaller and smaller drives to be produced—from the original 14-inch drives, to the 8-, 5.25-, 3.5-, 2.5-, and 1.8-inch architectures. This is because these changes were disruptive in nature.

Each generation of smaller disk drives did not at first offer the same storage capacity as the established one. Yet each generation offered a performance rate of improvement on this dimension (the critical performance dimension) far superior to the speed with which computer manufacturers required greater storage capacity. As a consequence, when the storage capacity of the smaller drives reached market needs, the incumbent's mainstream customers switched to the new entrants. No longer having storage capacity concerns, they now valued the other characteristics offered by the new technology (i.e., smaller size, reduced power consumption). Many have suggested that the electric car may turn out to be a disruptive technology (Figure 4.33). In line with this, perhaps mindful of lessons learned by other incumbents in the past, or perhaps due to the steep costs associated with research and development in this area, auto manufacturers are beginning to roll out their own electric car models.

Implications for Managers

Familiarity with the dynamics of disruptive technologies is important for modern general and functional managers because disruptive technologies typically blindside leading firms (i.e., the incumbents in the market), who see their position of dominance lost to those upstarts that were able to ride the disruptive technology wave.

Differential Rates of Improvements   The deadliest characteristic of disruptive technology is their rate of evolution on the currently established performance metrics. As shown in Figure 4.32,

Figure 4.33 "Fueling" an electric car in London (Created by Frankh at the English Wikipedia Project.)

a disruptive technology begins with performance that is well below the needs of the firm's mainstream customers. Moreover, the disruptive technology will likely not improve at a rate sufficient to overcome the existing or sustaining technologies available. However, this is misleading information for a manager!

In truth, it is irrelevant whether the disruptive technology will ever outstrip the current one on key performance metrics. Rather, you should estimate whether, in the foreseeable future, the disruptive technology will catch up to market needs on the critical performance dimensions (i.e., become good enough for mainstream customers).

It is often the case that, focused on its most demanding and most advanced customers, a firm will push the performance of its products using new generations of sustaining technologies. However, such relentless focus on the most demanding customers may end up pushing the firm to increasingly overshoot the needs of its mainstream customers. When this is the case, the incumbent firm becomes particularly vulnerable to disruptive technologies.

Different Sets of Attributes Become Relevant   As disruptive technologies close the gap between the performance level they offer and mainstream customer needs, the novel set of attributes they offer may become increasingly attractive to potential customers. In other words, as the disruptive technology closes the gap on the primary performance metrics, their other characteristics may become a source of positive differentiation. At this point, customers defect from established suppliers offering the standard products and begin to adopt the new technology—but it is typically too late for established players to make the switch to the new technology.

Listening Closely to Customers May Spell Trouble   Conventional business wisdom suggests that a firm is well served by closely listening to its customers in an effort to develop the products and services that best serve their needs. While you should not ignore this suggestion, we add a word of caution: Listening attentively to your most aggressive customers will create a bias toward prompt adoption of sustaining technology and a reluctance to buy into disruptive technology.

Your best customers are constantly pushing the envelope of your product performance. Consider again the hard drive industry. High-end computer manufacturers, seeking to outdo each other, will seek larger and faster hard disks to be included in their machines. As a consequence, they will create an incentive for you to adopt those technologies that offer improved performance on the accepted set of performance metrics. A technology that enables the development of smaller hard disks is not valued, even though these smaller devices have other interesting characteristics, such as compact size, lower energy consumption, and less need for heat dispersion. They simply are not good enough on the "important" dimensions that your best customers are clamoring for. However, if the new, smaller hard disks are a disruptive technology, their performance will soon meet the needs of your mainstream customers. When this happens, all those other characteristics may become valuable and you'll be left with a rapidly shrinking market.

What to Do?

Those studying disruptive technology change suggest the following approach to managing organizations that face the emergence and development of disruptive technologies:

- Monitor market developments for the emergence of new technologies and determine whether they are of the sustaining or disruptive kind.

- When disruptive technologies emerge, envision the new market they would likely be best suited for. One of the greatest challenges faced by the incumbent firm is to identify what customers will likely appreciate the new blend of features and functionalities that the disruptive technology supports. While a producer of large mainframes does not care much about the power requirements and physical size of hard disks, these are critical characteristics for laptop manufacturers.

- Spin off a new division that focuses exclusively on the commercialization of products based on the disruptive technology. Separating the group that is blazing the trail for the new technology may be necessary to create the appropriate financial incentives. Disruptive technologies start off serving the needs of a small niche market. As such, it is difficult for large companies to get excited about, and more importantly divert resources to, such small markets. A separate entity, focusing on that business and competing with the other small firms in the new market, would have no difficulty creating the appropriate incentives.

 ## SUMMARY

This chapter provides you with a framework to understand how new technologies are shaping the competitive landscape you will encounter as you enter the job market. Specifically, in this chapter we discussed three broad topics: network economics, information economics, and disruptive technologies.

- Value creation in networks, physical ones such as the telephone network and virtual ones such as eBay's online community of buyers and sellers, is created by plentitude. This value driver is the opposite of the principal value driver of most other goods and services: scarcity.

- Because the most valuable networks are the largest ones, the act of joining a network by an individual creates value for the other members of the network—a phenomenon termed network effects. In industries subject to strong network effects, particularly when the demand for variety is low and networks are mutually exclusive, winner-take-all dynamics ensue and the market is dominated by one organization.

- Information, a prevalent resource in the modern competitive landscape, has unique economic characteristics. In its pure form, information has high production costs, which are sunk, and negligible replication and distribution costs. The production of information faces no natural capacity limits, and information is not consumed by use. As a consequence, information is infinitely reusable, highly customizable, and often time valued.

- When discussing information as an organizational resource, it is important to distinguish the information itself from the carrier of the information. Historically, information as a resource or product has been constrained by the economics of the carrier. The advent of the Internet, a global infrastructure for information exchange, has in many cases separated the two. New technology continues to push the frontier of the richness/reach trade-off and in the process threatens established business models in information industries and beyond.

- New technologies can be characterized as sustaining or disruptive. Sustaining technologies are those that maintain or rejuvenate the current rate of performance improvement of the products and services that use them. Conversely, disruptive technologies are those that offer a different set of attributes than the technology the firm currently uses in its products, and their performance improvement rate is higher than the rate of improvement of market needs. Disruptive technologies are particularly dangerous for established firms, which typically tend to underestimate their potential impact on the firm's current business. Proper monitoring and management of disruptive technologies by the incumbent is necessary because, due to the rate of performance improvement and the different set of features they offer, once a disruptive technology has achieved acceptable performance improvements on the traditional dimensions of performance, customers quickly defect to products that use it.

STUDY QUESTIONS

1. Define the term *Internet* and offer examples of its principal services. What is the difference between the Internet and the World Wide Web?

2. What do you see as the likely evolution of the Internet in the near future?

3. Explain each of the following concepts: positive feedback, network effects, and tippy market. Explain how the three concepts relate to one another.

4. Offer an example of a tippy market, and an example of a market that does not tip.

5. Can you differentiate physical and virtual networks? Can you provide examples of each?

6. Explain the defining characteristics of a two-sided network and provide an example.

7. What is the defining characteristic of classic information goods? How do they differ from information-intensive goods? Provide examples of each.

8. Information, as an economic entity, behaves quite differently than traditional goods. Identify the principal economic characteristics of information and draw the primary implications for strategy.

9. Explain what we mean by the richness/reach trade-off. Why is this concept important today for general and functional managers? Provide examples of recent technologies that have pushed the richness/reach trade-off frontier further out. What industries or organizations are under pressure as a consequence of this development?

10. Do you believe that "the Internet changes everything" or is it "just another technology"? Be sure to defend your position.

11. What is the difference between sustaining and disruptive technologies? Can you offer one example of each?

12. What would you advise an incumbent firm to do in the face of the emergence of new technology? For example, if you were an executive for American Airlines, what would you do about the recent introduction of Very Light Jets (VLJ)—such as the 2,000 preordered Eclipse 500 VLIs from Eclipse Aviation, which are able to reach 300 mph and a range of 1125 nautical miles?[15] Is "air taxi" a disruptive technology? What should major airlines do about it, if anything?

FURTHER READINGS

1. Bower, J. L., and Christensen, C. M. (1995). "Disruptive Technologies: Catching the Wave," *Harvard Business Review*, January/February, pp. 43–53.

2. Christensen, C. M. (1997). *The Innovator's Dilemma: When New Technologies Cause Great Firms to Fail*. Boston, MA: Harvard Business School Press.

3. Evans, P. B., and Wurster, T. S. (1999). *Blown to Bits: How the New Economics of Information Transforms Strategy*. Boston, MA: Harvard Business School Press.

4. Evans, P. B., and Wurster, T. S. (1997). "Strategy and the New Economics of Information." *Harvard Business Review*, September/October, pp. 70–82.

5. Porter, M. (2001). "Strategy and the Internet." *Harvard Business Review*, March, pp. 62–78.

6. Rayport, J., and Sviokla, J. (1994). "Managing in the Marketspace." *Harvard Business Review*, November/December, pp. 141–150.

7. Shapiro, C., and Varian, H. R. (1999). *Information Rules*. Boston, MA: Harvard Business School Press.

8. Tapscott, D. (2001). "Rethinking Strategy in a Networked World." *Strategy and Competition*, Third Quarter, pp. 1–8.

9. Shirky, C. (2001). "The Internet Revolution Rages On," *Business 2.0*, March.

GLOSSARY

- **Classic information goods:** Those purchased for the only purpose of gaining access to the information they contain.

- **Data:** Codified raw facts—things that have happened—coded as letters of the alphabet and numbers and stored, increasingly, by way of a computer.

---

[15]http://edition.cnn.com/2006/TRAVEL/03/31/private.jet/ (Accessed 01/10/2011).

- **Disruptive technologies:** Technologies that offer a different set of attributes than the technology a firm currently uses in its products, and whose performance improvement rate is higher than the rate of improvement of market needs.
- **Information:** Data in context.
- **Information-intensive goods:** Those tangible products and services (i.e., not classic information goods) for which information is either one of the critical components or a necessary resource during the production process.
- **Internet:** A global, publicly accessible network of digital networks relying on distributed ownership and open standards.
- **Message reach:** The number of possible recipients of the message.
- **Message richness:** The amount of information that can be transmitted, the degree to which the information can be tailored to individual needs, and the level of interactivity of the message.
- **Negative feedback:** The self-reinforcing process by which the strong get weaker and the weak get stronger.
- **Network effects:** The process by which a network becomes more valuable as its size increases. That is, when a new node, while pursuing his or her own economic motives, joins the network, the network is more valuable for all the other members.
- **Network node:** Any device connected to a network.

- **Physical networks:** Networks where the nodes are connected by physical links (e.g., railroad tracks, telephone wires).
- **Positive feedback:** The self-reinforcing process by which the strong get stronger and the weak get weaker.
- **Protocol:** An agreed-upon set of rules or conventions governing communication among the elements of a network (i.e., network nodes).
- **Sustaining technology:** Technologies that maintain or rejuvenate the current rate of performance improvement of the products and services that use them.
- **Tipping point:** That moment in the evolution of a market where one organization or technology reaches critical mass and goes on to dominate it—the point of non-return where winners and losers are defined.
- **Tippy market:** A market that is subject to strong positive feedback, such that the market will "tip" in favor of the firm that is able to reach critical mass and dominate it. A tippy market is therefore a market with "winner-take-all" tendencies.
- **Virtual networks:** Networks where the connections between nodes are not physical, but intangible and invisible. The nodes of a virtual network are typically people rather than devices.
- **World Wide Web:** One of the most popular services available on the Internet. It consists of "pages" and other resources that can be easily created and published as well as accessed by way of uniform resource locator (URL) addresses.

5

Electronic Commerce: New Ways of Doing Business

What You Will Learn in This Chapter

This chapter covers almost two decades of electronic commerce history and trends. The objective is to help you develop a solid grounding in electronic commerce concepts and vocabulary—a vocabulary that is no longer the exclusive province of Silicon Valley insiders, but an integral part of the language of modern business. After laying the foundations, we look ahead to coming electronic commerce trends. Specifically, after reading this chapter you will:

1. Understand and be able to clearly articulate what the Internet is, its principal characteristics, and the principal services it makes available to users.

2. Broaden your definition of the Internet from a network of computer networks to an information grid connecting a staggering range of devices, both wired and wireless.

3. Be able to compare and contrast *electronic commerce* and *electronic business*, and provide examples of each. Identify and understand the enablers of electronic commerce trends.

4. Categorize electronic commerce phenomena on a number of different dimensions, including the type of transactions taking place and the structure of the organizations involved.

5. Understand and apply the concept of *business model*, and explain why the Internet has led to so much business model experimentation. Identify the principal *revenue models* employed in electronic commerce and explain the dominant business model in use today.

6. Understand and evaluate the principal implications of electronic commerce for both established firms and new entrants.

7. Be able to evaluate the *Web 2.0* phenomenon and be able to discuss both its technological and organizational manifestations.

8. Discuss some of the more relevant future electronic commerce and electronic business trends.

MINI-CASE: THE QUEST FOR DIFFERENTIATION AND PROFITS AT EPICTRIP.COM

The phone started ringing as you arrived in the office. You picked up the receiver and immediately recognized the familiar soft voice: "Hey there, it's Steve-O!" You had not heard from him in a few months, but in a split second his whole work history flashed in your brain. Steve Yu, Steve-O as his closest friends called him, went to work for a large corporation right after college. As the executive assistant to the president of one of the largest hotel chains in the United States, he had the luxury of being involved in high-stakes strategic decisions, without much of the responsibility. But, as an entrepreneur and a dreamer at heart, Steve quickly became disenchanted with the corporate lifestyle. As a former Marine, he was fond of saying, "Life's too short not to chase your dream."

The genesis of Epic Trip started from Steve's interest in collecting television commercials while attending college. He believed commercials told compelling stories when emotionally connecting with consumers about the possibilities of what the product could help the customer realize or achieve. About a year and half ago,

Steve resigned from his job as executive assistant and founded his own firm. With one childhood friend and a lot of ramen noodles, they began developing what would soon become EpicTrip.com (Figure 5.1). An arts enthusiast, Steve brought significant design sensitivity to the team while his partner brought the technical skills. The vision behind EpicTrip.com was to revolutionize how people purchase travel.

The Epic Trip website read, "Epic Trip is a new and unique way for travelers to know what their destinations and their hotels are all about, even before setting off. By connecting our travelers with videos, virtual tours, reviews, and the wealth of experience brought to bear by the very users of Epic Trip, it is our mission to spark people's desire to discover their own epic trip."

As the Internet travel market was crowded with sites that focused on listing as many options as possible and finding customers the "best deals," Steve believed there would be value in focusing on the experience of travel, even before the trip started. Through the use of rich media (videos, virtual tours, photos, and

Figure 5.1   Epic Trip's home page

audio), Epic Trip was designed to help travelers get a feel for the unique offerings of their destination before arriving—and to dream about new ones. Epic Trip also focused on community, with tools for members to share their experiences and photos, and to connect with other like-minded travelers.

Still in beta version, without having begun any formal marketing campaign, EpicTrip.com was attracting some attention from bloggers, travel industry insiders, and travel enthusiasts. The consensus was that the Epic Trip site was visually appealing and extremely easy to navigate.

"What's up, Steve-O!" you screamed into the receiver, a bit too loud for the early hour. "I know that you've been doing some eCommerce consulting for the travel industry as of late," said Steve, adding with a chuckle, "I keep up with you, my friend." You fire back: "I've been monitoring your progress, too. I see you have launched in beta already." "We're at a cross roads," Steve said, his voice becoming serious. "We have the site up and running, and we have the partnerships in place with the major travel distributors. The site is fast, and we have rolled out the members' area and the platform for featured destinations" (Figure 5.2).

"Nice going, Steve-O!" you exclaim, excited about the progress. "Time to make some dough now, buddy," Steve replies. "As you know, we originally thought about a referral model, taking a cut when people follow a link from our site and purchase some travel product." "That's a tough business," you interject. "Exactly," Steve replies. "It appears we have people doing research on the site, but they don't go straight through. They may come back over and over, and later book or even call an agency or a hotel themselves. We don't get paid that way. In addition, we just learned that Expedia is now offering free production of virtual tours to hotels to be featured on their site."

With very limited resources, Steve knew he had to quickly come up with a solid value proposition that differentiated Epic Trip and a revenue model to approach potential investors. "You're my eCommerce guru; I need some guidance. I have some ideas, but I would love your take. I need to start monetizing this platform we've built," said Steve. "Absolutely!" you reply without hesitation. "Give me until the end of the week to study this and I'll call you with some ideas." Steve answers, "Thanks bud, I knew I could count on you. Talk to you at the end of the week."

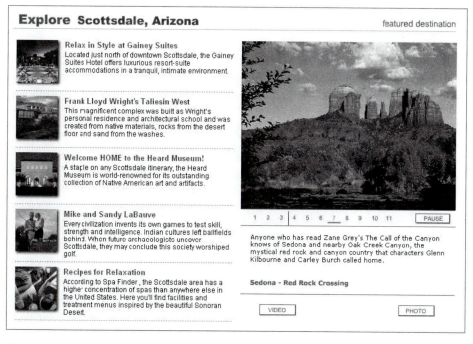

Figure 5.2   Epic Trip's featured destination area

continued

MINI-CASE (*continued*)

DISCUSSION QUESTIONS

1. What kind of information do you think you need to seek out as you formulate your recommendations for Steve?
2. How do you suggest that Epic Trip think about driving revenue? What are some of the options? How would you rank them relative to each other?
3. What would you suggest Epic Trip do to differentiate itself? How can Steve ensure the long-term viability of Epic Trip?

INTRODUCTION

In the previous chapter, we introduced concepts and techniques to understand the implications of recent technological advancements for the modern firm. We introduced the notions of network economics and information economics, and the role of disruptive technologies in shaping the competitive landscape. These concepts are critical for general and functional managers, who increasingly find themselves managing in the network economy. With this theoretical background firmly in hand, we now formally discuss the Internet and its associated services, and then focus on the business innovations that have been spurred by the widespread adoption and rise to prominence of the Internet. Our objective here is to help you become familiar with the language, history, and manifestations of the electronic commerce phenomenon by providing useful categorizations and examples.

A basic understanding of how the Internet works and a mastery of the business vocabulary that has developed around it since its commercialization in 1993 is important because the Internet is critical to modern business. A recent McKinsey study shows that the Internet is a powerful economic engine in developed economies and that its impact on economic growth has increased as the technology has become increasingly mainstream (Figure 5.3). The research found that the Internet contributes directly as a vehicle for economic activity (e.g., online sales, advertisement) and indirectly as an element of economic progress. It is also a catalyst for job creation adding 2.6 jobs for every technology job lost by a sample of 4,800 small and midsized enterprises that McKinsey surveyed. It follows then that, aside from the fact that you may be one of those people getting an Internet-enabled job soon, at a minimum you will need to understand and leverage the opportunities for growth enabled by the Internet.

THE INTERNET

A brief look at any information systems textbook quickly reveals that the Internet is, simply put, "a network of networks." In other words, the Internet is broadly defined as a collection of networked computers that can "talk to one another." This simple definition points to a fundamental issue: The Internet is an infrastructure upon which *services*—such as e-mail, the Web, instant messaging, and many others—are delivered.

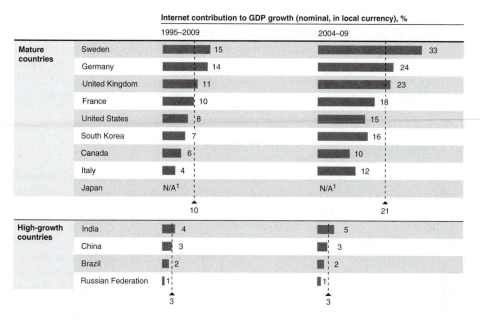

Internet contribution to GDP growth (nominal, in local currency), %

¹Negative growth due to deflation.
Source: Organisation for Economic Co-operation and Development (OECD) national accounts, McKinsey analysis

Figure 5.3   Internet contribution to economic growth[1]

Wikipedia, the free Web-based encyclopedia, provides a more complete definition: "The Internet (also known simply as the Net) is the worldwide, publicly accessible system of inter-connected computer networks that transmit data by packet switching using the standard Internet Protocol (IP). It consists of millions of smaller domestic, academic, business, and government networks, which together carry various information services, such as electronic mail, online chat, file transfer, and the interlinked Web pages and other documents of the World Wide Web."[2] From this definition follow a number of observations, but before discussing them you should carefully note that the definition of the Internet is very general and "device agnostic." In other words, as a collection of computer networks, the Internet can connect any intelligent device based on the digital computer architecture—such as a laptop, a Smartphone, a face-recognition digital camera, etc. Today we can confidently estimate that there are more intelligent devices connected to the Internet than there are people with access. In fact, Hans Vestberg, President and CEO of telecommunications equipment giant Ericsson, recently predicted that by the year 2020 there will be 50 billion Internet connected devices.[3] Vestberg recently stated: "Today we already see laptops and advanced handsets connected, but in the future everything that will benefit from

---

[1]McKinsey Global Institute (2011). Measuring the Net's growth dividend, McKinsey Report.

[2]http://en.wikipedia.org/wiki/Internet (Accessed 01/10/2010).

[3]"CEO to shareholders: 50 billion connections 2020," Ericsson Press Release, April 13, 2010 (Available 31/03/2011 at http://www.ericsson.com/thecompany/press/releases/2010/04/1403231).

being connected will be connected," including heart monitors, house appliances, and sensors of all kind. The extreme flexibility of the Internet protocol is what allows such scalability and variety of devices. Note as well that the general definition above does not restrict the type of channel connecting these intelligent devices across the Internet. In other words, if you are imagining an Internet made of computers and cables you should revise this mental picture, as the channels are increasingly wireless—using radio signals, satellites, or even cellular technology.

INTERNET SERVICES

As the Wikipedia definition suggests, the nodes of the Internet "together carry various information and services." A common misconception is that the terms *Internet* and *World Wide Web (or Web)* are synonymous. This is incorrect, and it is important to differentiate the two. The Internet is the infrastructure upon which many services are made available. Typically, you will connect to the Internet, the infrastructure, to access the services you want to use (e.g., Instant Messaging).

The Web is a service available on the Internet and, alongside electronic mail, is the most popular. However, there are many other services that we use on a daily basis—for example Instant Messaging (IM), Voice over IP (VoIP), Blogs, Real Simple Syndication feeds (RSS) (Figure 5.4), discussion groups (asynchronous electronic discussion), chat rooms (synchronous electronic discussion), and even the old trusty File Transfer Protocol (FTP) (Figure 5.5).

Distributed Ownership

The Internet is "publicly accessible," meaning that no single entity owns it, regulates its use, or otherwise controls it. In fact, the Internet has many owners but no one who centrally controls it. In other words, different portions of the Internet (i.e., different networks connected to other networks) are owned by different entities—literally millions of them. For example, your university network, while connected to the public Internet, is privately owned by your university. Your university manages and pays for it. Similarly, if you decide to launch your start-up upon graduation and need it to have a Web presence, you may decide to run your own infrastructure

Figure 5.4   RSS reader
Source: © AKP Photos/Alamy Limited

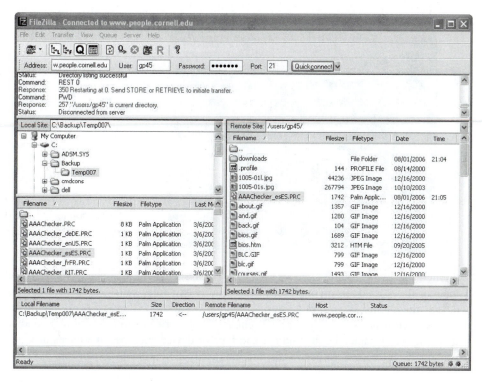

Figure 5.5   FTP client

rather than purchase it as a service. In this case, you would maintain your own Web server and your own dedicated connection to the Internet, thus becoming one of the many entities owning a small piece of the global network. Distributed ownership has been perhaps the main strength of the Internet, limiting regulation, fostering experimentation, and ensuring widespread access leading to significant growth.

Multiplicity of Devices

The Internet is a digital network consisting of millions of smaller digital networks. Each of these smaller digital networks encompasses a collection of digital devices, called nodes. The simplest digital network to visualize is perhaps a home network. Your home network may be composed of a couple of personal computers and a printer to which both computers can send documents. Using a home router, wired or wireless, and a broadband modem (e.g., cable or DSL), you connect to the Internet. Each of these digital devices—the two computers, the printer, the router—are nodes on your home network.

Your home network is a tiny contributor to the larger Internet. The fancier ones among us may have more cutting-edge devices, such as wireless VoIP phones to make free Skype-powered phone calls all over the world, a wireless media center to stream MP3 music from a computer

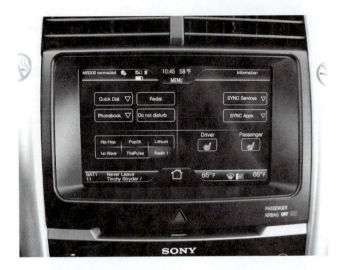

Figure 5.6   Prototype of Internet-connected car (Created by Randy Stern at the English Wikipedia project.)

through the living room stereo or to listen to Internet radio stations, a wireless Web cam to monitor the front door, a couple of tablets, and even cooler stuff! A car equipped with a GPS device, the OnStar system, or a satellite Internet connection (Figure 5.6.) is another example of a networked node, as is a modern cell phone. As the price of microchips and bandwidth keeps dropping (see Chapter 1), the number and type of devices that become nodes of a network will continue to increase. In other words, the Internet is in continuous expansion.

Open Standards

The Internet relies on open technology standards and protocols. A protocol is an agreed-upon set of rules or conventions governing communication among the elements of a network (i.e., network nodes). For example, case study discussion in your class follows a (stated or implicit) protocol. Typically the professor sets the stage for the case discussion. You listen and, when the floor is open, you might raise your hand. When you are called on, you contribute your perspective. You may disagree with the professor or classmates, but you do so in a polite manner, addressing ideas rather than individuals. Respect of the protocol by all is necessary to enable constructive communication rather than unproductive classroom chaos.

Similarly, in order to communicate, network nodes need to follow an agreed-on set of rules. On the Internet such a set of rules is the TCP/IP protocol mentioned in the Wikipedia definition. Nobody owns the TCP/IP protocol; as such, it is an open (i.e., freely available) standard, as opposed to a proprietary one. The same holds true for the other technologies that enable the Internet and its services, such as HTML (the language used to write Web pages). While there are standard-setting bodies that decide how each of these technologies should evolve (in the case of HTML it is the World Wide Web Consortium, W3C), no entity can charge for their use. Thus, anyone who wants to embed support for these standards in their applications can do so... and innovation continues to thrive on the Internet!

The Network, More than the Internet of Today

The definition of the Internet as a network of networks can be very misleading. It typically conjures up a vision of computers, of various shapes and sizes, hooked together by a maze

	Panasonic Senior Partner	Apple iPhone 4	Δ
Year	1983	2010	
CPU speed	4.77 MHz Intel 8088	800 MHz Apple A4	16,771%
Weight	14.9 Kg	137 g	0.92%
RAM	128 Kilobytes	512 Megabytes	409,600%
Storage	20 Megabytes	32 Gigabytes	163,840%
Price	$5,520 (infl. adj)	$998 (unlocked)	18.1%

Figure 5.7 New versus old portable devices (© 2011 Zachary Ruben.)

of cables of different shapes and colors—the Internet as a bunch of interconnected computers. While this image more or less correctly captures what the Internet looked like in the past, it is more confusing than helpful when trying to understand the current state of affairs. For example, while it may not look like it at first glance, modern cell phones are full-fledged digital computers, and the cell phone network, while not a cable, is a data transmission channel. In fact modern smartphones are way more powerful than the portable computers of just a few years ago (Figure 5.7).

Don Tapscott, a consultant and author, put it best when he wrote in 2001 that it is "an all-too-common mistake [to assume] that the Internet we see today—a network that connects desktop PCs—is the same Internet we will see tomorrow. This is nonsense. The Internet of tomorrow will be as dramatic a change from the Internet of today as today's Internet is from the unconnected, proprietary computing networks of yesterday."[4] He went on to describe a vision that has, in large part, already become reality: "Mobile computing devices, broadband access, wireless networks, and computing power embedded in everything from refrigerators to automobiles are converging into a global network that will enable people to use the Net just about anywhere and anytime. No facet of human activity is untouched. The Net is a force of social change penetrating homes, schools, offices, factories, hospitals, and governments."

For an example of the Internet as a force of social change, recall what happened to food giant Nestlé, maker of Kit-Kat bars and other snacks, in early 2010. A report by Greenpeace, supported by a YouTube video, alleged that Nestlé was sourcing palm oil from suppliers who were destroying rainforest habitat in Indonesia, contributing to the extinction of the local orangutan

---

[4]Tapscott, D. (2001). "Rethinking Strategy in a Networked World," *Strategy and Competition*, Third Quarter.

Figure 5.8　Modified Nestlé and Kit-Kat logos

Source: Greenpeace (http://www.greenpeace.org)

population. Activists started posting their protests right on the wall of Nestlé's Facebook page, using modified Nestlé logos (Figure 5.8). Nestlé contacted Google to have the video removed for copyright infringement. However, the protest gained traction and many regular consumers joined in, bringing the issue to international attention and turning the story into a public relations nightmare for Nestlé. The firm later committed to develop a new policy to identify and exclude companies from its supply chain that own or manage high-risk plantations or farms linked to deforestation.

Others have discussed a vision of the Internet as a pervasive network using the word "grid."[5] The idea is that distributed intelligent devices and high-volume network connections will soon make it possible to turn computing into a utility, much like water or electricity. In the near future, the proponents of grid computing claim, we will not have to wonder whether we will have access to the Internet and all its services when we travel, just like we don't worry about whether we will have access to electricity or water now. With such a pace and magnitude of evolution awaiting you as you enter the workforce and get ready to make decisions as a general or functional manager, you must be equipped with some fundamental concepts to navigate the new environment.

THE eCOMMERCE VOCABULARY

The concept of electronic commerce (or eCommerce for short) has been widely investigated since its advent in the early 1990s. We recall a quote we read in the late 1990s that suggested

---

[5]Heingartner, D. (2001). "The Grid: The Next-Gen Internet?" Wired News (Accessed 7/12/2006 at http://www.wired.com/news/technology/0,1282,42230,00.html).

"in five years there will be no eCommerce, just commerce." This statement is perhaps a bit bold, and certainly designed to be attention grabbing. However, history has proven it largely true. It is hard to imagine organizations today, beyond those of very small size, that would be well served by ignoring the Internet as a vehicle for commerce, whether as a tool for back-office operations (e.g., purchasing and logistics), a channel of distribution (e.g., online sales), or as a complement to the customer service experience.

eCommerce and eBusiness

A number of definitions of the terms *electronic commerce* (eCommerce) and *electronic business* (eBusiness) have been proposed over the years. Perhaps the simplest definition of the term *electronic commerce* is the broadest one: an online exchange of value. A more specific one, adopted in this book, is the following: Electronic commerce is the process of distributing, buying, selling, marketing, and servicing products and services over computer networks such as the Internet. This definition succinctly captures the essence of the electronic commerce phenomenon as the coming together of parties in an exchange that is mediated by networked information technologies.

The term *electronic business* originally referred to the digital enablement of internal organizational business processes, such as logistics and the use of Intranets. However, recognizing the increasingly interconnected nature of business operations upstream and downstream in the value chain, the term rapidly evolved to encompass interorganizational processes spanning such areas as electronic purchasing and supply chain management. Thus we broadly define the term *electronic business* as the use of Internet technologies and other advanced IT to enable business processes and operations.

Today the definitional boundary between the two terms, *electronic commerce* and *electronic business*, has largely blurred, and regardless of definitional differences both phenomena rely on the same set of enablers.

The Enablers

While much of the attention-grabbing electronic commerce headlines date back to the dot-com era (1993–2000),[6] electronic commerce and electronic business concepts, as defined above, are not a new phenomenon. Electronic transactions have been completed over computer networks since their early development in the 1970s and 80s.

Consider, for example, the Minitel in France, launched in the early 1980s by France Telecom (Figure 5.9). The Minitel, introduced as a tool to check telephone directories, quickly evolved into a platform for accessing a wide range of services, from ordering flowers to purchasing train and airline tickets—even chat rooms to socialize with other Minitel users.

Another early example is offered by Electronic Data Interchange (EDI) technologies, pioneered conceptually in the late 1960s. EDI enabled the computer-to-computer exchange of structured data by two or more organizations that agreed on message standards to be used by their respective applications. In fact, in a business-to-business setting, electronic business has been around since the introduction of telecommunication and networking technologies. The

---

[6]While there is no agreed-on timeline of the dot-com era, we can think of it as beginning with the commercialization of the Web in 1993 and ending with the crash of the NASDAQ security market in March of 2000.

Figure 5.9   Minitel terminal (Created by Jef Poskanzer at the English Wikipedia Project.)

hospitality industry, often regarded as a technology laggard, was engaging in electronic business as early as the 1970s using proprietary networks to sell reservations.

Yet if electronic commerce and electronic business transactions have been around for such a long time, why have the last two decades been so ripe with innovation and opportunities? A number of enablers, discussed in previous chapters, are at the heart of the meteoric rise to prominence of eCommerce and eBusiness. We briefly summarize them here:

- *Affordable computing equipment*. Euromonitor International data indicate that in 2005, 27.5% of households in the world possessed a computer. That percentage had grown to 39.5 by 2010. The number increases still further when access at work or in public venues (e.g., schools, libraries, Internet cafés) is also considered.

- *Access to the Internet.* There is an estimated two billion people with access to the Internet worldwide (about 30% of the world's population).[7]

- *Ease of use.* Technology adoption is strongly influenced by its perceived usefulness and ease of use. The emergence of the World Wide Web created an easy-to-use, graphical method for navigation of the Internet. This tool dramatically broadened the potential audience for the Internet and its services. The trajectory toward increasing ease of use is continuing to this day with direct manipulation interfaces (e.g., iPad) and voice recognition software.

- *Open standards*. Open standards—technology standards that are readily available and can be used for free—created the bedrock for the expansion of the Internet.

Categorizing Electronic Commerce Initiatives

The electronic commerce and electronic business landscape literally exploded during the dot-com era. It was a unique period of time when venture capital was plentiful and a sense of

---

[7]Internet Usage Statistics: The Internet big picture (Available online 4/4/2011 at http://www.internetworldstats.com/stats.htm).

possibility pervaded Silicon Valley and other hotbeds of information technology innovation. To make sense of the seemingly endless number and type of innovations, a specific vocabulary was introduced. This vocabulary has now become part of the language of business circles, and you should therefore master it.

Note that the process of creating categories is useful in that it enables us to identify and quickly refer to different entities. However, categorizations are a simplification of reality and, as a consequence, you may find that the different categories introduced below overlap somewhat.

Categorizing Ventures by Transaction Type   The most immediate way to classify different types of electronic commerce ventures and innovations is to identify the parties involved in the transaction.

Business-to-Consumer (B2C)   Business-to-consumer transactions are those that involve a for-profit organization on one side and an end consumer on the other. This category includes online retailers, such as Amazon.com or Target.com, as well as business models where a firm offers value to a consumer without selling any physical goods. Take, for instance, Edmunds.com, which provides information and referrals to consumers seeking to purchase automobiles. Edmund's revenue model is based on referrals and advertisement revenue (Figure 5.10).

We recall a conversation with an executive at uBid.com, the online auction pioneer, who told us that the biggest question in 1995 for electronic commerce trail blazers was "whether consumers would feel comfortable providing their credit card information to a web site." That question, with many similar others, has long been answered, and the B2C electronic commerce model is now a mature one, as well as the most visible kind of eCommerce.

Business-to-Business (B2B)   Businesses-to-business transactions are those in which two or more business entities take part. The transactions can range from one-time interactions, very similar to the ones described above (e.g., your company purchases printer toner through Staples.com), or they can be highly unique and tailored to the relationship between two firms. For instance, Dell.com offers a B2C site, where all consumers can purchase computing equipment. Dell also offers an extensive B2B site, called Premier Pages, which offers services tailored to the individual needs of its larger business customers. On Premier Pages authorized employees can access tailored services, such as maintenance history and a knowledge base of identified issues,

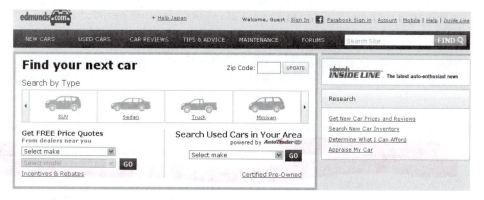

Figure 5.10   Edmunds.com's website (Courtesy of Edmunds.com, Inc.)

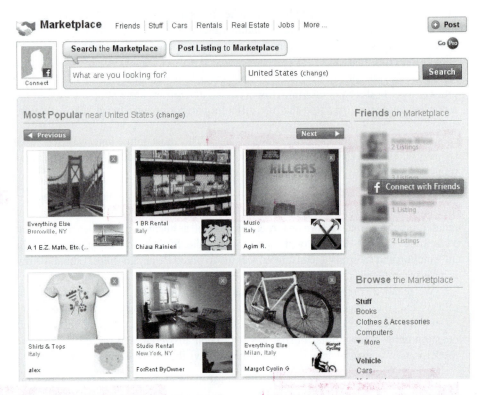

Figure 5.11   Marketplace on Facebook

and purchase items with agreed-upon contract terms (e.g., warranty, returns) and preferred prices due to volume discounts.

Consumer-to-Consumer (C2C)   Consumer-to-consumer transactions are those that enable individual consumers to interact and transact directly. The classic example of a firm that enables C2C transactions is eBay, Inc., the marketplace that lets any one of us trade goods with other consumers. Since its inception as a pure C2C player, eBay has provided an opportunity to retail shops and other businesses to reach its large audience of buyers. As a consequence, eBay is no longer a pure example of C2C, but rather employs a blended C2C/B2C model. A more recent example of pure C2C is offered by Facebook Marketplace (Figure 5.11).

Business models built around community and social networks, such as YouTube or mySpace, fall into this category as well. For example, in 2005 Yahoo! launched Yahoo! Answers, a Web site where individuals can post questions that other people respond to. Interactions occur between members of the Yahoo! community, while the firm benefits from the traffic they generate.

Consumer-to-Business (C2B)   Consumer-to-business transactions occur when individuals transact with business organizations not as buyers of goods and services, but as suppliers. eLance.com represents an example of this (Figure 5.12). The company enables firms to upload the specifics of a project or job they need completed, and allows individuals (or other firms) to offer their services to do the project or job. Typical projects are those amenable to simple

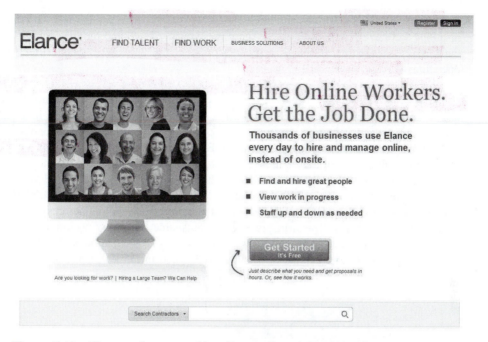

Figure 5.12   Elance value proposition (Image Copyright 1999–2011 Elance, Inc. All rights reserved.)

outsourcing and delivery, like graphic design, research, or programming, but any type of project can be posted.

eGovernment   Electronic government, or eGovernment, refers to all transactions involving legislative and administrative institutions. eGovernment transactions can occur with individual citizens, businesses, or other governments. An example of an eGovernment transaction may be electronic filing of income tax. Another example is offered by electronic voting or the use of Web portals to solicit public input on upcoming regulation and legislation.

Categorizing Ventures by Company Structure   Beyond the type of transaction being investigated, another way in which observers have been trying to make sense of the electronic commerce landscape is by categorizing the companies involved in it on the basis of their structure.

Brick and Mortar   Brick and mortar is a term used to refer to "traditional" organizations—in other words, those firms that have physical operations and locations (i.e., stores), and don't provide their services exclusively through the Internet. In the early days of the dot-com era, brick and mortar firms were regarded by many observers and commentators as dinosaurs soon to be swept away by nimble online firms. This prediction proved incorrect, and today most brick and mortar organizations have substantial eBusiness and eCommerce operations. Consider, for example, General Electric (GE), the largest company in the United States. GE is certainly a business with substantial brick and mortar operations. Yet, under the leadership of Jack Welch, GE moved very aggressively to incorporate the Internet in the very fabric of its operations.

Bricks and Clicks   Bricks and clicks, or click and mortar, is a label used to refer to organizations that have hybrid operations. These are typically brick and mortar operations that saw the potential offered by the Internet and aggressively used the new channel. Bricks and clicks operations evolved in one of two ways.

Some developed independent ventures to take advantage of the opportunities, and capital, available to online ventures. A classic example of this model is offered by Barnes & Noble, the largest bookseller in the United States. Barnes & Noble was thrust, much to its dismay, into the eCommerce limelight once Amazon.com opened its virtual doors selling books as its very first category. In response to the online threat, Barnes & Noble developed a separate subsidiary focusing on online sales of books, music, DVDs, video games, and related products and services.

Borders Group, Inc., once the number two bookstore operator in the United States, provides another example of bricks and clicks strategy. In a perfect example of co-opetition,[8] Borders struck a partnership agreement with rival Amazon.com to have the online retailer run its online bookstore (Figure 5.13). The firm preferred to outsource its online operations to the best in the business—which also happened to be a competitor—rather than shoulder the considerable investment necessary to create its own online selling and fulfillment capabilities.[9]

Figure 5.13   Borders' bookstore
Source: © Newscast/Alamy Limited

---

[8] The term co-opetition is a combination of the terms cooperation and competition. It represents situations where competitors strike mutually beneficial partnership agreements.

[9] Despite this move, Borders could not capture some of Amazon's "magic" and filed for bankruptcy in February 2011.

Figure 5.14   CVS' website

A competing approach consists of running the online channel as part of the bricks and mortar operations in a highly integrated fashion. An example of this strategy is offered by the drugstore chain CVS/pharmacy. The firm launched CVS.com in 1999 with the objective of fully integrating the online pharmacy with store operations. Doing so enabled it to offer a seamless experience to shoppers, allowing them to interact with the firm online, offline, or (most likely) in different manners at different times (Figure 5.14).

Whichever approach is better for bricks and clicks firms is a matter of debate. On the one hand, the independent operation allows the online channel to make decisions with only limited concern for the impacts on store operations. On the other hand, proponents of the integrated model point out that combining online and offline operations yields potential synergies.

Pure Play.   Pure play is a term used to identify those organizations "born online"—that is, firms that have no stores and provide their services entirely through the Internet. Google, Amazon.com, Yahoo!, Monster.com, Match.com, and eBay are some of the traditional pure play brands. Skype, YouTube, Facebook, Foursquare, Gowalla, Groupon, LivingSocial, and many others have more recently emerged. Note, however, that not having stores does not equate to not having physical operations—unless the firm deals exclusively in classic information goods (e.g., Google). Amazon, for example, has its goods stored in about fifty fulfillment centers and warehouses located around the United States and the globe to ensure its ability to rapidly deliver goods to customers.

MANIFESTATIONS OF eCOMMERCE AND eBUSINESS

The dot-com era was intriguing for many reasons, not least of which was the breathtaking pace of innovation that took place during less than a decade. Beyond technology innovation, much of the creativity pertained to uses of the Internet as a business platform—the notion of business model innovation. With a lesser dose of "irrational exuberance," Internet inspired innovation continued to pervade the latter part of the first decade of the new millennium.

Business Models: Definition

A business model captures the firm's concept and value proposition while also conveying what market opportunity the company is pursuing, what product or service it offers, and what strategy the firm will follow to seek a dominant position. The business model may also identify what organizational capabilities the firm plans to leverage to turn the concept into reality. In short, the business model tells us what the firm does for its customers, how it does it, and how it is going to be compensated for what it does. There are a number of tools that can help entrepreneurs and managers alike to think through their business model in a disciplined fashion (Figure 5.15).

The term business model acquired prominence with the emergence of electronic commerce because up until the commercialization of the Internet, with few exceptions, it was clear what a firm did and what its value proposition was (i.e., its business model) once we knew its industry.

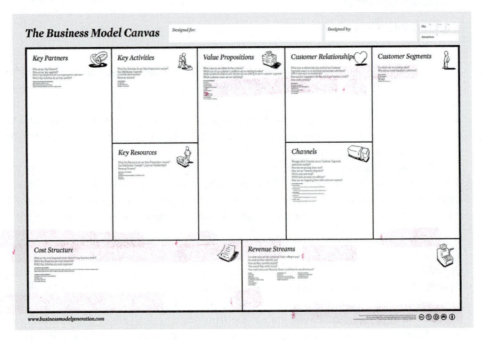

Figure 5.15   The business model canvas (Created by Business Model Alchemist www.businessmodelalchemist.com.)

The statement "I produce beer," or "I sell groceries," or "I am a real estate agent," clearly conveyed what the firm did, what its cost structure was likely to be, and, most importantly, how the firm would create and sustain a revenue stream. In other words, the underlying business model was implicit.

However, the emergence of the network economy created a seemingly unending stream of new business models and new ways to leverage the Internet infrastructure for business opportunity. Consider Priceline.com, for example. The Priceline name-your-own price business model is predicated on the notion that real-time B2C communication made available by the Internet would enable customers to trade-off convenience for discounts. In other words, travelers with more time than money—perhaps students—can communicate to Priceline how much they are willing to pay for a ticket between two city pairs. Priceline then shops for the customer's price at top airlines to see if anyone is interested in selling a ticket with such characteristics (e.g., city pairs, dates, price). If any provider accepts the price, the customer's credit card is billed, the flight is ticketed, and Priceline collects a commission. Today, with its "negotiator" app that leverages GPS functionality, Priceline allows travelers to name their own price for hotels in the vicinity of their current position (Figure 5.16).

Revenue Models   An important consideration for organizations doing business online, particularly pure plays, is the revenue model they adopt. A firm's revenue model specifies how the firm intends to draw proceeds from its value proposition—in short, how it plans to make money. The dominant revenue models include the following.

Pay for Service   The pay for service model is the most straightforward revenue model. The firm offers a product (e.g., books) or a service (e.g., insurance) for sale, and it is compensated much like a traditional store or service provider.

Subscription   The subscription revenue model is similar in nature to the pay for service model, in that customers pay for the service they receive, which in this case is content (e.g., news, sports highlights). Unlike pay for service, though, subscription models are typically based

Figure 5.16   Searching for a hotel nearby
Source: I Love Images/Glow Images

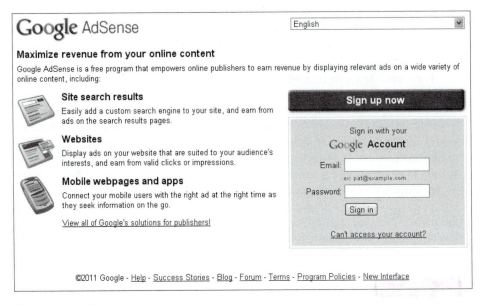

Figure 5.17   Google Adsense

on access rather than usage. In other words, customers pay for the right to access the content and then are able to use as much of the service (i.e., content) as they need.

Advertisement Support   Perhaps the most used (and abused) revenue model of the network economy is the advertisement-supported model. The firm's content or services are made available for free in an effort to attract a large audience. The firm then "sells access to its audience" to interested advertisers, much like radio stations do. A critical difference between the traditional and online ad-supported models is that traffic to, and behavior on, a Web site can be tracked very precisely at the individual level—something that print media, television, and radio advertisements could never offer. Google, for example, provides a complete suite of tools for advertisers to maximize results from their online advertising efforts (Figure 5.17).

The unprecedented level of accountability offered by online advertisement, however, proved to be a mixed blessing. On the one hand, advertisers value the ability to monitor who is consuming their message, as well as when, how, and what they are doing afterwards. Specifically, sites that require logon id (e.g., *New York Times*) can collect precise demographics and serve up targeted ads. On the other hand, precise data quickly demonstrated that most sites did not get the significant traffic (i.e., hits) they expected. More importantly, exact click-through data (the percentage of people who take action spurred by Web-based advertisements) shows that very few of the people visiting a Web site respond to the ads online by clicking through.

This ability to collect precise data about customers viewing the ads and their behavior spurred a number of innovations. Advertising syndicates, such as Doubleclick and Criteo, are able to offer targeted ads that leverage previous customer behavior—a practice called retargeting. Say you have been looking to take a vacation using Booking.com, the travel intermediary. One property you looked at is the beautiful Geovillage Resort near the town of Olbia in the pristine island of Sardinia. After shopping however you left the site. Two days later, while viewing a YouTube video you notice a banner ad from Booking.com featuring the Geovillage... and the

Figure 5.18   A highly targeted and actionable advertising banner

hotel is directly bookable by clicking directly on the ad (Figure 5.18)... that's retargeting! The aim is to increase customer conversions by leveraging all possible available customer behavioral information. On the balance, however, online advertisement has been garnering increasing attention, also thanks to the introduction of local and mobile targeting (see Figure 5.19 for advertising priority trends over the last decade). The research firm IDC estimates that worldwide Internet advertising spending is set to surpass $106 billion in 2011.[10]

[In millions of dollars (175,777 represents $175,777,000,000). See source for definitions of types of advertising]

Media supplier	2000	2003	2004	2005	2006	2007	2008	2009
Total supplier ad revenue	**175,777**	**174,355**	**186,366**	**194,463**	**203,079**	**204,527**	**193,730**	**163,610**
Total [1]	**173,811**	**174,012**	**184,382**	**194,190**	**200,876**	**204,200**	**191,335**	**163,129**
Direct	29,528	33,962	37,372	40,445	44,273	47,511	47,665	42,799
Direct mail	16,585	18,601	19,920	20,567	22,178	22,677	21,613	18,732
Direct online [2]	560	2,894	4,377	6,374	8,794	11,373	13,567	13,664
Directories[3]	12,382	12,467	13,075	13,503	13,301	13,461	12,485	10,403
National	53,494	52,018	55,632	59,230	61,897	64,578	63,241	56,982
National television [3, 4]	25,574	29,049	31,457	33,236	33,718	34,836	35,136	33,700
Magazines [3]	19,025	17,112	17,961	19,351	20,373	20,975	19,533	15,609
National digital/online [5]	5,665	3,244	3,469	3,955	5,100	-6,161	6,171	5,703
Network and satellite radio	1,065	1,118	1,175	1,161	1,178	1,226	1,220	11,00
National newspapers [3]	2,165	1,495	1,570	1,527	1,527	1,379	1,180	870
Local	90,791	88,032	91,377	94,515	94,706	92,111	80,429	63,348
Local newspapers [3]	46,506	43,444	45,133	45,880	45,074	40,830	33,559	23,951
Local TV [3, 6]	18,389	19,385	19,845	21,089	20,781	21,790	19,538	16,872
Local radio [3]	18,819	18,570	18,932	19,018	19,031	18,476	16,536	13,203
Emerging outdoor	195	281	377	426	553	790	995	1,010
Other outdoor	5,040	5,224	5,457	5,875	6,252	6,493	5,997	4,891
Local digital/online [5]	1,843	1,129	1,633	2,227	3,015	3,732	3,804	3,421
Political [7]	1,180	343	1,280	273	1,553	327	1,795	482
Olympics [8]	785	–	704	–	650	–	600	–

– Represents zero. [1] Excludes political and olympic revenue. [2] Includes paid search, lead generation and Internet yellow pages. [3] Excludes Internet-based advertising revenues. [4] Includes English and Spanish-language network TV, national cable and national syndication. Excludes incremental olympic revenues. [5] Includes rich/online video, Internet classifieds, e-mail, digital display and mobile. [6] Includes local broadcast and local cable TV. Excludes local political advertising revenues. [7] Total political advertising revenue on local broadcast and local cable TV. [8] Incremental advertising revenue from olympics on network TV.

Source: MAGNAGLOBAL, New York, NY, (copyright), <http://www.magnaglobal.com>.

Figure 5.19   Advertising revenue by category (2000–2009) (*Source*: Accommodation, Food Services, and Other Services; U.S. Census Bureau, Statistical Abstract of the United States: 2011.)

---

[10]IDC (2009). *Worldwide New Media Market Model.*

Figure 5.20   Online Shopping *Source*: Christian Barthold/Image Source

Affiliate   In similar fashion to the advertising model, the affiliate model, pioneered by Amazon.com, seeks to generate revenue from a third-party based on customer traffic to the firm's Web site. In this case the referring site receives a commission once a customer who originated from the site makes a purchase on another site. This model is enabled by the ability to link pages directly to products (Figure 5.20).

Freemium   The label freemium is the contraction of the term 'free premium.' In this model, the firm gives away its product or service for free, and attempts to build a large customer base by reducing the obstacle created by the payment. Once the firm has gained traction and enlisted a large customer base, it offers premium services or enhanced versions of the product for a fee (Figure 5.21). While the freemium model should be more associated with the software industry than the Internet, the term freemium was coined during the rise to prominence of the Web 2.0 phenomenon, and it is therefore associated with Internet based ventures.

Dominant Business Models

As the Internet and the Web emerged as a stable platform for commerce, a number of business models were proposed by entrepreneurs and organizations seeking to profit in the "network economy." The sense of possibility offered by the new technology (and plentiful cash from venture capitalists!), and the limited knowledge of the new landscape, created the precondition for significant business model experimentation. Some of these business models spawned successful and profitable companies, while others proved to be flawed. We address the most relevant of these models below. Note, however that, just like industrial age conglomerates, modern firms may have a portfolio of business models and you may not be able to categorize them neatly into one or the other type.

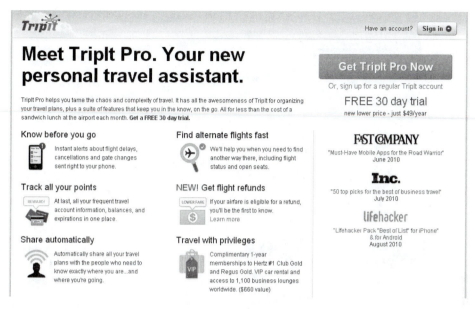

Figure 5.21   TripIt Pro—premium services of the free utility TripIt

Online Retailing   The poster child of eCommerce business models, due in large part to the attention garnered by Amazon.com, is online retailing. Examples abound with both pure play, such as Buy.com, and bricks and clicks organizations, like Staples.com or BestBuy.com. The defining characteristic of online retailers is the fact that they take control of inventory that they then resell at a profit. Fulfillment is a critical capability for these organizations. The revenue model is pay for service.

Infomediaries   Information intermediaries, or infomediaries, are organizations that use the Internet to provide specialized information on behalf of product or service providers. The value proposition of the infomediary consists in the gathering of product and service specifications and reviews, and creating a system to quickly search and organize the data. Unlike online retailers, though, infomediaries do not sell the goods and services that they review, or take ownership of inventory. Rather, they link to online retailers and receive compensation for referrals as well as advertisement. Infomediaries are typically segment or product focused, so as to offer domain-specific expertise. Examples of infomediaries abound, from retail products (e.g., MySimon.com) to travel (Skyscanner.com) to autos (e.g., Edmunds.com).

Content providers   Content providers are organizations that develop and publish content. The content offered ranges from news (e.g., Reuters.com), to gossip (e.g., Eonline.com), to historical and reference information (e.g., Britannica.com), and travel information and tips (e.g., TripAdvisor.com). Traditionally, content providers relied on largely owned content generated by the organization's staff, but there is now a consolidated trend toward user-generated content (Figure 5.22). User-generated content offers two advantages. First, it is considered more honest and less prone to marketing influence or manipulation. Second, it has a limited cost of production, since the community typically volunteers its input.

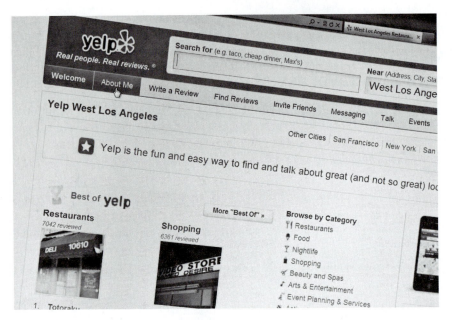

Figure 5.22 User-generated content in the form of reviews *Source*: © Ingvar Björk/Alamy

The technologies used by content providers are increasingly converging, with most providers employing a mix of text, images, animations, streaming audio, and video. Because the product being offered by these organizations is information (i.e., classic information goods), fulfillment is not a major concern. The revenue model for content providers can be advertisement supported, subscription, or pay per download.

Online Communities An online community is a group of people brought together by a common interest (e.g., windsurfing) or goal (e.g., to initiate a class action lawsuit). The community is virtual in that its members primarily interact using information technologies and are brought together through a network. Virtual communities work because they alleviate one of the constraints of the physical world: physical distance. Imagine three cities—say, Milan, Italy, Durham, North Carolina, and Sacramento, California—and three individuals who share a passion for windsurfing (e.g., Gabe, Fernando, and Anthony). Before the advent of the Internet, these three individuals would have likely never met each other. However, by virtue of being members of the same online community, they can trade tips, pick each others' brains about equipment and repairs, and even coordinate trips together to meet (physically) in world-class windsurfing destinations.

Before the advent of the Internet, these individuals may have been isolated in their respective cities, unable to find a critical mass of like-minded persons who shared the same interest (Figure 5.23). Today, however, you can find thriving online communities devoted to almost any interest—from tall people on Facebook to timbale collectors on Yahoo Groups. Virtual communities are particularly valuable for niche interests, where a critical mass of community members can only be found in large cities. In many cases they offer business opportunities, but, perhaps more importantly, they have created unprecedented opportunities for non-mainstream interests to thrive because those who share them can now easily find each other.

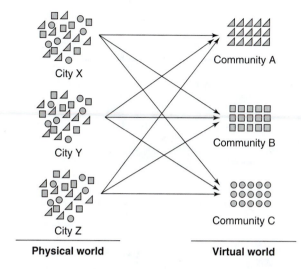

City X

City Y

City Z

Community A

Community B

Community C

Physical world

Virtual world

Figure 5.23   Virtual communities of interest

Business models crafted around online communities became extremely popular once the business community realized their potential to harness network effects (see Chapter 4). A great example of an online community is offered by Yahoo! Answers (Figure 5.24). The site allows anyone with a Yahoo! account to post questions that are immediately read by other members of the community. The wealth of content on Yahoo! Answers, ranging from where to find historical

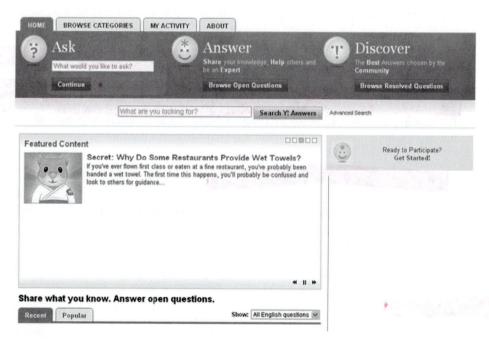

Figure 5.24   Have a question? Ask the community!

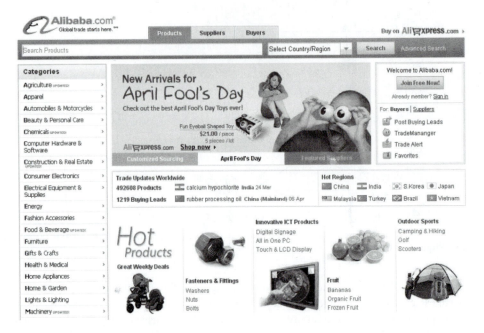

Figure 5.25   Alibaba.com

weather data to how to best exact revenge on an enemy, is generated by the community at no cost to Yahoo!, the sponsor of the network.

Exchanges   Exchanges are organizations that create a marketplace for buyers and sellers to come together and transact. Thus, an exchange does not take control of inventory or worry about fulfillment. Rather the exchange provides a "market making" service and is compensated with fees, commission on sales, or consulting fees on more complex business-to-business transactions. The prototypical example of an exchange is eBay. Others include Alibaba.com (Figure 5.25) and Ariba—both mainly targeting the business-to-business domain.

THE IMPLICATIONS OF eCOMMERCE

As we discussed in the introductory chapters, the emergence of new technologies often has dramatic impacts on organizations. The rapid adoption of the Internet and the emergence of the network economy proved to be no exceptions. General and functional managers must proactively manage these effects. In order to do so, you should be familiar with some of the main effects caused by the evolving use of Internet technology in business.

Disintermediation

The hallmark of the Internet is connectivity. As such, its emergence and widespread adoption by consumers enabled any organization that so chose to establish (at least technically) a direct relationship with its customers. All of a sudden it was practical for companies as diverse as hotels and computer manufacturers, automakers, and insurance companies to reach customers directly rather than through one or more middleman.

The term disintermediation refers to the process by which a firm's distribution chain is shortened through the elimination of one or more intermediaries. Disintermediation has a direct impact on those organizations that find themselves being... well, disintermidiated—such as travel agents and car dealers. Those organizations that were caught in the middle had to recast their value proposition in order to survive. For example, many travel agents have found it difficult to stay in business after airlines, and increasingly hotels, have eliminated commissions. Many others, though, have been able to leverage their superior knowledge about the travel product and rules, and are now prospering using a consulting, rather than commission, model (i.e., they receive fees from travelers who value their service and knowledge). In the worst-case scenario, a firm facing disintermediation may be forced to harvest and close the business.

Disintermediation has less direct impacts on organizations that, while unable to dismantle their distribution chain, can circumvent some parts of it (for example, by improving after-the-sale service).

Reintermediation

As managers and observers tried to make sense of the Internet as a business opportunity, many thought that disintermediation would lead to the demise of distribution channels in most industries. While disintermediation failed to eliminate traditional intermediaries, the Internet created opportunities for new intermediaries to exist alongside their brick and mortar counterparts—a process known as reintermediation. Consider the insurance industry, for instance. Today, insurance companies reach consumers directly (e.g., Progressive.com), through traditional insurance brokers, and through independent online insurance brokers (e.g., insure.com).

Another example is offered by many of the infomediaries discussed above. While it is true that traditional travel agents have been forced to reinvent their value proposition, a number of Internet travel agents (e.g., Orbitz, Opodo) have emerged and are thriving due to their ability to help travelers gather information and uncover low prices. Similar dynamics have occurred in traditional retail and in many other industries.

Market Efficiency

Since their advent, information technologies have contributed to reduced search costs and improved efficiency of markets. The Internet and its related technologies continued and perhaps accelerated this process, empowering customers with the instruments and technologies they need to sift through large amounts of product and service data.

Prior to the arrival of the Internet, customers faced significant costs when searching for products and services. They would have to either visit physical stores or call multiple outlets to describe what they were looking for and inquire about availability and price. In either case the process would be fairly time consuming and, therefore, costly. The outcome of this process has been heightened competition and an increasing difficulty in profiting from strategies rooted in asymmetry of information or high search costs. Perhaps the best illustration of market efficiency is provided by travel metasearch infomediaries such as Skyscanner (Figure 5.26).

Channel Conflict

The emergence of the online channel created a conundrum for many organizations that had an established distribution chain. Should they disintermediate, following the promise of reduced

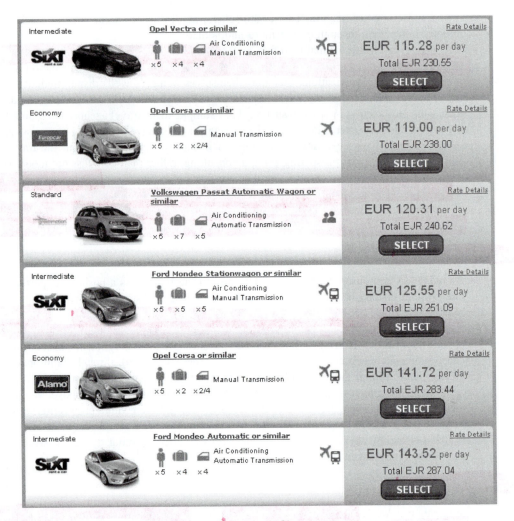

Figure 5.26   Subset of results from metasearch Skyscanner

distribution costs and a direct relationship with customers, or should they work with the channel in an effort to identify mutually beneficial Internet-enabled initiatives? At the heart of this dilemma is the inherent difficulty of moving distribution from the traditional channel, the one currently producing the revenue stream the organization needs to survive, to the online direct channel, the one that promises the highest profitability in the long run. The term "channel conflict" captures this dilemma.

Two examples highlight the difficulty faced by organizations confronting channel conflict. When Dell began selling computers through its Web site, it faced no objections from distributors because it had none. When Compaq, Dell's principal competitor, sought to respond by creating its own direct-sale Web site, it faced significant resistance from electronics store chains carrying its devices (e.g., Circuit City).

Figure 5.27 Renaissance Cruises *Source*: SENA VIDANAGAMAAFP/Getty Images/Newscom

Renaissance Cruises had an even more traumatic encounter with the channel conflict dilemma (Figure 5.27). Taking a page out of the airline and lodging industries, the company decided to embrace the Internet channel in the late 1990s and drastically reduce travel agent commissions. In retaliation, the travel agent community boycotted the Renaissance product and the firm quickly encountered financial difficulties. A public apology in the pages of the Wall Street Journal notwithstanding, these difficulties culminated in bankruptcy once the events of September 11, 2001 severely hampered the travel industry.

Customer and Employee Self-Service

Another important implication of the widespread adoption of electronic commerce and electronic business has been the emergence of customer and employee self-service. Aided by easy-to-use Web sites and the increasing degree of comfort that the general public has developed with information technologies of all kinds, IT-enabled self-service is a growing trend requiring managerial attention (Figure 5.28).

Examples of this trend abound, from kiosks at airline counters, in hotel lobbies, and in fast food restaurants, to self-checkout counters at grocery stores, and Web-based software that allows you to compute fairly complex tax returns without ever speaking to a professional. While kiosks have indeed made great strides, it appears that the new frontier of self-service is the mobile platform (see Chapter 12).

eCOMMERCE: FROM NOVELTY TO THE MAINSTREAM

In the little over ten years since the Internet opened for business, electronic commerce and electronic business became mainstream—searching for information and transacting via the Web became the norm for many individuals. As a consequence, the volume of business transacted

Figure 5.28   Self-service kiosk *Source*: © Kevin Foy/Alamy Limited

through the web increased to \$134.9 billion in North America (3.7% of total retail sales) and \$49.1 billion (3.4% of retail sales) in Western Europe. No modern organization would ignore the impact of the Internet and the technologies that leverage it. However, innovation did not stop at what many are now calling Web 1.0, and both technology advances and business innovations continue to emerge at a rapid pace. Below we discuss some of the most recent trends.

The Web 2.0 Phenomenon

With the success and widespread adoption of the Internet, and the technologies associated with it, has come the need to categorize and conceptualize its evolution. The underlying infrastructure and its defining characteristics (see Chapter 4) did not change dramatically since its inception. Moreover, many of the technologies at its core (e.g., the TCP/IP protocol, HTML, JavaScript) are still the bedrock of Internet operations and the pillars upon which innovation happens. However, we have witnessed a significant evolution of the front-end and the way in which the Internet is utilized by both organizations and individuals. The term Web 2.0 was coined to label the second wave of innovation and evolution occurring on the Internet after the shakeout following the original thrust of mainstream internet innovation during the dot-com era (1993–2001).

While skeptics consider Web 2.0 a hollow marketing term, proponents of the label draw a distinction between the first incarnation of the World Wide Web (Web 1.0) as made of web pages populated with text and static images (Figure 5.29), and the dynamic nature of Web 2.0 sites (Figure 5.30). They consider Web 2.0 a useful umbrella term for categorizing both emerging technologies and business innovations that represent a significant departure from the paradigm of Web 1.0. More specifically, the proponents of Web 2.0 identify a number of defining features that differentiate it from its predecessor.

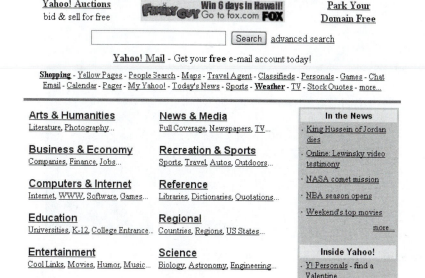

Figure 5.29 Yahoo.com website (1999)

Two-way conversations The metaphor for the Web, when it first became widely utilized in the early 1990s, was the printed publication. The Web was made of pages (not a coincidence in terminology!) filled with text, and later images. One key difference between traditional printed publications and Web publishing, however, was presented by the information navigation possibilities offered by links in hypertext documents. Despite its navigational interactivity, however, in the early days the Web was a one-way broadcasting medium. Organizations and individuals would *create* Web pages, and an audience of visitors would *visit* those pages. Today the metaphor for individual and organizational web presence is a two-way conversation. Blogs, a prototypical example of Web 2.0 technology, are a vehicle for individuals to communicate with the (potentially) huge audience of web surfers. However, a staple of all major blogs is the possibility for that "audience" to comment and respond to the original blog post. Those responses are themselves public, searchable, and linkable—making them an intrinsic and valuable component of the blog itself. The bloggers themselves can in turn comment on the comments of the "audience," thus turning the blog into a full-fledged asynchronous conversation. The power

Figure 5.30 Youtube. *Source*: © STANCA SANDA/Alamy Limited

of blog-enabled conversations is exemplified by a story reported by CNN online.[11] A JetBlue customer, outraged at having to pay $50 for a regular-size box just because it contained a foldable bicycle, blogged about it. As others responded, the story was picked up from blog to blog, receiving increasing attention. As the story picked up steam, JetBlue refunded the passenger's money and proceeded to change the rule "discriminating" against bicycles.

While blogs present an apt example, two-way interactivity is a staple of all technologies associated with Web 2.0 (see below). For example, YouTube enables its user-base to comment on posted videos with text comments and—as you would expect from a video-sharing community—even with video responses!

Interactive user experience   If the metaphor for the early Web was the printed page, relatively static and unchanging over time, Web 2.0 sites are designed to be more akin to desktop applications than documents. Using a set of programming technologies centered on the AJAX framework (see below), Web 2.0 sites dynamically respond to user behavior and to other events. Such applications are generally referred to as Rich Internet Applications (RIA). Consider for example the popular Google e-mail client—Gmail (Figure 5.31). Unlike previous web-based e-mail clients, where the inbox was a static page of text and images, the Gmail inbox behaves like a local e-mail client (i.e., a software program that resides on the user's own computer). If a new e-mail arrives, the page is automatically updated with the new information without any user intervention (i.e., you don't need to refresh the page).

User-generated content   If the "surfers" of the early web were consumers of content, the modern web surfer could be better labeled a "prosumer."[12] This evolution is in large part

---

[11]Elliott, C. "Pushy bloggers to travel industry: Be nice," CNN.com/Travel (Available 05/29/2009 at http://www.cnn.com/2009/TRAVEL/traveltips/03/23/blogging.travel.complaints/index.html).

[12]*Prosumer* is a term that represents the combination of *pro*ducer and con*sumer*—thus indicating that individuals both create and utilize content and resources available on the Web.

Figure 5.31   Gmail logo

due to Web 2.0 technologies that dramatically lower the barriers to the production of content by the general population of Web users. One example of user-generated content is the blog comments discussed earlier. But examples of user-generated content abound today on the Web, from videos on YouTube, to images on Flickr, to descriptions of locations in Foursquare—the list is seemingly endless and growing daily. However, more subtly, user generated content also encompasses comments on the content uploaded by other users in any of the above services, reviews produced by travelers on intermediary sites such as Expedia or TripAdvisor, ratings of products on Amazon or eBay, and so on. Perhaps the starkest example of user-generated content is offered by Wikipedia, a complete encyclopedia entirely co-authored by its readers through their voluntary contributions, editing, fact-checking, and quality assurance. As a testament to the power of user generated content and the crowds of users contributing it, Time magazine recognized the generic "you" (i.e., the mass of individuals cooperating and communicating through the Web) as the person of the year. In the explanation, *Time*'s editors wrote: "Who are these people? Seriously, who actually sits down after a long day at work and says, I'm not going to watch *Lost* tonight. I'm going to turn on my computer and make a movie starring my pet iguana? I'm going to mash up 50 Cent's vocals with Queen's instrumentals? I'm going to blog about my state of mind or the state of the nation or the steak-frites at the new bistro down the street? Who has that time and that energy and that passion? The answer is, you do. And for seizing the reins of the global media, for founding and framing the new digital democracy, for working for nothing and beating the pros at their own game, TIME's Person of the Year for 2006 is you."[13]

Emergent structure   The publishing metaphor of the early web, along with the technical restrictions imposed by the technology of the time, made it so that content on the web had to be structured by a designer and that users would accept it and work within its limits. However, as technology progressed, making it easier for users to interact with and customize online applications to suit their needs, it became possible to allow structure to take form dynamically. The best example of this principle is the notion of a "folksonomy"—as opposed to a taxonomy.[14] While a taxonomy implies a preordained categorization mechanism developed by some expert, a "folk[15] taxonomy" (indeed a folksonomy!) emerges by aggregating and compiling the individual categories created by users. The best example of this principle is a tag cloud, used for example to organize pictures in online sharing services such as Flickr (see below).

There is no clear date marking the transition from Web 1.0 to Web 2.0. There is no clear test to establish if a firm should be considered to have a "Web 2.0 presence." However, the value of discussing Web 2.0 for general and functional managers is not in being able to precisely mark the transition to Web 2.0 (assuming such a transition has even happened), but it is in

---

[13]Grossman, L. (2006). "Time's Person of the Year: You," *Time Magazine*, Dec. 13, 2006.

[14]A taxonomy, or taxonomy scheme, is a classification of the elements of a given universe (e.g., animals) in a hierarchical form.

[15]Folk is an English term that represents a group of people.

developing an appreciation for how Internet technology has evolved and for the implications that this evolution has had, and continues to have, for organizations and businesses.

Web 2.0 Technologies

While the term Web 2.0 is relatively general and not precisely defined, it has the value of enabling us to group a wave of technologies and IT innovations that helped move the Web from a static platform made of flat pages, to a dynamic place both in terms of user experience and content. This technological innovation has resulted in services that are free and easy to use, less structured, and more interactive than traditional Internet services. Interestingly, these services do not lack structure but, in true Web 2.0 form, they allow for structure to emerge, based on the interests and objectives of their community of users. The following are some examples of these services:

Wiki   Wiki is a technology, introduced in 1994, that enables simple coauthoring and editing of Web content. Wikis are extremely conducive to online collaboration, they can be set up as private or public, and they can require authentication or enable anyone to write and make changes to the shared documents. The primary example of a Wiki is Wikipedia (Figure 5.32), a global, free, community-written encyclopedia. Wikipedia is literally a phenomenon, having started with little funding in 2001. Wikipedia does not commission any articles; the writing, editing, and quality assurance are all done by the global virtual community of Wikipedia contributors.

In early 2011, Wikipedia counted encyclopedias in 29 languages, with over 600,000 individual encyclopedia entries in each of the 10 most popular languages, and over 3.5 million entries in the English language encyclopedia alone. As a community-supported repository of knowledge, with a staff of less than ten people and no professional or editorial personnel, it is legitimate to wonder about the quality of the entries in Wikipedia. An article in the journal

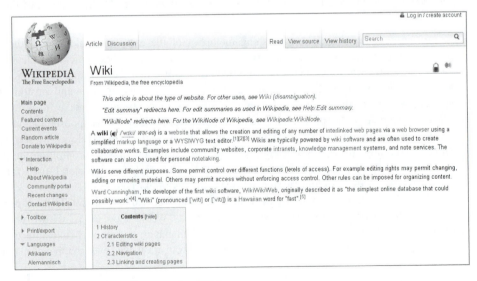

Figure 5.32   Wikipedia entry for Wiki

Nature asked that very question and concluded, based on a peer-review test, that Wikipedia is of equivalent quality to the Encyclopedia Britannica Online, a repository of knowledge with a decidedly more august pedigree.[16] The test by *Nature*, while certainly not definitive, suggests that harnessing the knowledge and efforts of a huge community may lead not to anarchy, but instead to robust content of a quality comparable to that produced by experts—an argument used by the proponents of Open Source software as well (see Chapter 12).

SideWiki   In September 2009, search giant Google formally launched SideWiki with the lofty goal of allowing people to help one another by adding useful information to any website. Based on the concept of a Wiki (an open, community-edited document), SideWiki enables visitors who have installed the Google toolbar and activated the side wiki to see a sidebar with comments from other visitors—all outside the control of the website owner! While at the time of its launch there were a number of obstacles (e.g., the need to install dedicated software to access the service), SideWiki's launch showed how simple it would be to democratize brand communication, and showed how difficult it could be for brand managers to influence perceptions in a Web 2.0 environment.

Blogs   Blogs, a shorthand for Weblogs, emerged along with the public Internet. Despite the techie-sounding term, a blog is nothing but an online journal that an individual keeps and publishes on the World Wide Web for the whole world to enjoy. While the early blogs were just static Web pages laboriously updated by their authors, today setting up a blog is matter of minutes using tools such as WordPress or Blogger (Figure 5.33). Launched in 2005, one of the most renowned blogs, the *Huffington Post*, was sold to AOL in 2011 for $315 million.

As a Web 2.0 technology, blogs enable their authors to modify their structure by including other media types beyond text—such as video and images. More importantly, blogs enable hyperlinking and discussion, thus making them not just a one-way communication medium, but one able to support interactive "conversations."

Figure 5.33   Blogger
Source: Imagebroker/Glow Images

---

[16]Giles, J. (2005). "Internet Encyclopedias Go Head to Head," *Nature*, 439, pp. 900–901.

SIDEBAR 1: BEHIND THE SCENES AT TRIPIT.COM

Running a Web 2.0 site (or any ecommerce site for that matter) is no easy feat. Behind the glitter and flash of the front end—the website or mobile app—there is an infrastructure that is both technically and managerially complex. The diagram below takes us behind the scenes at TripIt.com, a high-profile Web 2.0 firm. TripIt provides a free utility, running on the Web and as a smartphone app (Figure 5.34), that simplifies travel for its users. TripIt creates a digital itinerary for travelers by combining all components of a trip—airline ticket, hotel room confirmations, rental car agreement, restaurant reservations, and even theater tickets. TripIt creates the itinerary by parsing (i.e., reading) e-mail confirmations that the suppliers send to customers. Its proprietary software, aptly named *The Itinerator*, does this process automatically adding contextual data (e.g., the location of a given airport, nearby points of interest) and other valuable information (e.g., maps, weather forecasts). Once compiled these master itineraries are available to the traveler who can share them with friends, families, co-workers, and any other one of his TripIt's connections (see case study in Chapter 12 for a complete description of TripIt).

To the typical user of TripIt, the provision of this valuable service seems simple enough. However, delivering the TripIt value proposition requires the reliable operation of a complex infrastructure the bulk of which is hidden—a technology iceberg of sort (Figure 5.34). The development of TripIt on stealth mode, prior to its public beta launch, took 10 months but its service is in a constant state of development and software engineers represent the bulk of the firm's staff.

Figure 5.35 shows the logical design of TripIt's infrastructure. As with any organizational software architecture you recognize three major layers: the interface, the logic, and data management. The interface layer is concerned with external communication, whether with users or other services. The logic layer is the *Itinerarator* itself, the software that extracts relevant data from the confirmation e-mails and combines them into the master itinerary. The data management layer is concerned with access to the database and storage of new data that is acquired when travelers send their confirmation e-mails.

Wrapped around the proprietary set of applications and systems that make up the TripIt infrastructure are layers of what is called middleware. Middleware is a general term that encompasses all those technologies, software programs, and services that are necessary to integrate the components of the TripIt's infrastructure as well as connecting it to the outside world. In general, the middleware of a modern ecommerce organization includes:

Figure 5.34 Itinerary in TripIt's iPhone app

- Access gateways that provide authentication for users and services
- Database interfaces that provide access to local and remote data repositories
- Network and communication interfaces that provide the rules of interoperability for applications and software services
- Directory services that provide a way to identify and reach resources on the network

Finally, for TripIt to operate effectively and reliably, a number programming environments and languages have to be mastered by its IT professionals. At TripIt the following feature prominently:

- Ruby, a programming language well suited for dynamic website development

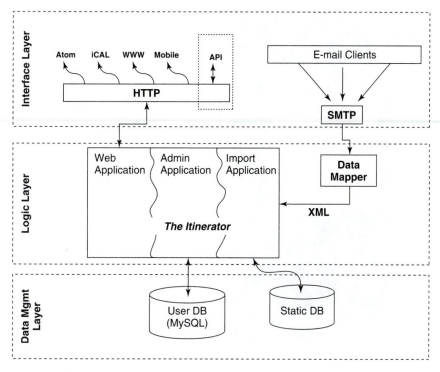

Figure 5.35   Logical design of the TripIt software infrastructure

- Ruby on Rails, a web application framework for the Ruby programming language
- XML, the eXtensible Mark-up Language used to transfer data
- SQL, a querying language for databases

While this sidebar is not intended to be a comprehensive list or analysis of the technologies that enable the proper functioning of enterprise class ecommerce eCommerce applications, it should help you appreciate how complex these operations are.

RSS   RSS stands for Real Simple Syndication (RSS). RSS technology enables an organization to create Web feeds, short summaries of content with a link to the full-fledged version, that are broadcast to everyone who subscribes to the feed once a trigger event occurs (Figure 5.36). For example, as a blogger you may want to use RSS to inform your faithful readers every time the blog is updated. Travelocity, the online travel agent, uses RSS to alert customers who signed up and provided information about their preferred city pairs and destinations about changes in fares of interest to them.

In many ways, RSS is a new twist on an early Internet idea: push technology. Push technology emerged in reaction to the explosion of Web content and the increasing difficulty of searching for relevant content. It enabled users to specify what content they were interested in, and such content would be delivered to them.

Figure 5.36 RSS alert *Source*: Imagebroker/Glow Images

Tags Tags, short descriptors associated with an object, are not a new technology by any means. However, tags are now widely used on the Internet to give structure to, and to categorize, the increasing amount of available content. One of the pioneers in the use of tags was Flickr, the online photo management and sharing application. Instead of providing users with a fixed set of predefined categories to use to index the photos they upload, Flickr allows individual users to create their own tags. Subsequently, Flicker uses custom software to identify the emergent structure of the aggregate image database by identifying sets of tags that correlate highly. This approach creates an intriguing emergent structure.

Ajax Ajax (Asynchronous JavaScript and XML) represents a group of Web programming technologies designed to enable the development of interactive client-side applications running on the Web. In other words, when using the Ajax technologies a Web designer can mimic the behavior of traditional desktop software applications by enabling the web site that the user interacts with (i.e., the client side) to interact, in the background, with a remote server-side application. A classic example of Ajax use is the Gmail application described above.

Microblogs Microblogs, brought to fame by the explosion of Twitter into the mainstream, represent the vehicle for unidirectional, short bursts of communication to a self-selected audience of followers. In and of themselves, microblogs are not interactive. However, users quickly figured out how to expand the capabilities of the application by enabling re-tweeting (i.e., forwarding of tweets), link embedding, and threading through hash tags. The rapid evolution of Twitter and its functionalities demonstrates once again the flexibility and malleability of information technology innovations, which can quickly morph and adjust to user interests and needs. Twitter's co-founder and CEO Evan Williams captured this concept: "The fundamental idea is that Twitter lets people share moments of their lives, whenever they want, be they momentous occasions or mundane ones. [....] What we didn't anticipate was the many, many other uses that would evolve from this very simple system." Microblogs are the gasoline on the word-of-mouth fire, enabling immediate communication and re-broadcasting with unprecedented ease. They also offer organizations a tool for real-time communication with interested customers. Leveraging this feature of the technology, for example, the low cost airline JetBlue has over 1.5 million followers.

Web 2.0 and Business Innovation

Web 2.0 technologies continue to spur business innovation driven by firms seeking to create value in the evolving environment. The following is a description of some of the principal business innovations that have paralleled the evolution of the Web 2.0 phenomenon:

Social Networking   Social networking is perhaps the most visible manifestation of the Web 2.0 phenomenon and in many respects its poster child. This is somewhat ironic, as the essence of social networking has pervaded the Internet since its inception. As early as 1968, when JCR Licklider[17] published a paper titled *"The computer as a communication device,"* the notion of computer-mediated social interactions had been clearly conceptualized. However, the current form of social networking applications, with member's individual profiles, private connections between friends, and easy communication and sharing within a social network, did not emerge until the 2003 public launch of Friendster.com. Following the launch of Friendster, a number of other social networking sites emerged, including familiar names such as MySpace, LinkedIn, and Facebook (Figure 5.37). By some accounts, in 2011 there were almost 200 separate active social networks, including highly targeted communities such as Livemocha.com (online language learning community), Geni.com (online family tree), and VampireFreaks.com (focused on the Gothic–industrial subcultures).

Long-tail strategies   In statistics, the notion of a long tail represents a power law relationship between two quantities. A power law between two quantities occurs when the frequency of an object occurs as a power function of certain characteristics of that object. The best-known example of this phenomenon in economics is the so-called Pareto principle, or the 80–20 rule (e.g., 80% of your sales will come from 20% of your customers). More generally, the long tail represents a phenomenon by which the frequency of an event is related to some characteristic of that same event. For example, Chris Anderson in his article on the subject noted that, according to the Recording Industry Association of America, only the top ten major label music CDs are actually profitable. However, Anderson observed that online stores could capture sales from non-hits as well. More specifically, he documented that the online retailer Amazon.com carried at the time 2.3 million books, and could fill orders of magnitude greater than the total inventory

---

[17]JCR Licklider was a computer scientist widely regarded as the driving force behind ARPAnet, the predecessor of the Internet we know today.

Figure 5.37   Facebook
Source: Imagebroker/Glow Images

of a typical physical bookstore (about 130,000). Importantly, he also documented that the total sales of books at Amazon.com from the 130,000 books one would also find in traditional stores (i.e., the high-volume "hits"), accounted for less than 50% of total sales. In other words, the long tail of "not-so-popular" products delivered a greater share of sales than the *fat head* of popular items. While one could argue that this is partly due to the fact that Amazon faced significantly higher competition for the popular items, the findings suggest that customer interests are highly varied, and that there is some demand for niche products. When this is the case, a firm has the opportunity to craft a strategy that leverages the dis-homogeneity in customers' demands. Such strategy should focus on minimizing inventory holding and distribution costs—easiest to do with information goods such as digital songs or eBooks (see Chapter 4)—as well as enabling customers to search for the more obscure items, and even be alerted about previously unknown items that would be of interest to them based on previous purchases through collaborative filtering[18] or similar technologies.

Mashups   Mashups represent a tangible and visible example of combinatorial innovation, whereby component parts (e.g., integrated circuits) are combined into novel creations (e.g., personal computers, laptops, digital cameras). In a mashup the component parts are software artifacts available on the Internet, such as programming standards, communication protocols, databases, and other resources. When a programmer creates a mashup she will use those components to string together available digital resources into a novel web application that delivers new functionalities. For example, the earth album (http://www.earthalbum.com) is a mashup that combines Google Maps with Flickr's public photos, offering a crowd-sourced album of images from all over the world.

---

[18]Collaborative filtering is the technique of alerting customers about products of potential interest to them, based on an analysis of their pattern of behavior relative to people who exhibit similar tastes. A famous example of the use of collaborative filtering is Amazon.com's purchase recommendations.

SUMMARY

The years between 1993 and 2000 saw the dawn of the network economy, a landscape of economic activity characterized by pervasive information networks. While the frenzied pace of experimentation has slowed since 2000, electronic commerce and electronic business trends and innovations spurred by the widespread adoption of the Internet have become mainstream.

In this chapter we sought to provide you with the tools to make sense of past developments and to understand future trends.

- The Internet, traditionally thought of as a network of computer networks, is evolving into a global information grid enabling ever-changing devices, and the people who use them, to easily connect and disconnect from it. The rapid pace of evolution and innovation on the Internet is enabled by its characteristics: distributed governance and the reliance on publicly available open standards supporting a multiplicity of compatible devices and offering a number of services.

- While today the two terms are used largely as synonyms, we defined electronic commerce as an online exchange of value, and electronic business as the digital enablement of internal organizational business processes. Electronic commerce and electronic business find their roots in the development of information technology and networking over the last forty years. But the recent acceleration of innovation in this area has been enabled by affordable computing equipment, widespread access to the Internet, the increasing ease of use of information technologies, and the availability of open standards.

- We have categorized electronic commerce phenomena on two dimensions. By looking at the type of transaction taking place, we classified electronic commerce as business-to-consumer (B2C), business-to-business (B2B), consumer-to-consumer (C2C), consumer-to-business (C2B),

and eGovernment. Focusing on the company structure of the organizations involved, we classified concerns involved in electronic commerce such as brick and mortar, bricks and clicks, and pure play.

- We defined a business model as the document that captures the firm's concept and value proposition while also conveying what market opportunity the company is pursuing, what product or service it offers, and what strategy the firm will follow to capture a dominant position. The dominant business models that have emerged in the network economy are online retailing, infomediaries, content providers, online communities, exchanges, and infrastructure providers.

- A key feature of a business model is the revenue model—the firm's plan for building a revenue stream. The dominant revenue models that have emerged are pay for service, subscription, advertisement support, and affiliate.

- The rapid adoption of the Internet and the emergence of the network economy have had some significant implications for both established organizations and upstarts. Disintermediation (the process by which a firm's distribution chain is shortened through the elimination of one or more intermediaries), reintermediation (the process by which new online intermediaries carve a niche for themselves alongside their brick and mortar counterparts), channel conflict (the dilemma faced by organizations deciding whether to disintermediate their legacy distribution channels), and the emergence of widespread IT-enabled self-service are the most relevant.

- While the dot-com boom may have slowed down, technology and business innovation is alive and well in the network economy. New technologies such as Wiki and RSS continue to redefine business models and determine how organizations can create value in the network economy.

STUDY QUESTIONS

1. What is the difference between the terms electronic commerce and electronic business? Why has the distinction largely faded in recent years?

2. What are the principal enablers of the continued importance of electronic commerce trends?

3. Define each of the following terms and provide examples: business-to-consumer (B2C), business-to-business (B2B), consumer-to-consumer (C2C), consumer-to-business (C2B), and eGovernment.

4. Define each of the following terms and provide examples: brick and mortar, bricks and clicks, and pure play.

5. Explain what we mean by the terms business model and revenue model. How do the two differ? What are the principal business models and revenue models adopted by modern organizations?

6. What are the principal impacts of the network economy for both established organizations and upstarts? Define each and provide examples.

7. Identify and provide examples of the most important recent technology and business innovations in the network economy.

 ## FURTHER READINGS

1. Anderson, C. (2006). *The Long Tail: Why the Future of Business Is Selling Less of More*, Hyperion, New York, NY.
2. McAfee, A. (2006). "Enterprise 2.0: The Dawn of Emergent Collaboration." *Sloan Management Review*, Spring, pp. 20–28.
3. Osterwalder, A., and Pigneur, Y. (2010). *Business Model Generation: A Handbook for Visionaries, Game Changers, and Challengers*, Wiley.
4. Rayport, J. F., and Jaworski, B. J. (2004). "Best Face Forward." *Harvard Business Review*, December, pp. 47–58.

GLOSSARY

- **Brick and mortar:** A term used to refer to "traditional" organizations, those firms that have physical operations and don't provide their services through the Internet.
- **Bricks and clicks:** Organizations that have hybrid operations involving both physical and online operations.
- **Business model:** A business model captures the firm's concept and value proposition while also conveying what market opportunity the company is pursuing, what product or service it offers, and what strategy the firm will follow to capture a dominant position.
- **Business-to-business (B2B):** A form of electronic commerce involving two for-profit organizations in the transaction.
- **Business-to-consumer (B2C):** A form of electronic commerce involving a for-profit organization on one side and the end consumer on the other side of the transaction.
- **Channel conflict:** A term that captures the dilemma faced by organizations deciding whether to disintermediate their legacy distribution channels.
- **Consumer-to-business (C2B):** A form of electronic commerce enabling individuals to transact with business organizations not as buyers of goods and services, but as suppliers.
- **Consumer-to-consumer (C2C):** A form of electronic commerce enabling individual consumers to interact and transact directly.

- **Disintermediation:** The process by which a firm's distribution chain is shortened through the elimination of one or more intermediaries.
- **eGovernment:** A form of electronic commerce involving legislative and administrative institutions in the transaction.
- **Electronic business:** The digital enablement of internal organizational business processes.
- **Electronic commerce:** An online exchange of value.
- **Pure play:** Organizations that have no physical stores and provide their services exclusively through the Internet.
- **Reintermediation:** The process by which new online intermediaries carve a niche for themselves alongside their brick and mortar counterparts.
- **Revenue model:** Specifies how the firm intends to draw proceeds from its value proposition—in short, how it plans to make money.
- **Web 2.0:** A term that identifies a collection of trends and technologies that mark the shift from a static, mostly broadcast, paradigm for the world wide web, to a dynamic paradigm centered around user participation and involvement.

The Strategic use of Information Systems

The potential for the strategic use of IT-enabled information systems has been a source of debate since it became clear that information technologies had important business applications. The love-hate relationship between business and information systems continues to this day, with stark examples of companies that have successfully harnessed the potential of ever-more-powerful information technologies grabbing headlines, market share, and profits, and others who have famously squandered large sums of money with little visible benefit. For example, eBay Inc., the multinational company managing online marketplaces in twenty-seven countries around the globe, has built an empire around the novel and clever use of information systems to enable the connection of far-flung buyers and sellers.

The ability of mega-store operator Walmart, Inc. to manage information for competitive advantage is the stuff of legends. The firm built its own satellite-based telecommunication network in the 1970s to support real-time communication with its stores located in rural areas of the United States. As a testament to his faith in the potential of information systems pervading the company, founder Sam Walton declared in 1992, "We've spent almost $700 million building up the current computer and satellite systems we have... What I like about it is the kind of information you can pull out of it on moment's notice—all those numbers."[1] Walmart's traditional competitor, K-Mart, never reached the same level of proficiency with information systems and IT use. Its resulting inability to compete in the battle for low prices took it perilously close to bankruptcy more than once.

So why are some firms able to exploit information systems for sustained competitive advantage while others cannot? Perhaps the most enduring research result that can help in answering this question is offered by executives' surveys, which show remarkable consistency with the finding that the average non-IT senior manager feels that technology and information systems decisions are well outside his or her comfort zone. To this day, many general and functional managers are uncomfortable with planning for the use and management of information systems. This state of affairs is best captured by the following quote from a beleaguered business executive: "What can I do? I don't understand IT well enough to manage it in detail. And my IT people—although they work very hard—don't seem to understand the very real business problems I face."[2]

---

[1] *Sam Walton: Made in America*, Sam Walton with John Huey. New York: Bantam, p. 271.

[2] Nolan, Richard, and McFarlan, F. Warren (2005). "Information Technology and the Board of Directors." *Harvard Business Review*, 83, no. 10 (October), pp. 96–106.

Compounding the above problem is the fact that the information systems function has traditionally been led by technologists. Because of the vastly different background and knowledge base of business executives and technology executives, the result has often been failed communication and a delegation of "all IT issues" to technologists. More recently, however, we have witnessed a trend reversal, with the IS function being led by many "new school" CIOs, who are well versed in the inner workings of the business. While this is a step in the right direction, it is hardly enough because, as talented as today's CIOs are, they are not spending their time addressing operations problems the way COOs do, marketing problems the way CMOs do, or financial problems the way CFOs do.

The above call to action is particularly important when it comes to using information and information technology to underpin value-adding strategic initiatives. General and functional managers must feel comfortable with planning and setting direction for the use of information systems resources, with identifying opportunities to use technology to create and appropriate economic value, and with deciding under what circumstances these initiatives can be protected against competitive retaliation.

Part III speaks to general and functional managers, and covers the key information systems decisions that all modern managers must be comfortable with making. Specifically, the chapters in Part III cover the following:

- *Chapter 6: Strategic Information Systems Planning.* This chapter provides an overview of the strategic information systems planning process, from the definition of an overall information vision to the identification of strategic initiatives.

- *Chapter 7: Value Creation and Strategic Information Systems.* This chapter sets the background for analyzing the use of information systems and technology to create and appropriate value. We define key terms and explain the framework used to analyze value creation and appropriation potential of specific strategic initiatives.

- *Chapter 8: Value Creation with Information Systems.* This chapter discusses a number of frameworks and analytical models that have been advanced over the years to help managers envision how to use information systems and technology to create and appropriate economic value.

- *Chapter 9: Appropriating IT-Enabled Value over Time.* This chapter completes the puzzle by focusing on sustainability. Once a firm has successfully created value with information systems and technology, it must be able to defend its position of advantage and appropriate the value created over time.

6

Strategic Information Systems Planning

What You Will Learn in This Chapter

This chapter focuses on the strategic information systems planning process and the role that general and functional managers need to play in it. Strategic information systems planning is a fundamental aspect of information systems management because it ensures that information systems and technology decisions are not made in a haphazard fashion. Rather, decisions are made with a clear understanding of business strategy and an overall sense of direction with respect to what the firm is trying to achieve with its use of information systems resources.

Specifically, in this chapter you will learn:

1. Why general and functional managers must be involved in information systems planning decisions despite their lack of technical expertise.

2. The purpose that strategic information systems planning serves in modern organizations.

3. What the key components of the strategic information systems planning process are, including information systems assessment, information systems vision, and information systems guidelines.

4. How to perform an information systems assessment.

5. How to decide what role information systems resources should play in your firm using available analytical tools to develop an information systems vision.

6. What role information systems guidelines play in the planning process, and how to develop them upon having established an information systems vision.

7. How to evaluate how well positioned your organization is to achieve its information vision following the guidelines, and to develop consistent strategic initiatives.

MINI-CASE: STRATEGIC INFORMATION SYSTEMS PLANNING AT CFCU

As you return to your hotel room in Athens, GA tired from your first day at the new client site, you start thinking about the challenge ahead. Your consulting firm was called in by a regional bank—Campus Federal Credit Union (CFCU). The small regional bank has long tradition in the community, having started in 1967 to serve the retail banking needs of local residents through 21 branches, a capillary network of ATMs and, since 2001, online banking facilities.

CFCU's operation centered on personal banking with a wealth of products, ranging from standard checking accounts, to certificates of deposit, to mortgages. While CFCU was a conservative player, offering the pledge of being a safe place for its customer's money, the recent evolution in banking afforded both the opportunity, and created pressure, to innovate and reach new customers. As you suspected and your meeting today confirmed however, the bank's main market were local residents with stable financial needs who would benefit from new services—such as online bill pay or flexible personal loans.

Your consulting firm had been engaged by the client to "develop a strategic information systems plan." Yet the series of meetings you had today left you with the distinct impression that the client had already formulated some ideas. In a meeting with you, the senior vice president of marketing said: "We're missing the boat. Large national banks like HSBC target our customers with precise marketing offers. We must invest in Business Intelligence and CRM tools or we will not survive." From the director of technology services you heard mostly frustration: "They want me to deliver a world-class infrastructure on a shoestring. The CFO, to whom I report, makes me justify every IT investment. ROI and net present value calculations are all he cares about! Yet two-thirds of my budget goes to keeping the lights on, and the remainder is spent on various pet projects for one or the other of the executives. How am I going to modernize our archaic infrastructure under these conditions?"

The CEO seemed to recognize some of these issues and thought your help would be instrumental in changing things for the better. In the opening meeting, he said, "Your firm is the best at this and you know our industry well. We need you to assess our current operations and draft a strategic plan; we will follow it at once!" As you organize your notes, a nagging feeling overcomes you—the firm does not seem to have great unity of purpose at the moment, so how does it expect you to be able get all members of the firm on the same page? Plans are vacuous without the commitment of those who have to follow them.

"Well," you tell yourself, "one step at a time." You have certainly been in more difficult situations.

DISCUSSION QUESTIONS

1. What do you see as the major pitfalls of the current manner in which the information systems budgeting and prioritization process is run?
2. What do you believe are going to be the major challenges you will encounter on this assignment?
3. What should be your next step as you get to work tomorrow morning?

 # INTRODUCTION

With information technologies increasingly embedded in all aspects of business operations, the most successful organizations are those that are able to establish a productive partnership between IT executives and their functional counterparts. Results of a *ComputerWorld* survey indicate that in all of the firms classified as "world-class businesses" in the study, the CIO had a seat on the primary management committee (e.g., executive committee), compared to only 56% in typical companies.[1] However, only 43% of CIOs in the most recent "State of the CIO" survey by CIO magazine report directly to the CEO (See Table 6.1).[2]

---

[1]Eckie, J. (2006). What it takes to be world class. *Computerworld* (Accessed http://www.computerworld.com/careertopics/careers/story/0,108901,108974,00.html).

[2]http://www.cio.com/article/591633/Why_Is_the_CFO_Still_Boss_of_IT_?page=2&taxonomyId=3000.

Table 6.1 To Whom Do CIOs Report?

Executive	2005	2006	2007	2008	2009	2010
CEO	40%	42%	41%	41%	47%	43%
CFO	30%	23%	24%	23%	16%	19%
COO	13%	14%	14%	16%	16%	13%

Being able to establish a productive partnership between your organization's technology professionals and the executive team is predicated on recruiting the right people and devoting significant attention to the development of the relationship. However, whether or not you are able (and lucky enough) to establish a productive partnership with the information systems professionals in your organization, you must be involved in the strategic planning and management of information systems in your firm. Failing to do so, and leaving all information systems decisions to your IT counterparts, will simply result in your joining the ranks of unsatisfied and disappointed general and functional managers scattered throughout the world.

A Word About Strategic and Operational Planning

The realm of strategy pertains to the decisions that an organization takes with respect to how it will develop and deploy its resources over time in an effort to achieve its long-range objectives. Consider for a moment the Roman proconsul Julius Caesar. When he set forth to conquer Gaul (Figure 6.1), he had to decide how to best create and deploy Roman military resources in order to succeed in the conquest—in essence, he had to devise a strategy for the conquest of Gaul. Caesar and his generals had to decide how many legions to raise, how to equip them, how to train them, where to locate camps, and how to organize the logistics of supplies and provisions to sustain the campaign.

As we see here, the realm of strategic thinking, and as a consequence, the realm of strategic planning, is concerned with long-range decisions about resource development and deployment. Conversely, operational decision making is concerned with local decisions in the present. For example, as the famed tenth legion took camp at Bibracte (near modern day Autun in Bourgogne), the camp had to operate with day-to-day routines for mounting guard, for cleaning, for provisioning, and so on.

As this simple example from a historic military campaign clarifies, there is a clear difference between strategic and operational decision making. While both strategic planning and operational effectiveness are critical to the success of a venture—whether military or organizational—the remainder of the chapter focuses on strategic Information Systems planning. Thus, we are concerned here with how the firm will build and deploy its IS resources in an effort to achieve its long-range objectives.

Strategic Alignment

A firm that has been able to achieve a high degree of fit and consonance between the priorities and activities of the IS function and the strategic direction of the firm has achieved strategic alignment. Research in this area has consistently shown that alignment has a direct impact on

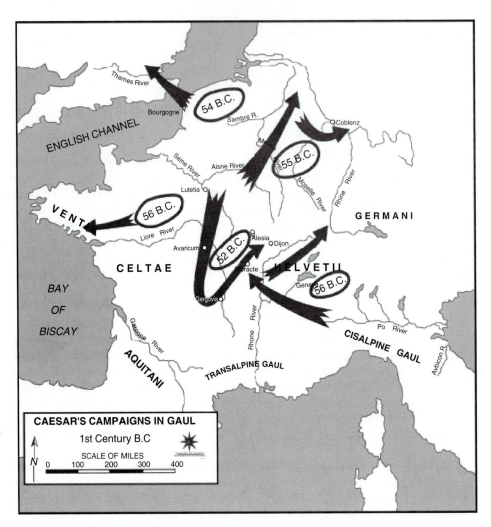

Figure 6.1   The Roman Gaelic campaign

firm performance, and alignment is perennially on the top-ten list of CIO priorities. Yet strategic alignment is very difficult to achieve and maintain, particularly in those highly competitive environments where opportunities arise and fade quickly, and strategic priorities change constantly. Thus, ensuring a high degree of strategic IS alignment requires as much improvisation as careful planning. Recent data from McKinsey provides some comfort, suggesting that IT executives have become adept at aligning IT strategy with the needs of the organization.[3] However, according to the same findings, the IS function still struggles to systematically propose new ways of creating value using technology resources (Figure 6.2).

---

[3]Craig, D., Kanakamedala, K. and Tinaikar, R. (2007). "The next frontier in IT strategy: A McKinsey survey," *McKinsey on IT*, Spring 2007.

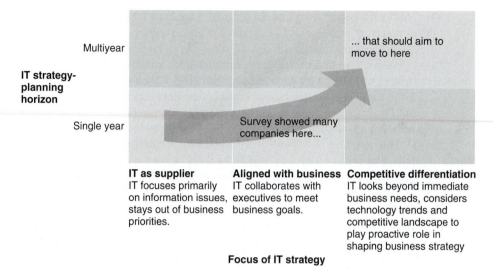

Figure 6.2   McKinsey IT strategy maturity matrix

SIX DECISIONS REQUIRING MANAGERIAL INVOLVEMENT

Jeanne Ross and Peter Weill, of MIT's Center for Information Systems Research (CISR), suggest that senior management get involved in IS management by taking the leadership role on six key information systems decisions (Table 6.2).[4]

Table 6.2   Six key information systems decisions managers must be involved with

How much should we spend on IT?	This question is designed to force senior executives to discuss and decide on what the role of information systems and technology should be in the organization.
Which business processes should receive the IT dollars?	This question requires executives to decide what business processes are most important to the firm at a given point.
Which IT capabilities need to be companywide?	This question requires executives to weigh the cost/benefits of standardization and flexibility.
How good do our IT services really need to be?	This question forces executives to make conscious decisions about the degree of service the firm needs and that they are willing to pay for.
What security and privacy risks will we accept?	This question forces executives to make conscious decisions about privacy and security risk management.
Whom do we blame if an IT initiative fails?	This question forces executives to clearly identify and assign responsibility for information systems projects.

---

[4]Ross, Jeanne W., and Weill, Peter (2002). "Six IT Decisions Your IT People Shouldn't Make," *Harvard Business Review*, November, pp. 84–92.

1. *How much should we spend on IT?* This is perhaps the most critical question that you, as a general manager or as a member of the executive committee, will be called on to ask because the answer informs all subsequent IT-related decision making.

   As we saw in Chapter 2, organizations are widely different with respect to their strategy and objectives, their culture, their history, their current infrastructure, and so on. It follows that even two head-to-head competitors may need very different investments in IT—different both in terms of quantity (i.e., how much to spend) and quality (i.e., what initiatives should be the recipient of the IT budget).

   This question is designed to force senior executives to discuss and decide on the role of information systems and technology in the organization—something that most executive committees don't do. Failing to ask and answer this question puts the firm's IT department in a reactive mode, having to decide on individual projects with little guidance as to the overall picture.

2. *Which business processes should receive the IT dollars?* This question requires executives to decide what business processes are most important to the firm at a given point—clearly a business decision—and as a consequence should attract IT funding. In other words, it is within the purview of business managers to decide on the allocation of resources among the many possible projects the firm can pursue—information systems and technology projects included!

3. *Which IT capabilities need to be companywide?* Large organizations constantly battle the trade-off between standardization and flexibility. Increasing standardization enables the firm to manage operations efficiently, while flexibility enables the firm to react more quickly and more effectively to local needs. Because information systems often enable the standardization or flexibility of operations, IS professionals are often left with the responsibility to make this decision. Yet this is a business decision that general and functional managers should not hand over. After all, the executive committee is in the best position to weigh the cost/benefits of standardization and flexibility.

4. *How good do our IT services really need to be?* The quality of service provided by an organization's information systems department is measured by the reliability and uptime of the IT infrastructure, data accessibility and flexibility, responsiveness to user needs, and the like. This question forces executives to make conscious decisions about the degree of service the firm needs and what they are willing to pay for.

5. *What security and privacy risks will we accept?* Remember the old adage, "You get what you pay for"? When it comes to computer security and privacy risks, this proverb is more accurate than ever. Security and privacy decisions are about managing, not eliminating, risk (see Chapter 13). Different organizations face different threats and have different degrees of risk aversion. For example, while a hospital cannot afford to skimp on redundancy and uptime of life support systems, a restaurant may not need to worry about (and pay for) more than basic security and backup procedures. The critical point is that security and risk management decisions are not information systems decisions. Rather, they are business decisions that can have a dramatic impact on the future viability of the business and, as such, need the full attention of the executive team.

6. *Whom do we blame if an IT initiative fails?* This question draws attention to the need to identify business sponsors for most information systems projects. Any project that involves users and organizational departments beyond the information systems group

should have a clearly identified business sponsor who is responsible for its successful implementation. It is the job of senior executives to allocate resources (e.g., create time for business managers to be involved with relevant information systems projects) and assign responsibility.

Note that these are wide-ranging business decisions, necessitating senior executives' input, but they require technical understanding of the various alternatives, costs, and implications. Thus they need to be made in partnership with the information systems professionals and the IS function. The planning process helps to structure this partnership.

THE PURPOSE OF STRATEGIC INFORMATION SYSTEMS PLANNING

The six decisions mentioned above are based on the premise that general and functional managers need to be involved in the decision making that affects their organization's investment in, and use of, information systems and information technology resources. In order to be an asset on the planning team, you must understand the planning process, its purpose, and the type of decisions to be made as it unfolds.

As we have established in this book, information systems are complex organizational systems that exist at the intersection of business and technology. For this reason, setting direction for their use and management requires a blend of skills, technical and organizational, that are rarely housed in one organizational function or department. The planning process must occur as a partnership among those with technical skills, the information systems group, and general and functional managers.

The planning process has a number of objectives, chief among them that of clarifying how the firm plans to use and manage information systems resources to fulfill its strategic objectives. Note that we used the term *planning process*, not *planning document*. As most executives will attest, the *process of planning* is as important as, if not more important than, the final documents that represent its output. The planning process requires discussion, clarification, negotiation, and the achievement of a mutual understanding. While these documents can serve to bring new hires, consultants, and vendors up to speed on what the company is looking to achieve with its adoption and use of IS resources, the time spent discussing and writing the documents is what cements mutual understanding for the individuals involved. The planning process offers a number of advantages, discussed next.

Plans Enable Communication

Perhaps the most important outcome of the information systems planning process is to enable and support intraorganizational communication. As the planning team members, composed of IS professionals as well as general and functional managers, assess current IS resources and set guidelines for their future use and management, a shared mental image of the role of each member of the team emerges. This communication is critical since individuals typically have different expectations, speak different languages, and often have different objectives and priorities.

Consultants are sometimes brought into the planning team because they bring significant experience and knowledge of the planning process, and they can serve as catalysts for discussion and facilitators of the communication process. Yet their firm-specific knowledge is limited, and it will be easy for the organization to dismiss a plan that is formulated by a consulting firm. Thus, it is critical that consultants serve as members of the planning team rather than as delegates of the firm.

Plans Enable Unity of Purpose

Organizations achieve their best results when a clear strategy and clear goals have been identified and lead to concerted efforts from the organizational units and employees. The information systems plan serves as a contract of sort, wherein the objectives of information systems deployment are specified and clear responsibilities are agreed upon. When this happens, coordinating action and achieving unity of purpose become simpler.

Plans Simplify Decision Making over Time

When a firm has not developed an IS plan, it has failed to create a context for decision making. Under these circumstances (all too common, unfortunately), the firm will find itself selecting projects to fund as part of the yearly budgeting process, with little sense of overall direction and purpose. As a consequence, projects will be funded year-to-year in a haphazard fashion, resulting in an uncoordinated infrastructure and redundancy of systems and efforts, and leading to a heightened risk of missing opportunities and wasting resources.

THE STRATEGIC INFORMATION SYSTEMS PLANNING PROCESS

While strategic information systems planning can be a lengthy and complex process, particularly for large organizations, its basic structure is fairly straightforward. It consists of gathering information about the current availability and performance of IS resources. It also involves a series of decisions, increasingly specific, designed to provide a roadmap for decision making about information systems. The strategic IS planning process typically evolves in five phases:

1. *Strategic business planning:* A strategic business plan consists of an organization's mission and future direction, performance targets, and strategy. Strategic plans are a prerequisite to information systems planning. Note, however, that strategic planning is itself informed by available IT and current IS trends. As discussed in Chapter 2, IT is a critical enabler for modern firms, often determining the strategic opportunities available to them.

2. *Information systems assessment:* An information systems assessment consists of the process of taking stock of the firm's current IS resources and evaluating how well they are fulfilling the needs of the organization.

3. *Information systems vision:* An information systems vision consists of a concise statement that captures what the planning team believes should be the role of IS resources in the firm. It provides an articulation of the ideal state the firm should strive for in its use and management of its resources.

4. *Information systems guidelines:* Information systems guidelines represent a set of statements, or maxims, specifying how the firm should use its technical and organizational IS resources.

5. *Strategic initiatives:* Strategic initiatives are long-term (three- to five-year) proposals that identify new systems, and new projects or new directions for the IS organization.

Note that while we are presenting the strategic planning process in a sequential manner, this is a simplification of reality and the process is really an iterative one (Figure 6.3). In other

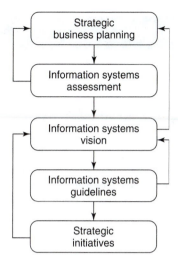

Figure 6.3   The iterative strategic IS planning process

words, downstream analyses may lead to a reevaluation and change in decisions made earlier. We now discuss each step in greater depth.

Know Who You Are: Strategic Business Planning

Information systems are enablers of business strategy and operations. They allow a firm to achieve its stated goals while also creating opportunities for new strategic directions and initiatives that new technologies make possible. Thus, effective information systems planning can only occur in concert with business planning. In other words, unless the planning team has developed a clear understanding of the firm and what makes it successful, as well as a deep understanding of the business strategy and its future goals and objectives, planning for the use and management of information systems resources is an exercise in futility.

Imagine trying to decide what car you should rent for your upcoming vacation before you have decided where you will go, with how many friends, and at what time of the year. A sporty two-seater may do wonders for you and your better half on a weekend trip to the south of France, but it won't help much if you and your four ice-fishing buddies planned a two-week outing roughing it in Norway.

Know Where You Start: Information Systems Assessment

Once the planning team has a clear grasp on the strategic direction the firm intends to pursue, more research is needed. The team needs to perform an information systems resource assessment that includes taking an inventory of the IS resources the firm is currently using and critically evaluating them in terms of how well they are meeting the business needs of the organization. The planning team should assess the firm's current use of, and satisfaction with, these resources. The objective is to understand what resources are available and whether they are currently satisfying organizational objectives. Note that we refer here to an information systems assessment, not an information technology assessment, as including technical resources, data and information resources, and human resources.

SIDEBAR 1: TECHNICAL RESOURCES

- What hardware comprises the organization's IT infrastructure?

- What platforms are currently in use?

- What is the current application portfolio?

- Are there any redundant systems?

- What networking infrastructure is currently in place?

- Does the IS organization provide any shared services to the business?

- Is the IT infrastructure centralized or decentralized?

- What systems are on-site, and what systems are off-site?

- Are any components of the IT infrastructure outsourced?

- How do the existing applications relate to one another as a system?

- What is the age of the current application portfolio?

- How are applications normally obtained (in-house development, acquisition)?

- Who owns the IT infrastructure?

- What rules are followed to determine ownership and responsibilities?

- Technical resources are composed of hardware, software, and networking components that make up the firm's IT infrastructure. Inventorying of these resources can be done by examining documents, such as IT schematics and speaking with selected IS professionals (see Sidebar 1 for some suggested questions to ask at this stage).

- Data and information resources are composed of databases and other information repositories. An assessment of these resources can be done by examining documents, such as database structure and data schemas, and by speaking with informants, including technical personnel and the customers of the data resource (see Sidebar 2 for some suggested questions to ask at this stage).

- Human resources are composed of IS professionals—those individuals who are responsible for creating and managing the IT resources—and the user community—including general and functional managers as well as end users. An assessment of these resources requires an examination of individuals and their skills, attitudes, and preconceptions, as well as an examination of reporting structures and incentive systems. This can be done by examining documents, such as the firm's organization chart, and speaking with informants from the various hierarchical levels of the IS function and the business (see Sidebar 3 for some suggested questions to ask at this stage).

During the assessment stage, the planning team reviews company documents and public literature, and interviews key informants. The documents analyzed and individuals interviewed depend on the size and structure of the organization. Note that obtaining the needed information requires skilled questioning. Often it is not enough to ask informants a direct question (e.g., how is the IS function performing?); they may not be willing to share the information or, more likely, they may be unable to answer a question posed in this way. But skilled questioning and probing from a number of different angles usually will surface the needed information (e.g., what IS services do you need that are lacking today?).

The output of the assessment stage should be a snapshot, using both text and graphics, of the current "state of IS resources" in the organization. A well-developed

SIDEBAR 2: DATA AND INFORMATION RESOURCES

- What data are currently collected?
- Where and how are the data collected?
- Where are the data stored? In what format?
- Are data shared across applications? How?
- What applications access the data?
- Who owns the data (e.g., the IS organizations, local departments)?

- Who is in charge of maintaining the accuracy of the data?
- Who is in charge of ensuring the security and backup of the data?
- What rules are followed to determine data ownership and responsibilities?

SIDEBAR 3: HUMAN RESOURCES

- How many full-time IS professionals are currently employed by the organization?
- How is the IS function organized?
- Who does the head of the IS organization report to?
- In what role has the IS organization been explicitly assigned in its mission statement?
- What is the current skill set of the in-house IS professionals?
- What is the IS sophistication level of the end users and user-managers?
- What are the industry performance benchmarks?

- How does the organization compare against industry benchmarks?
- Who are the leading competitors?
- What performance levels have leading competitors attained?
- What are the user-managers' opinions of the current IT infrastructure and application portfolio (e.g., alignment with business objectives, accessibility of accurate and comprehensive information)?
- What are the users' perceptions of the current IT infrastructure and applications (e.g., usability, reliability, information accuracy)?

assessment document should clearly convey to the reader what IS resources are currently available and how well they are serving the needs of the organization. It should also inherently suggest potential areas of concern.

Know Where You Want to Go: Information Systems Vision

With a clear understanding of the organization's business strategy, an inventory of the current resources available, and a solid assessment of their present performance, the planning team begins its real work—looking forward. The first step at this point is to spell out the role that information systems should play in the organization. In some organizations, information systems operations and technology resources are critical to the firm's survival, let alone its success. For other firms, information systems operations are not so critical to their survival and continued success.

Consider the case of eBay, Inc. In June 1999, a 22-hour outage at eBay's popular auction Web site cost the firm between $3 and $5 million in revenue, and a 26% drop in stock price, resulting in a $4 billion decline in capitalization. Obviously, flawless IT operations at eBay are a must, at least according to the stock market! Contrast the above case with that of Morton's Restaurant Group, Inc., the world's largest owner and operator of company-owned upscale steakhouse restaurants, with upscale steakhouses in the North American, Singapore, and Hong Kong markets. The company has several applications, ranging from unit-level point-of-sale to corporate procurement and financial systems. Disruptions to the performance of these applications, even if protracted, do not endanger the viability of the organization. Imagine, for example, a twenty-two-hour outage of the network or of the point-of-sale systems. Morton units can revert to a manual system and continue with operations. While this is certainly not a scenario that Morton's executives would like to experience, the impacts are much less severe than those that eBay experienced.

With more and more organizations relying on computer based information systems, protracted disruptions to the firm's IT infrastructure are going to create problems. However, the impact of these disruptions can vary dramatically from organization to organization.

Aside from the impact on day-to-day operations, information systems play a more strategic role in some firms and a tactical one in others. Some organizations' success in the marketplace depends heavily on their ability to introduce IT innovations and manage information systems strategically. Google and Apple, Inc. come easily to mind, as do United Parcel Service of America (UPS) and Federal Express.

For these firms, information systems must play a strategic role, and the organization must constantly look for applications of IS that enable it to be more competitive. For others, typically those organizations in more mature and less IT-intensive industries, being cutting edge is less important. In fact, in some firms information systems are nothing more than a "necessary evil"—a resource the company needs to have and use, but not one that will provide a leg up on the competition.

Information Systems Vision   Whether information systems are crucial to the firm's success, or merely useful, whether they are strategic or a necessary evil, it is important that the planning team is able to clearly articulate what the role of IS *should be* for the firm. We refer to this statement as the information systems vision (see Sidebar 4).

The IS vision is a concise statement that captures what the planning team believes should be the role of information systems resources in the organization. It provides an articulation of the ideal state the firm should strive for in its use and management of IS resources.

SIDEBAR 4: INFORMATION SYSTEMS VISION OF THE LARGE CRUISE LINE[5]

The IS function will assume more of a leadership role within the corporation. While the IS function will continue to service the organization by providing a solid IT infrastructure, supporting and maintaining existing systems, the IS function will no longer be considered exclusively a support arm to the rest of the organization.

In order to maintain our leadership position, we must use information to

- Set the customer service standard in the industry for consumers and business partners by using customized

and personalized information, beginning with the first contact and continuing throughout the relationship.

- Enable the company to be the employer of choice in our industry by empowering a workforce with accurate, timely information and thus to accelerate change and innovative decision making.

- Assume a leadership role as innovators in the use of the Internet as an enabling technology that drives business growth, internal and external communications, operating efficiencies, and new sources of revenue.

---

[5]Sidebars 4 to 7 all refer to the same company, a large cruise line operator with multinational operations. The examples are adapted from the actual firm's 2000 information systems planning document. We refer to this company as The Large Cruise Line.

The information systems vision must be aligned with and reflect the firm's business strategy and, as a consequence, will be unique and highly specific to your company. While the industry your firm competes in, the product or service it offers, and the competitive environment will have some influence on the role that information systems should play in your organization, the position and role of the IS function should ultimately depend on a conscious decision by senior management and the planning team. Thus, companies that compete in the same industry, even head-to-head competitors, will have different information systems visions as reflective of their strategic posture.

For example, while the Ritz-Carlton and the W Hotels compete in the luxury segment of the lodging industry, the former positions itself to offer traditional luxury while the latter has a much more edgy image catering to a younger and more tech-savvy customer base. We can therefore expect the two hotel chains to have developed very different IS visions.

Deciding what the role of information systems in your organization should be, and developing a concise IS vision that encapsulates it, is a difficult task. Two analytical tools that have been developed to help managers involved in this process are the critical success factors (CSF) methodology[6] and the strategic impact grid.[7]

Critical Success Factors   A technique that has been used over the years to help focus managers' attention to the firm's information needs is the critical success factors (CSF) methodology. Critical success factors are defined as the limited number of areas, typically three to six, that executives must effectively manage to ensure that the firm will survive and thrive. CSFs represent those fundamental things that "must go right" for the business to flourish. At the risk of oversimplifying things, the CSF methodology has the merit of focusing attention on fundamental issues and of helping to ensure that the planning team is able to prioritize. Note that the CSF methodology asks that managers focus not on information systems, but on business objectives. That is, the CSF methodology asks that you identify what the firm must do right (not what the IS department must do right) to ensure the ongoing success of the organization. With the CSFs identified it becomes easier to think about the role of IS in achieving them.

Let's return to the eBay example. Given that eBay's revenue stream is highly dependent on its Web site being operational, and given the significant disruptions (and stock market reaction) that follows protracted downtime, one of eBay's CSFs in 1999 was likely "to ensure the optimal performance (i.e., reliability and speed) of online store operations." Other CSFs we could imagine for eBay at the time are as follows:

- Continue to grow the size of the marketplace in terms of buyers and sellers.
- Increase online buyer and seller confidence and trust in the marketplace by ensuring the security of transactions, reliable payments, and high levels of customer service.

The Strategic Impact Grid   Another tool that helps in defining the role of information systems in a specific company is the strategic impact grid. The main advantage offered by the strategic impact grid is its ability to enable simultaneous evaluation of the firm's current and future information systems needs. This is achieved by plotting the firm on the following two dimensions: the

---

[6]Rockart J., "Chief Executives Define their Own Data Needs," *Harvard Business Review*, 57, March/April 1979, pp. 81–93.

[7]Nolan, Richard, and McFarlan, F. Warren (2005). "Information Technology and the Board of Directors," *Harvard Business Review*, 83, no. 10 (October), pp. 96–106.

current need for reliable information systems and the future need for new information system functionalities.

Current Need for Reliable Information Systems   This dimension focuses on current day-to-day operations and the functionalities of the existing systems. Not all organizations, even fierce head-to-head competitors, need the same information systems and the same degree of reliability of their technology infrastructure. The planning team should achieve some consensus about where the firm falls on this dimension by determining whether

- There is the risk of a tangible loss of business if one or more systems fail for a minute or more.

- There are serious negative consequences associated with even small degrading response time of one or more systems.

- Most core business activities are online and require real-time or near-real-time information processing.

- Even repeated service interruptions of up to twelve hours, while troublesome, will cause no serious consequences for the viability of the business.

- The company can quickly revert to manual operations for the majority of transaction types when systems failure occurs. While unwelcome, such disruptions do not endanger the business as a viable concern.

Future Needs for New Information System Functionalities   This dimension is forward looking, and is concerned with the strategic role that new IT capabilities play for the organization. While the industry the firm competes in has some bearing on this question, different organizations pursuing different strategies will fall on different locations of the spectrum. The planning team should achieve some consensus about where the firm falls on this dimension by determining whether

- New systems and new functionalities of existing systems promise major process and service improvements.

- New systems or new functionalities of existing systems promise major cost reductions and efficiency improvements.

- New systems or new functionalities of existing systems promise to close (or create!) major gaps in service, cost, or process performance with competitors.

- Systems work is mostly maintenance of the current state of the art and functionalities. The firm foresees no major new systems that are crucial to business success within the current planning horizon.

- New systems promise little strategic differentiation, and customers do not expect any major new functionalities or services.

At the intersection of these two dimensions we find four possible roles that information systems can play in the organization (Figure 6.4). A common error is to use the strategic impact grid to separately map the firm's current and future position (i.e., where the firm is today and where it should be). The strategic impact grid simultaneously captures current operations and future impact. Therefore, if used correctly, it will show where the planning team thinks the firm falls and, as a consequence, what the use of information systems resources should be going forward.

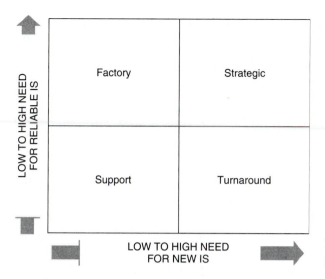

Figure 6.4 The strategic impact grid

Support Quadrant The organization falls in the support quadrant when information systems are not mission critical for current operations, and this state of affairs is not likely to change in the foreseeable future. A mining company may be an example of a firm that falls in this quadrant, as is the Morton's Restaurant Group, Inc., discussed above.

When a firm finds itself in the support quadrant, it should view information systems as a tool to support and enable operations, but one that offers little potential to significantly harm or benefit the organization. As a consequence, firms in this quadrant are typically cost conscious and conservative in their IS investments decision making, with the head of the IS function typically reporting to the chief financial officer.

Factory Quadrant The organization falls in the factory quadrant when it currently has a technology infrastructure that enables the business to operate with the needed degree of efficiency and effectiveness. Disruptions to this infrastructure, even small ones, can endanger the firm's well-being and future viability. Yet within the planning horizon under consideration, the firm appears to be in a stable state and the planning team foresees a limited potential for new systems and functionalities to make a substantial contribution. Like a factory working steadily, if the current state of information systems affairs is maintained, the firm will be in good shape. NASDAQ, the company that runs the largest U.S. electronic stock market, is an example of a firm that must ensure flawless operation of its current systems. Airlines and large chemical plant operators represent other examples.

When a firm finds itself in the factory quadrant, it must closely monitor its current systems and must be willing to fund their maintenance and upgrade. Yet because of the minor future potential for impact of new systems, the organization may take a conservative stance toward future investments.

Turnaround Quadrant The organization falls in the turnaround quadrant when information systems are not considered mission critical for current operations. Yet unlike firms in the support quadrant, the planning team believes that the current state of affairs is due for a change in the near future, and new information systems or new functionalities of existing systems will be critical for the business's future viability and continued (or expected) success. As the term *turnaround* suggests, the firm is (or should be) readying to change its information systems posture. Consider, for example, Caesars Entertainment, the Las Vegas–based casino operator, in the late 1990s. A firm historically in the support quadrant, Caesars (at the time still called Harrah's) foresaw the opportunities afforded by emerging business intelligence techniques and spent over $100 million to secure a leadership position in guest data analysis. When a firm finds itself in the turnaround quadrant, it typically needs to engage in some reorganization (for example, by reevaluating its organizational structure and creating a CIO position with a seat on the executive team). In the case of Caesars, the $100 million investment was associated with a major internal reorganization that closely aligned the information systems and marketing functions. Finally, when in the turnaround quadrant, the firm will also need to take an aggressive stance with respect to IT investments and the acquisition of necessary skills.

Strategic Quadrant   The organization falls in the strategic quadrant when information systems are both critical to the firm's current operations and the planning team foresees new information systems or new functionalities of existing systems to be critical for the future viability and prosperity of the business. In other words, outstanding IS operations and a relentless attention to information systems innovation are a must for companies in this quadrant. Amazon.com and eBay are two examples of organizations whose survival depends on flawless IS operations, and who must constantly be on the lookout for new systems. Large banks find themselves perennially on this list as well.

When a firm is in the strategic quadrant, it must be extremely proactive with respect to information systems and IT investments. This is typically done by having CIOs with a strong voice on the executive team. For these organizations, information systems are part of the firm's DNA. For example, Amazon defines itself as a technology company that happens to be in the retail business, rather than a retail company that uses technology. Walmart (definitely not an eCommerce pure play!) also defines itself as a technology company.

Know How You Are Going to Get There: Information Systems Guidelines

While the information systems vision articulates the destination, the ideal state the firm should strive for when it comes to using and managing information systems resources, it provides little guidance as to how the firm should deploy its resources to achieve this goal. Thus, the next stage in the information systems planning process consists of identifying a parsimonious set of guidelines that, if followed, will enable the firm to achieve its information vision. This set of guidelines, sometimes referred to as the information systems architecture, is prescriptive in nature—identifying the guiding principles that the firm will follow when using and managing information systems resources.

Why Develop Information Systems Guidelines?   The building of a custom home offers a good metaphor for understanding the role of information systems guidelines. While you have a vision for what you'd like your dream home to be like—including location, style, size, number and types of rooms—you probably know very little about construction codes, materials, and the like. Thus, you engage an architect to whom you describe your vision, and rely on her to formalize it in the form of blueprints and schematics (Figure 6.5).

When the architect delivers the drawings and the floor plans, you will be able to see if she captured your vision and to suggest any changes. A good architect will also make suggestions

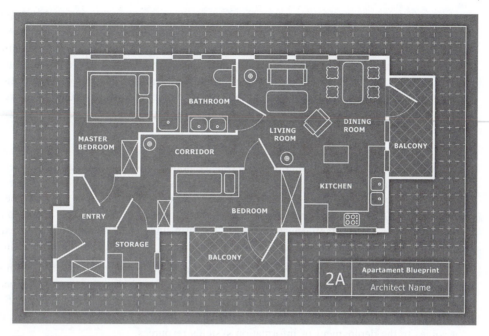

Figure 6.5   The blueprint of the floor plan of a custom house   *Source*: © pagadesign/iStockphoto

about what changes will make the house better, reduce cost, speed up construction, and so on. Once you sign off on the blueprints, they become binding—a sort of contract. Armed with them, you or your architect on your behalf will engage a builder who will actually create the house.

The blueprints enable the contractor to develop the house according to your vision, without having to interact much with you—or even knowing what your overall vision was. Contractors will know where they should locate the rooms, their size, and where to install plumbing, windows, door frames, and electrical outlets. They will also know what materials they should use. If you change your mind during construction and request changes, you will be responsible for the cost. On the other hand, if the builder makes a mistake and forgets to create a window opening in the master bedroom, he or she will be responsible for the cost of the modifications. The blueprint serves as the guideline for what should happen and for dispute resolution.

The process and purpose of creating information systems guidelines are very similar to those described above in the context of custom home building. The firm executives have a vision for what they want the business to achieve and how they want it to operate. Working in partnership with information systems professionals, as part of the planning team, they will refine their vision and establish a blueprint that will enable communication, establish responsibility, and guide future decision making.

Communication   The primary objective of the information systems guidelines is to simplify tactical and operational decision making, and to ensure that future decisions are aligned with the information systems vision. By establishing a coherent set of rules stemming from the information systems vision, these guidelines ensure that future information systems and technology decisions are made in accordance with the overall objectives of information systems use and management in the firm, rather than haphazardly and in an uncoordinated manner.

Imagine, for example, an organization that opts for a strictly supporting role of information systems. Such a company will likely strive to buy low-cost IT products (e.g., buying refurbished or older hardware) and will be conservative when it comes to IT innovation (e.g., waiting to buy applications until they have become a competitive necessity). Conversely, an organization in the strategic quadrant of the strategic impact grid that has identified flawless personalization of the customer experience as a critical success factor may decide to move to a centralized architecture with centralized servers that gather all customer data in one location for easy retrieval and analysis.

Identify Responsibilities   The information systems guidelines also set expectations for behavior, serving a similar binding purpose as policy rules or the custom home building blueprints and schematics described above. Decisions that are made in accordance with the information systems guidelines are in line with expectations and will typically be deemed appropriate. Decisions that are made outside of the guidelines are treated as exceptions and will typically need substantial justification. If the firm finds itself regularly making exceptions, it will need to reevaluate the quality and accuracy of the information systems guidelines.

Long-Range Decision Support   Because the firm will not engage in the IS planning process every year, the information systems guidelines must be general enough to provide direction over a number of years. Yet it is crucial that they be actionable. Thus, they need to be specific enough to clearly spell out what the firm should do, and, as a consequence, what it should not do, when it comes to the deployment of information systems resources.

Imagine that you just got an internship with The Large Cruise Line (discussed previously). You are eager to make a contribution and, after reading the company's information systems vision (see Sidebar 4), you remember your long-lost cousin Vinnie, who just launched a startup. The brochure of his flagship product reads, "Our personalization software solution enables your company to track customer preferences and offer outstanding service." A light bulb goes off, and you run to your CIO and suggest: "We should buy and implement this software; it is perfectly aligned with our vision!" She ponders your suggestion for all of five seconds and then denies your request, adding: "I'm glad you read the planning document, but you seem to have stopped reading too early. The second technical guideline (see Sidebar 5) rules out relationships with new and not established vendors for core systems like those housing our customer data. "

Technical and Organizational Guidelines   Information systems guidelines address every aspect of information systems decision making, both technical and organizational. While technical guidelines and organizational guidelines are deeply intertwined, it helps to separate them out during the planning process and in the planning documents.

Technical Information Systems Guidelines   The information systems guidelines that focus on the technical components of the firm's information systems must address future decisions pertaining to the hardware and software infrastructure, networking services, and the storage and protection of organizational data and information (see Sidebar 5 for an example).

Technical guidelines will not typically specify the vendors to be used, or particular platforms or applications. Instead they are broad enunciations of direction for the technical components of the infrastructure. As the example in Sidebar 5 shows, the statements produced by the planning team of the cruise line are aligned with the firm's information systems vision (see Sidebar 4) and are both general, thus making them relevant and useful for years to come, and precise, thus specifying what decisions are legitimate and what decisions should not be made.

SIDEBAR 5: TECHNICAL INFORMATION SYSTEMS GUIDELINES OF THE LARGE CRUISE LINE

1. The movement toward standardization will evolve over time, and we will remain flexible in our approach. However, our major objective is to achieve centralized and standardized products that are more easily managed and controlled, especially across multiple continents with limited staff to maintain them.

2. We will follow the trends of dominant vendors and be guided by these leaders rather than the niche market players for both hardware and software core systems.

3. We will buy software packages (rather than develop custom code) that provide generic solutions for business functions that are not part of our core competency and not part of what constitutes our competitive advantage.

4. We will not obtain monolithic packages that drive significant duplicate code and data.

5. We will store data centrally for all mission-critical applications.

6. Mission-critical systems will have complete fall-back solutions to redundant systems to minimize the impact of any disaster.

Organizational Information Systems Guidelines   The information systems guidelines that focus on the organizational components of the firm's information systems must address those decisions that pertain to human resources, the organization of the information systems function, reporting and hierarchical structures, and the like (see Sidebar 6 for an example).

These statements focus on IT governance issues (e.g., the relationship between the IS function and the other departments in the organization, who is responsible for proposing and sponsoring application development, how maintenance and new purchases should be evaluated), on outsourcing and vendor relationships, on human resources decisions (e.g., what type of individuals the IS function is looking to hire, the type of IS skills that the firm deems necessary), and the like.

SIDEBAR 6: ORGANIZATIONAL INFORMATION SYSTEMS GUIDELINES OF THE LARGE CRUISE LINE

- We will focus our expenditures on projects of strategic value and long-term importance over short-term fixes that deviate from our overall strategy.

- Outsourcing will be considered for IS operations and legacy applications where possible and feasible.

- Business-supported projects will be governed by the business case and will be evaluated by the full project costs and values in terms of people, process, and technology.

- Business-supported projects will require the participation of the business throughout the engagement.

- While the IS function will be developing systems, at all times our mindset will be that of a business professional first and will always consider the business opportunity and/or impact of systems that we develop or purchase.

- The IS function will create a mixed environment of both seasoned professionals and new, eager, recent graduates. The persona of [company name]'s IS function will be that of a level-headed, technologically excited individual.

- We will strive to avoid silos of data and silos of skill sets within our company and thus enable our staff to grow and to minimize disruption when specialized staff are moved to other assignments and/or leave the company.

Know How Well-Equipped You Are to Get There: Information Systems SWOT

Having defined the information systems vision and the broad maxims to achieve it—the information systems guidelines—the planning team must now review how well equipped the firm is to achieve their vision in accordance with the stated guidelines. This step is the last piece of analysis before the team develops an action plan and proposes tangible initiatives. It consists of a Strengths, Weaknesses, Opportunities, and Threats (SWOT) analysis focused on the firm's current information systems resources and capabilities.

The iterative nature of the planning process becomes clear at this stage. As the planning team members evaluate how well positioned the firm is to attain the information systems vision, they may realize that they are attempting to do too much and the vision, as stated, is not achievable given the current set of strengths and weaknesses, and the landscape of opportunities and threats. In this case, the information systems vision should be revised to be more realistic. Failing to do so will create an unattainable, not actionable, vision that will make people cynical and defeat the purpose of the planning process.

As shown in the example (see Sidebar 7), this stage of the analysis is designed to surface the internal factors that can be exploited to achieve the vision, as well as highlight the internal weaknesses that must be carefully managed. It also enables an externally focused analysis that seeks to uncover new technologies and trends that generate opportunities for the firm, as well as threats that may undermine the ability of the firm to achieve its information systems vision.

SIDEBAR 7: INFORMATION SYSTEMS SWOT AT THE LARGE CRUISE LINE

Strengths:

- The IS staff is competent in the implementation and maintenance of new technology.
- User-managers, on average, understand information systems concepts and have a good relationship with the IS function.

Weaknesses:

- There are currently four nonintegrated systems housing customer data.
- The current IT infrastructure supports a silo, function-centric approach and does not support flexible timely response to customer needs.

Opportunities:

- New technology, such as the XML standard and data warehousing applications, is now robust enough to warrant migration to integrated data repositories.

- No competitor is currently offering IS-enabled integrated customer solutions.

Threats:

- [Competitor's name] is moving swiftly to establish itself as the customer service leader in our industry through the deployment of integrated, channel-independent customer service systems.
- Our preferred suppliers have developed the capability for electronic data communication, but we are currently unable to connect to their systems. This inability to communicate hampers our efficiency and may drive suppliers to the competition.

In a well-developed plan, this section of the analysis is consistent with the previous ones and forms the basis for the next section. In other words, having read the SWOT analysis, and given the proposed vision and the guidelines, it should become clear what the firm needs to do during the current planning cycle.

From Planning to Action: Proposed Strategic Initiatives

After so much discussion and analysis, it is time to move to action. The last component of the strategic information systems plan is the identification of strategic initiatives. Strategic initiatives are long-term (three- to five-year) proposals that identify new systems and new projects (e.g., supply chain management) or new directions for the IS organization (e.g., create a CIO position reporting directly to the CEO). These initiatives need not be precisely articulated, but they do need to identify a set of future avenues for exploitation of the IS resources. They also must be tightly aligned with the information systems vision and the proposed role of IS in the organization. For example, it would not be appropriate for the planning team to propose a change to the organizational structure, seeking to establish a new CIO position who reports to the CEO, after having decided that information systems play a support role in the organization and having crafted a defensive information system vision.

A number of frameworks and techniques have been developed to support the identification and analysis of strategic initiatives, and they will be discussed in the remaining chapters of Part III.

 SUMMARY

This chapter provides the basis for the ensuing chapters and describes the strategic information systems planning process. Specifically, in this chapter we discussed the goals of the strategic information system planning process and its components, with a focus on the role played by general and functional managers.

- Strategic information systems planning is the process by which the firm, by way of the planning team, develops a shared understanding of the role of information systems resources use in the organization.

- General and functional managers play a crucial role on the planning team, despite the fact that they typically lack technical knowledge. Their role is to help identify the firm's strategy, and, in light of that business strategy, to help decide how information systems resources should be used to achieve it.

- General and functional managers should also take the lead in answering questions, such as how much

money should be spent on IT, to what business processes these funds should be directed, what IT capabilities should pervade the organization, what levels of IT service should be achieved, what degree of IT risk the firm will accept, and who is responsible for IT initiatives.

- As critical members of the planning team, general and functional managers will help in crafting the firm's information systems vision and guidelines. The information systems vision provides an articulation of the ideal state of information systems resource use, while the guidelines offer a context for decision making.

- With the basic planning mechanisms in place, the firm moves to action and identifies strategic initiatives to be implemented in order to achieve the stated information systems vision. These strategic initiatives often stem from what the organization believes are available opportunities, as well as weaknesses that must be managed.

STUDY QUESTIONS

1. Why should general and functional managers be involved in information systems planning decisions despite their lack of technical expertise?

2. Jeanne Ross and Peter Weill, of MIT's Center for Information Systems Research (CISR), suggest that senior managers be involved in six information systems management decisions. What are these decisions? What is the guiding principle behind this need for senior executives' involvement?

3. What is the purpose of strategic information systems planning? Who needs to be involved in this process? Why?

4. What are the key components of the strategic information systems planning process? Can you define and describe each one?

5. What purpose do the critical success factors methodology and the strategic impact grid play in the planning process? Can you provide examples of firms in each of the four quadrants of the strategic impact grid?

6. What is the purpose of the information systems vision? Can you provide an example?

7. What is the purpose of the information systems guidelines? Given the information systems vision you have proposed in response to Question 6, can you provide an example of guidelines that are aligned with it?

FURTHER READINGS

1. Drucker, Peter (1954). *The Practice of Management*, Harper and Row.
2. Freedman, Thomas (2005). *The World Is Flat: A Brief History of the Twenty-first Century,* Farrar, Straus and Giroux.
3. Nolan, Richard, and McFarlan, F. Warren (2005). "Information Technology and the Board of Directors." *Harvard Business Review*, 83, no. 10 (October), pp. 96–106.
4. Ross, J. W., and Weill, P. (2002). "Six IT Decisions Your IT People Shouldn't Make." *Harvard Business Review*, November, pp. 84–92.
5. Yolande E. Chan (2002). "Why Haven't We Mastered Alignment? The Importance of the Informal Organization Structure." *MIS Quarterly Executive*, 1(2) pp. 97–113.

GLOSSARY

- **Information systems assessment:** The process of taking stock of the firm's current information systems resources and evaluating how well they are fulfilling the needs of the organization.

- **Information systems guidelines:** A set of statements, or maxims, specifying how the firm should use its technical and organizational information systems resources.

- **Information systems vision:** A concise statement that captures what the planning team believes should be the role of information systems resources in the firm. It provides an articulation of the ideal state the firm should strive for in its use and management of information systems resources.

- **Planning team:** The set of individuals, company employees and hired consultants, who work together to develop the firm's strategic information systems plan.

- **Strategic alignment:** The degree of fit between the priorities and activities of the IS function and those of general and functional managers involved in the day-to-day operations of the business.

- **Strategic information systems planning process:** The process by which the planning team develops the planning documents.

- **Strategic initiative:** A long-term (three- to five-year) proposal that identifies new systems and new projects, or new directions for the IS organization.

- **Strategic plan:** An organization's mission and future direction, performance targets, and strategy. Strategic plans are a prerequisite to information systems planning.

Value Creation and Strategic Information Systems

What You Will Learn in This Chapter

This chapter focuses on the strategic role of information systems and the information technologies that enable them. The definitions, analytical frameworks, examples, and exercises in this chapter will help you develop a knowledge base that allows you to confidently identify and evaluate the added value creation potential of IT-dependent strategic initiatives.

Specifically, in this chapter you will become well versed in the language of the added value analysis and strategic information systems. You will learn:

1. To define key terminology, including the concepts of total value created, customer willingness to pay, supplier opportunity cost, and added value.

2. To compute total value created and added value.

3. To estimate the portion of the total value created that will be appropriated by each of the entities who contributed to its creation.

4. To differentiate between strategic information systems and tactical information systems.

5. To define and utilize the concept of IT-dependent strategic initiatives.

MINI-CASE: CONSULTING FOR THE ROYAL HOTEL

The Royal Hotel in New York City is a luxury all-suite hotel primarily serving an executive clientele who are visiting Manhattan on business. Typically, these business guests stay for three to six days, during which time they use their hotel suite as a temporary office. Thus, Royal Hotel's management has positioned the property to cater to the many needs of this busy and demanding audience. Amenities include in-suite plain paper fax, printer, and copier, three two-line telephones with voicemail and remote message alert, 24-hour business center, wired and wireless Internet access in rooms and public areas, fitness center, in-suite dining, laundry service, complimentary shoe shine, complete stereo system with CD and cassette player, dedicated high-speed elevators, and more.

Even though most suites feature an in-room combo device (fax, printer, and copier), and the Royal Hotel has the technical ability to route incoming faxes to these combo devices, most guests prefer to have faxes sent to a central number. In-room combo devices are used mainly for sending outgoing faxes. In order to fulfill the demand for incoming faxes, the IT department at the Royal Hotel runs four "industrial strength" Canon fax machines (twenty pages per minute or ppm), with rollover numbers (i.e., one incoming fax number automatically allocated to the available machine). On a typical day the fax machines run almost nonstop. They cost the Royal Hotel $1,000 each and have operating costs of about $200/ year each (e.g., toner, electricity, maintenance). The fax machines have a usable life of five years.

Over the years the Royal Hotel has developed a formal process for delivering the faxes, and maintains a full-time "fax operator" position. The process has the following steps: (a) retrieve the fax; (b) log the receipt

in a dedicated log book recording time of receipt, recipient, recipient's room number, and sending fax number; (c) place the fax in a bright orange envelope; and (d) make it available to the bell staff for immediate delivery to the guest's room.

WizTech, a California-based hi-tech firm specializing in printing solutions, has recently contacted the Royal Hotel. This contact is very timely as the Royal Hotel was about to replace the four Canon fax machines and assume the costs discussed above. WizTech is beginning to commercialize a "driverless printing" solution that enables regular printers to be contacted by fax machines without any need to install drivers (a driver is a software program that manages the interaction between two devices). Thus, the printer equipped with driverless printing software is a *perfect substitute* for the industrial strength fax machines. Moreover, to ensure a degree of redundancy, WizTech offers, free of charge, a backup service that enables temporary rerouting of incoming faxes to any other printer in the hotel if the main printer fails; this service is secure and managed seamlessly by WizTech until the main printer is back in operation. WizTech's high-end solution offers a "driverless printer" performing at eighty ppm with annual operating costs of $500. The printer's useful life is comparable to that of the industrial strength fax machines (five years). Each printer equipped with the software costs WizTech $1,500 to produce.

DISCUSSION QUESTIONS

1. What should the Royal Hotel's IT department do?
2. Does WizTech enjoy a competitive advantage (or disadvantage) in this market?
3. Can you quantify such advantage (or disadvantage)?

INTRODUCTION

Perhaps the primary role of functional and general managers in business organizations is to contribute to the *creation* and *appropriation* of economic value by their firm. Consider, for example, the following episode as recounted by Jack Shewmaker, former President and COO of Walmart Stores, Inc.:

Glen Habern was our data processing manager, and he and I had this dream of an interactive [satellite-based] communication system on which you could communicate back and

Figure 7.1   A communication satellite

forth between all the stores and the distribution centers and the general office. Glenn came up with the idea and I said: "Let's pursue it without asking anybody."[1]

This quote speaks to the importance of a strong partnership among a firm executive, the COO, and an IT professional, who together envisioned a better way to manage information and to create economic value in their organization—in the case of Wal-Mart, this satellite network (Figure 7.1) became the backbone of many of the firm's future strategic initiatives and competitive advantage.

But what does it mean to create value? Why would an organization want to engage in value creation? And, perhaps most importantly, how can you ensure that your organization benefits from its value creation strategies and initiatives?

THE ANALYSIS OF ADDED VALUE

Added value is one of those terms that we all too often hear being used in presentations and press releases to convey the idea that a firm is doing something worthy of attention. Consider the following:

- From the website of a State Information Technology Agency: "We will work hard to make sure that everything we do is "value-add" for our customers and achieves [the agency's] vision."

- Bill Gates: "Analytical software enables you to shift human resources from rote data collection to value-added customer service and support where the human touch makes a profound difference."

- From the title of an article published by *The Washington Times*: "Wi-Fi Going from an Added Value to an Expected Amenity."

---

[1] *Sam Walton: Made in America*, Sam Walton with John Huey. New York: Bantam, p. 270.

The Benefits of Disciplined Analysis

What does it really mean to create value or to have added value? Can you carry out a disciplined analysis or compute a number for the value added by an initiative you have envisioned? What would this number mean? What decisions could you make based on this analysis?

The analysis of added value is a formal mechanism that managers and analysts use to answer these questions, and to evaluate how much of the value created the firm can appropriate in the form of profits. While the analysis of added value can be applied to any firm's initiative, we will constrain our focus to those projects that leverage IT at their core. This analysis is an essential step in the decision of whether or not you should go ahead with the initiative. It stands to reason that, if the proposed initiative creates no tangible value, you should shelve it. More insidiously, if the initiative does contribute to the creation of value, but your firm will be unable to appropriate such value created, then you should also not go on with it, in most cases.

This type of analysis is useful not only when you are innovating—in other words, when you are endeavoring to create value in novel ways and offering things that no competitor is currently offering—but also when you are evaluating how to respond to a competitor who took the leadership position. The analysis of added value can help you measure how much benefit your competitor is drawing from the innovation and what benefits are likely to accrue to you if you choose to replicate the initiative. While in many cases you will only have limited information and you will not be able to create precise estimations for value created and added value, a disciplined analysis will nonetheless help you carefully analyze the potential of the initiative.

The Definition of Value

Economic value is generated when *worthwhile things* that did not exist before are created. Thus, value is generated not when something novel is done, but only when this "something novel" is deemed worthwhile by someone else. As entrepreneurship scholars have long recognized, this is the crucial difference between inventors and entrepreneurs. Inventors are those individuals who create new products and new technologies—in short, new things. These new technologies or products can be amazing, technically flawless, and beautifully engineered, but they will not create value until they solve a problem in some market. Entrepreneurs know this full well and focus on *market opportunities* and the development of *solutions* to meet these opportunities—that is, entrepreneurs look for new ways to create value rather than new technologies or new products. Often the novel solution being marketed relies on a new technology, but it is the invention that serves the market opportunity, not the other way around. While the solution offered may not be technically superior or beautifully engineered, it will be commercially appealing precisely because it does contribute to the creation of economic value.

The Firm's Transformation Process   Economic value is created through a transformation process when some input resources that have a value of $x in their next best utilization are transformed into outputs for which customers are willing to pay $x + $v. When such a transformation process takes place, it can be said that value, in the amount of $v, has been created. In other words, this new value was not there before and would not come to be unless the transformation process did occur, since the input resources would remain untransformed and simply maintain their original worth of $x. Enacting the transformation process is typically a firm that engages in it while seeking to monetize (at least) some of this value created in the form of profits.

Figure 7.2   Entrance of a Tesco store (Image created by Michael Lee at the English Wikipedia Project.)

Input resources are represented by any factor of production, such as raw materials, labor, equity and debt capital, managerial talent, support services like transportation and storage, and so on. In other words, anything that is used to generate the product or service, and then market it, sell it, and support it is to be considered an input resource.

The output of the transformation process is the product and/or service that the firm engaging in the transformation process is seeking to sell and that a customer is interested in acquiring.

Let's return to the example of a large retailer (e.g., Walmart, Carrefour, Tesco). As a retailer, Tesco (Figure 7.2) uses input resources such as labor, physical stores, warehousing facilities, trucks and transportation equipment, energy sources (e.g., diesel fuel for the trucks, electricity for the stores), equity and debt capital, and so on. By employing these resources in its transformation process, which consists of acquiring products in bulk, warehousing them, and then distributing them to conveniently located stores, the firm is able to offer something that its customers are willing to pay for: convenient access to a large selection of mainstream products.

Defining the Components of Value Created

A formal analysis of added value requires some key definitions:

- *Supplier opportunity cost (SOC):* Supplier opportunity cost is the minimum amount of money the suppliers are willing to accept to provide the firm with the needed resources.
- *Firm cost (FC):* Firm cost is the actual amount of money the firm disbursed to acquire the resources needed to create its product or service.
- *Customer willingness to pay (CWP):* Customer willingness to pay is the maximum amount of money the firm's customers are ready to spend in order to obtain the firm's product.
- *Total value created (TVC):* The total value created in the transaction is computed as the difference between customer willingness to pay and supplier opportunity cost. TVC = CWP − SOC.

Supplier Opportunity Cost   Supplier opportunity cost, the lower bound of value creation, is an important figure as it represents the value that the needed resources would have in their next best use. For this reason it is defined as an opportunity cost. A rational supplier will only provide the firm with its services (e.g., labor, managerial talent, raw materials) if it receives at least the same sum of money it would have received from any other buyer (i.e., another firm seeking to use the resource the supplier offers).

Note, however, that suppliers will typically not be paid an amount equal to their supplier opportunity cost. This is because the firm acquiring the resources will not be able to precisely estimate this number—in fact, in most cases the suppliers themselves may not have a precise estimate available—and the suppliers will happily accept any offer exceeding their opportunity cost.

For an example, think back to the latest job offer that you received and accepted. During the interview, you, the supplier of labor to the hiring firm, formulated some idea regarding your willingness to work for the company and how much you'd want to get paid. When the offer came through it most likely exceeded this minimum requirement you had established, and you took the job... without returning the "excess salary" you received.

The simple example above addresses a very important issue. Supplier opportunity cost is a theoretical minimum; the actual amount of money the firm will disburse to acquire the needed resources (i.e., the firm cost) is the outcome of a negotiation effort in the presence of an asymmetry of information between the negotiating parties. We will see that this important point resurfaces later when we discuss price considerations.

Customer Willingness to Pay   The other end on the value continuum is represented by the customer willingness to pay. As we noted above, an inventor is someone who generates a new idea and creates a new product or technology. An entrepreneur is someone who matches a novel product or service to a market opportunity. This difference should be clear now with the terminology of value creation. Unless some customer is willing to part ways with his money to acquire whatever the inventor has created, and this amount is larger than the supplier opportunity cost, no value has been generated and no economically viable venture has been created. In other words, value is in the eyes of the customer. The most elegantly engineered and technically beautiful product is valueless unless a customer is willing to pay for it.

The history of information technology products and services is littered with examples of innovations that, while perhaps technically amazing, met with cool customer response and dwindled into market oblivion as a consequence: Do you remember the picture phone (Figure 7.3), the Apple Newton, Audrey (3Com's Internet appliance) (Figure 7.4), WebTV, and Webvan's online grocery service? Unless you are a historian of sorts, the answer is most likely no.

Computing the Total Value Created

Simply defined, value is the difference between customer willingness to pay and supplier opportunity cost. That is, value is created when resources that in their next best use would be worth a given amount are transformed into something that a customer is willing to pay more for.

Consider a simple fictitious example.[2] Your grandmother was famous for baking a great-tasting cake. In her will, she entrusts the secret recipe to you, so you decide to become an

---

[2]While this example could be considered trivial, we encourage you to pay close attention since it elucidates every aspect of the analysis of added value. The example is clearly fictitious in that it assumes perfect information by all parties involved.

Figure 7.3 The PicturePhone—an innovation introduced 35 years before its time

Figure 7.4 Audrey, the Internet appliance

entrepreneur and start baking the specialty cake. You can bake a single cake using amounts of eggs, flour, sugar, and the secret grandma ingredients worth about $4.00 together. An hour of your time invested in making the cake is valued at $6.50, under the assumption that you only qualify for minimum-wage jobs (i.e., if you used the same amount of time to work for the best other job you qualify for, you would earn $6.50). Finally, you use electricity to bake the cake, and some gas and wear and tear on your car to deliver it, in the amount of 50¢. The local gourmet coffee shop, whose owner knew your grandma personally and who had tasted the cake, is willing to pay you as much as $20.00 for each one of your homemade cakes. This is because she thinks that she can get twelve slices out of every cake and sell each one for $2, thereby making a nice $4.00 profit.

This information allows us to precisely compute the total value created (TVC) in this *cake making and selling* transaction. TVC = CWP − SOC (see Figure 7.5). That is, TVC = $20.00 − ($4.00 + $6.50 + $0.50) = $9.00. Or, more formally, taking resources valued at

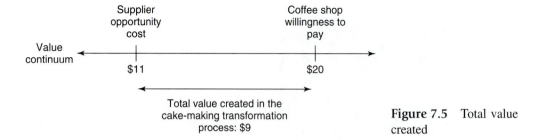

Figure 7.5   Total value created

$11.00 in their next best use and producing a good valued at $20.00 by a customer, you have contributed to creating value of $9.00 through a "cake-making transformation process."

Appropriating the Value Created

Up to this point we have discussed the process of value creation—a process in which suppliers, the focal firm (i.e., you), and the customer partake. However, total value creation only tells us if there is *an opportunity* to make a profit. That is, if the total value created is greater than zero, someone will benefit, but we still don't know who.

Value appropriation is the process by which the total value created in the transaction is split among all the entities who contributed to creating it (i.e., suppliers, the firm, and the customer). It is typically the outcome of a negotiation process between the firm and the suppliers, to determine the firm cost, and between the firm and the customer, to establish product prices (see Figure 7.6). When a firm appropriates value, it does so in the form of higher profits. When customers appropriate value, they do so in the form of savings (i.e., paying less than what they would have been willing to pay).[3]

Let's return to the example of your grandma-recipe cake-making venture. Note that at this point we have said nothing about either your actual cost of making the cake (i.e., the firm cost)

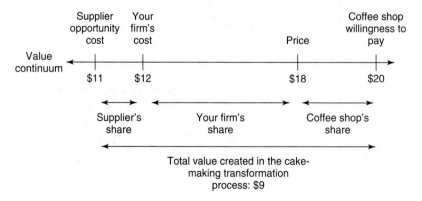

Figure 7.6   Value appropriation

---

[3]As customers, we have all come across a "good deal" a few times in our lives. A good deal is nothing but a situation where the price we are asked to pay is lower than our customer willingness to pay.

or the price you and the coffee shop have agreed on for each cake you will deliver. In other words, at this point we know how much total value has been created (a theoretical amount), but we know nothing about how this value is going to be realized and who is going to appropriate it.

Let's assume that, while the store that provides you with the ingredients for your cake may be willing to drop the price to about $4.00 per cake because of your bulk buying, you are unaware of the store's supplier opportunity cost and do not negotiate hard. You simply pay the published price of $5.00 per cake in ingredients. Thus, your firm cost[4] equals ($5.00 + $6.50 + $0.50) = $12.00.

Now, since you do not know that the coffee house's actual customer willingness to pay is $20.00 (they certainly are not going to tell you!), you accept the coffee house's first offer and do not negotiate hard... should you consider a negotiation class at this point?!? The price you agree on is $18.00 (see Figure 7.6).

We now have all the information we need to compute value appropriation and to determine how much of the total value created each of the entities involved will retain. Here is how the total value created, $9.00, would break down in this case:

- The suppliers appropriate $1.00 in excess profits—that is, one dollar more than the minimum amount of money they would have been willing to accept to provide you with the needed resources (i.e., supplier opportunity cost).

- You appropriate $6.00 in excess profits—that is, six dollars more than the minimum amount of money for which you would have been willing to stay in this venture (i.e., your firm cost).

- The customer, the gourmet coffee shop, appropriates $2.00 in savings—that is, two dollars less than the maximum amount of money it would have been willing to disburse to acquire your specialty cake (i.e., their customer willingness to pay).

The Definition of Added Value

With the terminology of value creation and value appropriation now in place, we are ready to discuss added value. A firm's added value is defined as *that portion of the total value created that would be lost if the firm did not take part in the exchange.* That is, the firm's added value is measured as that portion of the value created in the transaction involving the firm minus the total value that could be created if the firm did not exist. A firm's added value is therefore the unique portion of the total value created that is contributed by the firm itself. Added value depends on the effects of existing competition.

Recall the example of your cake-making venture. In that example your firm was the only one in the market that could take the ingredients that were valued at $11.00 and, using the secret grandma recipe, transform them into a final product, this one-of-a-kind cake that customers would be willing to pay a maximum of $20.00 for. We established that the total value created in the transaction was $9.00.

What was your firm's added value then? It was the full $9.00. If you decide not to bake the cake, as the only person who has knowledge of the secret recipe (i.e., the unique transformation

---

[4]Note that in this simplistic example, you are playing two roles. On the one hand, you are a supplier of the labor resource. At the same time, you are the entrepreneur, the firm, who will retain any profits the business is able to generate.

process), none of the potential value would be realized. That is, all $9.00 of the new value would be lost as we would be left with the raw resources worth the original $11.00.

Added Value in a Competitive Market

Let's now assume that you were not the only one who had been given the secret recipe in your grandma's will. Much to your surprise, your estranged cousin Bettie also received the secret recipe, and you just found out that she is entering the cake-baking business in your area! In fact, she just contacted the gourmet coffee shop you have been in talks with and is attempting to undercut you. She has the exact same cost structure as you do, and produces a cake that is no different in any respect than yours. In other words, you and Bettie produce two products that are perfect substitutes for one another.

Mapping this scenario to the added value model demonstrates that the total value created has not changed (see Figure 7.7), since both you and Bettie encounter the same supplier opportunity cost[5] and produce a cake that the coffee shop owner would pay the same amount of money for.

What has changed in this scenario is your firm's added value. In the first scenario you were the only one who could create the cake. Now, if your firm were to leave the exchange, Bettie's firm could step right in and, using the exact same resource, produce the exact same cake. You do *nothing unique* and, as a consequence, your added value is now $0.00.

Pricing Considerations

Again, while we don't need to know price to compute added value (a theoretical value), price becomes important to gauge what portion of the value created each entity partaking to the transaction can appropriate. In our first scenario, when you were the only person who knew the secret recipe for the cake, we assumed you'd agree to the first price the coffee shop owner proposed (Figure 7.6)—$18.00. It should be clear, though, that you were in a position of bargaining power

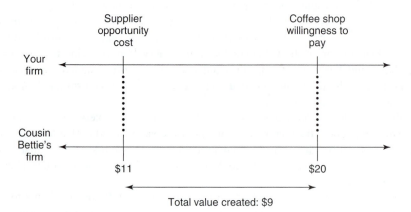

Figure 7.7   Total value created

---

[5]This assumes that Bettie also has a minimum-wage job as the next best use of her time.

and could have pushed the envelope. In fact, since we know the coffee shop owner's customer willingness to pay, we can assert that you could have charged as much as $20.00.

Once your cousin Bettie enters the market and begins to offer her cake, a perfect substitute of yours, you are no longer in a position of bargaining power. We can therefore expect a price war to cause prices to drop as low as your firm cost since neither of you offers anything unique (your added value is zero). Under this circumstance, any price you quote that exceeds your firm cost would provide an incentive to the coffee shop and cousin Bettie's firm to strike a deal to cut you out. Cousin Bettie would quote a price lower than yours to get the business, and a lower price would be a better deal for the coffee shop. This would force you to underbid Bettie, and the process would only end when either one of you is willing to quote a price equal to the firm cost. In this case, neither competitor will make any extra profit, while the customer, the coffee shop, will reap big savings.

The lesson is clear: No matter how much value your firm contributes to creating, unless you can be (at least in part) unique in your value creation, you will quickly compete this value away to customers. This is, of course, the essence of competition, and a force that in your capacity as a manager you need to learn to manage.

The Relationship between Added Value and Competitive Advantage

The insight about pricing discussed above is critical and it should clarify that a firm should focus on creating value, through innovation and the use of IT, not just for the sake of doing so, but in order to be able to appropriate at least a portion of the total value created. In theory, the maximum amount of value that a firm can appropriate equals its added value. Thus, the imperative when engaging in new strategic initiatives is for a firm to create *added value*. The firm's added value is also a measure of its competitive advantage because it measures the extent to which the firm is able to do something unique and valuable.

How Is Added Value Created?

Now imagine one last twist in the story of your cake-making venture. Imagine that, since you have some artistic talents, you are able to garnish the cake with some icing that makes it unique. The coffee shop owner thinks that she can sell each slice of your "personalized" cake at a premium, say $2.25, claiming that the cake is a "coffee shop exclusive."

Personalizing the cake takes you fifteen minutes of extra labor, and the value of the extra ingredients needed is 37.5¢. In this case, your supplier opportunity cost has risen by $2.00. But the extra investment of resources leads to an increase in customer willingness to pay of $3.00. Cousin Bettie has no artistic talents and is unable to personalize her cakes. Your firm's added value is now positive (Figure 7.8).

Perhaps a bit simpler is to focus on the value of the different characteristics of your product. That is, with an incremental investment of $2.00, you create an increment in customer willingness to pay of $3.00, over what the competition can do, thus generating added value in the amount of $1.00. Note that price will be once again determined as a consequence of a negotiation process, but you certainly now have a competitive advantage over Cousin Bettie's firm, and you can expect to appropriate as much as one dollar (e.g., charging the coffee shop no more than $14.00).

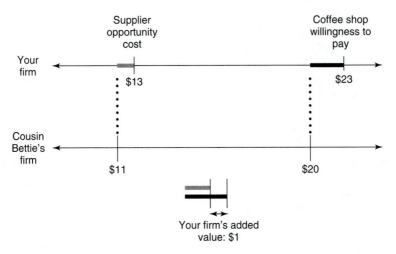

Figure 7.8   Added value under competition

Two Ways to Create New Value

More important than the calculations produced above is the meaning of this analysis and the considerations that follow from it.

Increasing Customer Willingness to Pay   Added value is created by doing something of value for customers, thereby increasing customer willingness to pay, through an investment of resources that does not exceed customer willingness to pay—otherwise we would be simply destroying value and wasting resources. Apple, Inc.—the consumer electronics firm lead by Steve Jobs—is a great example of value creation through increased willingness to pay. Steve Jobs, speaking at D,[6] articulated his firm's great success in digital media as focusing on making great products, pricing them aggressively, and going for volume. Translated into the terminology of this chapter, this approach reads: "Our strategy is to drive customer willingness to pay as high as we possibly can (i.e., great products), and then try to price low enough so that people perceive that they are appropriating significant value when they buy our products, and therefore buy them in large volumes."

The most visible competitive battles take place on this end of the value continuum. The firms that have innovated use marketing to educate customers about their new products and services, and to drive up customer willingness to pay (Figure 7.9). However, this focus on customer facing initiatives can be misleading.

Decreasing Supplier Opportunity Cost   By definition, value can be created by increasing customer willingness to pay over supplier opportunity cost, but also by reducing supplier opportunity cost without a comparable reduction in customer willingness to pay. In other words, there is

---

[6]The *all things digital conference*—or D for short—is the annual event for the executives of the computer and software industry hosted by the *Wall Street Journal*.

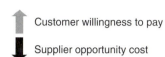

Figure 7.9   How value is created

great potential to create value by working with the firm's suppliers and creating incentives for them to supply you with needed resources for less money (Figure 7.9).

The prototypical example of this strategy is offered by Walmart, Inc., a firm that has made "everyday low prices" its slogan and the key driver behind most of its decisions. In the late 1980s, Walmart worked with one of its largest suppliers, Procter & Gamble, to find creative ways to lower its cost structure. Walmart pioneered a technique now called "continuous replenishment."

Continuous replenishment is based on the idea of "pulled logistics", whereby a supplier (e.g., P&G), not a customer (e.g., Walmart), is in charge of managing the customer's inventory. In the specific case of the Walmart/P&G partnership, leveraging its data network (remember the opening quote?), Walmart provided P&G with real-time purchase data from each of its stores. That is, anytime a box of Pampers or a carton of Tide detergent are sold at any Walmart store, P&G receives an electronic notification. This near-real-time knowledge of actual consumer demand enabled P&G to optimize its production schedules and its supply chain operations. As a consequence, P&G's own costs decreased and P&G became willing to supply Walmart for less money than it charged other customers who could not engage in continuous replenishment. In other words, P&G supplier opportunity cost for dealing with Walmart, and only Walmart, decreased thanks to this data-sharing initiative. On the other end of the value continuum, where Walmart serves the end consumer, no change occurred, as customers didn't need to know about continuous replenishment or see any changes in what Walmart offered, and Walmart still commanded the same customer willingness to pay for its service.

Some Considerations About the Analysis of Added Value

The above discussion of the analysis of added value and the above examples suggest a few important concluding remarks.

Value Is in the Eye of the Customer   We define customer willingness to pay as the maximum amount of money that a customer is willing to give the firm to acquire its products or services. Unless there is a market for the innovation, no value has been generated.

Customer Willingness to Pay Is Not the Same as Price   Price is a consequence of a negotiation between the firm and the customer, depending on the available information and the degree of competition in the market. Note, however, that a firm that is able to create higher customer willingness to pay does not need to charge higher prices to benefit. Imagine two firms vying for customer business and charging the same price. If one is able to command a slightly higher customer willingness to pay, for example by having a stronger brand, it will get the customer's business.[7]

---

[7]Note that in some industries (for example, the lodging or airline industries), where the cost structure involves significant fixed costs and small variable costs, attracting more customers, even if at the same price as the competition, can result in significant profitability gains. This is because any revenue from incremental business will mostly flow through to the bottom line.

Value Can Be Tangible or Intangible   Our cake-making example suggests that the coffee shop is willing to buy your cake because they can resell it and turn a profit. We buy clothes because of the tangible outcomes they provide (e.g., warmth). However, we also buy them for looks, style, fashion, for the way they make us feel, to fit within a certain group, to support a particular manufacturer, and so on. All these "intangible" drivers of value are as important as the tangible ones. As much as possible, goodwill, brand effects, loyalty, and all other intangible drivers of value should be estimated and measured. Techniques such as focus groups and market research are typically used to do this.

Creation of Value Is Not Appropriation   Beyond increasing customer willingness to pay, there is much opportunity to create added value by focusing on suppliers' opportunity cost and by providing advantages to suppliers to work with the firm. Yet, as a firm, it is crucial only to create value that you can appropriate (i.e., added value). Creating value can be done even in circumstances when this value can be appropriated by others (often customers). You must have added value (which is unique to your firm) to be sure to appropriate it.

Competitive Advantage and Added Value Are Closely Related   While the framework for the analysis of added value is a simplification of reality as it assumes perfect information of all entities involved and the absence of switching costs, it highlights what a firm must do to gain a competitive advantage. True competitive advantage is a function of added value (see Sidebar 1).

SIDEBAR 1: HOW TO PERFORM ADDED VALUE ANALYSIS

Depending on the specific characteristics of the initiative under investigation, the analysis of added value can be more or less straightforward. You should:

Clearly Define the Initiative and Understand What It Entails
The first step in the analysis requires that we are very clear about what the firm will do for customers or suppliers and what resources are necessary to create the product or perform the service being sold by identifying the intended value proposition.

Identify the Comparison
Because added value is defined in comparative terms, it is critical to identify a baseline comparison. This baseline can be the competitor's initiative or the firm's own offers—when the firm is innovating with products or services that improve on the current state of the art in the industry.

Estimate Customer Willingness to Pay
Estimating customer willingness to pay can be a very complex process requiring substantial approximation and research. In order to simplify and focus this process, it

helps to start by listing all of the positive customer willingness to pay drivers—defined as what the firm does, as part of its offer, to increase customer willingness to pay. Note that any initiative has both positive and negative effects. That is, any initiative entails trade-offs; as the firm does some things of value for its customers, it also forgoes doing other things. It is therefore critical to also surface these negative customer willingness to pay drivers and discount their effect.

Estimate Supplier Opportunity Cost
This analysis is similar to the one above, and includes both positive and negative change. When the initiative's main contribution to value creation is on the supplier opportunity cost side, supplier opportunity cost must be used. When the main effect of the initiative is on customer willingness to pay, then a simplifying assumption using firm cost as a proxy for supplier opportunity cost is acceptable.

Estimate Added Value
With the above information in hand, you can measure added value and begin to draw value appropriation considerations.

Note, however, that the analysis of added value is focused on the short term and tells us nothing about the long-term resilience (e.g., resistance to erosion) of the firm's competitive advantage. An analysis of sustainability, the focus of Chapter 9, is the analytical tool needed to evaluate if any added value we create can be appropriated over time. As we learned in this chapter, it is not enough to be able to create value; we must be able to appropriate it. To do so we must protect any added value we created from erosion by competitors.

STRATEGIC INFORMATION SYSTEMS

Without a doubt, information systems and technology engender a plentitude of confusing lingo, technical terms, and acronyms—a problem compounded by the crowds of half-prepared, fast-talking individuals using terminology incorrectly. In Chapter 2 we were very careful in defining what an information system (IS) is, and in differentiating it from information technology (IT). We defined an information system as a sociotechnical system that includes IT, processes, people, and organizational structure.

The distinction between IT and IS is a critical prerequisite to understanding the strategic potential of information systems, and the role that information technologies play in the creation and appropriation of added value. This distinction also shows why the firm that focuses solely on IT investments to become competitive (i.e., blindly purchasing computer systems) is wasting its money. IT investments are only appropriate within a larger IS design and only as components of information systems.

Definition: Strategic Information Systems

As you may intuitively expect, not all information systems that an organization seeks to design, develop, and use may be strategic. The foremost objective of strategy in for-profit business ventures is to achieve and sustain superior financial performance. To do so the firm uses its resources to create value by either reducing supplier opportunity cost or by increasing the customers' willingness to pay for its product and services, or both. A firm achieves competitive advantage when it is able to generate added value by creating a unique and positive difference between customers' willingness to pay and supplier opportunity costs. At that point, the firm is in a position to appropriate, in the form of profits, the added value it has created. In short, competitive strategy can be defined as the art and science of *being unique*.

We define *strategic information systems* as those information systems used to support or shape the competitive strategy of an organization. More succinctly, with the terminology discussed in this chapter, we can define *strategic information systems* as those that enable the creation and appropriation of value.

Strategic or Not? Depends on the Purpose Strategic information systems are not defined by their functionality or the organizational function they support (as categorized in Chapter 3), but are instead defined in terms of their objectives and the purpose they serve (e.g., improving the firm's competitive standing). Consider two examples from American Airlines:

- The SABRE reservation system, typically considered to be the foremost example of a strategic information system, was originally created as an airline seats inventory system (i.e., a transaction processing system).

Figure 7.10 eBay dominates the online auction market

Source: Imagebroker/Glow Images

■ The SMARTS system, also considered a tool that enabled American Airlines to gain a competitive advantage, was expressly designed to enable AA regional sales representatives to craft highly tailored incentive schemes for travel agents. SMARTS was an analytical tool (i.e., a decision support system).

No Need for Proprietary IT Contrary to conventional wisdom, strategic information systems do not have to rely on proprietary technology. eBay, Inc. has provided the starkest example of this rule (Figure 7.10). eBay has dominated the online auction market since its inception using commonly available technology—namely, Internet technologies and the Web.

A simple look at a competitor's auction site (Figure 7.11) shows remarkable similarities, and that the competitor offers comparable functionalities. eBay deploys little in the way of proprietary IT, and its technology has been duplicated by competitors. However, such replication of the

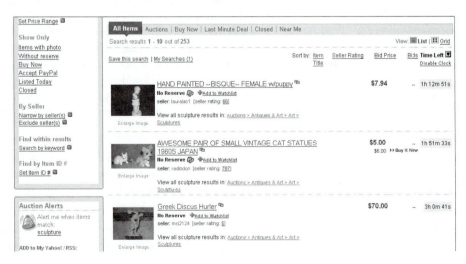

Figure 7.11 Yahoo's auction site (now discontinued)

technology is not enough, as it is the whole of eBay's initiative, and its information system, that underpins the firm's value-creating strategy and determines its added value. As we discuss more fully in Chapter 9, replicating the IT at the core of defendable strategic information systems is often a useless move.

Strategic versus Tactical Information Systems The definition of strategic information systems that we use is helpful in discriminating and identifying the many systems that are not strategic. These are systems that do not position the firm to create added value, even though they are important (often crucial) for the business's operations. We refer to these as *tactical* information systems. Consider the following examples:

- All organizations that have salaried or hourly employees must pay them and maintain a complex set of records to compute tax withdrawals, accrued vacation time, sick leave, and so on. These software applications, typically called human resource systems, are critical for the smooth operation of organizations. Can you imagine working for a company that consistently sent you a paycheck with errors? You'd be looking for another job fast! Human resource systems are critical. Yet they are not strategic. They typically do not enable the creation of added value—rare is the firm that offers a unique value proposition based on its ability to correctly cut paychecks!

- A restaurant's primary information system, anchored by its point of sale (POS) software, is used to manage reservations, seating, order taking and delivery, and billing. Clearly, most modern restaurants could not operate as effectively without such a system. Yet POSs are generally tactical in nature, not strategic, because they rarely allow the restaurant to create unique value.

- Similarly, no matter how well it is run, an e-mail system is unlikely to be the foundation of a strategic information system, and the same argument can be made for productivity software such as Microsoft Word and Excel, no matter how advanced their features may be.

No modern organization could run without e-mail and productivity software such as Microsoft Excel. Yet it is important to recognize that, as vital as they are, these systems are not strategic, and implementing or upgrading tactical systems will not create competitive advantage.

IT-Dependent Strategic Initiatives

As a general or functional manager, you may often propose new initiatives that need information systems and IT to be enacted. You will also be called upon to help in the analysis, design, and development of strategic information systems early in your career. As a graduate of a management program, you will be paid for your analytical and decision-making abilities. This will likely include being involved with strategic information systems decisions.

In this capacity, you will be focusing on specific projects and initiatives. We use the notion of *IT-dependent strategic initiatives* in this book to refer to identifiable competitive moves and projects that enable the creation of added value, and that rely heavily on the use of IT to be successfully implemented. IT-dependent strategic initiatives have three defining characteristics:

Initiative IT-dependent strategic initiatives consist of specific projects, with clear boundaries that define what the initiative is designed to achieve, as well as what it is designed to do and not do. For example, a freight shipper's package tracking initiative has very clear boundaries. It is designed to allow customers to gain visibility with respect to the current location of their parcels by logging onto a Web site. Tracking tools for online transactions are now available in lots of industries—you can even track your pizza as it is being made and delivered (Figure 7.12)!

Figure 7.12   Domino's Pizza tracking website

Strategic   The firm introduces IT-dependent strategic initiatives with the definite objective of producing new value that the firm can appropriate. In other words, the firm seeks to create competitive advantage through the initiative. The freight shipper's package-tracking initiative, originally pioneered by Federal Express in the mid-1990s, was primarily designed to improve customer service (and therefore customer willingness to pay). Note, however, that, as it happened, this initiative also had the potential to shift much of the current volume of tracking inquiries away from call-center operators and onto the Web, thereby reducing firm cost as well.

IT Dependent   IT-dependent strategic initiatives cannot be feasibly created and executed without the use of information technology at their core. Note that this IT core need not use cutting-edge or new breakthrough technologies, as was the case at FedEx, where the technology core of the initiative was certainly not of the bleeding-edge sort. While the Internet and the Web were relatively new to the shipping public in the mid-1990s, the technology at their core had been around for over twenty years. FedEx's package-tracking initiative is clearly IT dependent, as it would not be feasible for the freight shipper to heavily promote a call-center-based package-tracking system due to the high costs of call-center operations versus online automated tracking systems.

Examples of IT-dependent strategic initiatives abound in modern businesses, and include some of the most important and most recent trends: ERP-enabled business integration, supply chain management, customer relationship management, electronic commerce, and electronic business initiatives. However, as we see in the FedEx example above, IT-dependent strategic initiatives can also have a much more limited scope, including projects such as introducing Internet cafés on cruise ships, online retailers creating recommender systems (e.g., Amazon), or start-ups leveraging the widespread mobile platform to promote flexible group buying (e.g., GroupOn).

IT-Dependent Strategic Initiatives Not IT Investments   The notion of the IT-dependent strategic initiative is a critical one to plan for the use and management of strategic information systems. Using this definition forces us to shift attention away from investments in technology, and to recognize that IT investments can only pay off if they are part of a larger and cohesive information system design. It is the ability of the IT-dependent strategic initiative to create added value that we must focus on, not the uniqueness or innovativeness of the technology at its core. Thus, IT-dependent strategic initiatives do not simply consist of the building of a computer system or application that, allegedly, generates competitive advantage until it is successfully replicated; rather, they consist of the configuration of an activity system, dependent on IT at its core, that fosters the creation and appropriation of economic value.

 ## SUMMARY

This chapter provides the background for understanding strategic information systems decisions by discussing fundamental concepts and analytical frameworks. Specifically, in this chapter we introduced the notion of value creation and appropriation.

■ Economic value is created when some input resources that have a value of $x in their next best utilization are transformed into outputs for which customers are willing to pay $x + $v.

■ The value thus created is partitioned amongst those entities involved in its creation: a firm, its suppliers, and its customers—a process known as value appropriation.

■ A firm is able to appropriate that portion of the total value created that would be lost if the firm did not partake in the exchange—a figure we termed added value.

- Strategic information systems are those that are designed and developed to create and appropriate value. They differ from tactical information systems, which are those systems that, while often critical for the firm's operations, do not enable the creation of distinctive value.

- IT-dependent strategic initiatives consist of identifiable competitive moves and projects that enable the creation of added value, and that rely heavily on the use of information technology to be successfully implemented. They should be the focus of the search for new value creation.

- General and functional managers, because of their understanding of the firm's processes and customer needs, take center stage in the identification and analysis of opportunities to create value with information systems. When doing so, they should focus on IT-dependent strategic initiatives rather than taking a narrow focus on IT investments.

This chapter laid the foundation for the analysis of value creation and appropriation of IT-dependent strategic initiatives. In the next chapter we examine frameworks and analytical tools designed to help you envision, and take advantage of, opportunities to deploy IT-dependent strategic initiatives.

STUDY QUESTIONS

1. Explain the value creation process. How does a firm contribute to the creation of economic value?

2. Provide two examples of firms that you think have been able to create value using information systems. The first one should be a firm that has done so mainly by focusing on customer willingness to pay. The second one should be a firm that has done so mainly by focusing on supplier opportunity cost.

3. Think about the last time you bought something that you felt was "a great deal." Why did you think the product or service was such a great deal? Do you believe that the transaction was considered "great" by the firm from which you acquired the product or service? Why or why not? Explain using the framework of value creation and appropriation.

4. What is the difference between value creation and value appropriation? Why is this difference important?

5. Provide an example of a well-known firm that you think currently has added value. Explain your example using added value analysis.

6. Define the concept of strategic information systems and provide an example.

7. Define the concept of tactical information systems and provide an example.

8. Define the concept of IT-dependent strategic initiative and provide an example.

FURTHER READINGS

1. Brandenburger, A. M., and Stuart, H. W. (1996). "Value-Based Business Strategy." *Journal of Economics and Management Strategy*, (5:1), pp. 5–24.
2. Brandenburger, A. M. and Nalebuff, B. J. (1997). *Co-Opetition: A Revolution Mindset That Combines Competition and Cooperation*, Currency Doubleday.
3. Porter, M. E. "What Is Strategy?" *Harvard Business Review*, November/December 1996.

GLOSSARY

- **Added value:** That portion of the total value created that would be lost if the firm did not partake in the exchange.
- **Competitive advantage:** The condition where a firm engages in a unique transformation process and has been able to distinguish its offerings from those of competitors. When a firm has achieved a position of competitive advantage, it is able to make above average profits.
- **Customer willingness to pay:** The maximum amount of money the firm's customers are willing to spend in order to obtain the firm's product.

- **Firm cost:** The actual amount of money the firm disbursed to acquire the resources needed to create its product or service.
- **IT-dependent strategic initiatives:** Identifiable competitive moves and projects that enable the creation of added value, and that rely heavily on the use of information technology to be successfully implemented (i.e., they cannot feasibly be enacted without investments in IT).
- **Strategic information systems:** Information systems that are designed to support or shape the competitive strategy of an organization. Those information systems that enable the creation and appropriation of value.
- **Supplier opportunity cost:** The minimum amount of money suppliers are willing to accept to provide the firm with the needed resources.

- **Tactical information systems:** Systems that do not position the firm to create added value. In other words, they do not enable distinctive initiatives that allow the firm to create unique economic value.
- **Transformation process:** The set of activities the company engages in to convert inputs purchased from suppliers, into outputs to be sold to customers.
- **Total value created:** The difference between customer willingness to pay and supplier opportunity cost.
- **Value appropriation:** The process by which the total value created in the transaction is split among all the entities who contributed to creating it (i.e., suppliers, the firm, and the customer).
- **Value creation:** The process by which new economic value is generated through a transformation process.

8

Value Creation with Information Systems

What You Will Learn in This Chapter

In the previous chapter we laid the foundations for our discussion of strategic information systems and IT-dependent strategic initiatives. In this chapter we continue the discussion by focusing on theoretical and analytical models that have been developed over the years to identify opportunities to create value with IT, and to design and develop value adding IT-dependent strategic initiatives.
Specifically, in this chapter you will learn:

1. How to think in a disciplined fashion about the question of value creation with information systems resources.

2. How to use traditional models of value creation with information systems and information technology to identify and craft IT-dependent strategic initiatives, including industry analysis, value chain analysis, and the customer service life cycle framework.

3. How to incorporate information resources in your search for opportunities for value creation using emerging frameworks, including the virtual value chain and the customer data strategies framework.

4. How to devise and select initiatives that create value using organizational data.

MINI-CASE: IPHONE ORDERING AT DOMINO'S UK

On Wednesday, January 5, 2011, *The Guardian* reported that Domino's, the international pizza delivery chain, had "once again smashed City expectations" showing a "double digit growth in sales."[1] There were many reasons for this success, but the article pointed to the role of online ordering, which now accounted for a third of total orders. In September 2010 the firm had also launched its iPhone app, which, according to Domino's, had been instrumental in the growth effort. Chris Moore—the CEO of Domino's Pizza UK & IRL, plc—commented in the article: "We have set ourselves some challenging targets to beat in the coming year, but we believe that a great product, supported by exemplary customer service and innovative marketing, will continue to recruit new and retain existing customers in 2011."

The iPhone app automatically detected the Domino's location closest to the customer (Figure 8.1). Once logged into the application they could either select from

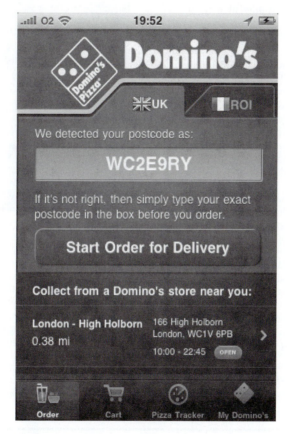

Figure 8.1   Domino's iPhone app welcome screen

---

[1]Wearden, G. (2011). "iPhone app helps Domino's smash sales forecast," *The Guardian* (Available online 01/05/2011 at http://www.guardian.co.uk/business/2011/jan/05/dominospizza-fooddrinks).

continued

Figure 8.2   Customers have playful ways to choose their toppings

Figure 8.3   Domino's order tracking feature

the standard menu or from an available list of specials from the chosen location. They could also request a custom order by selecting pie size, crust type, toppings (Figure 8.2) and any other possible personalization (e.g., extra sauce). One of the advantages of the iPhone ordering application is that it did not require the customer to talk to a restaurant employee on duty. As a consequence the app enabled customers to place orders, even during store closing times, and schedule delivery for a specific date/time.

James Millett, multimedia manager at Domino's Pizza, emphasized the usefulness of the iPhone ordering system. However he also stressed the need for brand consistency: "While the main function was ordering, it was essential the app also included other features to maintain the brand's funky, playful characteristics."[2]

Upon completing their order, customers would pay and then could track the progress of their pizza up to the delivery stage, through the preparation, backing, and quality assurance steps (Figure 8.3).

DISCUSSION QUESTIONS

1. Do you believe that Domino's iPhone ordering is an example of an IT-dependent strategic initiative? Explain.

2. Do you believe that this initiative has the potential to create added value? Substantiate your answer.
3. Do you believe that the Domino's iPhone ordering initiative improves customer service? How?
4. What would you do next if you were put in charge of the initiative?

---

[2]Kats, R. (2011). "Domino's Pizza iPhone app generates more than $1.3M in sales," *Mobile Commerce Daily* (Available online 01/12/2011 at http://www.mobilecommercedaily.com/2011/01/12/domino%E2%80%99s-pizza-iphone-app-generates-more-than-1 million-in-sales).

INTRODUCTION

We concluded Chapter 6 by showing how the strategic information systems planning process is designed to create an overall context for information systems decision making. The planning documents conclude with the identification of strategic initiatives. In Chapter 7 we laid the foundation for our discussion of strategic information systems and IT-dependent strategic initiatives by explaining how you can analyze the impact of such initiatives. In this chapter we get to the heart of the matter and introduce the frameworks and analytical models that information systems professionals, as well as general and functional managers, use to identify opportunities, and to design and evaluate IT-dependent strategic initiatives.

TRADITIONAL MODELS OF VALUE CREATION WITH IT

Considerable attention began to be devoted to the strategic potential of information technology in the mid-1980s. It was at this time that, prompted by a critical mass of success stories and case studies, academic researchers and consulting firms began to systematically explore and document the role of information systems and IT beyond automation of work and the creation of efficiencies. The use of IT as a "competitive weapon" became fertile ground for research and practice alike.

Prompting this attention toward the strategic role of information systems was the emergence of influential strategic models focusing on competitive positioning and competitive advantage. Three analytical tools were introduced or adapted to the search for strategic information systems opportunities:

- Industry analysis
- Value chain analysis
- Customer service life cycle analysis

Industry Analysis

The industry analysis framework is grounded in the basic notion that different industries offer different potential for profitability.[3] A simple analysis lends support to this assumption (see Figure 8.4). Based on this idea, the industry analysis framework suggests that industry differences can be analyzed *a priori* by managers using an analytical framework now known as the five forces framework (see Figure 8.5). Armed with the results of this analysis, executives can decide whether to enter an industry or forgo investment.

More importantly, for an organization that is already a player in a given industry, such analysis can offer guidance as to what to do to increase the appeal (i.e., average profit potential) of the industry. Thus, from a simply analytical framework, the industry analysis model becomes a prescriptive one. It is in this capacity that it can be used to surface opportunities to introduce IT-dependent strategic initiatives.

---

[3]Porter, M. E. (1980). *Competitive Strategy: Techniques for Analyzing Industries and Competitors*, Free Press, New York.

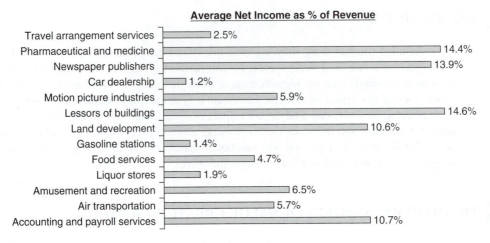

Figure 8.4 Industry differences in average profitability

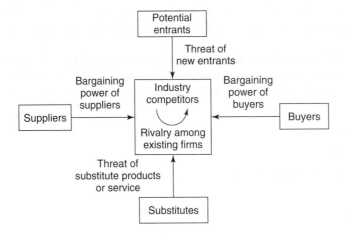

Figure 8.5 Industry analysis

Five Competitive Forces The industry analysis framework, often referred to as the five forces model, identifies five structural determinants of the potential for profitability of the average firm in a given industry. Each is discussed next.

The Threat of New Entrants This force represents the extent to which the industry is open to entry by new competitors, or whether significant barriers to entry make it so that the existing firms need not worry about competition from outside.

Consider car manufacturing, for example. Car manufacturing is characterized by a substantial need for capital investments in research and development, as well as a need for significant production capacity. Moreover, the automotive industry is characterized by strong economies of scale, such that it is important to produce a large number of vehicles to stay competitive. For these reasons, the auto industry is characterized by a low threat of new competitors due to strong barriers to entry.

Figure 8.6   The Sony Walkman

The Threat of Substitute Products or Services   This force represents the extent to which the products or services marketed by the firm in the industry of interest are subject to potential substitution by different products or services that fulfill the same customer needs.

For example, new products such as the iPod and digital music files, introduced by firms traditionally in the computer industry, are rapidly substituting CD players and other devices traditionally offered by consumer electronics firms. In a clear sign of the times Sony announced in October 2010 that it would stop manufacturing the iconic Walkman cassette player (Figure 8.6). Music cassette players have now been fully substituted by CDs and MP3s!

The Bargaining Power of Buyers   This force represents the extent to which customers of those organizations in the industry have the ability to put downward pressure on prices. Highly concentrated buyers and low switching costs (see Chapter 9) typically conspire to increase the bargaining power of buyers.

Consider, for example, a company like Walmart, which, because of huge sales in its more than 9,000 stores worldwide, can purchase the bulk of a manufacturer's production capacity. With its size and focus on low prices, Walmart is famous for influencing prices set by its suppliers—some would even say dictating prices to them!

The Bargaining Power of Suppliers   This force represents the extent to which those individuals and firms who sell production inputs to the organizations in the industry have the ability to maintain high prices. This force is the same as the previous one, where the firms in the industry of interest have taken the role of the buyer rather than the seller.

As a future supplier of labor resources, you should pay significant attention to this force. If you can put yourself in a position of bargaining power toward the industry of your interest (for example, by choosing to concentrate in a field of study that is highly sought after but in short supply), you stand to reap significant benefits in terms of salary.

The Rivalry among Existing Competitors   This force represents the extent to which fierce battling for position and aggressive competition occur in the industry. The degree of competition

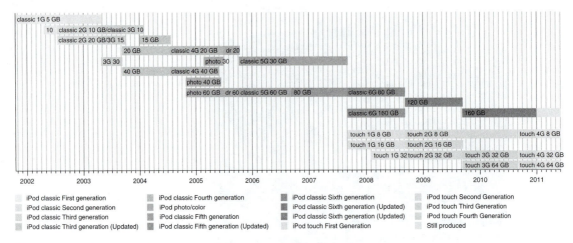

Figure 8.7 Consumer electronics—A hypercompetitive industry

in an industry can vary dramatically. The term *hypercompetition* refers to industries character-ized by fierce rivalry among existing firms and a very rapid rate of innovation leading to fast obsolescence of any competitive advantage and a consequent need for a fast cycle of innova-tion. The search engine industry may be an example, as is the consumer electronics industry (Figure 8.7).

Industry Analysis and the Role of Information Systems   Researchers and consultants who have adapted industry analysis to the search for opportunities to introduce IT-dependent strategic initiatives suggest looking for ways to use information systems to affect one or more of the industry forces, thereby tipping it to the firm's advantage. The following are some of the questions that are typically asked:

Can the Use of IT Raise or Increase Barriers to Entry in the Industry?   Investments in information systems may be such that they reduce the threat of new entrants. Consider, for example, the need for an automated teller machine (ATM) network in the banking industry (Figure 8.8). Entry into the banking industry nowadays requires access to a network of ATMs and, increasingly, online banking facilities. Likewise, access to the lodging industry requires access to a computerized central reservation system (CRS) and a substantial number of interfaces to the plethora of traditional and emerging distribution channels.

Can the Use of IT Decrease Suppliers' Bargaining Power?   With the emergence of the Internet and its related technologies as viable business tools, examples abound of information systems that have contributed to shift power away from suppliers and toward buyers. Con-sider, for example, Alibaba (Figure 8.9), the sourcing, procurement, and expertise provider that enables companies to easily access global suppliers. Alibaba enables organizations to dramati-cally increase their bargaining power with suppliers by reducing the search costs for identifying qualified suppliers.

Can the Use of IT Decrease Buyers' Bargaining Power?   As much as the Internet has helped firms strengthen their bargaining position toward suppliers, it has also reduced their bargaining

Figure 8.8   Automatic teller machines, ubiquitous in the banking industry

Figure 8.9   Global sourcing through Alibaba (Image courtesy of Alibaba.com.)

power toward customers. Just as companies can rapidly shop for alternatives when looking for production inputs, so can their customers. Yet some opportunities to strengthen relationships with customers, thus reducing their incentive to shop around, still exist.

Consider travel intermediaries like Orbitz.com. While competitors are literally one click away, by storing personal preferences (e.g., preferred airlines), personal data (e.g., frequent flier

Figure 8.10   Example of one-click buying button   (*Source*: C. Gray/F1 ONLINE/Glow)

miles), and billing information, travel intermediaries can levy switching costs and reduce their customers' bargaining power. This approach was made popular by Amazon's 1-click buying, an innovation for which the firm even received a process patent in 1999 (Figure 8.10).

Can the Use of IT Change the Basis of Industry Competition?   The introduction of a new information system by a firm, whether an incumbent or a new entrant, sometimes spurs a revolution that forces competitors to take notice and react. A stark example of this dynamic was presented by the advent of online retailing in the mid-1990s.

When Amazon.com burst onto the scene, with its ability to offer huge selection and high levels of customer service without a single store, shock waves reverberated in the retail sector. Firms such as Amazon that seized the opportunity presented by the Internet to sell direct to consumers trained consumers to self-serve in ways unheard of before and changed forever the notion of what it means to be a retailer. Today, it would be a grave mistake for any large retailer to neglect the online channel of distribution. We can find similar examples in online banking and throughout the travel and tourism sector.

Value Chain

While useful in identifying potential opportunities to improve the profitability of the industry and suggesting ways in which managers can deploy information systems to neutralize or minimize the unattractive features of an industry, much of the potential for the employment of strategic information systems concerns intra-industry competition. In other words, much of the time that you, as general or functional managers, will be spending analyzing opportunities to deploy strategic information systems will be with respect to the ability to create added value. Thus, you will not worry so much about average industry performance; rather, given the industry that you are competing in, you will seek to outperform your competitors by using information systems to create added value and competitive advantage.

In Chapter 7 we stated that value is created when a firm employs its transformation process to use resources that have a value of $x in their next best use, and to generate a product or service that customers are willing to pay $x + $v for. If what the firm does is unique, such that no competitor is able to offer comparable value, the firm creates added value and has achieved a position of competitive advantage. But what does the firm's "transformation process" look like? How do these input resources become the final product or service that customers pay for?

Primary and Support Activities   The classic framework that has been used to logically represent a firm's transformation process is the value chain (Figure 8.11).[4] The value chain model maps the set of economic activities that a firm engages in and groups them into two sets: primary activities and support activities.

---

[4]Porter, M. E. (1985). *Competitive Advantage: Creating and Sustaining Superior Performance*, New York, NY: Free Press.

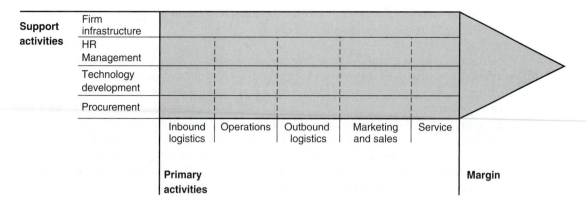

Figure 8.11   Value chain framework

Primary Activities   Primary activities represent the firm's actions that are directly related to value creation. These are the activities that define the firm's unique transformation process, such that they are typically performed by all firms engaged in the same, or similar, line of business. The classic value chain identifies five primary activities: inbound logistics, operations, outbound logistics, marketing and sales, and service. It is the execution of these activities that enables the transformation of the input resources in final products or services—and, as a consequence, the creation of value.

Let's return to the automotive industry. We can think of the car manufacturing transformation process in terms of these five primary activities. A car manufacturer needs to procure and receive component parts (i.e., inbound logistics), have assembly lines that take these components and put them together in the various car models (i.e., operations), deliver the vehicles to the distribution channel and its dealership network (i.e., outbound logistics), create a demand for its make and models (i.e., marketing and sales), and ensure that any problems with its products can be addressed by a network of repair shops (i.e., service).

Support Activities   Support activities represent the firm's actions that, while not directly related to the transformation process, are nevertheless necessary to enable it. These activities do not define the organization's unique transformation process, which is to say that they are typically performed by a wide range of firms offering diverse products and services. The classic value chain identifies four support activities: firm infrastructure, HR management, technology development, and procurement.

Take HR management, for example. Any firm that relies on labor resources, from car manufacturers to hospitals, must be able to recruit, train, evaluate, pay, promote, fire, and generally manage the labor force. Yes, these activities do not directly impact the product (e.g., the car traveling down the assembly line). However, no firm without an HR function would be in business for long!

As we discussed in Chapter 7, competitive advantage stems from the ability of the firm to transform input resources into a product or service that is both valuable and unique—thereby having created added value. Thus, in order to have a competitive advantage, the firm must perform a different set of activities than competitors, or it must perform the same set of activities but in a different (and value adding) manner. Information systems and IT have a long tradition of enabling such unique transformation processes.

Value Chain Analysis and the Role of Information Systems   Using the value chain to identify opportunities to deploy IT-dependent strategic initiatives requires managers to identify, understand, and analyze the activities the firm performs so that they can be enhanced or transformed using IS resources. This approach is grounded in the assumption that a firm's value chain has both physical and information processing components, and that information is a critical enabler of the firm's activities. Thus, the search for the strategic deployment of IT should focus on the role that information technologies can play in evolving and enhancing current activities.

An example is offered by an IBM commercial. A malicious-looking character is seen walking the aisles of a supermarket stuffing various goods into the pockets of his trench coat under the suspicious eye of a security guard (Figure 8.12). As he walks out of the store, apparently without paying, he is called to by the guard, who, after some suspense-inducing delay, says, "Sir! You forgot your receipt."

This is an example of how the grocery store checkout process may change in the future using radiofrequency identification (RFID) chips embedded in everyday goods. If this vision comes to bear, grocery stores no longer will have checkout lines. Instead we will simply walk out the door after making our selections and our bank account or credit card will be charged with the full amount of our purchases. In this case the checkout process is radically transformed, leading to substantial efficiency improvements and creating the potential for new initiatives (e.g., tracking household purchases over time).

The Value Network   Another insight that emerged from the introduction of value chain analysis is that a firm has relationships both upstream and downstream. In other words, the firm's own value chain exists in a larger value network that comprises the firm's suppliers upstream and the firm's customers downstream (Figure 8.13). The points of contact between these separate value chains are called linkages, and they offer significant opportunities for the deployment of IT-dependent strategic initiatives.

Figure 8.12   (*Source*: John Dowland/Altopress/NewsCom)

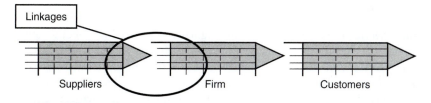

Figure 8.13   Linkages in the value network

For example, the inbound logistics activities of your firm can be thought of as an extension of the outbound logistics activities of your suppliers. Recognizing these linkages enables firms to create partnerships and develop interorganizational systems that may benefit all parties involved. Continuous replenishments, the initiative pioneered by Walmart and Procter & Gamble and described in Chapter 7, is a classic example.

A Word of Caution   Managerial frameworks are designed to map and simplify the complexity of real organizations in order to enable a disciplined analysis of complicated phenomena. In the case of the value chain model, the objective is to help you as a manager to identify opportunities to change the transformation process your organization engages in and thus uncover ways to create new value. It is therefore critical to recognize that a general framework, like the value chain, often needs to be adapted to the specific realities of your firm.

For example, the original model portrayed in Figure 8.11 is clearly best suited to represent the realities of manufacturing companies where raw materials and component parts are transformed into final products that need to be marketed, sold, and later serviced. Service businesses (e.g., consulting and law firms, banks, entertainment venues, laundry services, restaurants) work very differently and, while they also have to complete primary and secondary activities, the activities they perform and the sequence of events can be very different. Figure 8.14, for example, portrays the value chain model mapping the sequence of primary activities as they occur in a hotel or resort.

It is imperative that when using the value chain, or any other managerial framework, you do not simply apply it "as is," but, using your in-depth knowledge of the specific firm you are analyzing, you adapt the model to your needs. After all, as supplier of managerial talent, this is what you are paid to do!

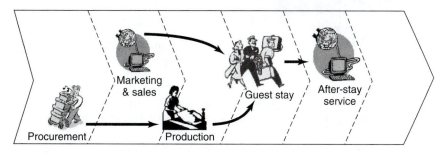

Figure 8.14   Sample value chain of a lodging outfit

Customer Service Life Cycle[5]

The customer service life cycle (CSLC) was originally introduced as a tool to spur managerial thinking about the potential of advanced information technologies under the label of customer resource life cycle.[6] While the CSLC framework has a time-honored tradition, its fundamental premise that a firm can use information systems to create value by offering superior customer service has received new impetus with the commercialization of the Internet and the introduction of the Web as a viable business tool. As more and more organizations have been able to establish direct relationships with customers (see Chapter 5), the potential for new value creation through superior customer service has increased.

The CSLC breaks down the firm-customer relationship into thirteen stages, grouped into four primary phases; for each one it shows how you can craft IT-dependent strategic initiatives to respond to customers' needs and create economic value.

Four Phases The CSLC framework suggests that managers step into their customers' shoes and think about the needs and problems that customers experience at each of four major phases in their relationship with the firm: requirements, acquisition, ownership, and retirement (Figure 8.15).

During the requirements phase, the customer realizes the need for a specific product or service and begins to focus on its attributes. During the acquisition phase, the customer orders, pays for, and takes possession of the product or service. The next major phase is ownership; here the customer has the product or is receiving the service and must deal with issues regarding its efficient and effective use. The final phase is retirement, in which the customer may begin to think about buying again, trading in, or dismissing old products.

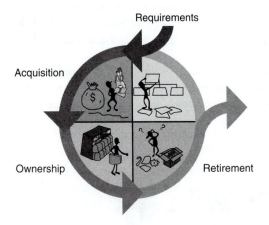

Figure 8.15 The customer service life cycle (CSLC)

---

[5]Portions of this section are adapted from Piccoli, G., Spalding, B. R., and Ives, B. (2001), "The Customer Service Life Cycle: A Framework for Internet Use in Support of Customer Service," *Cornell Hotel and Restaurant Administration Quarterly* (42:3), pp. 38–45.

[6]"The Information System as a Competitive Weapon," with G. P. Learmonth, *Communications of the ACM*, Vol. 27, No. 12 (December 1984), pp. 1193–1201.

Table 8.1   Customer service life cycle (CSLC) stages

Requirements

Establish requirements	Establish a need for the product or service
Specify	Determine the product or service attributes

Acquisition

Select Source	Determine where to obtain the product or service
Order	Order the product or service from a supplier
Authorize and pay for	Transfer funds or extend credit
Acquire	Take possession of the product or receive service
Evaluate and accept	Ensure that the product or service meets specifications

Ownership

Integrate	Add to an existing inventory or integrate with existing internal business processes
Monitor	Control access and use of the product or service
Upgrade	Upgrade the product or service if conditions change
Maintain	Repair the product as necessary

Retirement

Transfer or dispose	Move, return, or dispose of product or service
Account for	Monitor expenses related to the product or service

Thirteen Stages   Each of the four main phases is then further broken out into sub phases, or stages (Table 8.1). These thirteen stages represent typical needs that customers encounter when obtaining, using, and retiring a firm's product or service. The primary objective of the CSLC is to help management identify stages where their organization's customers are frustrated or underserved, and where the interaction can be improved through the use of the Internet or the deployment of IT-dependent strategic initiatives. As a creative planning framework, the CSLC is designed to stretch your thinking and help you view your business with a fresh perspective.

Note that the life cycle model covers the entire range of activities a customer goes through in identifying, acquiring, using, and owning a product or service. However, it is typically a subset of these thirteen stages that present particular challenges for the firm's customers—and therefore particular opportunity. Moreover, the stages that have the potential to yield the highest payoff will vary by customer segment, product, and over time.

Consider a firm that has recently developed an innovative new product. In this case the very first stage, establish requirements, may be ripe for innovation. Priceline.com, with its innovative model for purchasing airline tickets, hotel rooms, and other products, encountered early problems in educating both consumers and operators about its benefits. On the other hand, for a mature product competing in a fiercely competitive industry, the real potential may lie in managers' ability to differentiate their product and services by identifying unresolved customer problems—such as the need to effectively account for the total cost of ownership or use of the product or service.

Stage 1: Requirement   In the first stage of the CSLC, the customer identifies a need for the firm's product or service. In many cases, at this point in the life cycle the customer may not even be aware of the emerging desire, or may have a limited idea about what possible products

Figure 8.16 Site59 reinvented the travel acquisition process (*Source*: © Ron Chapple/Ron Chapple Stock/Corbis/Glow Images)

or services he or she needs. The ability to reach and communicate with a customer at this stage may enable the firm to gain his patronage.

Site59, the last minute weekend getaway site now part of Sabre holdings, billed itself as "your source for spontaneous escape and entertainment." It did so by cleverly positioning its offering in the requirement stage. You would tell Site59 what mood you were in and ask, "What should we do this weekend?" Site59 would respond with offers ranging from half-day suggestions as simple as going to visit your local museum, to an elaborate night out, including prepaid dinners and theater tickets (Figure 8.16). Site59 recognized that with more disposable income and less free time, customers appreciated novel suggestions that were prepackaged and ready to go.

Stage 2: Specify Once customers have established the need for a new product or service, they must specify the characteristics of that product or service in order to know which particular one to acquire. In the specification stage, customers select the product features that best suit their needs.

A nice example is offered by Nike, the sports apparel manufacturer, which allows prospective customers to customize many of the features of its sneakers through the NIKEiD initiative. Using the Internet to interact with customers in the specification stage is, of course, something that is now fairly common. Today consumers can purchase made-to-order personal computers, consumer electronics, and even clothes online.

Another example of providing superior service in the specify stage is offered by Homewood Suites, the extended stay brand of the Hilton Hotels family. Homewood Suites pioneered a program that enabled customers who booked online to see a complete floor-plan of the hotel in order to allow them to choose the specific room they wanted: near or far from elevators or

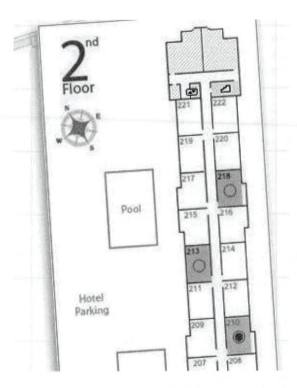

Figure 8.17 Selecting a specific room in the floor plan

vending machines, facing East (so as to be awoken with the rising sun) or West, to sip a drink while watching the sunset (Figure 8.17).

Stage 3: Select a Source   The Internet provides a new source for finding desired products, and one that can significantly reduce the vendor's distribution costs. The emergence of the Internet and the Web has created significant opportunity for new intermediaries in a wide range of industries to create value by focusing on this stage. Consider firms like MySimon.com that provide information and tips about buying popular products to attract traffic and then enable customers to rapidly find and rank purveyors of the chosen product.

Stage 4: Ordering   After selecting a source for their product or service, customers must order it. As with all other stages of the CSLC, the primary objective of the firm is to make it as easy as possible for clients to do business with it. This is often easy to do for returning customers, as certain elements of their second and subsequent orders typically are repeated from the first.

Wyndham Hotels and Resorts uses a dedicated application and the Internet to allow customers enrolled in its frequent guest program, Wyndham ByRequest, to configure rooms to their liking. Guests can select whether they want upper or lower floors, whether they want to be near or far from the elevator, even what kind of pillows they would like and what drinks or snacks they prefer to receive as welcome tokens. This customer service design has a number of potential far-reaching advantages and risks, yet it also helps to ensure that Wyndham differentiates itself at the ordering stage of the CSLC. If Wyndham can deliver the room as configured by customers, they are more likely to be satisfied.

Stage 5: Authorize and Pay For   Once customers have placed an order, they need to authorize and issue payment. Convenience and security are the determinants of customer service and satisfaction at this stage. Most firms that accept online orders enable clients to store payment method, shipping location, and preferences details for quick and easy future reordering. With the emergence of the mobile platform as a viable business instrument, many organizations are enabling payment through cellular phone to simplify their customers' lives.

Stage 6: Acquire   At this stage the customer takes possession of the product or begins to use the service. Some perishable or sensitive products may not be able to be shipped, while some information-based products or services may be delivered online directly. Information-based products are far more widespread than most of us realize. They include financial, medical, legal, and accounting services as well as airline tickets, reservations, music, education, books, software, magazines, games, films, and so on—a very sizable, and growing, percentage of the economy.

One of the most familiar products that have dramatically changed the traditional acquisition stage is the digital song. Consider Napster, for example. After its early days as an outlaw, Napster now offers a legal service enabling subscribers to gain access to its database of digital songs. The "song acquisition process," once confined to complete albums on physical CDs available for purchase in stores, is now available for individual tunes on a subscription basis from the comfort of your home (Figure 8.18).

Stage 7: Evaluate and Accept   After customers have acquired their new product or service, they may test it out to verify that it works as expected. This is particularly true for businesses

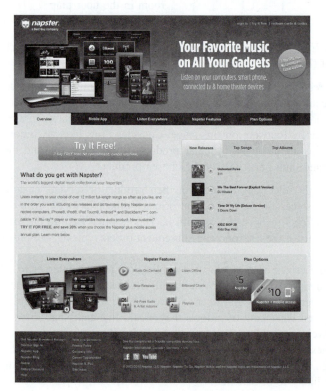

Figure 8.18 Napster music streaming (Napster logo and are used with the permission of Napster, LLC.)

purchasing equipment, but it is also the case for consumers purchasing big-ticket items, such as cars. When a very innovative product or service is introduced, customers need to be extensively educated about its features and how to maximize the benefits of its use. This is particularly important for products and services that require the customer to undergo a certain degree of process change.

Although the evaluate-and-accept process historically has taken place after purchase, we increasingly see firms in service- and information-based industries letting customers "try out" products prior to purchase. Examples include virtual tours, sample consulting reports, and demo software.

Stage 8: Integrate   Once the product or service is acquired and accepted for use, the customer must add it to his or her existing inventory of resources. Often customers must also adjust their internal business processes to take full advantage of the new product or service.

FedEx offers Ship Manager, a Web-based tool for the creation and editing of FedEx labels. Using Ship Manager, customers can develop an address book of frequent shipment receivers and seamlessly create and print package labels, and automatically price the shipment. Through Ship Manager, FedEx devised an IT-based solution to the challenge that customers face when they integrate the FedEx service with their existing operations.

Stage 9: Monitor Use and Behavior   Customers must ensure that resources remain in an acceptable state of operation while they are in use or during the time they receive service. Using the Internet, suppliers can provide customers with the facilities to simplify this monitoring stage. By reducing clients' effort in monitoring usage of the product or service, the provider may be able to command a higher price or simply create a tight bond that customers may find difficult or costly to forego.

Otis Elevators mastered this stage long ago. During the 1980s, Otis introduced self-monitoring equipment that reduced unavailability, service calls, and overall maintenance costs. The new version of this service, called eService, is now Web-based and allows customers to monitor their elevator system through a Web browser and place service calls as needed, 24 hours a day. Another example is offered by Facebook, as it is used by businesses that create a presence on the dominant social network. These organizations have access to Facebook Insight, a monitoring tool that enables them to assess how well they are engaging their customers and Facebook friends online (Figure 8.19).

Stage 10: Upgrade   When customers are using the product or service, it may become necessary to modify or improve it so that it will better fit their unique needs. As competition has heated up in the airline industry under continued pressure from low-cost carriers, the legacy airlines have attempted to differentiate service for their best customers. Many of them now offer preferential seating (for example, in exit rows) and automatic upgrades to their best customers, who can request upgrades and receive confirmation online (Figure 8.20).

Stage 11: Maintain   Helping the customer to analyze, diagnose, and repair the product or service, or suggesting solutions to problems as they occur, affords the firm many opportunities to take what would be a source of dissatisfaction and offer outstanding service.

The software industry has led the way in this area. Nowadays, upgrading apps is a seamless process, as our iPhones and iPads simply tell us that there is a new version available and we tap the screen to get it. But this process has a time honored tradition. Like most other programs, Microsoft Windows, the software program we all love to hate and the favorite target of hackers

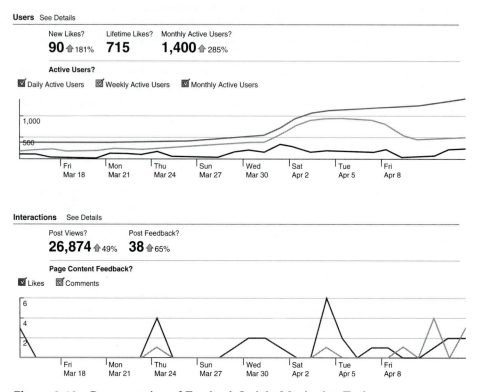

Figure 8.19   Representation of Facebook Insight Monitoring Tool

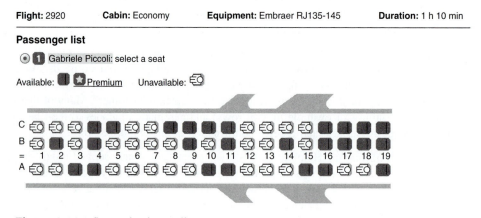

Figure 8.20   Seat selection online

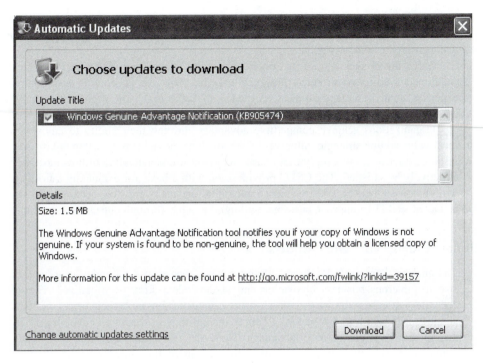

Figure 8.21   Patch management dialog box

and virus authors, has a facility that will automatically identify, download, and install security patches and bug fixes (Figure 8.21).

Stage 12: Transfer or Dispose   Customers will eventually transfer, resell, return, or dispose of the product or service. As this sometimes happens after a considerable amount of time, the original supplier may not be involved. In some instances this step may be complicated by regulation and restrictions (for example, with regard to disposal of old computer equipment).

Some organizations have made support of this process a staple of their offering, recognizing that a customer problem, the need to dispose of an item no longer needed, may be the start of another customer service life cycle. Dell is a firm that realized this very early on with its business clients. With its Dell asset recovery service, the company will pick up, within two days and at the client's site, any end-of-life machine, format its hard disk to eliminate all of the customer's data, and dispose of it according to current legal requirements. At the end of the process Dell sends a statement to the client detailing what was done and certifying that the equipment was disposed of correctly. Another great example of this strategy is offered by manufacturers of networked printers and copiers that can automatically re-order toner and ink cartridges when they are running out. Customers don't have to worry about the reordering process, while manufacturers ensure themselves a steady stream of consumable sales.

Stage 13: Account For   The final stage of the life cycle focuses on evaluation and accounting of the experience. This stage is particularly important, for example, for large corporations that are constantly attempting to better measure, manage, and control their travel and entertainment (T&E)

budgets. Given the complexity and magnitude of this process, an organization may willingly limit its portfolio of T&E suppliers in exchange for the ability to precisely monitor and control total spending while enforcing company policies.

Large travel agents, such as American Express, have long recognized this fact, and have developed Web-based products designed to offer tools for accounting and control of travel expenses to their large customers. Armed with these tools, the organization achieves better control of its travel budget while being able to use a larger pool of providers.

Organizations achieve competitive advantage through their ability to envision and implement value adding strategic initiatives. The most innovative ideas are often not the most costly or resource intensive, but simply those based on the best understanding of how customer needs can effectively be satisfied. The CSLC provides you with a basis for evaluating a firm's relationship with customers, benchmarking against competitors, and uncovering opportunities to use the Internet and advanced IT to improve customer willingness to pay through outstanding customer service.

Traditional Models, Not "Old" Models

The analytical frameworks discussed above have been in use for many years and have helped spawn numerous business innovation and IT-dependent strategic initiatives. They continue to accurately represent the way in which many companies organize their work, and therefore offer significant insight to those seeking to apply increasingly powerful and evolving IT in the never-ending quest for competitive advantage. Note that the value chain and CSLC are somewhat complementary. The value chain mostly focuses internally while the CSLC draws attention to the relationship between the firm and its customers.

 ## EMERGING FRAMEWORKS

The strategic role that information systems and IT can play in the modern organization was acknowledged over thirty years ago. However, recent trends have provided new impetus for the search for IT-dependent strategic initiatives. Perhaps the most important event was the commercialization of the Internet in 1993, an event that took the global network of computers from an unknown tool used by scientists and the military to business organizations. The Internet took the world by storm, and today many of us, both consumers and businesses, could not imagine working (and living?) without it.

Parallel to this upsurge of global networking was the continuance of trends we discussed in Chapter 1—the declining cost/performance ratio of computing equipment, the declining cost of storage, and the consequent widespread adoption of computing in consumer and business life. More recently, the Web 2.0 phenomenon (Chapter 5) and the rise to prominence of the mobile platform (Chapter 12) have continued to rejuvenate and strengthen the potential of information systems to contribute to business success.

One of the most successful users of IT for strategic advantage during the mid-'90s was Dell Computers, Inc. Michael Dell, founder and chief executive officer of the firm, in describing how his firm had been able to dominate the personal computer industry, said, "We substitute information for inventory and ship only when we have demand from real end consumers." While the fortunes of Dell, Inc. started to turn in the new millennium, this quote captures the power of information to create economic value and competitive advantage.

Inventory of parts in a manufacturing company are typically held to reduce uncertainty of demand and inbound logistics. Clearly this insurance against uncertainty comes at a cost—the cost of capital tied up, as well as the cost of write-offs for obsolete inventory. A firm that is able to gather and use superior information, and thereby reduce uncertainty, can limit its inventory stocks and run a leaner operation. This is all the more important in computer manufacturing, where technological innovation is rapid and the value of inventoried parts drops significantly when a new, more powerful component is developed (e.g., new generation microchips). Dell significantly reduced uncertainty by turning the production process on its head and gathering demand before building, rather than manufacturing computers that it then sold through a distribution channel.

Affordable, powerful, interconnected computers and cheap storage have created the backdrop for a number of new ways to create economic value with information systems. Traditional models were characterized by a view of information as a support resource to the production and transformation processes that the firm engages in. Thus, the search for value creation with IT-dependent strategic initiatives focused on using IT to affect physical activities. Recently developed frameworks, however, recognize that the data that modern organizations generate through their day-to-day operations may have significant value in their own right. These frameworks therefore are designed to help managers identify opportunities to harness information for value creation.

Virtual Value Chain

The virtual value chain (VVC) model[7] maps out the set of sequential activities that enable a firm to transform data in input into some output information that, once distributed to the appropriate user, has higher value than the original data (Figure 8.22). The virtual value chain builds on the generally understood value chain model. In a value chain, through a series of logically sequential activities, raw materials are transformed into products or services that the firm then distributes to customers (Figure 8.11). The process is a value adding one, such that the products or services being distributed have a higher value (and command higher customer willingness to pay) than the inbound materials and services.

The critical insight underpinning the VVC is that information is no longer just a support resource for physical activities, those described by the physical value chain model,[8] but can itself be treated as an input of a productive transformation process. In the physical value chain

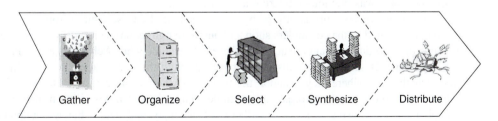

Gather   Organize   Select   Synthesize   Distribute

Figure 8.22 Virtual value chain framework

---

[7]Rayport, J. and J. Sviokla (1995). "Exploiting the Virtual Value Chain," *Harvard Business Review*, 73 (November–December 1995), pp. 75–85.

[8]In this section, to avoid confusion, we use the term physical value chain to refer to the traditional value chain model.

information is treated as a support element, designed to enable the physical activities of the value chain. The virtual value chain model uses the same logic, but recognizes information as the entity being transformed (the value of which is being enhanced) through the chain of activities. When fed through the activities of the virtual value chain, organizational data can be transformed into valuable insights, new processes, or new products or services.

Five Activities   The proponents of the virtual value chain identify five sequential activities that must be complete in order to harness its power:

- *Gather.* In the first activity the firm collects information from transaction processing systems and any other sources—both internal to the organization (e.g., orders received) and external (e.g., census data).

- *Organize.* In the second activity the firm stores the gathered data in a way that makes later retrieval and analysis simple and effective.

- *Select.* In the third activity users identify and extract the needed data from the data repository created in the previous step.

- *Synthesize.* In the fourth activity the firm packages the selected information so that it can be readily used by the intended consumer for the specific purpose to which it is directed (i.e., decision making, sales, etc.)

- *Distribute.* In the fifth activity the firm transfers the packaged information to its intended user or customer.

Three Classes of Strategic Initiatives   The proponents of the virtual value chain offer three classes of strategic initiatives that firms typically create once they adopt virtual value chain thinking: visibility, mirroring capabilities, and new customer relationships. These three classes of activities are in increasing order of complexity and uncertainty of results, with visibility being the most intuitively appealing and easy to justify financially, and new customer relationships being the toughest to sell to senior management. Note that the five value adding activities of the virtual value chain are performed with each one. What changes is the level of complexity and departure from the traditional way of doing business of the organization.

Visibility   The first application of the virtual value chain is termed visibility. In this case, the firm uses the sequential activities in the virtual value chain to "see through" organizational processes that it was previously treating as a black box.

An example of visibility is offered by online retailers. Because their customers' behavior is computer mediated as the consumers shop and purchase online, online retailers collect significant amounts of individual and aggregate data. These data include what Web pages a customer views, which Web pages seem to go unused, what path through the site customers are taking as they shop, whether and where they abandon the transaction, how customers react to advertising and banners, and so on. In other words, online retailers have significant visibility in their customers' shopping and purchasing processes, a degree of accuracy and detail that was unprecedented in brick and mortar stores. A similar example is offered by the not-for-profit educational site Khanacademy.org. Through Khanacademy students of all ages and classes can watch over 2,100 explanatory videos on a wide range of academic subjects. They can then practice the skills

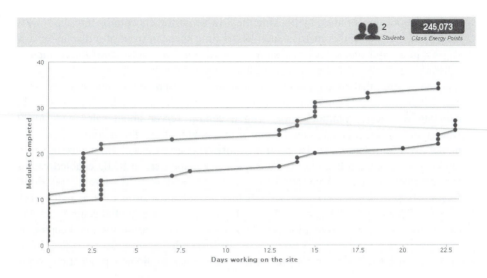

Figure 8.23   Sample progression through mathematics modules in Khanacademy

they have learned using engaging online test banks. As students practice and progress in their understanding, the computer records their behaviors. All kinds of metrics, from what exercises they complete and how fast, to what questions they have difficulty with and what topics they master, are recorded. The results are available to teachers (or coaches, as they are called in Khanacademy) to review (Figure 8.23). Armed with this superior visibility in their pupil's learning progression, coaches can take precise corrective action to help their students master the material.

The power of visibility strategies is not only available to pure-play eCommerce firms and Web-based not-for-profits. It is available to any organization that digitizes some aspect of its operations. For example, using micro cameras embedded in store mannequins and shop windows (Figure 8.24), physical retailers in the fashion industry are today attempting to replicate the level

Figure 8.24   Modern digital camera—smaller than a coin   (*Source*: Park Ji-Hwan/AFP/Getty Images/NewsCom)

of visibility available online by tracking the flow of customers coming into the store and relating their purchases to various metrics such as the time spent in front of a display or a window.

As more and more devices become "intelligent," by embedding microchips and running software, the firms that use them have more opportunities to harness the power of visibility. Imagine a firm that manages vending machines, which are increasingly computerized and network-connected. What decisions could you make if the vending machines where able to maintain real time communication with a central server about sales and inventory level? How much more efficient could your firm be with this information? What new strategic initiatives would you implement with this infrastructure in place? In one example of innovative thinking, Coca-Cola rolled out the Freestyle drink dispenser, an RFID-enabled vending machine that draws ingredients from 30 flavor cartridges and is able to mix 100 different drinks (Figure 8.25). While we may debate whether any of these drinks are actually worth drinking, here lies Coca-Cola's strategy. The Freestyle machine is connected to central servers through the cellular phone network. By letting people mix and match their drinks, and keeping track of their tastes over time through the RFID reader that identifies each customer, the firm is betting on being able to perform extremely precise taste tests that will aid new product development. Moreover, Coca-Cola leases the machines to fast food outlets, enabling them to access real-time drink consumption data in their outlets... all the while providing greater variety to those soft-drink-crazed individuals who have to have 100 different flavors!

Figure 8.25   Coffee drink dispenser
(*Source*: © alam/Alamy Limited)

Mirroring Capabilities   A further application of the virtual value chain, termed mirroring capabilities, consists of shifting some of the economic activities previously completed in the physical value chain to the information-defined world of the virtual value chain. That is, some of the activities that were previously physical in nature (i.e., completed by employees) become completely information based.

Examples of mirroring capability are pervasive in firms that need to perform much testing and simulation. For example, a recent trend among drug manufacturers is to test the effect of new drugs using computer models rather than real patients, thereby drastically speeding up trials and reducing the cost of new drug development. Another example that may be particularly dear to your heart, as busy students, is offered by electronic library reserves. Typically your instructor will place some materials on reserve in the library so that you can check them out for a short period of time and study them. Due to copyright restrictions, only a few copies of the material can be put on reserve.

As you painfully know, the day before the exam, the early bird gets the worm, and if you are late you will be unable to consult the readings. Electronic reserves solve this problem (Figure 8.26). Because material that is digitally uploaded is not tied up when checked out (information goods are not consumed by use; see Chapter 4), all those who want to consult it can, and can do so any time they like, day or night, from the comfort of their own room.

Another great example of mirroring capabilities is offered by training in second life, the virtual reality massive multiplayer game we have discussed a few times before in this book. Many organizations, from hospitals, to police departments, to the military, are creating virtual learning environments in second life where they can leverage the immersive reality characteristics

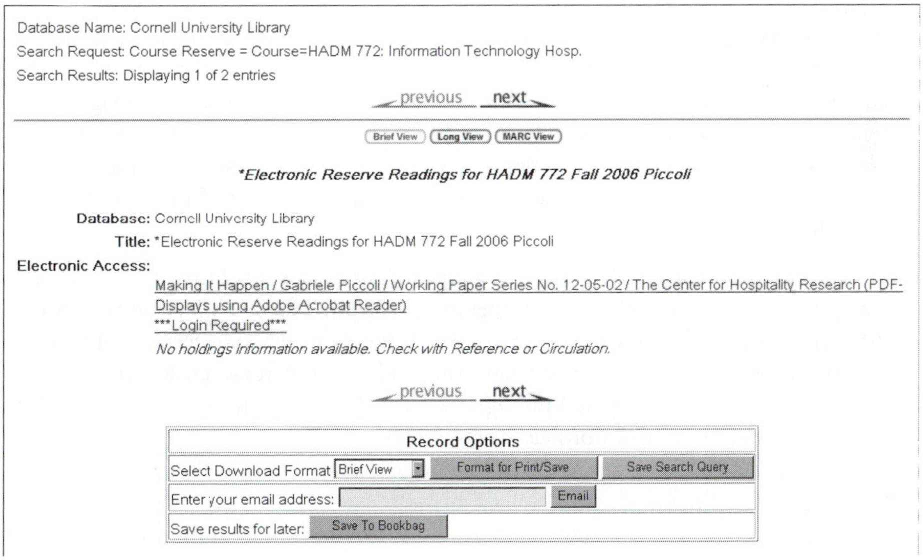

Figure 8.26   A library's eReserve application

Figure 8.27   A simulated emergency room in *Second Life*

of second life and create situations that would be extremely expensive and time consuming to design in real life (Figure 8.27). Imagine staging a terrorist attack or a blackout in the emergency room to train crisis response skills! In fact, the traditional approach to this type of training is classroom cases—a technique that pales in comparison to the virtual world in terms of realism and skill acquisition potential.

Note that mirroring capabilities are beneficial when transferring the activity to an information-based platform if they enable the firm to perform the activity more efficiently and effectively. They are also beneficial when the activity can be transformed with significant performance improvements. For this reason a mirroring capability approach is different from a mere automation of the existing activity using computers. To fully grasp this concept, think about the Ergo Bike Premium 8i from Germany's Daum Electronics. The Premium 8i looks like a regular, albeit high tech, stationary bicycle. However, it allows you to race other bicycle enthusiasts across the world on some of the greatest bicycle race segments on the globe (e.g., Hawaii's Ironman Triathlon). The bike simulates the terrain, giving you the sensory feeling of being there. It allows you to monitor your heart rate and other statistics as well, while talking to your racing partners over headsets. Imagine climbing the Alp d'Huez along with your friends, following in the footsteps (or bike tracks) of the great racers in the history of the Tour de France—Gino Bartali, Fausto Coppi, Eddy Merckx, Greg LeMond, Miguel Indurain. Perhaps then, a better term for this strategy would be digitizing capabilities rather than mirroring capabilities.[9]

New Digital Value   The above two types of strategies, visibility and mirroring capabilities, are mainly concerned with internal operations and the creation of value within the confines of the organization. The third stage, new digital value, is instead concerned with the organization's relationship with the customer and the firm's ability to increase customers' willingness to pay, using the information generated through the virtual value chain to create new value in the form of new information-enabled products or services.

Consider a classic example of this strategy: personalization through suggestive selling initiatives. Using your individual purchase history, as well as a technique known as collaborative filtering that compares your purchases to those of others with similar interests, online retailers are able to propose items that may be of interest to you in an effort to increase their sales. This approach, pioneered in retail, is now common in many industries. Recent examples come from

---

[9]We do maintain the original terminology in the framework to keep consistency with the original authors.

Figure 8.28   Spotify related artists suggestions

the music service Spotify (Figure 8.28), and apparel store Stylefeeder.com, which developed a proprietary recommendation engine based on your browsing behavior as it compares to other Stylefeeder.com patrons.

Value Matrix   When introduced to the virtual value chain and the potential for value creation through the use of organizational data, it is natural to gravitate to this way of thinking. However, it is important to remember that most organizations today need to pay significant attention to the traditional environment and their established operations. For as relevant as the potential to create value through information is, much of the opportunity for value creation remains in the firm's physical transformation processes. Thus, combining the traditional (physical) value chain and the virtual value chain offers a cohesive framework, termed the *value matrix*, that general and functional managers can use to seek and exploit opportunities for the deployment of IT-dependent strategic initiatives in their organizations (see Figure 8.29).

By being mindful of the five steps of the virtual value chain as they apply to data generated throughout the physical value chain, managers can uncover opportunities for new value creation and appropriation. The caveat expressed before about analytical frameworks holds here as well, and you need to map the value matrix that most accurately represents your firm's individual context (see, for example, Figure 8.30).

Value Creation with Customer Data

A class of initiatives for value creation that the proponents of the virtual value chain model have identified is new digital value. The objective of these types of initiatives is to use customer

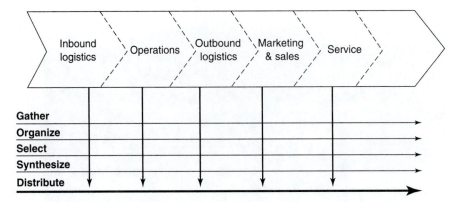

Figure 8.29   Value matrix

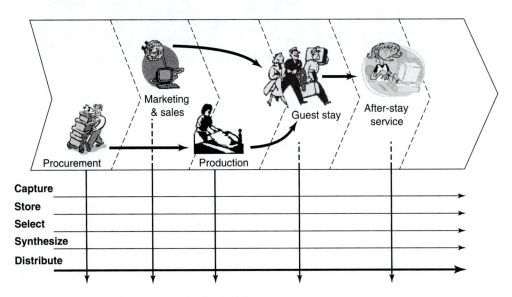

Figure 8.30   Sample value matrix for lodging

data and information to do something of value for them—thereby increasing their customer willingness to pay. To do so requires significant analysis and an understanding of the firm's characteristics and value proposition.

Analysis of the Value Proposition   Business firms specialize in the production and sale of a specific set of goods and services—the firm's value proposition. The characteristics of these products and services are, barring changes in product mix or significant innovation, fixed. For example, large resorts such as the Hilton Waikoloa Village on the Big Island of Hawaii, or the Atlantis Paradise Island in the Bahamas, offer customers a vacation experience characterized by length of time, amenities offered in the resort, and excursions; a car manufacturer offers

Figure 8.31   Magnetic strip cards are today the norm in large resorts

customers personal transportation vehicles with different characteristics of size, performance, safety rating, and so on. As you join a specific firm, in a specific industry, it is within the constraints of its unique value proposition that you may be called on to craft a customer data strategy.

Imagine, for example, that you join the workforce at one of these large resorts. As you do, you hear from the large consulting firms that personalization and customization are all the rage and that "customers are demanding it"—you must "go personal!" Their argument is that, since you can collect so much data about your customers' habits and preferences, you can create extensive profiles of your returning customers.[10] Once you know that Joe Resort likes Corona beer, you can have a few chilled bottles waiting for him in his room. He had a long trip all the way to Hawaii, it's hot outside, and he is tired, but as soon as he checks in he can unwind with his favorite drink. He'd love you for that surprise, and wonder how you did it. He will never want to spend his vacation in another resort! This is at least what you are told. Is it true? How do you know if a personalization strategy is the best way to use customer data?

Repurchase and Customizability: The Dimensions of Decision Making   An analysis of your firm's value proposition and characteristics of customer behavior in your industry helps in identifying initiatives that fit with the context and those that don't. Specifically valuable is information about the theoretical repurchase frequency in the industry and the degree of customizability of the product or service being offered.

Theoretical Repurchase Frequency   The dimension of theoretical repurchase frequency represents the regularity with which the average customer acquires goods and services offered by the firms in the industry or segment of interest (e.g., how often do people visit the Hilton Waikoloa Village in their lifetime). Note that this measure is concerned with the potential for high repurchase frequency, not with the actual repurchase rates any one individual firm is experiencing—hence the use of the term *theoretical repurchase frequency*. A firm that has very

---

[10]Resorts use room key cards (Figure 8.31) to obviously let customers into their respective rooms, but most importantly, as a debit card to pay for any one of the hundreds of on-premise services. Since the introduction of these cards, resorts have had the ability to unobtrusively collect large amounts of individual level behavioral and preference data.

few returning customers in an industry characterized by high theoretical repurchase frequency is either doing a poor job or missing an opportunity.

Imagine going to a McDonald's in your neighborhood and finding it dirty and painfully slow in service. If this state of affairs is not quickly rectified, you most likely will not return to the same store. However, you will not stop patronizing fast food restaurants—you'll just shift your demand to a store that does an acceptable job. The key point here is that theoretical repurchase frequency is a function of the industry the firm is in and the characteristics of the value proposition it offers. It is not a characteristic of any one individual firm's current performance.

Car manufacturing and real estate are typical examples of industries characterized by relatively low theoretical repurchase frequency. Perhaps the ultimate low repurchase frequency is the "Master of Business Administration (MBA) product"—once you have obtained one MBA, no matter how satisfied you were with the experience, you have no need for another. Coffee shops and grocery stores are at the other side of the spectrum and enjoy high theoretical repurchase frequency.

Degree of Customizability   The degree of customizability represents the extent to which the product or service your firm offers can be tailored to the specific needs and requirements of individual customers or a segment of the customer base. This dimension is a function of the complexity of the product or service itself.

Gasoline, as with most commodities, is an example of a product with a very low degree of customizability. Airline service and vending machine operations also belong in this category. At the other end of the degree of customizability spectrum are large resorts and destination spas. The Grand Wailea Resort Hotel and Spa, on the Hawaiian island of Maui, is a perfect example: Along with top-notch accommodations in paradise, the Grand Wailea offers high-end shopping at the Grand Wailea Shops, seven dining options, a world-class spa with hundreds of services, a golf course, a tennis club and fitness center, a number of pools, beach services, excursions, and events, all immersed in a setting characterized by beautiful scenery and art work.

Cruise lines, meeting and conference planning, and home building represent other examples of industries selling products and services characterized by a relatively high degree of customizability.

General Customer Data Strategies   Based on the specific theoretical repurchase frequency of an organization and the degree of customizability of the product and services it offers, we can identify four general customer data strategies (see Figure 8.32). Note, however, that these

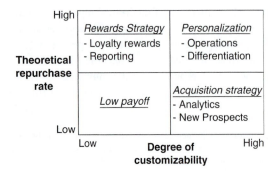

Figure 8.32   Customer data strategies

strategies are not a prescription or a silver bullet solution. Like any analytical framework, the matrix presented is a thinking tool designed to help you analyze the potential offered by an organization's operations.

The matrix does offer insight as to what strategies are likely to fit best with the characteristics of a given industry and a firm's value proposition. This does not mean that other strategies will not work, but simply that they will encounter obstacles and may be difficult to implement—something that as a general or functional manager responsible for their success you'd rather know up front.

While the firm you are analyzing may or may not fit neatly in one quadrant, the matrix will help you evaluate the advantages and disadvantages of each general strategy and, more importantly, the natural fit of each of the four approaches to your firm's characteristics and value proposition.

Personalization Strategy   A typical service personalization or product customization strategy is most appropriate for firms competing in industries characterized by both a high theoretical repurchase frequency and a high degree of customizability. Under these conditions the potential is there to collect significant individual-level data because of the repeated interactions the firm has with its returning customers. Moreover, the high degree of customization affords management many opportunities to use this information to tailor the product or service to the specific needs—learned or inferred—of the returning customers. Thus the firm can use the information to modify its operations and differentiate its product or services.

Event planning may be a good example of an industry that fits in this quadrant—particularly those firms that work closely with customers who need the organization of many recurrent events (e.g., large investment banks). Another example may be large IT vendors (e.g., Sun Microsystems, now Oracle corporation) catering to business customers with complex business and IT requirements.

Rewards Strategy   A rewards strategy is predicated on the notion that the firm's product and service will be purchased frequently. Yet these same products are fairly standardized, and it is difficult for the organization's managers to tailor them to specific customer requests. Under these circumstances the firm can use customer data to evaluate the profitability of each customer—actual and potential—and use this information to reward behavior in an effort to increase customer loyalty or boost share of wallet (i.e., make sure that customers consolidate their purchase behavior in the industry by sourcing from the firm rather than its competitors).

The firm can also use the individual level data collected to generate accurate reports and improve its operations (e.g., grocery stores performing basket analyses). Note that this means understanding customer profitability as well as customers' propensity to repurchase without incentive—a strategy much more complex and sophisticated than the "buy nine coffee cups and receive the tenth one free" that many firms seem to settle for (Figure 8.33). The airline industry represents a classic example for this quadrant.

Acquisition Strategy   Even in the face of low theoretical repurchase frequency, a firm in an industry with a high degree of customization may benefit from an acquisition strategy. Following this approach, the firm collects exhaustive data about its current customers in an effort to profile them and develop predictive models to identify and attract new profitable customers while avoiding unprofitable or marginal ones.

Figure 8.33 Coffee punch card

A good example of an industry that falls in this quadrant is the wedding reception business (Figure 8.34)—an industry offering highly customizable products but typically enjoying low repurchase frequency.

Another example may be the Grand Wailea Resort Hotel and Spa profiled earlier. Given the significant cost of a vacation in Hawaii, and even more so in a luxury resort such as the Grand Wailea, theoretical repurchase frequency for such a product may be very low. Yet given the complexity of the product and the high degree of customizability it offers to talented managers, an acquisition strategy may work well in this case.

Figure 8.34 The uniquely complex choreography of a wedding reception
(*Source:* Courtesy of www.flowershopnetwork.com)

No Potential   When a firm is in an industry characterized by low theoretical repurchase frequency and relatively low degree of customizability, there seems to be little potential for crafting a strategy around customer data. This is because very little data will likely be generated and managers' hands are tied with respect to what they can do with it. A chain of budget or limited service tourist hotels in an exclusive fly-in destination (e.g., Hawaii, Fiji) offers an apt example. Midscale hotels in these locations, such as the Ohana brand of Outrigger Hotels and Resorts (see Chapter 6) are generally a "window on an experience" rather than the experience themselves, and their value proposition is to offer guests an affordable opportunity to experience a great location. Because of the time commitment and cost of reaching these destinations, repurchase is relatively infrequent. Thus, there is little opportunity to enact any of the three strategies discussed above. Under these conditions the firm may be better off focusing on efficiency and low prices, and avoiding the cost of collection, management, and analysis of customer data.

Applying the Model   Let's return to the scenario we used earlier: your job at the Hilton Waikoloa Village. When analyzed through the lens of the general customer data strategies matrix, it becomes clear that a personalization strategy, while intuitively appealing, is probably not optimal. A product like the Hilton Waikoloa Village is characterized by relatively low repurchase frequency—for as affordable and mainstream as travel has become, a week in a large resort remains a fairly expensive vacation option, and the cycle of repurchase is relatively long (e.g., honeymoon in Hawaii followed by a five- or ten-year anniversary trip).

How likely is your company to be able to profit from the (considerable) investment in a full blown personalization strategy? Would it not be better to focus on an acquisition strategy designed to attract profitable first-time resort-goers based on what the firm learns from analyzing and clustering the profiles of its past guests?

Acquiring the Needed Data: The Third Dimension   The strategic initiatives described above are predicated on the firm's ability to capture the needed customer data in a format and a manner that make them amenable to the needed analysis. As with theoretical repurchase frequency and degree of customizability, the immediacy with which customer data can be captured and used varies by industry and context.

The expanded model acknowledges that different industries, because of the general norms about how business is conducted within them, offer a different potential for data capture. In other words, the degree to which data collection can be done easily can vary dramatically by industry and is an important early consideration. Let's examine a simple example. When purchasing hospital services (something that we typically prefer not to do!) we don't think twice about providing our social security number and intimate details about our personal life. In fact, if the doctor came in, looked at us, and said, "Take these pills twice a day, they'll fix you up," we would be outraged. Given the nature of hospital services, it is part of the natural course of good business to be asked many (personal) questions about our medical history, our family history, allergies, and symptoms before receiving a diagnosis.

Compare the hospital experience with the "get paid for your opinions!" e-mails that clog our inboxes, the guest satisfaction surveys we rarely fill out in hotels, or the dreaded twenty-minute dinner-time phone call on behalf of a company we recently transacted with asking us to rate their service. We largely consider them all to be a disruption and a waste of our time. Of course, the firm would be quite happy to gather the information in a different manner, but for many of these companies it is just not natural for customers to provide lots of information during the interaction. There is an emerging model to measure customer satisfaction that could save us from this annoyance. Firms like new Brand Analytics, Inc. (nBA) that capture and aggregate online mentions and reviews to construct a comprehensive picture of customer satisfaction based on comments of actual customers. But, as the ringing phone at dinner reminds us every so often, this new less intrusive approach has yet to become mainstream.

In summary, it is customer expectations as to what the encounter with the firm should be like—the norms within the industry—that determine what options the firm has when collecting data. While it is acceptable and accepted for a hospital to ask us for our social security number, as it is for a bank or an insurance company, we would be startled if the coffee shop, restaurant, or grocery store in our neighborhood did so.

These simple examples show that some firms are highly constrained when it comes to gathering customer data, and may have no better way to obtain it than to pay a representative sample of customers to take the time to respond to surveys. Others have more data than they can ever hope to use. We refer to this as the degree of unobtrusive data capture. Despite being a mouthful, this is a largely intuitive concept that indicates the extent to which, in the normal course of business, customer data are collected and stored in a readily usable format (see Figure 8.35).

An early analysis of practices in your industry can be illuminating. Imagine, for example, a fine dining restaurant. Fine dining is an industry with relatively high repurchase frequency and a relatively high degree of customizability of the experience. A personalization strategy is highly suitable for such an establishment, yet much of the data needed to carry it out are generated in fleeting customer-server exchanges that are difficult to capture and codify for easy storage and retrieval. Add to this mix the high employee turnover typical of the food service industry and it becomes clear why, for as much patronage as we give to our favorite restaurants, we generally don't receive a commensurate degree of personal service.

Compare the difficulty a restaurant has with collecting and storing its customer data in a readily usable format to the relative simplicity of the same task at an online retailer. Granted,

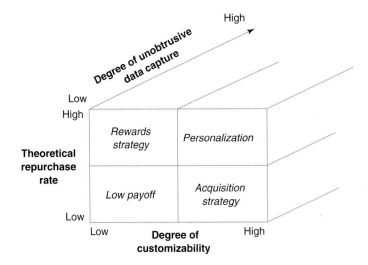

Figure 8.35   Data capture constraints

the potential depth of the relationship is lower, but the ease with which online shops can collect, store, and process the data you provide is much greater—enabling them to provide a more personalized experience than your favorite restaurant!

The degree of unobtrusive data capture for a firm is largely given at any point in time. However, technology improvements and innovation may pay off here if you are willing to shoulder the cost of changing people's habits. For example, while much of the information about customers' gambling behavior in casinos was traditionally left to busy and fallible casino hosts and pit bosses, the advent of electronic slot machines ushered in a new era. Casino executives realized that a modern slot machine is in essence a digital computer and that a computer records all the transactions it performs with great speed and accuracy. Tying these transactions to individual customers once they were convinced to use magnetic strip cards was a relatively small step. Today the natural course of business in the casino industry is such that a company can have an accurate, real-time picture of each of its customers' slot-playing behavior. With the declining price point of RFID tags, this same level of precision will soon be extended to table playing as well, not just slots.

Crafting Data-Driven Strategic Initiatives

Given the wealth of information available to the modern business, it can be extremely confusing to decide where to start looking for opportunities. The amount of data and information generated by the IT infrastructure of modern organizations often overwhelms those who look for opportunities. As a result, general and functional managers often face frustration when they attempt to extract value out of the business data locked into their computer systems. "All this software comes with great reporting capabilities, but who has time to look at them?" they often lament.

In this section we present a methodology that can be used to identify opportunities to create value with organizational data and then select the ones that hold the greatest potential for value creation and appropriation.

1. Identify relevant transaction processing systems (TPS).
2. Inventory data currently available in these systems.
3. Conceptualize initiatives that use the available data.
4. Prioritize among the selected initiatives.

Identify Relevant TPS   This first step is designed to allow you to narrow the scope of the analysis and focus on the systems that are most likely to hold relevant data—given your functional area and scope of responsibility. For example, a hotel revenue manager is mainly focused on decisions pertaining to room pricing and stay restrictions. While this narrowing of the scope may not be necessary in smaller operations, like a small independent retail store, it is crucial in larger outfits where functional areas must be clearly defined. At this stage the primary objective is to focus attention on the computer systems that hold data relevant to the area you are focusing on—typically a relatively small set of software programs.

Inventory the Data Currently Available   Once the relevant TPS have been identified and listed, you can inventory the data that are currently readily available in them. A first step in this phase may be to gain access to the system and explore its reporting functionalities. The key here is to focus not so much on the analyses that the reports yield, but instead to identify the underlying data that are tracked by the application in the natural course of business.

When you are not very familiar with the application, this step may be best accomplished by meeting with power users—those individuals who have intimate familiarity with the software, its capabilities, and the data it stores. This is often the best alternative because power users in your area will speak the same language and will be intimately familiar with the opportunities and challenges that you are likely to focus on. Alternatively, particularly in larger organizations, a meeting with the IT professionals who support the software may be necessary. The outcome of this phase should be a comprehensive list of data items that are reliably tracked within each TPS.

Conceptualize Initiatives   Having laid out all the available data currently being tracked by your TPS, you can simply ask yourself, "Given what I have, what would I like to know?" For this phase very little formal guidance can be offered; there is no substitute here for creativity and insight.

As you examine the data you have inventoried, some ideas and potentially beneficial analyses will emerge. This is a crucial part of the brainstorming stage, and you should focus at this point on generating ideas without worrying much about their feasibility or financial viability.

Prioritize Initiatives   Once you have articulated a number of potential initiatives, it's time to evaluate their actual feasibility. At this stage you should make a series of pragmatic decisions regarding the order in which the suggested initiatives should be implemented. This is because justifying data-driven initiatives to acquire the necessary funding is a very difficult task. Financial justification measures, typically requested by executives, are ill-suited to the task. Initiatives that are based on data analysis are qualitatively different from automation initiatives, where ROI is much easier to compute. As a consequence, the reputation of the initiative's champion, and the trust executives put in his or her judgment, is of paramount importance. How do you establish such a reputation in the domain of business data initiatives?

The prioritization matrix described in Figure 8.36 may help. It is based on the evaluation of two dimensions: upside potential and data availability.

Upside Potential   The first dimension provides an assessment of the financial benefits associated with the initiative in terms of revenue lift or cost reduction. The extent to which data analysis initiatives have upside potential typically depends on their

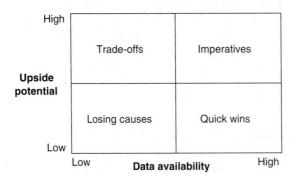

Figure 8.36   Initiative prioritization matrix

■ *Time sensitivity:* The degree to which the impact of the decisions that analysis of the data allows depends on how closely to the time of data collection it is made.

■ *Impact immediacy:* The degree to which the information is directly usable after it is generated as opposed to needing aggregation or manipulation.

■ *Aggregation requirements:* The extent to which the benefits of the analysis are dependent on substantial aggregation of multiple data sources.

■ *Trending requirements:* The extent to which the benefits of the analysis are dependent on substantial trending of data over time.

Data Availability   The second dimension provides an assessment of the immediacy with which the initiative can be implemented and a measure of the costs associated with it—the higher the availability of the needed data, the cheaper and more immediate the initiative's successful implementation. The following are critical dimensions of data availability:

■ *Accuracy:* The extent to which the available information is reliable without duplication, inaccuracies, or outdated elements.

■ *Comprehensiveness:* The extent to which the data needed to carry out the initiative are complete and free of missing elements and/or values.

Note that this dimension becomes crucial when resources are limited and/or executives are not easily sold on the potential of data as a strategic resource. Developing initiatives around high-availability data enables the firm to establish a track record of project success.

When the initiatives identified earlier are mapped to each of the four quadrants, it becomes apparent which ones can be quickly implemented, maybe as proof of concept or to gain support from other executives. It will also become clear what initiatives are resource intensive and require a much higher level of organizational commitment.

Imperatives   In this quadrant, classified as imperatives, fall projects that have significant upside potential and rely on readily available information. These initiatives can be implemented quickly and with limited investment of resources beyond sunk costs. Consider, for example, a grocery store that has been using checkout scanners for quite some time. With a relatively small investment, the store could compile checkout data and, after comparing it to current inventory levels, provide the store manager with an exception report flagging items that are running dangerously low. While the incremental investment is minimal, the potential upside of this initiative, reducing costly stockouts, can be significant.

Quick Wins   In this quadrant fall projects that, while not having much upside potential, can be readily implemented based on immediately available information. These initiatives are labeled quick wins because they do not require significant resources and a demanding approval cycle. In the absence of clear imperatives, these initiatives can often be used as proof of concept to gain momentum and to establish a track record of successful implementation designed to build credibility with other executives. The credit so built can then be put to use when making the case for harder-to-sell trade-off initiatives. Consider a firm running an online store that uses banner ads on referring sites. Further, imagine that your firm receives a limited amount of traffic and business from these referrals. Using currently available data and log analyzer software, the various referral sites can be evaluated, enabling a ranking with respect to the volume of traffic and business each one provides. If customers referred by one Web site consistently leave the online store after a few seconds, there is a mismatch between your offer and the referring Web site's audience. This type of analysis can be very valuable in contract negotiations, even though given the limited amount of traffic coming from referrals in this example, upside potential is limited.

Trade-Offs   In this quadrant fall projects that have significant upside potential but rely on information that is not readily available and consequently tend to be quite costly. This may be because the information is not easy to capture, it is not in a readily usable format, or the initiative requires the pooling of substantial information from multiple sources and substantial data integration. These initiatives are called trade-offs, as they require substantial cost benefit analysis and a rigorous approval cycle before the allocation of the needed resources can be justified. Consider, for example, customer preferences elicited through the waiter-guest interaction at a restaurant. While such data can be very valuable to improve customer service and elicit loyalty, the data are hard to capture and store in a manner that makes them easily usable for analysis.

Losing Causes   In this quadrant fall projects that are deemed to have little upside potential and that rely on information that is not readily available. Initiatives that fall in this category should not be implemented unless the cost associated with making the needed data available can be justified and assigned to other projects with positive ROI. In other words, these initiatives should be shelved until a change in circumstances moves them to another, more attractive quadrant.

 ## CONCLUSIONS

In this chapter, we continued our discussion of strategic information systems, initiated in Chapter 7 with foundation concepts. Crafting successful IT-dependent strategic initiatives is part art, requiring creativity and insight, and part science, requiring disciplined analysis and attention to detail. The primary goal of this chapter was to support both the creative and analytical aspects of this process by introducing you to traditional and recent frameworks for value creation with information systems and IT. Each of them offers a different focus and a different perspective which, collectively, should provide you with a comprehensive toolset. Using these frameworks requires an analytical mindset, lots of discipline, and a good dose of creativity. There is no substitute for experience and practice here. For this reason this chapter is full of short cases and examples that we hope will help you put the analytical models into a practical context.

 ## SUMMARY

In this chapter, we focused on IT-dependent strategic initiatives, discussing the frameworks and analytical models that have been proposed over the years to help you identify opportunities to create value with IT, and to design and develop value adding IT-dependent strategic initiatives.

Specifically, in this chapter we introduced the following frameworks:

- Industry analysis, focusing on the characteristics of the industry your firm competes in, seeks to help you identify opportunities to deploy information systems to improve the profitability of the industry.
- Value chain analysis focuses on the firm's own unique transformation process. It seeks to spur your thinking about how information systems and

technology can be used to introduce new activities and/or change the way the firm's activities are currently performed.

■ The customer service life cycle (CSLC) suggests that there is ample opportunity to create value by using information systems and technology to enhance the relationship with customers and enable superior customer service. The CSLC identifies four major phases and thirteen stages in which the relationship between the firm and its customer can be mapped. Each one offers opportunities for value creation.

■ The virtual value chain recognizes the importance of the wealth of information available to today's organizations in the search for value creation. It identifies five sequential activities that a firm can use to transform raw data input into information outputs that have more value than the inputs. Using this approach, a firm can develop one of three classes of strategic initiatives: visibility, mirroring capability, and new digital value.

■ Customer data can also offer the potential to create value with different strategies best fitting different organizations depending on two dimensions: the theoretical repurchase frequency of the firm's product or service, and its degree of customizability. Depending on where the firm finds its offer falling on these two dimensions, it will find a personalization, rewards, or attraction strategy to fit best. The viability of the chosen strategy depends also on the degree of difficulty the firm encounters in collecting and using the needed customer data.

■ Once the firm identifies a potentially value adding strategy, it must ensure that it can appropriate the value created over time. In other words, the firm that has created competitive advantage by way of an IT-dependent strategic initiative must ensure that the advantage is sustainable; this is the topic of the next chapter.

STUDY QUESTIONS

1. Describe the focus and principal objectives of industry analysis applied to information systems. Select one of the five competitive forces, and offer an example of a firm that you believe has been able to influence it by way of an IT-dependent strategic initiative.

2. Describe the focus and principal objectives of value chain analysis applied to information systems. Why is it important to contextualize the value chain? Provide an example of a firm you think has been able to create competitive advantage using information systems. Identify the primary activities most impacted by information systems in this firm.

3. Describe the customer service life cycle (CSLC) and its primary objectives. Provide an example of a firm that, in your opinion, has created competitive advantage

using information systems to enable superior customer service. What stages of the CSLC are mostly impacted by the firm's IT-dependent strategic initiative?

4. Describe the basic tenets of the virtual value chain. How does it differ from the physical value chain? Can you identify an example for each of the three applications of the virtual value chain?

5. Think about your last job, or the job you'd like to have once you graduate. Where would you place this firm's product or service on the dimensions of theoretical repurchase frequency and degree of customizability? How difficult is it for the firm to collect and use customer data? Is the firm engaging in a customer data strategy? If not, is it missing the boat?

FURTHER READINGS

1. Ives, B., and Learmonth, G. P. (1984). "The Information System as a Competitive Weapon." *Communications of the ACM*, Vol. 27, No. 12, pp. 1193–1201.
2. Piccoli, G., Spalding, B. R., and Ives, B. (2001). "The Customer Service Life Cycle: A Framework for Internet Use in Support of Customer Service," *Cornell Hotel and Restaurant Administration Quarterly* (42:3), pp. 38–45.
3. Piccoli, G. (2005). "The Business Value of Customer Data: Prioritizing Decisions." *Cutter Benchmark Review* (5:10), pp. 5–16.
4. Porter, M. E. (1980). *Competitive Strategy: Techniques for Analyzing Industries and Competitors*. New York, NY: Free Press.

5. Porter, M. E. (1985). *Competitive Advantage: Creating and Sustaining Superior Performance*. New York, NY: Free Press.

6. Rayport, J., and Sviokla, J. (1995). "Exploiting the Virtual Value Chain." *Harvard Business Review*, 73 (November–December), pp. 75–85.

 # GLOSSARY

- **Acquisition strategy:** A customer data strategy most appropriate for firms competing in industries characterized by a low theoretical repurchase frequency and a high degree of customizability.
- **Customer service life cycle:** A framework designed to draw managers' attention to the potential for value creation offered by the relationship between the firm and its customers.
- **Degree of customizability:** The extent to which the product or service offered by a firm can be tailored to the specific needs and requirements of individual customers or a segment of the customer base.
- **Degree of unobtrusive data capture:** The extent to which, in the normal course of business, customer data can be collected and stored in a readily usable format by a firm.
- **Industry analysis:** A framework that identifies the five forces shaping the profitability potential of an industry.
- **IT-dependent strategic initiatives:** Identifiable competitive moves and projects that enable the creation of added value, and that rely heavily on the use of information technology to be successfully implemented (i.e., they cannot feasibly be enacted without investments in IT).
- **Linkages:** The points of contact between the separate value chains of the firms in a value network.
- **Mirroring capabilities:** An application of the virtual value chain that enables the firm to perform some economic activities previously completed in the physical value chain to the information-defined world.

- **New digital value:** An application of the virtual value chain that enables the firm to increase customers' willingness to pay for new information-enabled products or services.
- **Personalization strategy:** A customer data strategy most appropriate for firms competing in industries characterized by both a high theoretical repurchase frequency and a high degree of customizability.
- **Reward strategy:** A customer data strategy most appropriate for firms competing in industries characterized by a high theoretical repurchase frequency and a low degree of customizability.
- **Theoretical repurchase frequency:** The regularity with which the average customer acquires goods and services offered by the firms within the industry or segment of interest.
- **Value chain:** A framework that maps a firm's transformation process as a set of sequential value adding activities.
- **Value matrix:** A framework combining the physical value chain and virtual value chain models.
- **Virtual value chain:** A framework that uses the basic value chain structure to draw attention to data as a valuable input resource in the transformation process.
- **Visibility:** An application of the virtual value chain that enables the firm to "see through" organizational processes that it was previously treating as a black box.

Appropriating IT-Enabled Value Over Time

What You Will Learn in This Chapter

General and functional managers have historically had a love-hate relationship with information technology. They recognize its potential to help the firm compete, but they often lack the tools to make sound decisions about its use. The plethora of pundits who comment on the strategic potential, or lack thereof, of information systems and IT only add to the confusion. In this chapter we provide a set of concepts and an analytical framework that will help you in establishing whether a given IT-dependent strategic initiative can be defended against competitors' retaliation. In other words, we will explore under what circumstances a competitive advantage rooted in an IT-dependent strategic initiative is sustainable.

Specifically, in this chapter you will learn:

1. To analyze the potential of IT-dependent strategic initiatives to ensure value appropriation over time.

2. To recognize the flaws in the arguments of those who suggest that information technology has lost its potential to enable sustained competitive advantage.

3. To recognize the four barriers to erosion that protect IT-dependent competitive advantage, and to estimate their size.

4. To identify the response lag drivers associated with each of the four barriers to erosion, and to provide examples of each.

5. To recognize how each of the four barriers can be strengthened over time in order to protract the useful life of an IT-dependent strategic initiative.

6. To use the concepts and frameworks described in this chapter in the context of future IT-dependent strategic initiatives when your firm takes a leadership position.

7. To use the concepts and frameworks described in this chapter in situations where your firm may be evaluating whether to retaliate against a competitor who pioneered an IT-dependent strategic initiative.

8. To identify the possible courses of action a firm should take based on your analysis, and to be able to recommend when the firm should or should not pursue a given IT-dependent strategic initiative.

MINI-CASE: IPHONE ORDERING AT DOMINO'S UK—SHOULD YOU FOLLOW SUIT

In early 2012, five years after graduating, your information systems consulting business is thriving. At 6:45 A.M., when you power up your computer to check e-mail and start the day, you see a late-night message from Gregg Yves, the vice president of marketing and customer service initiatives at Regional Chain of Pizza Shops (RCPS) headquartered in Bristol, UK. He is an old friend you met through your university alumni network when you were in school and with whom you have kept in touch.

Why would he be e-mailing so late? As you read his message, it becomes clear: "Do you remember when we discussed the Domino's iPhone ordering initiative?[1] At the time we were focused on rolling out in-store ordering kiosks in our restaurants and did not pay much attention. However, I noticed that Pizza Hut quickly replicated Domino's initiative.

I've been thinking about this all night. Should we follow suit as well? Do we need to move rapidly? I'd rather take a wait-and-see approach here, but I'm afraid that if we miss the boat on this initiative, the repercussions could be significant.

You're an expert on this strategic information systems stuff; can you give me your insight and direct my thinking a bit?"

DISCUSSION QUESTIONS

1. Do you believe that the Domino's iPhone ordering initiative is sustainable?
2. What are the pros and cons of the wait-and-see approach that Gregg prefers?
3. What is your recommendation? What should RCPS do next?

INTRODUCTION

As we discussed in Chapter 7, when it comes to using information systems and IT, the primary objective of the modern general and functional manager is to use them to create added value. However, creating added value is just one facet of the job; the firm must be able to appropriate the value created over time to truly benefit. In other words, any competitive advantage the firm has created with the implementation of its IT-dependent strategic initiative must be defended over time to ensure that the firm will be able to reap the benefits of its innovation. Failing to do so will quickly lead to a situation where competitors match the leader, and customers rather than the innovator end up appropriating the value created.

Can a firm really protect an advantage based on the innovative use of information systems and IT? Can IT-dependent strategic initiatives deliver sustained competitive advantage? These seemingly simple questions engender much debate and continue to stir up controversy—they have for over two decades now! On the one side are the skeptics who claim that, as the very success of IT continues (i.e., technology becomes cheaper, easier to use, and more pervasive than ever before), its strategic value declines.

Most information systems researchers and professionals, who are on the other side of the debate, disagree. Such disagreement is based on the findings of over forty years of information systems research, which has demonstrated that not all information technologies are created equal or behave the same—particularly when used strategically.

---

[1] See the mini-case in Chapter 8 for a description of the Domino's UK initiative.

NOT ALL IT IS CREATED EQUAL

The examples described below show how two different IT-dependent strategic initiatives, based on two different technologies at their core, can produce opposite results when it comes to creating and appropriating economic value.

High-Speed Internet Access in Hotel Rooms

During the dot-com days of the late 1990s, as the number of Internet users was increasing at a staggering rate, a host of organizations—ranging from airport operators, to coffee shops, to malls—began offering high-speed internet access (HSIA) and wireless connectivity to their customers. Lodging operators also followed this trend, offering in-room HSIA capabilities in their hotels. Soon HSIA became one of the hottest technologies to come to the lodging industry in a while. Companies offered HSIA as a paid amenity, with $9.95 for unlimited daily use being the most popular pricing option.

While take rates (i.e., guests' actual usage) were much lower than expected, HSIA quickly became a "must-offer" amenity, based on the assumption that business travelers, who were used to high-speed connections at home and in the office, would snub hotels that could not have them surfing in the fast lane.

The inevitable result was an increasing number of properties that offered HSIA, and quickly the amenity became free of charge. For example, in February 2001 the Sheraton Vancouver Wall Centre announced that it was offering HSIA free of charge to all guests. In the press release introducing the initiative, the HSIA vendor declared, "Offering this service as an amenity with no charge to the guest will certainly differentiate the Sheraton Vancouver Wall Centre from its competitors." Any hoped-for differentiation did not last long, however, as more operators had to join the "HSIA as a free amenity" trend. Soon free HSIA moved from a property-level amenity to a brand-level free amenity. Omni Hotels began offering HSIA systemwide to all guests starting in February 2003, and Best Western and Holiday Inn quickly followed suit, as did many other major chains (Figure 9.1).

Figure 9.1   Free Wi-Fi is a standard in three-star hotels
(*Source*: Media Bakery)

Following the trend of countless amenities before it, HSIA was rapidly becoming just another cost of doing business in the lodging industry and a competitive necessity. HSIA is valuable indeed; after all, consider how hard it is to use a dial-up connection when you are used to high-speed at home and in the office! However, because it could not be protected from rapid imitation, all of the value it created is now largely appropriated by hotel guests rather than the hotel companies that introduced it.

The same dynamic played out in restaurants and coffee shops, as the experience of McDonald's and Starbucks demonstrates. McDonald's started its HSIA initiative in 2003, initially charging $4.95 for two hours. It then went to $2.95 for two hours, before finally offering unlimited free Wi-Fi in its stores starting in December 2009. Starbucks went to free Wi-Fi in September 2009 in the UK, and then in all of its U.S. stores starting July 1st, 2010.

Business Intelligence at Caesars Entertainment

Caesars Entertainment (Figure 9.2) has been widely celebrated for its innovative use of information systems and IT in support of its efforts to better understand its customers—a type of initiative known as business intelligence (see Chapter 3). To do so, Caesars (which at the time was known as Harrah's Entertainment)[2] had to invest heavily in IT—an investment estimated to exceed $100 million in the year 2000. While the expenditure may seem significant, the firm made a conscious decision to invest the money in technology rather than follow the industry trend of creating elaborate resorts that would "wow" visitors with their size and design (e.g., MGM Mirage's, The Bellagio, The Venetian). Harrah's used a fraction of the money necessary for these developments, often exceeding the $1 billion mark, to create a sound technological and organizational infrastructure brand-wide.

Technology is only the beginning of this story, however. Harrah's did not simply buy a bunch of computer systems, flip on the switch, and watch the dollars roll in. Instead, the firm embarked on a large-scale reorganization, centralizing and focusing operations around the brand

Figure 9.2 Harrah's Casino in Atlantic City

---

[2] In this chapter, we refer to Caesars Entertainment as Harrah's to preserve reference to the historical name the firm had at the time. It is interesting to note that Harrah's success enabled it to acquire Caesars Entertainment but the firm decided to retain the latter's name after the merger.

and away from individual property interests. As part of the reorganization, Harrah's hired a new breed of analysts, known as decision scientists. These individuals had the mindset and the skills to gather and analyze data about gamblers' characteristics and activities. By carrying out scientific experiments, Harrah's was able to become both more efficient (i.e., spend less) and effective (i.e., spend better) in its use of funds to attract and retain gamblers while also increasing share-of-wallet (i.e., the percentage of the gambling budget a gambler would spend with Harrah's rather than its competitors) and customer satisfaction.

The returns on Harrah's use of technology have been considerable, even in the face of a slowing economy. At the same time, the centralized IT infrastructure and the processes it has developed enable Harrah's to expand its distribution with relative ease and control. Clearly, Harrah's Entertainment has been able to reap significant long-term results from its IT-dependent strategic initiative, and continues to appropriate a large portion of the value created.

The Need for A Priori Analysis

If nothing else, the above examples raise the question of whether managers should approach distinct IT-dependent strategic initiatives differently. Put another way, is there a way, a priori, to reduce uncertainty about whether an IT-dependent strategic initiative can lead to a sustainable advantage? In the remainder of this chapter we introduce a framework designed to support this analysis.

 # APPROPRIATING VALUE OVER TIME: SUSTAINABILITY FRAMEWORK

The major criticism levied by skeptics against the potential for sustained competitive advantage associated with IT innovation is that technology is easily replicated by competitors, who can quickly offer the same functionalities. Put in the framework of value creation, the accusation is that IT helps companies create value that they cannot appropriate over time because competitors can easily imitate any IT innovation.

By now, however, it should be clear to the attentive reader of this book that this argument simply misses the point. Because information systems are not IT, as we established in Chapter 2, creating and appropriating value hinges on successfully deploying a defendable IT-dependent strategic initiative. It follows that the focus on the analysis of sustainability should be the IT-dependent strategic initiative, in all its facets, not just the IT core. In other words, even if the IT components used by the firm are (at least in theory) replicable by competitors, it does not follow that the firm's IT-dependent strategic initiative built on that (replicable) technology will be easily copied as well.

Sustainable Competitive Advantage

The ability of a firm to protect its competitive advantage, known as sustainability[3] of the advantage, is often thought of as a binary condition—it is either possible or impossible for competitors

[3]The term sustainability is used here in its business strategy connotation. The term sustainability has gained much currency lately to refer to environmental sustainability. The role of information systems for environmental sustainability will be discussed in Chapter 12.

Figure 9.3   Amazon's UK warehouse

to erode the leader's advantage by matching the added value it creates. However, this can be a misleading approach. After all, short of very few resources, such as patents or exclusive access to raw materials, almost anything is replicable—in theory! Thus, it isn't whether the advantage is theoretically replicable that matters in practice, but the difficulty that competitors face in matching the leader's offer.

Consider the example of Amazon.com, a firm that is famous for its relentless pursuit of customer service and customer satisfaction. In an effort to improve these important metrics of success, by the year 2000 Amazon had deployed nine highly automated distribution centers that were strategically located throughout the United States, and a number more throughout the world (Figure 9.3). While it is true that competitors (for instance, Buy.com), could theoretically replicate Amazon's distribution, it would be very difficult—time consuming and expensive—for them to do so.

Resource Based View

In the last couple of decades, much of the thinking in strategic management has coalesced around the Resource Based View (RBV) of the firm. Within this approach, a firm is modeled as a bundle of resources. A key contention of the RBV is that a firm's competitive advantage depends upon the characteristics of the resources at its disposal and that, when the firm controls resources that are rare, valuable, inimitable, and non-substitutable, the advantage will be difficult for competitors to overcome.

- **Rare:** A resource is rare when it is idiosyncratically distributed. In other words, it is scarce and not readily available for acquisition by competitors. Consider a firm that has developed a deep understanding of consumer electronics experience design, such as Apple, Inc. While there is a market for design talent (perhaps you have such talent!), there is no market to which competitors can go to acquire a design capability. The same argument could not be made for office space, a resource for which (generally) there is a market with adequate supply.

- **Valuable:** A resource is valuable when it is necessary to underpin a value adding strategy (see Chapter 7). In other words, valuable resources enable the firm to offer a value proposition that is either superior to competitors' or, while equivalent, it can be offered with a lower investment. Valuable resources are also those that enable the firm to curtail its own weaknesses. In that case, however, the valuable resource enables the firm to overcome a competitive handicap rather than provide an advantage.

- *Inimitable:* A resource is inimitable when competitors find it impossible, or difficult, to duplicate it. Returning to the example of Apple's seemingly magic touch in designing consumer electronics that have immediate appeal with a loyal customer base, competitors who seek to imitate such capability find that it is rooted in more than just the hiring and "aggregation" of talent. The very difficulty of articulating how this capability comes to be and how it works in practice—a notion labeled as causal ambiguity in the literature—makes it difficult to replicate.

- *Non-substitutable:* A resource is non-substitutable when competitors are unable to replicate the firm's overall value proposition (e.g., an IT-dependent strategic initiative) using surrogate resources for the ones that are rare, valuable, and inimitable. In other words, if competitors can achieve the same results as the innovator using different resources, the advantage of the leader will be eroded and the inimitability of some of its resources will be rendered irrelevant.

Response Lag

A practical way to implement the ideas of the RBV framework in the technology arena is to think about sustainability not as a binary condition, but rather in terms of how much time and money it would take competitors to erode the advantage that the leading firm has been able to create with its IT-dependent strategic initiative. The higher the "time and money" obstacles—termed here barriers to erosion—the more resilient the firm's advantage.

Competitive retaliation occurs in stages. Once a firm's rivals find themselves at a disadvantage, they search for the sources of the firm's competitive advantage. If they are successful in identifying those sources, the competitors must decide whether they are able and willing to respond and, if they are, what approach they should take. Response lag, the time it takes competitors to respond aggressively enough to erode a firm's competitive advantage, is a measure of the delay in competitive response.

The longer the time and the higher the cost of replication, the more resilient is the firm's advantage. Thus, response-lag drivers are defined here as the characteristics of the technology, the firm, its competitors, and the value system in which the firm is embedded that combine to make replication of the IT-dependent strategic initiative difficult and costly. Response-lag drivers combine their effects to levy barriers to erosion.

Four Barriers to Erosion

Response-lag drivers can be grouped into one of the following four barriers to erosion of IT-dependent competitive advantage: (1) IT-resources barrier, (2) complementary-resources barrier, (3) IT-project barrier, and (4) preemption barrier. The magnitude of each barrier to erosion is determined by the number and strength of its response-lag drivers (Figure 9.4). We briefly describe each barrier to erosion below, and detail each of the response-lag drivers associated with them in the sidebars.

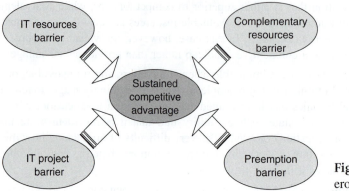

Figure 9.4   Four barriers to erosion of advantage

Barrier 1: IT Resources   IT-dependent strategic initiatives rely on access to the assets and capabilities necessary to produce and use the technology at their core. Two classes of response-lag drivers contribute to the height of the IT-resources barrier; these are IT resources and IT capabilities (Figure 9.5). As an initiative becomes more reliant on preexisting IT resources and capabilities, it becomes increasingly difficult to copy (Sidebar 1 lists and explains in detail all the response-lag drivers associated with this barrier).

Consider, for example, a firm that controls some highly specific and difficult to imitate IT resources, such as Walmart Stores, Inc. In earlier chapters we described the notion of continuous replenishment, an IT-dependent strategic initiative pioneered by Walmart in conjunction with Procter & Gamble. Continuous replenishment relies on real-time or near-real-time scanner data transfer between a retailer (e.g., Walmart) and a supplier (e.g., P&G). Walmart, having access to the satellite-based network infrastructure among its stores, found this initiative easier and less costly to implement than any of its competitors. In other words, it should not surprise us that continuous replenishment was pioneered by Walmart, as it already had the network infrastructure to do so. Competitors who wanted to replicate this initiative had to first deploy the same (or a comparable) infrastructure.

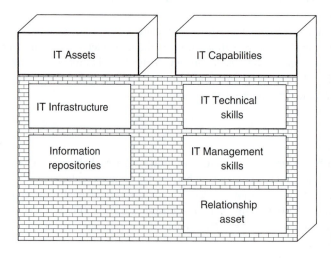

Figure 9.5   IT resources barrier

SIDEBAR 1: IT RESOURCES BARRIER

IT Assets

IT assets are technology resources available to the organization, including hardware components and platforms (e.g., a private network connecting globally distributed locations), software applications and environments (e.g., a proprietary software using custom-developed analytical models), and data repositories. These resources contribute to building response lag directly, by simplifying and speeding up the development and introduction of the initiative's IT core, or indirectly, by making it difficult for competitors who have no ready access to the needed IT resources to replicate the leader's initiative.

IT Infrastructure

An IT infrastructure is a set of IT components that are interconnected and managed by IT specialists with the objective of providing a set of standard services to the organization. Thus, the IT infrastructure provides the foundation for the delivery of business applications. With IT infrastructure-development times generally estimated to exceed five years, the response lag and ensuing barrier to imitation is likely to be substantial.

Information Repositories

Information is now widely recognized as a fundamental organizational resource, and firms are investing significantly to improve their ability to collect, store, manage, and distribute it. Information repositories are often large data stores containing extensive information about customers, suppliers, products, or operations, organized in a structured form that is accessible and useable for decision-making purposes. A firm's information repositories can contribute to the development of substantial response lag by supporting strategic initiatives. Competitors attempting to replicate the leader's strategic initiative must not only duplicate the IT at its core, but they must also accumulate a comparable information resource—a feat that often takes substantial time.

IT Capabilities

IT capabilities are derived from the skills and abilities of the firm's workforce. These capabilities directly influence the response lag associated with the introduction of IT at the core of IT-dependent strategic initiatives because they facilitate the technology's design and development. These capabilities also play a fundamental role in enabling effective and timely implementation, maintenance, and use of the technology.

IT Technical Skills and Business Understanding

IT technical skills relate to the ability to design and develop effective computer applications. They include proficiency in system analysis and design, software design, and programming. Another element is the depth of business understanding of IT specialists. Business understanding enables the IT specialists charged with developing the technology supporting IT-dependent strategic initiatives to envision creative and feasible technical solutions to business problems. A high level of business understanding also contributes to the creation of response lag by mitigating the risks associated with the introduction of the strategic initiative and the relative investments in technology.

IT Management Skills

IT management skills refer to the firm's ability to provide leadership for the IS function, manage IT projects, integrate different technical skills, evaluate technology options, select appropriate technology sources, and manage change ensuing from the introduction of IT. IT management skills, because of their idiosyncratic and socially complex nature and the learning curve associated with their development, are a source of sustainable competitive advantage. Managerial IT skills can contribute to creating substantial response lag when techniques and routines developed over time can substantially reduce development costs and development lead times. Competitors who attempt to replicate the initiative but lack the same high level of managerial IT skills as the innovator face substantial obstacles to imitation.

Relationship Asset

The relationship asset is accumulated over time and finds its roots in a mutual respect and trusting rapport between the IS function and business managers. When a firm has developed a substantial relationship asset, IS specialists and business managers are able to work together effectively by coordinating and communicating extensively. Having developed the relationship, they share a vision for the role of IT within the business. Business partners share the risk and accept the responsibility for IT projects, and IS specialists are able to anticipate a business's IT needs and devise solutions that support these needs.

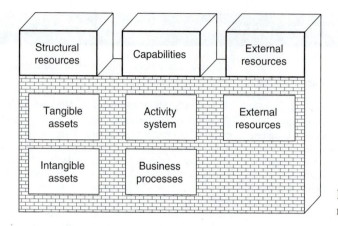

Figure 9.6   Complementary resources barrier

Using the terminology of the sustainability framework, we can assert that the difficulty Walmart's competitors found in quickly and successfully imitating Walmart's continuous replenishment strategy was in part due to the need to first acquire a prerequisite IT asset—the networking infrastructure enabling real-time scanner data transfer from stores. Walmart's ownership of this unique asset translated into a response-lag driver (IT infrastructure) that contributed to increase significantly the magnitude of the IT resources barrier to erosion.

Barrier 2: Complementary Resources   While IT is by definition a fundamental component of any IT-dependent strategic initiative, successful implementation of such an initiative requires that complementary organizational resources be mobilized as well (Figure 9.6). Thus, to implement an IT-dependent strategic initiative, the firm must develop or acquire the necessary complementary resources (e.g., physical assets such as warehouses and distribution centers, intangible assets such as a brand).

As an initiative becomes more reliant on distinctive complementary resources, the complementary-resource barrier to imitation strengthens, and replication of the strategy becomes slower, costlier, and more difficult. In this situation, competitors will have to acquire or develop not only the IT at the core of the strategy, but also the complementary resources that underpin the initiative (Sidebar 2 lists and explains in detail all of the response-lag drivers associated with this barrier).

Consider again the example of Harrah's Entertainment and its business intelligence initiative. While the firm spent a significant amount of money to acquire IT resources, it also engaged in a radical reorganization when launching the initiative in the late 1990s. This reorganization challenged decades of casino management practice, where each casino within a chain operated in a highly independent fashion. Through its reorganization Harrah's asked the general managers of each property to report to divisional presidents, who in turn reported up to Harrah's Entertainment's chief operating officer. The firm also created transfer mechanisms and incentives to support cross-property traffic and a general sense that customers "belonged" to Harrah's corporate office, not to each individual casino that signed them up to the program. This change in organizational structure enabled the success of Harrah's brandwide initiative.

Figure 9.7 A popular conveyor belt sushi bar (Image created by Chenyun at the English Wikipedia Project.)

Fast forward now to the year 2001, when Harrah's was receiving substantial praise and attention for its use of guest data and putting pressure on competitors to imitate. How well positioned were its competitors to replicate Harrah's highly centralized customer data strategy? Not very well, since the typical competitor still treated each property as unique and independent, with a unique brand and little incentive to share customers and customer data with the other casinos in the chain.

Using the terminology of the sustainability framework, we can assert that Harrah's competitors are likely to find it costly and time consuming to successfully imitate Harrah's business intelligence initiative. This is because, at least in part, their organizational structure is not conducive to the strategy, and a change would be very risky, costly, and time consuming. In other words, Harrah's has access to a unique complementary resource, namely its idiosyncratic organizational structure, which creates substantial response lag and contributes to heighten the complementary resource barrier.

The analysis of complementary resources is important because during the design of the initiative it is often possible to use IT to leverage the impact of some idiosyncratic complementary resources. Imagine managing an upscale conveyor-belt sushi restaurant (Figure 9.7). Your restaurant prides itself (and justifies its premium prices) on the superior quality and freshness of its sushi.

Using RFID tags your restaurant can keep constant track of the amount of time each dish has been out on the conveyor belt and thereby ensure that dishes that have been rotating for more than 25 minutes are removed to maintain freshness. With this infrastructure in place you decide to add a display to each dish in order to show the time each dish has been rotating around. This seems like a simple addition, and technologically it is not overly complex. However, it is not simple for your lower rate competitors to replicate, as they would in fact be advertising that their sushi is not nearly as fresh as yours. The lesson is simple. By using technology to leverage an idiosyncratic complementary resource, you have made replication of your strategy much more difficult for competitors.

SIDEBAR 2: COMPLEMENTARY RESOURCES BARRIER

Structural Resources

Structural resources comprise non-IT-related tangible and intangible internal assets used by the firm in the enactment of its IT-dependent strategic initiatives.

Tangible Assets

In theory, any tangible resource available to the firm can underpin an IT-dependent strategic initiative. Among these are competitive scope, physical assets, scale of operations and market share, organizational structure, governance, and slack resources.

Intangible Assets

As in the case of tangible resources, nearly any of a firm's intangible resources can support an IT-dependent strategic initiative. Examples of commonly cited intangible resources that can be so applied include corporate culture, top management commitment, and the ability to manage risk. As with tangible IT resources, complementary intangible resources create response lag by making a strategic initiative difficult, costly, and time consuming to imitate.

Capabilities

A firm's capabilities define how the firm carries out its productive activities. These resources specify what activities are performed and what steps or business processes make up those activities. The activities that the firm performs and the manner in which it performs them contribute to response lag and help sustain the competitive advantage created by the initiative.

Activity System

A performance-maximizing activity system relies on a set of economic activities that are both interlocking and mutually reinforcing, expressly showing internal consistency (internal fit) and appropriately configured given the firm's external environment (external fit). Although IT is one of the fundamental components of the strategy, it still must fit within the entire activity system. When a firm has implemented a given configuration of activities and has developed the IT core supporting the linked activities, replication of the technology alone is insufficient for successful imitation. Indeed, narrowly replicating just the IT core leads to further decline of the imitator's position by wasting time, money, and management attention without eroding the leader's competitive advantage. A classic example of a firm that has an idiosyncratic activity system is Southwest Airlines. Because Southwest does not cater flights, does not offer seat assignments, has a standardized fleet of aircrafts, uses less crowded airports, and focuses on point-to-point travel for price-sensitive customers, it is relatively resistant to competitive imitation. Merely imitating one aspect of Southwest's activity system will not suffice, but attempting to duplicate the entire package generates considerable response lag.

Business Processes

We defined a business process as the series of steps that a firm performs in order to complete an economic activity. The notion of business process is related to, but distinct from, that of the economic activities discussed above. Economic activities describe the set of undertakings that the firm performs, while business processes describe the way in which the firm performs them. The contribution that business processes make to response lag and to the height of barriers to imitation depends on their distinctiveness and strategic value. When a firm is able to introduce an IT-dependent strategic initiative built around a business process with characteristics of uniqueness and differentiation, the firm creates a significant barrier to erosion.

External Resources

External resources are assets (such as brand, reputation, and interorganizational relationship assets) that do not reside internally with the firm but accumulate with other firms and with consumers. Generally intangible, external resources are usually developed over time. When a firm's IT-dependent strategic initiative can make use of or contribute to the development of these external resources, response lag increases considerably and barriers to imitation are augmented. Thus, the firm forces competitors to develop a comparable level of external resources before producing an effective response.

Barrier 3: IT Project IT-dependent strategic initiatives rely on an essential enabling IT core. Thus, they cannot be implemented until the necessary technology has been successfully introduced. The response-lag drivers of the IT project barrier are driven by the characteristics of the technology and the implementation process (Figure 9.8).

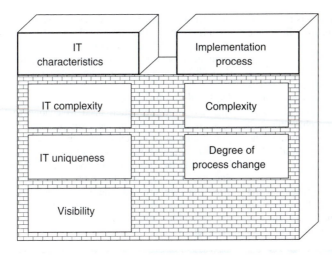

Figure 9.8 IT project barrier

Information technologies are not homogeneous, undifferentiated entities. To the contrary, they differ substantially with respect to their intrinsic characteristics, their ability to complement other organizational resources, the context in which they are introduced and used, and the degree of organizational change that needs to occur during the implementation process (Sidebar 3 lists and explains in detail all of the response-lag drivers associated with this barrier).

Consider, for example, a website. No matter how complex they are, websites are typically relatively quickly designed and deployed, particularly compared with large infrastructure projects (e.g., data warehouses) that are complex, lengthy, and prone to failure. Returning to the Harrah's Entertainment example, it should not surprise you that the IT project barrier associated with its $100 million investment in technology is substantial in and of itself.

SIDEBAR 3: IT PROJECT BARRIER

IT Characteristics

Information technologies differ with respect to their complexity, distinctiveness, and visibility to competitors.

IT Complexity

Different IT applications have different degrees of complexity. The complexity of the technology is a function of the bundle of skills and knowledge necessary to effectively design, develop, implement, and use it. Technology complexity raises the IT project barrier by increasing development lead times for a competitive response.

IT Uniqueness

On the low end of the IT uniqueness continuum are self-contained, off-the-shelf IT products that need little integration or customization (e.g., an electronic mail system).

At the high end are custom-developed applications or infrastructure subsystems that are unavailable in the open market. When the IT underlying the innovator's strategy is not distinctive, competitors can engage consultants or service firms to aid them in reducing knowledge barriers, thereby reducing the imitation response lag. Unique IT makes this process much more difficult.

Visibility

Visibility is the extent to which competitors can observe the enabling technology. The visibility dimension can be conceptualized as a continuum spanning from custom developed internal systems, which are virtually invisible to competitors, to immediately visible interorganizational or customer-facing systems that require extensive education and selling to external users or customers (e.g., an online purchasing system). IT that is highly visible and is readily available for inspection by competitors limits the strength of the IT project barrier.

Implementation Process

Since different kinds of information technology are inherently dissimilar, the processes by which they are implemented and become available to the organization also differ. Depending on the implementation characteristics of the IT core of the strategic initiative in question, the strength of the barriers to imitation changes considerably.

Implementation-Process Complexity

Implementation-process complexity is a function of the size and scope of the project, the number of functional units involved, the complexity of user requirements, and possible political issues, among other things. IT

infrastructure projects represent a powerful example of complex systems that have a substantial lead time. While the components may be commodity-like (e.g., personal computers, server, telecommunication equipment), it is difficult to integrate them in an effective system.

Degree of Process Change

Business processes often need to change to fit a new system—particularly in the case of large, highly integrated enterprise systems. The challenges escalate when several organizations or operations use the technology involved in the strategic initiative. The more departments that are involved and the more organizational boundaries that are crossed, the harder and the riskier the change becomes. Yet as complexity increases, so do the difficulties encountered by competitors in imitating the strategy.

Barrier 4: Preemption   You may now be wondering why we term the four forces ensuring sustainability as "barriers to erosion" rather than "barriers to imitation." We do so because in some cases, even if a competitor is able to replicate an IT-dependent strategic initiative, the response may bear no fruit for the laggard. A discussion of the preemption barrier will clarify this point (Figure 9.9).

In some cases, the IT-dependent strategic initiative pioneered by the first mover creates a preferential relationship with customers or other members of the value system and introduces substantial switching costs. Under these circumstances it is not enough for competitors merely to imitate the leader's strategy; they need to either compensate the customer for the cost of switching or provide enough additional value to justify the customer's decision to incur the switching costs. That is, imitators must be "that much better," where "that much" is an amount

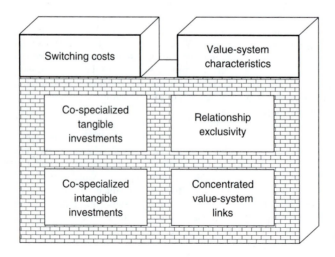

Figure 9.9   Preemption barrier

greater than the current value of all co-specialized investments[4] that the customer has made (Sidebar 4 lists and explains in detail all of the response-lag drivers associated with this barrier).

eBay, Inc., the dominant online auction site, provides a perfect example. Aware of its success, two formidable competitors, namely Amazon.com and Yahoo!, launched their own online auction sites. Despite having an e-commerce pedigree, brand recognition, and technical capabilities just as good as eBay's, both firms achieved lackluster results when imitating eBay's IT-dependent strategic initiative. Interestingly, a brief look at both competitors' Web sites would show that they were remarkably similar to eBay's own. Clearly an imitation strategy didn't pay, but why? So lackluster were their results, in fact, that both had to close their respective auction sites as it was not viable to compete with eBay (at least in the North American market).

The reason for eBay's dominance can be found in its ability to harness a dynamic that occurs in its industry—strong network effects. As you recall from Chapter 4, when strong network effects are present, the dominant player will be the one that first reaches critical mass (in this case eBay, at least in North America). At that point both buyers and sellers face daunting switching costs, and only "wholesale defection" of a large portion of the customer base will enable competitors to catch up to the leader—an extremely unlikely event. Being second in the online auction market is not a good place to be![5]

SIDEBAR 4: PREEMPTION BARRIER

Switching Costs

Switching costs represent the total costs borne by the parties of an exchange when one of them leaves the exchange. They include not only economic costs, but also psychological and physical costs. "Switching costs are the norm, not the exception, in the information economy."[6] IT-dependent strategic initiatives, which rely heavily on the collection, storage, manipulation, and distribution of information, are particularly suited to the creation and exploitation of switching costs.

Co-Specialized Tangible Investments

When an IT-dependent strategic initiative is deployed, it may require that the firm's customers acquire the physical assets necessary to participate in the initiative. The total capital outlay necessary to obtain these assets is termed co-specialized tangible investments. These range from computer hardware and telecommunication equipment to software applications and interfaces between the existing customers' systems and the firm's IT. For example, hotel franchisees buy costly interfaces for the franchising brands' reservation system. These interfaces become valueless if the property is re-branded. The extent to which the IT-dependent strategic initiative requires co-specialized tangible investments determines the potential for strong barriers to imitation associated with the initiative.

Co-Specialized Intangible Investments

As is true of tangible investments, the deployment of an IT-dependent strategic initiative often necessitates a firm's customers or channel partners to invest time and money to take part in the initiative. An investment of this kind is known as a co-specialized intangible investment. For instance, to benefit from customer relationship management initiatives, customers often need to take the time to complete a profile. Co-specialized intangible investments might include "set-up" costs as well as ongoing costs

---

[4]The term co-specialized investment simply refers to investments made in conjunction with a specific IT-dependent strategic initiative. Because these investments are specific to the initiative, they will lose part or all of their value if those who made the investment switched to a competitor (see Sidebar 4).

[5]Interestingly, the eBay example shows that using proprietary IT is not a necessary condition for superior long-term performance.

[6]Shapiro, C., and Varian, H. (1998). *Information Rules: A Strategic Guide to the Network Economy* (Boston: Harvard Business School Press), p. 111. Also see this book for an excellent treatment of switching costs in the information age.

(e.g., retraining new travel associates using a reservation system). Data and information repositories represent perhaps the most important class of co-specialized intangible investments in the information age. Considerable switching costs can be built on information accumulated over time. An interesting example is offered by information that is valuable only as long as the customer is using the firm's products or services (e.g., revenue-management models and historical records that are brand specific and become valueless if the hotel is re-branded).[7]

The same situation occurs even when switching costs are not readily apparent. Some forward-looking banks are attempting to take advantage of their long-standing relationships with customers to reach a position of "trusted consolidator" of top clients' complex financial positions. This strategy entails the collection of extensive information about customers' banking profiles and services used; insurance holdings; investment portfolio; mortgage, credit, and loan positions; and scheduled bill payments. The bank in this instance need not provide all of the services in question, but it strives to offer a consolidated view that customers find valuable and costly to transfer to competitors. Note that even when switching costs appear to be low, their presence can be critical for strategy development.

Value-System Characteristics

A firm does not engage in economic activity in isolation, but as a link in a larger value chain or system that includes upstream and downstream members. The structure of this value system can provide opportunities for preemptive strategies, and for the exploitation of the response-lag drivers discussed here. The structure of the value system does not directly affect the strength of the preemption barrier to imitation, but instead magnifies or diminishes the preemptive effects of switching costs.

Relationship Exclusivity

An exclusive relationship exists when participants in the value system will elect to do business with only one firm that provides a particular set of products or services. The firm's counterpart (i.e., customer or supplier) places a premium on dealing with either the firm or one of its competitors, but not both. Relationship exclusivity is the norm

with IT-dependent initiatives that provide integration services and that benefit from the accumulation of historical information. When first introduced, the American Airlines SABRE terminal for travel agents created strong incentives for relationship exclusivity, as travel agents did not want to waste valuable office space for competitors' proprietary terminals (e.g., United's Apollo), which were considered essentially duplicates of the SABRE terminal.

When a business relationship benefits from exclusivity, the customer faces penalties for hedging behavior and for sourcing the needed product or service from multiple firms, and when competitors introduce competing offers, customers are already invested in their relationship with the incumbent.

Concentrated Value-System Link

At each of the various stages or links in the value system, the degree of concentration in the link is inversely proportional to the number of suitable business entities populating that link—where suitability depends on whether the firm would find the products or services offered by the vendors populating the link acceptable. A highly concentrated link is one where there are relatively few organizations or consumers available for the firm to use or serve. In the case of airline reservation systems, for instance, the total number of travel agents serving the market targeted by the airline sponsoring the system represents the concentrated link.

A market of given size will support only a finite number of competitors, and achieving a substantial penetration in the concentrated value-system link—by definition, a small market—is necessary to successfully preempt imitation. As the degree of concentration increases, the time necessary to secure a relationship with a substantial proportion of the link decreases—all else being equal. Consequently, the leader has a better chance of capturing a substantial proportion of relationships and being able to use switching costs to "lock out" competitors and maximize its barriers to imitation. Conversely, when a link in the value system comprises a large number of business entities, a firm is unlikely to effectively reach a critical mass of entities and raise substantial barriers to imitation in the same amount of time.

---

[7]The software here is neither proprietary nor brand specific, and the data are not acquired over a network or hosted by the brand. Yet the historic data and the models the hotel has developed assume that the hotel has a given brand (e.g., Four Seasons). If the hotel is re-branded, while the software, the data, and the models are retained, their value is much lower because the data and models are specific to the original brand and assume that the hotel sports the related flag (e.g., has access to Four Seasons' brand equity, reservation systems, and loyal customer base).

With the language of the sustainability framework, we can assert that eBay, by virtue of being the first company to reach a critical mass of buyers and sellers in a market with strong network effects, was able to erect an insurmountable preemption barrier to erosion.

The Holistic Approach

While the framework for evaluating the sustainability of IT-dependent strategic initiatives breaks the analysis into its component parts—barriers to erosion and response lag drivers—you should always be mindful of the fact that appropriation of value is dependent on these components working together. In other words, when thinking about value creation appropriation, you must think holistically. Attentive readers of this chapter will undoubtedly note that those who suggest that IT does not have the characteristics of rarity and inimitability—and as a consequence cannot be considered a strategic resource—have failed to think holistically.

Recent information systems research[8] corroborates this holistic approach by showing how the combination of information technology and organizational resources—termed IT-enabled organizational resources—display both emergent properties and sustainability potential. In other words, the combination of IT and organizational resources creates a system that often has properties of neither the IT itself nor the organizational resources individually, but rather emerges from the combination (i.e., they are emergent properties). Consider the example of telemedicine. Telemedicine is the notion that a doctor can operate on a patient at a distance with the aid of local staff and robotic equipment that she controls remotely via a computer (Figure 9.10). Australian doctors in Adelaide recently performed heart surgery in this manner. A telemedicine system of this sort is a socio-technical system that displays emergent properties. For it to work, you need remotely located doctors with the competencies to perform the surgery and skills in operating the telemedicine equipment. You also need local medical staff to prepare both the patient and the telemedicine robotic equipment. The emergent property is the ability to perform

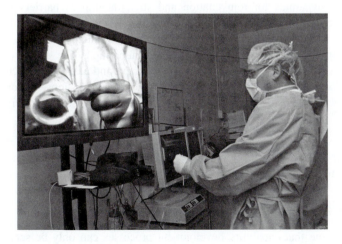

Figure 9.10   Telemedicine equipment   (*Source*: Nati Harnik/ © AP/Wide World Photos)

---

[8]Nevo, S., and M. R. Wade. (2010). "The Formation and Value of IT-Enabled Resources: Antecedents and Consequences." *MIS Quarterly* (34:1) pp. 163–183.

remote heart surgery, a resource that neither the remote doctors nor the local equipment have independently. Only when the local technology and staff work in combination with the remote heart surgeons can the surgery successfully happen.

The telemedicine example clearly shows the value of holistic thinking. IT-enabled organizational resources have properties than neither IT nor the organization alone possess. However, you will quickly note that these IT-enabled organizational resources do have the potential to be valuable, rare, inimitable, and non-substitutable. In other words, they have the potential to provide for creation and appropriation of value to the organization that controls them—demonstrating the short-sightedness of those who suggest that IT cannot be instrumental to sustained competitive advantage because it is easily imitable. The sustainability framework places IT-enabled organizational resources in the context of specific initiatives the firm may introduce. By doing so, it is a valuable analytical tool that helps you as a manager make decisions.

The Dynamics of Sustainability

As high as the barriers to erosion may be, when launching IT-dependent strategic initiatives, a firm has an advantage but still shouldn't "fall asleep at the wheel." Rather, general and functional managers proposing IT-dependent strategic initiatives should have a plan for continuously remaining ahead of the competition. This means looking for opportunities to reinvigorate and reinforce the barriers to erosion described above. Consider the example of Dell Inc., a firm that maintained its leadership position in personal computer manufacturing for more than a decade. At the heart of Dell's strategy was its high-velocity, built-to-order production model for direct sales. The firm continually improved the performance of its production system, as well as introducing further initiatives that leverage its core advantage. For example, in the mid-1990s Dell took its direct sales model to the Internet and began to sell to individual consumers. More recently the firm has extended its high-velocity production model to other products, such as high-end servers and consumer electronics—albeit with less positive results.

There are two main dynamics for rejuvenation and strengthening of barriers to erosion over time: capability development and asset-stock accumulation. There is a mutually reinforcing dynamic between barriers to erosion and a firm's IT-dependent strategic initiative. Available response-lag drivers offer the firm a "head start" on the competition. The enactment of the strategy allows the leader to engage in the capability development and asset-stock accumulation processes described below, in turn leading to further development of the response-lag drivers and the preservation of barriers to erosion (see Table 9.1 for a list of response-lag drivers affected by each dynamic).

Capability Development Capability development refers to the process by which an organization improves its performance over time by developing its ability to use available resources for maximum effectiveness. When it comes to IT-dependent strategic initiatives, capability development consists of the ability to engage in "learning by using," defined as the process by which a firm becomes more effective over time in using and managing an information system and the technology at the core. Note that capability development processes can only be set in motion once the IT-dependent strategic initiative is introduced. In the case of Dell Inc., repeated practice with its high-velocity, built-to-order production model enabled the computer manufacturer to consistently increase inventory turns—thereby strengthening its direct sales initiative over

Table 9.1 Barriers to erosion response-lag drivers

Barriers to Erosion	*Response-Lag Drivers*
IT Resources Barrier	IT Assets • IT infrastructure* • Information repositories* IT Capabilities • Technical skills[†] • IT management skills[†] • Relationship assets*
Complementary Resources Barrier	Complementary Resources*[†]
IT Project Barrier	Technology Characteristics • Visibility • Uniqueness • Complexity Implementation Process • Complexity • Process change
Preemption Barrier	Switching Costs • Tangible co-specialized investments* • Intangible co-specialized investments* • Collective switching costs* Value-System Structural Characteristics • Relationship exclusivity • Concentrated links

*Response-lag drivers subject to asset-stock accumulation processes.

[†]Response-lag drivers subject to capability development processes.

time—and subsequently to leverage its advantage to reach previously unserved consumers and small accounts through the Internet.

Asset-Stock Accumulation   Critics of the sustainability potential of information systems and IT contend that information technologies today are easily imitable and readily acquirable in the open market. However, many of the assets underpinning an IT-dependent strategic initiative cannot be readily acquired, particularly when they are internally developed. For example, specialized databases and ad-hoc forecasting models need to be custom developed; the same goes for an IT infrastructure (e.g., Walmart). This also holds true for many complementary resources as well.

Asset-stock accumulation represents the process by which a firm accrues or builds up a resource over time. Assets of this kind must be built up and developed as a result of a consistent process of accumulation. For example, at the core of Harrah's initiative discussed throughout this chapter, there is a comprehensive centralized repository of personal and behavioral data about each gambler, and a set of predictive computer models that forecast a player's projected worth. Harrah's ability to collect data and develop the predictive models depends on having information systems for data collection, storage, analysis, and distribution. These only became available when Harrah's launched its IT-dependent strategic initiative. Moreover, no matter how committed a competitor may be, the process of data accumulation requires time to complete. Consider a destination customer who visits a Las Vegas property once per quarter to play blackjack—collecting six data points about her (i.e., information on six visits) requires one and a half years.

For these reasons, sustainability often does not stem from visionary one-time initiatives, but rather from evolutionary initiatives predicated on a commitment to capability building and asset-stock accumulation. On this basis, the firm can develop the strategic initiative, offering a moving target to its competitors by reinforcing its barriers to imitation over time.

 ## APPLYING THE FRAMEWORK

When looking to be innovative with information systems and IT, you can easily get wrapped up in wishful thinking about the potential of new ideas and new technologies. Importantly, the sustainability framework is as useful in helping you to decide when *not* to pursue an IT-dependent strategic initiative as it is in suggesting when to do it. You can use the framework when evaluating IT-dependent strategic initiatives either as the innovator looking to protect an existing advantage or as the laggard looking for ways to respond. This is done by asking a series of increasingly specific questions.[9]

Prerequisite Questions

Since the focus of the analysis here is on sustainability (i.e., appropriation of value over time), you must assume that the IT-dependent strategic initiative under investigation does indeed create value and is consistent with the firm's priorities. The set of prerequisite questions discussed next can be used as a check.

Is the Proposed Initiative Aligned with the Firm's Strategy?   This crucial question often goes unasked until late in the analysis. (Sometimes it never gets asked!) This question is important because it is necessary for the proponents of the initiative to be able to formulate how the initiative advances the firm's positioning and strategy. If the firm has developed a strategic information systems plan (see Chapter 6), this question is relatively easy to answer by ensuring that the proposed initiative follows the information systems guidelines.

Is the Proposed Initiative Focused on Reducing the Firm's Cost or Increasing Customers' Willingness to Pay?   Rare, but particularly coveted, initiatives have the potential to accomplish both—decreasing the firm's cost while increasing customers' willingness to pay. As we discussed in Chapter 7, the value of this question is in requiring managers to clearly define the value proposition of the planned initiative.

What Is the IS Design Underpinning the Proposed Initiative?   This question is designed to formalize even more the analysis begun with the second question. At this stage in the analysis, one needs to achieve clarity with respect to the information processing functionalities of the

---

[9]We frame the analysis here by referring to a proposed initiative. Thus, we take the perspective of the innovator evaluating a new initiative. The same script can be used, with minor adjustments, by followers as well.

information system supporting the proposed initiative. Each of the four components—IT, people, processes, and organizational structures—also needs to be discussed to evaluate what changes to the current information systems will have to be made, and what new resources may be needed. This question is also crucial because it is the first step in evaluating the chances of implementation success of the needed information system (see Chapter 2).

Sustainability Questions

While it is impossible to estimate perfectly the magnitude of any particular barrier to erosion, the purpose of this analysis is to refine the design of the IT-dependent strategic initiative, identify areas of potential weakness, and identify areas where changes to the initiative—often small ones at this stage—can substantially strengthen it. Perhaps the most important aspect of this analysis is to identify initiatives that are not sustainable. Because it is important to understand when to avoid investing in expensive projects, the following questions can raise red flags before substantial resources are committed to the initiative.

What Competitors Are Appropriately Positioned to Replicate the Initiative? Based on a clear understanding of the characteristics of the proposed IT-dependent strategic initiative, the objective of this competitor analysis is to evaluate the strength of the IT-resource and complementary-resource barriers to erosion. Competitor analysis allows the innovator to identify sources of asymmetry that can be exploited and amplified through the deployment of the proposed initiative. The objective is to design the initiative so that it takes advantage of the existing sources of asymmetry, and provides a basis to reinforce them over time through capability development and asset-stock accumulation.

A powerful opportunity here is to take advantage of competitors' rigidities, which are resources that hamper competitors' ability to replicate an innovation. A classic example is provided by firms with strong distribution ties (e.g., Compaq computers, Levi's), which could not easily replicate direct sellers' use of the Internet (e.g., Dell, Lands' End) because of channel conflict. While Compaq, for example, may have had the ability to sell directly from its website, as Dell does, it wasted precious time early on because it could not risk upsetting its dealers, who were responsible for the bulk of its distribution. As a consequence, it experienced a substantial delay in responding to Dell's move online.

The result of this analysis is a clearer understanding of which competitors are in a position to respond quickly to the IT-dependent strategic initiative, and which will instead need to first acquire necessary resources or capabilities. This analysis may also provide guidance as to how hard it would be for competitors to acquire these prerequisite resources. It is clear that when fundamental resources are heterogeneously distributed, substantial response lag can be created. Developing initiatives that amplify and leverage this heterogeneity is a critical step in your analysis.

How Long before Competitors Can Offer the Same Value Proposition? This question is primarily concerned with the response lag associated with the creation, rollout, and infusion of the information systems at the heart of the IT-dependent strategic initiative. This analysis yields an assessment of the strength of the IT project barrier.

After a visioning stage, where the main characteristics of the initiative are envisioned by managers, the information system at the core needs to be developed and implemented. This process follows a sequential set of stages from inception to full functionality (see Chapter 11). It generally includes the following sequential stages: system definition, system build, and system implementation. Upon completion of the process, the cycle often restarts with maintenance and enhancements to the system.[10]

Competitors looking to have the same information processing functionality in place, and thus be able to offer the same value proposition, need to enter a similar development and implementation cycle. The only difference is that a follower will start the process with an awakening phase rather than a visioning phase.

The awakening stage occurs when the competitor realizes that the innovator has an advantage. The timing of the awakening depends on the characteristics of the initiative and can occur when the competitor begins to witness losses (e.g., market share, revenue), when the innovation is first introduced (typically for customer-facing systems), or even before the innovator has launched the initiative. Knowledge of behavior patterns exhibited by competitors may help in gauging the timing of the awakening and of the subsequent stages.

For example, Burger King has traditionally shown a propensity to quickly enter geographical markets pioneered by McDonald's. While not technology related, this type of knowledge of the competition is what allows the innovator to more precisely estimate lead time. In some rare cases, some competitors will find imitation so daunting that they will elect not to follow. The SABRE reservation system, pioneered by American Airlines, and the Apollo reservation system, built by United Airlines, emerged as the dominant airline reservation systems because other airlines elected early on not to follow the lead of these two carriers. The decision not to engage in the design and development of their own reservation systems was based on a consideration of the expense and risk associated with such projects.

Will Replication Do Competitors Any Good?   Armed with an understanding of which competitors will be in a position to respond to the innovator's IT-dependent strategic initiative, and a general idea of how long it may take them to have the same functionality in place, the innovating firm must estimate the magnitude of the preemption barrier to erosion. The fact is that being second sometimes means being left behind (remember the eBay example?). Exploiting the characteristics of the innovation and the industry in which they compete, innovators can sometimes preempt any meaningful response by competitors.

Even when outright preemption is not possible, the attentive innovator often has the ability to create substantial obstacles for any prospective imitator by levying switching costs. Preemption is strongest when the firm can identify a link in the value system where few customers or partners (e.g., suppliers) exist, and the partners that do exist place a premium on having an exclusive relationship with only one firm. In this scenario, they may eventually sever their relationship with the firm and do business with a competitor, but they won't trade with both at the same time.

Consider, for example, a five-unit restaurant operation that wants chainwide forecasts and historical analyses of trends, such as those offered by business intelligence-data consolidators like Avero Inc. In this case, for the software to be useful, all five units must use it (Figure 9.11). From Avero's standpoint, customers (in this case, the restaurant chain) place a premium on an exclusive relationship. The restaurant chain will either use Avero for all five

---

[10]Thoughtful readers will note that the rationale offered by those who suggest that IT is not strategic because it is easily imitable is that the technology can easily be replicated. In other words, this rationale addresses only the build and implementation phases of the IT development cycle. The attentive readers of this book know that there is much more to IT-dependent strategic initiatives than simply technology development!

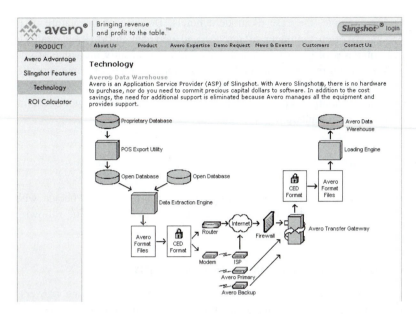

Figure 9.11   Avero Slingshot architecture (Image courtesy of Avero, LLC.)

restaurants, or it will switch them all to a competitor's software program. In either case, it will not work with two software vendors at the same time, as that would defeat the original purpose of data consolidation.

When such conditions are present or can be created, switching costs have the most power in raising the preemption barrier. When switching costs are high, competitors must indemnify any newly won customers for the cost of switching. As we stated previously, competitors must be that much better than the leader, where "that much" is determined by the magnitude of the switching costs.

The set of three questions offered above should provide the innovator, or any follower who is using this analysis as a diagnostic tool to study the leader's IT-dependent strategic initiative, with an idea of how defendable the initiative is and the available options to improve its barriers to erosion. No initiative is static, though, and barriers to erosion decay over time as competition runs its course. As a consequence, you should ask one more question to complete the analysis.

What Evolutionary Paths Does the Innovation Create?

Sheltered by its lead time, the innovator can and should seek ways to reinforce its barriers to erosion. Based on their understanding of the capability development and asset-stock-accumulation processes described previously, the leading firm's managers can chart an evolutionary path for the initiative. While the evolutionary paths thus identified must be revised as the situation changes, the analysis to this point can highlight important response-lag drivers that can be strengthened over time. Performing this analysis will also ensure that the evolution of the initiative is intentional rather than haphazard, and minimizes the likelihood that opportunities will be missed.

Consider, for example, the case of modern hotels. Because of the nature of the lodging service, where guests often volunteer preference and personal information, many hotels have assembled vast databases of guest needs and likes. Yet until recently the value of guest data for analyses (e.g., customer lifetime-value analysis) was not recognized by managers (cynics may suggest that it still largely isn't). A careful analysis of guest-reward initiatives may have shown that the substantial information repositories that accumulated as a byproduct of the initiative are subject to asset-stock accumulation.

 MAKING DECISIONS

On the basis of the analysis discussed above, you are in a position to decide whether to go forward with a proposed initiative or shelve it for future reevaluation. The following are three possible broad outcomes from the analysis:

Develop the IT-Dependent Strategic Initiative Independently

Independent development is warranted if the analysis suggests that strong barriers to erosion exist, and the firm foresees the ability to appropriate the value created by the initiative over the long term (i.e., sustainable advantage can be attained). Independent development is also warranted if the leader can reap an acceptable return on its innovation, even though the analysis shows that competitors will eventually be able to overcome the barriers to erosion.

Note once again that focus should be on the IT-dependent strategic initiative as a whole. The determination of whether the technology at the core of the initiative should be developed in a proprietary manner will depend on the role that the response lags associated with it play in the sustainability of the advantage (i.e., the IT project barrier).

Develop the IT-Dependent Strategic Initiative as Part of a Consortium

When the initiative is unlikely to yield sustainable competitive advantage for the innovator, but, even after replication by competitors, it will improve the overall profitability of the industry, the firm should attempt to create a joint venture with competitors or engage them in a consortium. In this scenario, the leader should strive to minimize costs and risks associated with the initiative and seek to share them with competitors since all will benefit in the long term.

Shelve the IT-Dependent Strategic Initiative

When the analysis suggests that the initiative will not offer strong barriers to erosion, and retaliation by competitors will degrade the average profitability of the industry (e.g., any value created is driven to customers by competition), the firm should shelve the proposed initiative. If the firm does go ahead with the initiative, the likely outcome is competitors' imitation and the creation of value that will be competed away and appropriated by customers. For these types of initiatives, the firm should refrain from being the innovator and instead plan to follow only when strictly necessary. Because of the fast-declining costs of IT and IT implementations, being a follower with nonsustainable innovations enables the firm at least to replicate the leader's initiative at a much lower cost.

SUMMARY

In this chapter, we demonstrated that quibbling about the strategic potential offered by information technology is not a productive use of management time and efforts. A large number of cases, including eBay Inc., Dell Inc., Harrah's Entertainment, and Walmart, provide evidence that IT-dependent strategic initiatives, with technology at their core, can be a source of sustained advantage for the modern firm.

More importantly, though, this chapter armed you with the tools to make recommendations about whether a specific firm should pursue a specific IT-dependent strategic initiative, or if it is better served by forgoing the financial investment and implementation effort. Specifically, we learned that

- When analyzing the potential to defend a competitive advantage created by an IT-dependent strategic initiative, you must estimate the magnitude of the following four barriers to erosion: IT Resources Barrier, Complementary Resources Barrier, IT Project Barrier, and Preemption Barrier. The extent to which an IT-dependent strategic initiative can be protected from competitors' retaliation is a function of the presence and significance of the response lag drivers that underpin it.

- An IT-dependent strategic initiative is defendable when the magnitude, in terms of time and money, of one or more of the barriers to erosion is such

to discourage imitation or to render it impossible or impractical.

- Information technology (IT) can be critical to the sustainability of competitive advantage. However, aside from rare occasions, it is not the IT itself that ensures sustainability, but rather the characteristics of the IT-dependent strategic initiative that the technology enables.

- The useful life of an IT-dependent strategic initiative (i.e., the span of time while the firm is able to protect the added value it created) can be extended by rejuvenating the barriers to erosion. Two processes, capability development and asset-stock accumulation, enable the firm to maintain its leadership position.

- The outcome of the analysis is one of three recommendations: (1) Pursue the IT-dependent strategic initiative independently, when the firm can protect it or reap an acceptable return on investment before competitors can successfully retaliate; (2) pursue the IT-dependent strategic initiative as part of a consortium, when the firm cannot protect it, but all the firms in the industry will be better off once replication has occurred; or (3) do not pursue the IT-dependent strategic initiative when the firm cannot protect it and industry profitability degrades once replication has occurred.

STUDY QUESTIONS

1. The CEO of your company, where you serve as the CIO, recently read the article title "IT Doesn't Matter" (see Further Readings list). He calls you into his office to "pick your brain," and asks, "Why do we invest money in IT when every one of our competitors can buy the same technology?"

2. Why is the difference between information systems and information technology so important to the analysis of sustainability?

3. Describe each of the four barriers to erosion.

4. For each barrier to erosion, provide an example of an IT-dependent strategic initiative that, in your opinion, leverages the barrier. Can you identify which response-lag drivers underpin the barriers to erosion in your examples?

5. Review your answers to the questions at the end of the opening mini-case. Have they changed? Why or why not?

6. Identify some businesses that currently appear to have a sustainable advantage. How does IS contribute to this sustainability? Highlight any cases where this sustainability appears to have a non-IS foundation or where there is no complementary IS to support the firm's value proposition.

7. Identify some businesses that currently appear to have no sustainable advantage and as a result are losing market share, are in (or close to) Chapter 11, or have gone out of business in the last year. Did a competitor's IS contribute to this decline or was there some other fundamental problem?

8. Can IS create a sustainable competitive advantage, or only support a firm in achieving a sustainable competitive advantage based on a compelling value proposition? Use evidence to support your argument.

FURTHER READINGS

1. Carr, Nicholas G. (2003). "IT Doesn't Matter." *Harvard Business Review*, May, Vol. 81, pp. 5–12.
2. Nevo, S., and M. R. Wade. (2010). "The Formation and Value of IT-Enabled Resources: Antecedents and Consequences." *MIS Quarterly* (34:1) pp. 163–183.
3. Piccoli, G., and Ives, B. (2005). "IT-Dependent Strategic Initiatives and Sustained Competitive Advantage: A Review and Synthesis of the Literature." *MIS Quarterly* (29:4), pp. 747–776.
4. Porter, M. E. (2001). "Strategy and the Internet." *Harvard Business Review*, March, Vol. 79, pp. 63–78.
5. Tapscott, D. (2001). "Rethinking Strategy in a Networked World." *Strategy and Competition*, Third Quarter.

GLOSSARY

- **Asset-stock accumulation:** The process by which a firm accrues or builds up a resource over time.
- **Barriers to erosion:** The difficulty, expressed in time and money, that competitors must overcome to match the value proposition offered by the leading firm.
- **Capability development:** The process by which an organization is able to improve its performance over time by developing its ability to use available resources for maximum effectiveness.
- **Competitive advantage:** The condition where a firm engages in a unique transformation process and has been able to distinguish its offerings from those of competitors. When a firm has achieved a position of competitive advantage, it is able to make above-average profits.
- **IT-dependent strategic initiatives:** Identifiable competitive moves and projects that enable the creation of added value and that rely heavily on the use of information technology to be successfully implemented (i.e., they cannot feasibly be enacted without investments in IT).
- **Resource:** Assets (i.e., things the firm has) and capabilities (i.e., things the firm can do) that the firm can deploy and leverage as part of its IT-dependent strategic initiatives.
- **Response lag:** The time it takes competitors to respond aggressively enough to erode a firm's competitive advantage. The delay in competitive response.
- **Response-lag drivers:** The characteristics of the technology, the firm, its competitors, or the value system in which the firm is embedded that combine to make replication of the IT-dependent strategic initiative difficult and costly. Response-lag drivers combine their effect to levy barriers to erosion.
- **Sustained competitive advantage:** The condition where a firm is able to protect a competitive advantage from competitors' retaliation.

Getting IT Done

The last part of this book is dedicated to the many issues that surround the management of information systems and technology in modern organizations—from budgeting and operational planning, to design and development, to ongoing operations. Keeping with the focus of the text, this section is not overly technical. Rather, it concentrates on what general and functional managers need to know to be actively involved in the management of their firm's or function's information systems resources.

Your involvement with the decisions discussed in this section is essential. While you can typically avoid worrying about hardware decision making, the same cannot be said of software applications and the issues that surround them. Software applications enable and constrain how work is done, and have a direct impact on organizational operations and climate. Thus, as the organizational expert and the person responsible for the success of your business function, you must have a say in the funding and prioritization of projects, you must be intimately involved in the design or selection of new systems, and you must be cognizant of the organizational risks associated with security and privacy failures.

In order to be an asset to the team making the aforementioned decisions, you must understand the processes that surround them, remain up to date on the information systems trends that concern these decisions, and be well versed in the vocabulary and issues pertaining to the management of information systems resources. Part IV of this book is devoted to these topics. Specifically,

- *Chapter* 10: *Funding and Governance of Information Systems.* This chapter focuses on the decisions and techniques pertaining to the funding and the governance of information systems. It also discusses outsourcing decisions and the outsourcing decision-making process.

- *Chapter* 11: *Creating Information Systems.* This chapter describes the process by which IT-enabled information systems come to be. It discusses the three main avenues for new systems creation: systems design and development, systems selection and acquisition, and end-user development.

- *Chapter* 12*: Information System Trends.* This chapter introduces the enduring and emerging information systems trends that concern general and functional managers. It then describes and discusses the characteristics and implications of each one.
- *Chapter* 13*: Security, Privacy, and Ethics.* This chapter makes the case for why general and functional managers need to be intimately involved in information security, privacy, and ethics decisions. It then provides the background to partake in the organizational debate of these issues.

C H A P T E R

10

Funding and Governance of Information Systems

What You Will Learn in This Chapter

We begin Part IV by discussing how modern organizations support, fund, and manage their information systems efforts.

In this chapter you will learn:

1. To understand the relationship between strategic information systems planning and the yearly budgeting and prioritization process.

2. To be able to articulate the role that general and functional managers play in the yearly budgeting and prioritization process.

3. To define, comprehend, and use the appropriate vocabulary, including concepts such as total cost of ownership (TCO), business case, and steering committee.

4. To evaluate the three main funding methods used by modern organizations: charge-back, allocation, and overhead. You will also learn their respective advantages and disadvantages.

5. To understand the yearly budgeting and prioritization project, and be able to evaluate individual and portfolio risks of information systems projects.

6. To define the terms *outsourcing* and *offshoring*, and identify the primary drivers of this enduring trend. You will also be able to articulate the principal risks of outsourcing and offer some general guidelines with respect to the outsourcing decision.

MINI-CASE: BUDGETING AT PERFORMANCE BOARDS, INC.

As the chief information officer (CIO) at Performance Boards, Inc., you chair the IT steering committee. Performance Boards has recently been acquired by Big Sporting Manufacturer, Inc. and is currently operating independently as a wholly owned subsidiary. During the yearly IT budgeting process, or the "ultimate fighting championship," as you call it, you are the unwilling center of attention—the arbiter of all disputes. It's that time of the year again, as shown by the calls you are receiving from other managers you hardly hear from all year.

Every July, the budgeting process starts with a call for projects. Every functional area responds with a rank-ordered list of initiatives that need funding, and their supporting business cases. Once the steering committee reviews the preliminary proposals, each executive sponsor presents the case for his or her proposed projects. Armed with this information, the steering committee deliberates and chooses the projects to be presented to the executive team for inclusion in the overall budget. Typically, whatever the steering committee proposes, the executive team approves. The executive team's main concern is overall IT spending. Bjorn Dunkerbeck, the founder and CEO of Performance Boards, is adamant that the firm should be in line with the manufacturing industry benchmark of 3.3% of revenue as a yearly IT budget.

This year, the third year of declining revenues for the firm, the ultimate fighting championship is shaping up as an all-time great—not a good thing for you! You had set aside 64% of the budget for the information systems function to control, in accord with industry allocation benchmarks. Your group needs the money for security, disaster recovery, general maintenance, infrastructure management, and administrative expenses. Yet, because of the tightening budgets, for the first time in your tenure as CIO you are being questioned and required to justify the allocation to the IS function.

At this point, the human resource project and the inventory management projects seem most likely to get green-lighted. The vice president of human resources has been asking for an upgrade to the benefits package management application for three years now. His business case shows both productivity improvements and higher retention of employees. The chief operating officer presented the business case for the manufacturing group. He has shown a substantial ROI associated with the proposed supply chain and just-in-time inventory management initiatives.

The VP of accounting and the new director of sales, Robby Naish, are exerting lots of pressure to obtain funding for their projects as well: an upgrade to the accounting management system, and a sales force automation (SFA) application, respectively. Naish has just finished reiterating his case to you on the phone. Being new to the firm, he is becoming quite frustrated with Performance Boards' approach to budgeting: "How am I supposed to compete with a project that increases productivity and one that improves efficiencies through automation? They can easily compute an ROI, but my project is not suited to that type of analysis. I can surely come up with some fictitious ROI number. I can pull them out of the thin air if this is how you guys do business!"

As you review the current informal ranking of projects, you can't help but think that you need to find a way not to alienate the functional managers and project sponsors. The last thing you need is for the IS function to be perceived as a roadblock to the success of the other functional areas, and ultimately of Performance Boards, Inc. as a whole.

DISCUSSION QUESTIONS

1. What should you do next? What are some of the options at your disposal to ensure that you do not alienate your colleagues?
2. Are there any structural problems with the budgeting process at Performance Boards, Inc.? What improvements would you suggest for next year—if any?

INTRODUCTION

In Chapter 6, we discussed the information systems strategic planning process. Strategic information systems planning involves identifying the long-term direction of information systems use and management within the organization. It provides a framework for decision making and project selection. Within this framework the firm develops yearly operational plans and budgets in order to prioritize information systems spending.

As a general or functional manager, you need to understand how the budgeting and prioritization processes work so that you can make the most of them. All too often we see organizations funding information systems using simple metrics, like percentage of revenue or fixed increments over the previous year's budget. While these metrics have a place in the budgeting process, the yearly budget is an opportunity to formally evaluate competing projects and make the (sometimes tough) comprehensive prioritization decisions necessary to align information systems with the firm's strategy. The firm that fails to do so misses the opportunity to offer guidance and a clear mandate to the IS function. The consequence is that a lack of direction and cohesive effort will degrade service (in many cases leading to outright failure) and demoralize the firm's IS professionals.

Note that this prioritization role should not be delegated to the information systems group, but should be made in concert with business managers (i.e., those who need the information systems) and IS professionals (i.e., those who make and manage the information systems). An IT group that does not deliver consistently is often the product of an executive team that fails to provide clear priorities. Note that this occurrence is not at all uncommon. The *Wall Street Journal* recently reported that only 26% of business unit executives they surveyed self-classified as "smart" about information technology—a paradoxical result given the importance that information systems resources have today for the success of most enterprises.[1]

INFORMATION SYSTEMS GOVERNANCE

Information systems governance is generally defined as the set of decisions rights and the guiding accountability framework designed to ensure that IT resources are employed appropriately in the organization.[2] IT governance in the modern firm has two principal aspects: the management of downside risk and the fostering of upside potential. The first facet, IT risk governance, is concerned with decisions for minimizing threats (e.g., security risks) and failures (e.g., unsuccessful project implementations). The second facet, IT value governance, is concerned with maximizing the value of IT investments and the firm's ability to leverage its information systems resources.

While to any casual observer it would appear obvious that the board of directors within an organization needs to pay close attention to information systems and IT decisions, one of the most enduring research findings is that most boards of directors abdicate this duty. For example, the consultancy company Deloitte recently reported that the great majority of 400 directors surveyed recognized the critical role the IT plays in their firm's success. However, only 14% of the respondents reported being actively involved in setting IT strategy[3]—and often executives can't quite articulate who should and why. Moreover, while 66% acknowledged that the board of directors should concern itself with IT decisions, only 11% reported discussing information systems decisions regularly.

As we stressed in Chapter 6, while firm executives need not evaluate every project, they do need to set up the framework for decision making about information systems resources within their organization.[4] There are a number of models and approaches that guide the design of an IT

[1]Special report on IT leadership: Editor's note, *The Wall Street Journal* (April 25, 2011).

[2]Weill, P., and Ross, J. (2004). *IT Governance*, Harvard Business School Press, Cambridge, MA.

[3]Deloitte Consulting, "You're Talking, not Walking," Corporate Board Member (March/April 2007).

[4]Weill, P., and Ross, J. (2011). Four questions every CEO should ask about IT, *The Wall Street Journal* (April 25, 2011).

Table 10.1 Five categories of risk the board of directors must address[5]

IT Competence Risk	This risk factor captures the degree of IT-related knowledge of the board of directors. While boards of directors need not all be as knowledgeable as CIOs or IT professionals, it is critical that they have the ability to follow IT discussions and ask relevant questions. Moreover, there should be a leading IT director who maintains an up-to-date competence on IT matters.
Infrastructure Risk	A firm's IT infrastructure represents the set of IT components that are interconnected and managed by IT specialists with the objective of providing a set of standard services to the organization. It provides the foundation for the delivery of business applications. The board of directors must be keenly aware of the weaknesses and risks associated with the firm's IT infrastructure.
IT Project Risk	In Chapter 3, we provide a sample of high-profile IT project failures. IT projects are generally complex and expensive undertakings that, if not properly managed, can put the organization in peril. The board of directors must ensure that the appropriate guiding framework for IT projects is in place. In large organizations this may require a project office, a certification process for project managers, and a portfolio approach to IT project management (see below).
Business Continuity Risk	Business continuity refers to the activities a firm performs to ensure that critical business functions remain operational in a crisis, and that the organization can withstand unforeseen disasters (see Chapter 13). The board of directors must ensure the existence of a business continuity plan and that such a plan is periodically tested and revised.
Information Risk	Information risk pertains to the many hazards associated with the collection and use of organizational, partner, and customer data (see Chapter 13). The board of directors must craft a governance system that ensures that an officer of the organization has clear responsibility for signing off and ensuring compliance with established privacy and security policies.

governance framework for an organization. The specifics of these models are beyond the scope of this book. However, recent research has highlighted five key areas of concern that boards of directors must proactively address (see Table 10.1). In order for a board of directors to take a proactive stance to IS governance, these five areas of potential risk must be monitored and cyclically evaluated.

Beyond the management of the principal risks associated with information systems use in organizations, the governance framework an organization puts in place must also ensure that the use of IT resources is aligned with organizational strategy and priorities.

Steering Committee

Larger organizations often formalize management involvement in information systems decision making by forming a steering committee. The steering committee brings together representatives from the various functional areas, the CEO (or other general management staff), and key IS professionals (e.g., CIO) who convene regularly to provide guidance to the IS function and share the responsibility for aligning its efforts with the larger business strategy. The steering committee is typically the venue where business cases are presented for approval, or as a filter

---

[5]Parent, M., and Reich, B.H. (2009). Governing Information Technology Risk, *California Management Review* (51:2), pp. 134–152.

before the budgeting process. The steering committee is also the main recipient and evaluator of progress during system development and implementation efforts.

 # FUNDING INFORMATION SYSTEMS

As with any other organizational asset, the firm must account for and fund information systems assets and expenses. Information systems are typically designed, built, implemented, and managed to achieve some business goal (e.g., improve factory floor efficiencies, increase sales effectiveness and customer repurchase). The exception is provided by shared services (e.g., security, planning and administration, business continuity initiatives) and infrastructure investments. There are three main methods used by modern organizations to fund information systems: chargeback, allocation, and overhead. Each one offers advantages and disadvantages.

Chargeback

The chargeback approach calls for direct billing of information systems resources and services to the organizational function or department that uses them. It is grounded in the pay-per-use principle. For example, a department may be charged for networking expenses based on the volume of traffic it initiates, and for personal productivity software based on the number of concurrent software application licenses it runs.

The main advantage of chargeback mechanisms is their perceived fairness, and the accountability they create for both users and the IS function. Another advantage of such systems is the degree of control they afford to general and functional managers, who can proactively control their function's information systems expenses. However, maintaining such detailed costing mechanisms can generate substantial direct and indirect expenses, including the cost of tracking and those for auditing and dispute resolution of charges.

Chargeback systems typically treat the IS function as a cost center. That is, the units are billed on the basis of actual costs. In some instances, particularly when the IS function has some unique skills, it may become a profit center and compete for service provision with external vendors. In rare cases it may also sell its services to other firms, not only to internal users, and return the profits to the organization.

Allocation

The allocation approach calls for direct billing of information systems resources and services to the organizational function or department that uses them. However, rather than a pay-per-use metric, it computes allocations based on more stable indicators such as size, revenues, and number of users. For example, a hotel chain may charge individual hotels in the chain on the basis of the number of rooms. A chain of retail outlets may charge each unit a fixed percentage of revenue or square footage.

The allocation method seeks to strike a balance between the pay-per-use fairness and the high cost of the chargeback method. Since rates are typically set once a year, the expenses each unit can expect are also more predictable. Some functional managers prefer the predictability of fixed allocations, while others prefer the higher degree of control offered by the chargeback mechanism.

Overhead

The overhead approach treats information systems as a shared expense to be drawn from the organization's overall budget rather than to be paid for by each unit. This is the simplest approach to funding information systems, since decisions are made once a year during the budget approval process. It also provides the most control to the IS function over spending decisions. As a consequence, the IS function is more likely to experiment and evaluate new technologies.

The main drawback of the overhead approach is a lack of accountability for both the functional areas and the IS department. On the one hand, since users are not billed directly, they are less likely to proactively manage their usage and filter their requests for service and new projects. Moreover, they remain largely unaware of their impact on the overall IS budget, which often leads to misconceptions about the cost of IT resources and the reasonable expectations for service. On the other hand, since the IS function has little accountability to the individual functional areas, it is more likely to be less responsive and to offer poorer service.

Recognizing their complementarities, some organizations adopt a blend of funding approaches for the Information Systems function. For example, while infrastructure services and maintenance may be billed based on the overhead method, new projects and new systems may be billed based on an allocation approach.

THE BUDGETING AND PROJECT PRIORITIZATION PROCESS

The yearly budgeting process is a tool organizations use to communicate plans and enforce control systems. As a planning tool, the budget provides an assessment of what the firm believes future financial flows will be. As a control mechanism, the budget helps encourage and enforce specific behaviors. More subtly, the budget can be used to allocate decision rights and power. In 2011, IT advisory firm Gartner found in its IT spending and staffing report that IT spending ranged from 0.7% to 6% of revenue in the industries surveyed (Figure 10.1).

For example, in an organization where the information systems function controls the bulk of the IT budget, decisions regarding the use of the IT resource will be highly centralized. In this case, the information systems group will be able to identify and create efficiencies, but users will enjoy limited flexibility. Conversely, if much of the IT budget is controlled by individual units, they will be able to fund tailored initiatives, but integration and firm wide efficiencies are left without a strong sponsor.

Typically, control over the IT budget is split, with a portion allocated to the information systems function for infrastructural expenses and projects that enable the business to operate in a reliable and secure manner (e.g., disaster recovery planning, business continuity initiatives, information systems security management). The remainder is controlled by the individual units, for funding operations of existing systems and for funding new projects (Sidebar 1).

Making the Budget

The budgeting process requires trade-offs between diverging interests, and the prioritization of projects under resource constraint. This can make for a very stressful process within which executives must argue and rally support for their initiatives, all the while attempting to ensure that information systems resources are deployed to meet the strategic demands of the business.

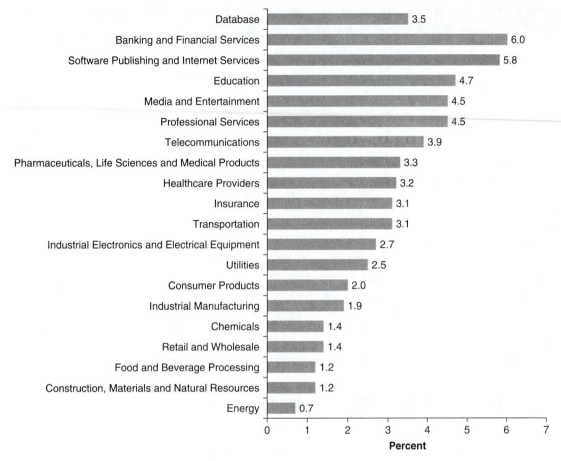

Figure 10.1   IT spending as a percentage of revenue[6]

The budgeting process varies by organization, but there are typically two decisions to be made: determining the appropriate budget for ongoing operational expenses (e.g., maintenance) and evaluating large capital expenditures (e.g., new systems). Published industry benchmarks can be instrumental in offering some guidance, but it is essential to stress that your firm's budget is dictated by its vision and architectural guidelines (Chapter 6), and the unique contingencies it faces. For instance, a firm that has been very successful in rationalizing and consolidating its infrastructure can be expected to have below-average ongoing IT expenses. Conversely, if a firm ran a number of legacy applications in need of substantial upkeep, it would be spending above average.

A sound appreciation for the role of information systems in the firm (i.e., the information systems vision) is even more important when evaluating capital expenditure and new information systems projects. This is critical, not so much for the evaluation of individual initiatives, but for the evaluation of the aggregate degree of information systems risk the firm is willing to accept.

---

[6]Potter, K., et al. Gartner, Inc., IT metrics: IT Spending and Staffing Report, 2010 (January 25, 2011).

SIDEBAR 1: SAMPLE OPERATIONAL IT BUDGET

This sample operational IT budget is loosely based on that of a major hotel chain.

Expenses	*Amount (U.S. dollars)*	*Percentage*
Payroll	3,140,000	31.4
Travel & entertainment	270,000	2.7
Depreciation*	450,000	4.5
Amortization†	1,080,000	10.8
Training	30,000	0.3
Equipment/hardware/software purchases‡	90,000	0.9
Maintenance	680,000	6.8
Telecommunications expense	520,000	5.2
Disaster recovery	10,000	0.1
Misc. other operating expense	180,000	1.8
Corporate IT allocation§	3,530,000	35.3

*Capitalized equipment is subject to depreciation.

†Capitalized software is subject to amortization.

‡Equipment below the capitalization threshold.

§IT allocation from the parent company. For firms without a parent company, this line would spread over the other items in roughly the same percentages.

FUNDING INFORMATION SYSTEMS PROJECTS: MAKING THE BUSINESS CASE

The business case is a formal document, prepared and presented by the general or functional manager sponsoring the project. It provides the rationale for pursuing the opportunity. Its primary objective is to explain and provide evidence to convince the executive team, typically during the budgeting process, that the initiative will pay off and its funding is warranted. Note that a firm will not only require a business case to be developed for new systems, but often the business case will be used to evaluate ongoing spending decisions and to evaluate existing systems as well.

Traditionally, business cases required fact-based investment analyses grounded in financial indicators such as internal rate of return (IRR), return on investment (ROI), or net present value (NPV). They required an analysis of the timeline of the project and its future cash flow stream, and supporting evidence for project benefits and cost estimates. However, in order to provide these analyses, project proponents all too often had to make assumptions and arbitrary judgments.

The business case approach is a standard in modern organizations, with 96% of respondents to a recent survey[7] reporting that they had to prepare some form of business case, and 68% reporting their belief in the value of the technique. However, despite their popularity, business cases have encountered significant criticism. Sixty-five percent of respondents to the same survey

---

[7]Ward, J., Daniel, E., and Peppard, J. (2008). "Building better business cases for IT investments," *MIS Quarterly Executive* (7:1), pp. 1–15.

reported some degree of dissatisfaction with estimating the benefits of the proposed initiative, while 38% reported having to overstate the value of the project benefits in order to get it green-lighted.

Limitations of the Business Case   The traditional business case technique is increasingly receiving criticism. The skeptics suggest that business cases strictly based on fact will often require so many assumptions and speculations that they will become based on fiction. This problem is less likely with "automation" initiatives (i.e., first-order change (see Chapter 2)), but it is particularly evident for projects that rely on business or technical innovation and, as a consequence, are characterized by significant uncertainty as to the final outcome. Financial projections are also difficult to make for projects that have mostly "soft" benefits. Consider as an example a firm that decides to invest significantly in social media, as the global pizza-delivery chain Domino's has done recently. Today, Domino's Pizza has over 2.5 million fans connected to its U.S. Facebook page. These fans participate in the chain's social media initiatives (e.g., contests, polls, specials)—a recent contest for the "super-secret pizza hand sign" was a winner with 1,223 "likes" and 169 comments in 11 hours (though I am still not sure what a pizza hand sign really is!). It is quite clear that Domino's has an established presence in social media and has gained significant traction with this initiative. However, what is the value of such customer engagement? How much more revenue would an initiative like this generate? These remain very difficult questions to answer.

The limitations of a traditional business case approach are clearly exemplified by the president of a large hotel chain explaining how his firm justified a recent customer relationship management project: "You can't justify such a project with traditional methods. There is too much uncertainty beforehand. You know this is the right project because it fits with your strategic positioning and brand. This is how we are going to differentiate our product in the marketplace."

Overcoming the Limitations of the Business Case   In order to overcome the limitations of a traditional business case, some observers point to the value of heuristics. A heuristic is a simple rule that is good enough to make decisions, recognizing that adjustments along the way will be necessary. This approach offers another advantage: It systematizes the reevaluation of both the costs and benefits of projects during their development. Another valuable approach consists of relaxing the focus on fact-based business cases and allowing proponents of a project to ground their request on faith (i.e., project rationale based on beliefs about market trends, customer expectations, competition, strategy) and fear (i.e., need to engage in projects to keep from falling behind the competition or to avert a likely negative outcome). Typically, a well-crafted business case will include all of the above: fact, faith, and fear-based arguments.

Recent literature has advanced a more formal approach to modern business cases, one that develops in six sequential steps:[8]

1. *Define Business Drivers and Investment Objectives:* Business case writers should begin by establishing the business drivers underlying the need for the project and by clearly spelling out the investment objectives and their relationship with the business drivers. If the firm has engaged in the strategic IS planning process (Chapter 6), much of the work underlying this first stage has already been completed.

---

[8]Ward, J., Daniel, E., and Peppard, J. (2008). "Building better business cases for IT investments," *MIS Quarterly Executive* (7:1), pp. 1–15.

2. *Identify Benefits, Measures, and Owners:* Business case writers should then identify all the potential benefits accruing to all stakeholders if the project is successfully implemented. Note that benefits could extend beyond the investment objectives, or even be un-intended. Once all benefits are identified, the business case writer should explain how benefits will be measured and who will own them (i.e., who will be representing the stakeholder group that the benefit will accrue to).

3. *Structure the Benefits:* The value, and the challenge, of business cases revolve around the ability to accurately assess the actual realizable benefits of the project. Structuring the expected benefits using the grid below (Figure 10.2), can foster deep, focused discussions that can significantly increase the precision of benefits evaluations.

4. *Identify Organizational Changes enabling Benefits:* Heading each column in Figure 10.2, benefits are categorized as the ones that accrue from doing new things (e.g., create Facebook- only pizza specials, thus being able to track demographics of interested customers), doing things better (e.g., improve call center operations by centralizing customer information for easy access by representatives during a call), and ceasing to do things (e.g., stop printing and shipping paper procedure manuals by transferring them online). While this may appear to be a simplistic categorization, it helps to make explicit the type of change that will bring about the change.

5. *Determine the Explicit Value of each Benefit:* Heading each row in Figure 10.2, benefits are categorized by the extent to which they can be made explicit. It is important to specify, during the writing of the business case, the extent to which a benefit is measurable in order to ensure the maximum degree of precision in their estimation. Benefits can be classified as:

   a. Financial Benefits: Computed by applying cost/price metrics or other recognized financial formula to measure the benefit.

   b. Quantifiable Benefits: Computed by gathering metrics, expressed in number form, that provide evidence of change univocally attributable to the project.

		Type of Business Change		
		Do New Things	Do Things Better	Stop Doing Things
High ↑	Financial Benefits			
Degree of Explicitness	Quantifiable Benefits			
	Measurable Benefits			
↓ Low	Observable Benefits			

Figure 10.2 Benefits evaluation grid for business cases

c. Measurable Benefits: A measure is available to monitor a given benefit, but changes in such metrics cannot be univocally tied to the project.

d. Observable Benefits: There exist agreed upon criteria, albeit not quantifiable, to evaluate the impact of the project on this class of benefits.

Failing to structure this evaluation often results in the business case writer overlooking potential benefits, or stopping at a level of precision in their evaluation that is unnecessarily coarse.

6. *Identify Costs and Risks:* A complete business case concludes with an estimation of the costs the firm will incur to see the project through to completion, as well as the degree of uncertainty and risk surrounding successful completion. Project costs will include all technology development expenses, licensing fees, training, and change management initiatives. Beyond the development costs, the firm should include the total cost of ownership (TCO). TCO is a financial estimate designed to explicitly recognize the full life cycle costs of IT assets. The costs of information systems and technology typically far exceed the costs of acquisition (e.g., selection, licensing, implementation), and include expenses that occur after the system is up and running but are necessary to maintain it in operation over its life span. These include ongoing training of users and support personnel, maintenance, upgrades, security, and business continuity investments. Even the end-of-life costs associated with retiring the asset should be included in TCO calculations. TCO is an imprecise measure that depends on substantial estimation and assumptions about feasible configurations and future events. Nonetheless, it is essential to estimate TCO as comprehensively as possible when developing the business case. Today there is commercial software that can be used to aid in TCO computations (Figure 10.3).

Figure 10.3   Computing TCO using commercial software   (*Source*: Grant Scott/Glow Images)

When discussed in the abstract, the business case development process can sound highly theoretical. Conversely, the technique discussed here is very practical and pragmatic. Sidebar 2 illustrates it in action.

SIDEBAR 2: WRITING THE BUSINESS CASE[9]

The Business Objective

This company is a major global provider of mobile telephone services to both consumers and businesses. Following an internal restructuring of its service and territorial divisions, the U.K. consumer division wished to improve the service provided to customers and its ability to promote new network services and features to existing customers. The company believed that excellent customer service was one of the few ways it could differentiate itself from competitors in a very competitive market. It had also invested considerable amounts of money in new network facilities and needed to increase sales of its higher end services to recoup this investment.

The company identified that service improvement and the promotion of its newer services could be achieved by upgrading its call center systems. Most service requests from customers came into the call center. If the request was dealt with promptly, the company believed the call center agent could then discuss newer service offerings with the customer.

In addition to dealing with incoming service requests, agents would also make outbound marketing and promotional calls to customers. A new customer-profiling system would be deployed so that the service being promoted, and the script used, could be tailored to the perceived customer needs. Agents would also collect data from customers during service and promotional calls, and record it in the profiling system. This data would be used both to improve future targeting and to develop new service offerings.

Business Drivers

External drivers

The company perceived competing mobile telephone services as being indistinguishable, so it was difficult to differentiate its offerings on brand alone. In the past, it had tried to compete on price but had found it difficult to sustain this. Hence it saw service as a differentiator.

Internal drivers

The company needed to recoup the high investment it had made in network access and infrastructure by increasing customer take-up of its higher-end services.

Investment Objectives

The company identified two objectives for the investment in upgraded call center systems:

■ Significantly improve the service provided by the call center and reduce service failures

■ Increase the take-up of newer services and collect customer profiling information to better target new services.

Benefits

The main benefits that would be realized by achieving the two objectives are shown in Figure 5. The total expected financial benefits amount to £1,805,000 ($3,587,400) per annum.

The benefits framework shown in Table 10.2 is typical of many IT investments. It includes a full range of benefit types, from observable to financial. While the senior managers involved were keen to show that the financial benefits provided an acceptable return to the organization, they recognized that the observable benefits were of most interest to the hundreds of call center agents who were required to use the new systems and adopt new ways of working. The agents' buy-in to the new system was key to making the investment a success.

The benefits in this example also cover the full range of business changes, from discontinuing things the company wished to avoid, such as call-backs to customers due to service call failures, to doing new things, such as promoting new higher-value services during service calls. The example also demonstrates that it is easier to put a financial value on things the company is already doing and either wishes to stop or do better. It is, however, harder to determine a robust quantity or financial value for benefits resulting from innovation.

---

[9]The case presented in this sidebar is minimally modified from Ward, J., Daniel, E., and Peppard, J. (2008). "Building better business cases for IT investments," *MIS Quarterly Executive* (7:1), pp. 1–15.

Table 10.2   Benefits evaluation grid

Objective Type	Doing New Things	Doing Things Better	Stop Doing Things
Financial		**Benefit:** Increased customer retention due to improved service provision **Measure:** Reduction in customer defections. Avoided defections due to service failure = 1,750 pa. Cost per defection = £500—saving of £875,000 pa **Benefit Owner:** Customer accounts manager **Benefit:** 20% reduction in call servicing costs **Measure:** Cost per service call. Number of calls pa = 5.6 million, total servicing costs = £1.2 million—savings of £240,000 pa **Benefit Owner:** Telechannel sales manager	**Benefit:** Stop call-backs to customers after failed service calls **Measure:** Number of call-backs. Number in previous years = 1.5 million. Cost per call-back = £0.46—savings of £690,000 pa **Benefit Owner:** Call center operations manager
Quantifiable			**Benefit:** Eliminate call waiting times of over 2 minutes for customers **Measure:** Number of calls currently waiting over 2 minutes = 1.1 million **Benefit Owner:** Call center operations manager
Measurable	**Benefit:** Call center staff able to undertake sales calls/promote new services **Measure:** Number of sales calls per staff member or sales per staff member. Current value = 0 (call center currently purely inbound) **Benefit Owner:** Telechannel sales manager	**Benefit:** Customers not switching to competitors' products and services **Measure:** Number of defections to competitors. Current number of customers switching = 5,500 pa **Benefit Owner:** Customer accounts manager	
Observable	**Benefit:** Call center staff motivated by being trained about newer services **Measure:** Increased call center motivation **Benefit Owner:** Call center staff manager	**Benefit:** Ability to develop future services based on customer data **Measure:** Quantity and quality of customer profile data **Benefit Owner:** New service development manager	**Benefit:** Stop customers becoming frustrated/rude because of service failure **Measure:** Call center staff opinion **Benefit Owner:** Call center staff manager

Investment Costs and Risks

In this section are detailed the investment costs that the mobile phone company incurred in implementing its new call center systems (Table 10.3) and the risks involved (Table 10.4).

Table 10.3   Investment costs

Investment Costs	
Purchase of new call center hardware and software:	£250,000
Cost of implementation technical consultants:	£120,000
Internal systems development costs (for configuration):	£150,000
Infrastructure upgrade costs:	£75,000
Business change costs:	£270,000
Training costs:	£80,000
Total:	**£945,000**
Net increase in annual systems support and license costs:	£80,000

Table 10.4   Risks of the project

Risk Analysis	
Technical Risks:	Complexity of the systems functionality
	Number of system interfaces and systems being replaced
Financial Risks:	Confidence in some investment costs—especially business change
	Confidence in the evidence for some of the benefits
	Business criticality of areas affected by the system
Organizational Risks:	The extent of changes to call center processes and practice
	Limited existing change management capability
	Call center staff capability to promote more technical services
	Customer willingness to share information for profiling purposes

Individual Project Risk

An important aspect of business case writing is the estimation of project risk. This is an important assessment, both when evaluating the risk of individual initiatives, and also particularly when measuring the overall risk of all projects under development in the organization at a given point in time. Information systems projects are renowned for their high degree of risk and incidence of failure. However, the risks associated with any one particular initiative can vary widely based on the following:

- *Project size.* Project size, expressed as the estimated monetary investment, is a proxy for project complexity and the potential consequences of failure. Note that you should focus less on the absolute size of the project (e.g., $12 million) than on its size relative to the typical kind of project the information systems group in your firm undertakes. In other words, a $12 million initiative carries different risk for a firm that typically handles $20 million projects than one that is mostly familiar with $150,000 efforts.

■ *Experience with technology.* The degree of experience a firm has with the technologies (e.g., hardware, software development, environment) at the heart of the project is a primary determinant of risk. Working with new and unproven technologies carries more risk than using mature ones. However, the relative novelty of the technology to the firm is also an important source of risk.

■ *Organizational change.* The degree of organizational change that the project requires is another important determinant of risk. As we discussed in Chapter 2, third-order change is much more difficult (and risky) to implement than second- and first-order change.

With respect to the cost/benefits that a system is expected to deliver, different initiatives vary significantly with respect to the size of the investment they call for and the expected useful life over which they will deliver the benefits. A large enterprise system will require a significant up-front investment but will deliver its benefits over decades. Conversely, a redesign of the company website will typically require a fraction of the investment but will also obsolesce much more quickly.

A portfolio approach can be used to optimize the blend of projects under development and ensure a balance of the overall risk, as well as proactively manage the cost/benefits of the applications under development.

Portfolio Management

After evaluating the risk of each proposed project, management should take a portfolio approach to information systems risk management. The set of ongoing information systems projects a firm has underway can be categorized into sub-classes based on the objectives of the initiative: Strategic projects seek new value creation and appropriation. Informational projects seek increased control and better information management. Transactional projects seek efficiency and cost cutting. Infrastructural projects seek integration and streamlining of the firm's IT infrastructure (Figure 10.4).

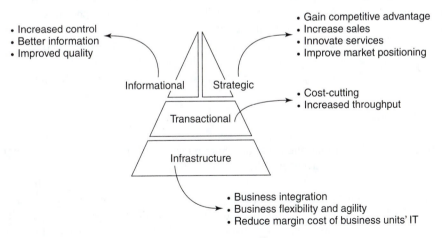

Figure 10.4 IT project portfolio components[10]

---

[10] Adapted from Weill, P., and Broadbent, M. (1998). *Leveraging the New Infrastructure—How market leaders capitalize on Information Technology*, Harvard Business School Press.

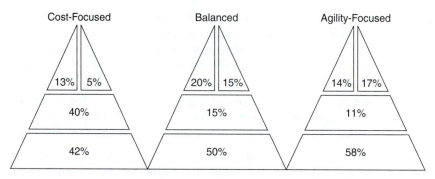

Figure 10.5   IT project portfolio profiles[11]

During the budgeting process, when the firm evaluates the collection of initiatives for the coming year, it should determine the appropriate level of aggregate risks it is willing to accept. The risk profile will change depending on the blend of strategic, informational, transactional and infrastructure projects the firm chooses to engage in (Figure 10.5). Note that this evaluation is a managerial decision, not an IT decision. While information systems professionals must help in evaluating project risk, it is the responsibility of the steering committee or the board of directors to decide what overall degree of risk the firm should accept given its overall strategic information systems plan.

A portfolio approach to managing information systems risk ensures that the funded initiatives fit the risk profile that the firm has deemed appropriate. For instance, firms in the strategic quadrant (Chapter 6) typically need to take on much higher aggregate risk than those in the support quadrant. The blend of projects they engage in is also different. This is due to the fact that in the first case information systems assets and initiatives are instrumental to the success and growth of the firm. The same cannot be said for those organizations that choose a very defensive approach to information systems use and management (e.g., support quadrant). In such a case, a high degree of aggregate portfolio risk is a signal that the firm is not managing information systems in accord with its strategic information systems plan. It may be that the organization needs to reevaluate and update its information systems vision, perhaps moving into the turnaround quadrant. Conversely, it could be that the firm is failing to take advantage of the budgeting and prioritization process to enforce the existing (and appropriate) plan.

OUTSOURCING

Information systems outsourcing is often used as a means of funding information systems operations by engaging outside providers. Outsourcing is the process of acquiring products or services that used to be created internally by the organization, from an outside provider. Information systems outsourcing is the process of contracting with an outside firm to obtain information systems services. Such services can range from automation of specific processes (e.g., payroll), to management of specific assets (e.g., data center), to development of new applications, to outright management of the IS function as a whole (i.e., full outsourcing). Outsourcing of information

---

[11] Adapted from Weill, P., and Broadbent, M. (1998). *Leveraging the New Infrastructure—How market leaders capitalize on Information Technology*, Harvard Business School Press.

systems services is now estimated to be a $284.9 billion industry, as measured by worldwide spending.

Drivers of Outsourcing

When outsourcing information systems and IT to a specialist, the outsourcing firm is typically driven by one or more of the following considerations:

Reduced Cost   Perhaps the primary driver for the outsourcing decision is the intention to capitalize on the provider's ability to create economies of scale in the production of IT services. Large providers of information systems services can consolidate their infrastructure (e.g., data centers) and enjoy superior bargaining power when dealing with technology vendors (e.g., hardware and software firms).

Access to Superior Talent   Many organizations find it difficult to attract top IT talent. The reason is simple: Top IT graduates want to be challenged and want to remain on the cutting edge of technological development. But many organizations cannot (and should not!) make this objective a priority. Conversely, IT service providers are in the business of continually seeking to improve their information systems operations, evaluate new technologies, and attract the best talent.

Because of these structural differences, outsourcing contracts offer the opportunity for organizations to access top IT talent and receive an infusion of technology and information systems management expertise.

Improved Control   In many organizations that resort to outsourcing, particularly full outsourcing, the driving force for the decision was an attempt to reclaim control over the IT function when it was perceived to be inefficient and unable to provide the appropriate level of service to the organization. By engaging in a contractual arrangement with an outside provider, the theory goes, the firm can surface costs, making them explicit, and hold the provider to its service level agreements.

Improved Strategic Focus   For many organizations information systems operations are considered (rightly or wrongly) a nuisance rather than a core strength of the firm. For these organizations outsourcing has considerable appeal because it enables the firm to focus on what it considers its strengths and eliminate what is often a little understood function that generates significant frustration for senior management.

Financial Appeal   Outsourcing arrangements where the service provider acquires the infrastructure and IT professionals of the outsourcing organization, liquidate some of the tangible and intangible assets tied up in the IT infrastructure. As such, these deals can strengthen the balance sheet and have considerable financial appeal.

The Risks of Outsourcing

While the drivers of outsourcing described above provide a strong case for the decision, the outsourcing literature and history have provided many examples of outsourcing deals gone bad. The following are the major potential drawbacks that must be carefully evaluated before taking the plunge:

The Outsourcing Paradox   Organizations that resort to information systems outsourcing often do so out of frustration with their current IT operations. Yet if you have little faith in your ability to manage information systems internally, how can you expect to be able to make sound outsourcing decisions (i.e., draft advantageous contracts) and monitor the performance of the service provider? How can you determine the appropriate amount to pay for the services, and the service levels you should expect? How do you know that you are getting what you paid for?

The Dark Side of Partnerships   The word *partnership*, when used in a business context in particular, can be very misleading. While the outsourcing firm and the service provider are "partners," as they work together to ensure the success of the operation, each has a responsibility to shareholders to maximize its own performance. This conflict of interest sometimes leads to friction and court battles. Imagine, for example, a service provider that is under pressure to cut costs and increase profitably. This result can be achieved by reducing customer service, particularly in areas where service levels are difficult to measure, hard to monitor, have no penalties attached, or have not been clearly specified in the contract.

Changing Requirements   One of the primary dangers in an outsourcing relationship is given by the length of the contracts in relation to the speed of technological and business needs evolution. For example, a ten-year contract will see significant change in organizational requirements before it is up for renewal. Yet outsourcing contracts are often very lengthy and specific in order to limit the possibility of self-interested behavior (e.g., service degradation).

Hidden Coordination Costs   One of the biggest surprises awaiting organizations that outsource information systems is the extent of coordination efforts needed to work with the provider. Coordination efforts include communicating requirements, monitoring and measuring the provider's activities and services, handling dispute resolution, and the like. These coordination efforts come at a cost of course, a cost that must be estimated beforehand and used in the decision-making phase.

The Deceptive Role of Information Systems   While many organizations outsource on the contention that they are not in the "IT business" or that "IT is not a core competency" for the firm, a lot of organizations underestimate the critical role that information systems play as enablers of business success.

Offshoring

Outsourcing has received substantial recent attention in the United States because of the prominence of the debate over loss of jobs to foreign countries allegedly brought about by one of its variants: offshoring. Offshoring, short for offshore outsourcing, is the process of engaging a foreign provider to supply the products or services the firm no longer intends to produce internally.

Offshoring has received much impetus since the commercialization of the Internet, which significantly lessened the impact of geographical and time differences on the transaction of information-based services (e.g., software design and development). Offshoring growth has been fueled by many of the same drivers of outsourcing, particularly cost and quality, with much of the business moving to India and China—countries that enjoy a significantly lower cost of living than the United States or Europe, and offer a seemingly endless pool of highly qualified IT talent.

Making Optimal Outsourcing Decisions

As with any other complex and far-reaching managerial decision, there are no silver bullet solutions when it comes to outsourcing. The outsourcing decision requires a clear understanding of the characteristics of the organization and of the relationship with the service provider—a debate that general and functional managers must be involved in.

The strategic grid (see Chapter 6) can provide helpful guidance by mapping the current and future role that information systems are expected to play in the firm. Typically, firms that find themselves in the support and factory quadrant may find it easier to outsource given the standardized and well-understood role played by information systems resources. More difficult is the decision for firms in the turnaround and strategic quadrants. Here, due to the critical role that information system assets must play in enabling the firm's strategy, outsourcing may be both challenging and risky. In this case, particularly for firms with limited access to new technologies or superior IT talent, outsourcing may be the only viable solution. However, these firms will typically provide critical information systems services in house.

In most cases, a firm should not resort to full outsourcing, locking itself into one provider, but should instead rely on selective outsourcing arrangements. Selective outsourcing arrangements are those where the firm relies on multiple providers offering different services. In such arrangements the firm often retains an internal information systems group and enables it to compete for the contract against outside service firms.

Perhaps the clearest advice that can be offered to firms considering outsourcing is to maintain a core group of information systems specialists and a strong CIO function: first, having the in-house expertise to match the organization's business needs to the appropriate information systems services—whether these services are provided in-house or not—is fundamental. Second, it is critical to have a group of internal employees, with an allegiance to your firm, who understand what the service firms are providing and how best to manage the relationship. Third, it is critical for the in-house information systems group to be skilled at negotiation, contract writing, and the on-going monitoring of service level agreements.

 # SUMMARY

This chapter begins our discussion of the techniques and methodologies that modern organizations use to introduce and manage information systems within the framework provided by the strategic information systems plan. As a general or functional manager, you must understand this process in order to fund initiatives of interest to your area and to partake in the overall budgeting and prioritization process in partnership with other executives and information systems professionals.

Specifically, in this chapter we learned that

- Total cost of ownership (TCO) is a financial estimate designed to explicitly recognize the life cycle cost of IT assets. The costs of information systems and technology typically far exceed the cost of acquisition (e.g., selection, licensing, implementation), and include expenses that occur after the system is up and running but are necessary to maintain it in operation over its life span.

- Project sponsors use TCO in the formulation of the business case. The business case is the formal documentation used to garner support and win funding for the initiative. The project sponsor presents the business case to the executive committee or, in larger organizations, to the steering committee. The steering committee, composed of representatives from the various functional areas and IS professionals, provides guidance for the use of information systems assets and shares the responsibility for aligning IS efforts with business strategy.

- Modern organizations use one of three approaches to the funding of information systems operations and projects: chargeback, allocation, and overhead. The chargeback method, requiring direct billing based on actual usage, gives the most control to users but has the highest administrative costs. The allocation method, requiring direct billing based on measures such as size or revenue, seeks to strike a balance between fair billing and administrative overhead. Finally, the overhead method, drawing funding directly from the overall organization's budget, is the simplest to administer but reduces accountability of both the IS function and units using the services.

■ The yearly budgeting process is the tool organizations use to assess future information systems requirements and prioritize funding. The budgeting process enables the firm to encourage and enforce specific behaviors and to allocate information systems decision rights and control. It can be a fairly stressful and emotionally charged process in which managers compete for funding of their projects.

■ During the budgeting process the firm has an opportunity to evaluate the risk of proposed projects, both individually and as a portfolio. The firm must take this opportunity to evaluate whether the degree of risk associated with its current portfolio of projects matches the risk profile the firm deemed appropriate during strategic information systems planning.

■ Information systems outsourcing is the process of contracting with an outside firm to obtain information systems services. Modern organizations outsource their complete IS function (i.e., full outsourcing) or some of their IS assets and services (i.e., selective outsourcing), seeking one or more of the following benefits: reduced costs, access to superior information systems talent, improved control over IS resources, a freeing up of resources to focus on core competencies, and liquidated IT assets. When evaluating outsourcing of information systems services, you need to consider the following risks: A firm with admittedly poor IS management will have difficulties evaluating providers and negotiating good contracts; outsourcing partners seek to maximize their own performance, which often creates friction; IS requirements evolve rapidly; and information systems operations are often more strategic than executives realize.

STUDY QUESTIONS

1. Describe the relationship between strategic information systems planning and the yearly budgeting and prioritization processes. What is the objective of each?

2. Why should general and functional managers be involved in decisions about the funding of information systems assets and services?

3. What is a business case? What is its purpose? Who should be developing and presenting the business case for a new information system?

4. Define the following terms: total cost of ownership (TCO) and steering committee.

5. Describe each of the three main information systems funding methods and discuss the advantages and disadvantages of each.

6. What are the key drivers of new information systems project risk? Why should a firm evaluate the aggregate risk of its portfolio of projects? What should the organization do if the current level of portfolio risk is not aligned with the degree of risk deemed appropriate according to the strategic information systems plan?

7. Define and differentiate the following terms: Outsourcing, information systems outsourcing, offshoring, full outsourcing, and selective outsourcing. What are the principal drivers and risks associated with information systems outsourcing?

FURTHER READINGS

1. Huff, S. L., Maher, P. M., and Munro, M. C. (2006). "Information Technology and the Board of Directors: Is There an IT Attention Deficit?" *MIS Quarterly Executive* (5:2), pp. 1–14.

2. Lacity, M., Willcocks, L., and Feeny, D. (1996). "The Value of Selective IT Sourcing." *Sloan Management Review*, Spring, vol. 37, no. 3, pp. 13–25.

3. Lacity, M., Willcocks, L., and Feeny, D. (1995). "Information Technology Outsourcing: Maximizing Flexibility and Control." *Harvard Business Review* (May–June), vol. 65, pp. 84–93.

4. McFarlan, F. W. (1981). "Portfolio Approach to Information Systems." *Harvard Business Review*, vol. 51, pp. 142–150.

5. McFarlan, F. W., and Nolan, R. L. (1995). "How to Manage an IT Outsourcing Alliance." *Sloan Management Review,* Winter, Vol. 36, no. 2, pp. 9–24.

6. Nolan, R., and McFarlan, F. W. (2005). "Information Technology and the Board of Directors." *Harvard Business Review*, vol. 83, no. 10 (October), pp. 96–106.

7. Parent, M., and Reich, B. H. (2009). Governing Information Technology Risk, *California Management Review* (51:2), pp. 134–152.

8. Ross, J. W., and Weill, P. (2002). "Six IT Decisions Your IT People Shouldn't Make." *Harvard Business Review*, November vol. 80, pp. 84–92.

9. Rottman, J., and Lacity, M. (2004). "Twenty Practices for Offshore Sourcing." *MIS Quarterly Executive*, vol. 3, no. 3, pp. 117–130.

10. Ward, J., and Elizabeth, D. (2006). *Benefits Management: Delivering Value from IS & IT Investments*, Wiley.

 ## GLOSSARY

- **Allocation:** A method of funding information systems where the cost of services is billed to the organizational function that uses them based on some stable metric (e.g., size, revenues, number of users).
- **Business case:** A formal document, prepared and presented by the general or functional manager sponsoring the project. It provides the rationale for pursuing the opportunity.
- **Chargeback:** A method of funding information systems where the cost of services is billed to the organizational function that uses them based on actual usage.
- **Chief information officer (CIO):** The individual in charge of the information systems function.
- **Information systems outsourcing:** The process of contracting with an outside firm to obtain information systems services.
- **Governance:** In general terms, governance represents the set of processes, policies, and practices for administering and controlling an entity.
- **IS governance:** Information systems governance is the set of decisions rights and the guiding accountability

framework designed to ensure that IT resources are employed appropriately in the organization.
- **Offshoring:** Offshoring, short for offshore outsourcing, is the process of engaging a foreign provider to supply the products or services the firm no longer intends to produce internally.
- **Overhead:** A method of funding information systems where the cost of services is not billed to the organizational function that uses them. Rather information systems assets and services are funded directly from the organization's overall budget.
- **Steering committee:** The steering committee, comprised of representatives from the various functional areas and IS professionals, provides guidance for the use of information systems assets and shares the responsibility for aligning IS efforts with business strategy.
- **Total cost of ownership (TCO):** A financial estimate designed to explicitly recognize the life cycle cost of IT assets.

11

Creating Information Systems

What You Will Learn in This Chapter

This chapter covers a very important subject: the process by which organizational information systems come to be. While as a general or functional manager you may not concern yourself with hardware decisions, you must partake in the software design, acquisition, and implementation processes. Your involvement is essential because technology professionals rarely can evaluate the cost/benefit trade-off and impact of new information systems on the organization and its business success drivers.

Specifically, in this chapter you will learn:

1. To appreciate how complex it is to design and implement information systems and the stable, robust, secure technology at their core.

2. To articulate the advantages and disadvantages of custom software design and development versus acquisition of an off-the-shelf product.

3. To describe and be able to use the main methodologies for custom software design and development. Specifically, you will be able to identify the major phases of the system development life cycle (SDLC) and discuss its advantages and disadvantages. You will also become familiar with the prototyping approach and will be able to identify its principal advantages and disadvantages.

4. To describe the systems selection methodology and be able to use it to choose a prepackaged software program for a specific organization.

5. To describe the reasons for the increasing prominence of end-user development in modern organizations and to articulate the benefits and risks of this approach to software development.

MINI-CASE: PROJECT MANAGEMENT BLUES

"What am I going to do now?" you found yourself asking out loud while staring at the ceiling in your office. "Should I de-escalate this project or press on?" It felt like you were in one of those management case studies—except that it was real and it was you!

You replayed the events leading up to this dilemma. It all started when you were appointed the lead of the HRBPS team—the project team in charge of creating the new human resources benefits package management system. You had made a very successful business case presentation and received public praise from the executive team. "Finally someone who does not speak techno-mumbo-jumbo but can present an IT project in business terms!" had exclaimed LJ Lalli, the CEO. It had been your ability to interface with both the developers and the business stakeholders that had landed you the project manager position. You were the first project manager in your firm to come from a functional area (human resources) instead of the information systems function.

The project had proceeded very well, with great support from the user community—your former colleagues, of course. This was due in large part to your knowledge of HR and your stakeholder-friendly approach. You had made a conscious choice to seek user feedback, and to honor as many requests for enhancements as possible. "You have to freeze the requirements," had objected Erik Khan, the lead system analyst, "otherwise it's going to be anarchy." But you had dismissed his complaints as "development team grumblings." Those guys were never happy with a little uncertainty anyway. Having been on "the other side," as a stakeholder in a number of system development projects, you knew full well that unhappy users were the fastest route to system failure.

Now you were beginning to second-guess your decision. The original schedule called for releasing the beta version of the application for user testing later this week. Instead you had only 40% of the approved functionality coded. Moreover, your team was looking at a list of twenty-two enhancements, two of which would require a change in the database structure. Projected completion, without the proposed enhancements, entailed seven more months (a 45% increase on the original).

It was now apparent that the original project had also been underfunded. The current estimate for finishing the project with the approved set of requirements called for a 62% budget increase (over the original). It was unclear how much more it would cost to exceed the requirements since the twenty-two proposed enhancements had yet to be evaluated by the system architect.

You were due to present a progress report to Ms. Lalli tomorrow afternoon, but you were still unsure about what course to take. The only certainty at this point was that you had to make your pitch for a project extension and ask for further funding at the meeting. Your plan was to report on the current state of affairs, paint a picture of the final product, and seek support. But what was the final product going to be?

DISCUSSION QUESTIONS

1. What should your agenda for tomorrow's meeting be? Should you press on with your strategy, or is a change of course in order?
2. What would you do differently, if anything, given the chance to start this project all over again?

INTRODUCTION

Once a firm has developed a strategic plan for the use of information systems resources (Chapter 6) and has gone through the budgeting and prioritization processes (Chapter 10) to identify what specific information systems it needs, it is ready to act. Whether the information systems rely on custom-developed technology or off-the-shelf software, it is critical that you as a general or functional manager understand how information systems come to be. Armed with this knowledge, you can proactively participate in the process.

While general and functional managers need not be concerned with hardware decisions, they must take part in the software design, acquisition, and implementation processes. Aside from the significant portion of your budget devoted to information systems management and development, general and functional managers' involvement in information systems funding and design is essential because never before has a firm's success depended so much on the use of the right software applications. Deciding what the characteristics of the "right" applications are is a business decision. It is a decision based more on the business case and the understanding of the business processes the software will enable (or constrain!) than on any technical consideration.

How Hard Can IT Be?

Consider the following three recent examples, each playing out in the last few years, and answer the question (write your answers on a separate sheet) before reading on to find out what really happened:

- The U.S. subsidiary of one of the major food producers in the world inked a deal to implement SAP (the leading enterprise system application), in an effort to centralize and rationalize operations across its nine divisions. The project required streamlining processes, standardizing software applications, and implementing the same organizational structure across the units. How much time and how much money would you budget for this project?

- A large hospitality company with over 2,000 branded hotels developed a customer information system to enable its customer relationship management (CRM) strategy. The custom-developed functionalities of the software application at the heart of the information system included a property-management system, the loyalty and CRM applications, and the reporting modules. How much time and how much money would you budget for this project?

- A major telecommunication carrier scheduled an upgrade of its customer service systems from version 6 to version 7 of a leading off-the-shelf application. The newer, more powerful version, exchanging information with fifteen other systems (e.g., billing), would simplify customer service representatives' access to customer data, and would increase the amount of customer information available for sales and service transactions. How much time and how much money would you budget for this project?

There are few technologies and products that have evolved as far and as fast as information technology has. However, the astounding successes of IT can be misleading, tricking you into severely underestimating what it takes to build and implement a stable, robust, secure system that will work under a wide array of organizational conditions.

Should you check your answers one last time before reading on? OK, here's what happened:

- The implementation of SAP by the major food service company took over six years and over $200 million. It was mired by setbacks and dead ends, with high-profile casualties, including the project leader, who was reassigned midway through the implementation.

- The large hospitality firm invested over $50 million in the design and development of the application and in integrating it with the other applications in the firm's infrastructure. The project took about two years and by its conclusion it had cost about $120 million. The resulting system, the firm's largest investment in recent history, was considered a success.

- The upgrade at the telecommunication company was a complete failure. The new system was unstable, crashing for days at a time, and the old system was no longer usable. The customer service difficulties translated into an estimated $100 million in lost revenue during the three months it took to complete the upgrade. A rival acquired the firm, which was mired in difficulties, for half of its original valuation.

The critical insight to be gained from this simple exercise is that organizational information systems usher in a wealth of complexities that go far beyond those associated with the personal computing environment that is most familiar to the typical end user (i.e., purchasing and installing Microsoft Office) (Figure 11.1). Unfortunately, managers are surrounded by the misleading rhetoric of statements like "IT is easy, the hard part is people." Or "today firms can easily develop or purchase technology to obtain the capabilities to rapidly match their competitors." Or "IT is a commodity."

These views are gross oversimplifications of reality. When they are held by those who have never been involved in large-scale information systems development efforts, they dangerously hide the truth: organizational information systems development efforts are very complex and risky endeavors. They are complex and risky precisely because they involve both technical and social challenges—and the intersection of the two. Rob Austin, a Professor at the Copenhagen Business School and author, captured this notion best when explaining why information systems projects will likely never be as disciplined and predictable as other engineering processes (e.g., the building of a factory). He stated: "In classic IT terms, important "requirements" are often not discernible in advance. If this statement sounds wrong to you, try on the alternative—that it's always possible to discern all the important requirements in advance, regardless of the size and complexity of the system and the rate of technological and business change. [....] Indeed, what makes a system great in the end, usually, is not just that it satisfies requirements that were known in advance. The difference between a great, value-adding IT system and a clunky dog that everyone hates is often in the details that are discovered along the way, as the system is implemented and users begin to have a more tangible sense of how it will work."[1]

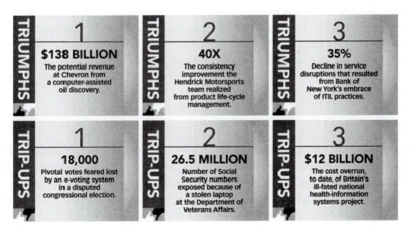

Figure 11.1   The potential and risk of IS projects (Image courtesy of Baseline Magazine www.baselinebag.com)

---

[1] Austin, R. (2005). "No crystal ball for IT," *CIO Magazine*.

The interplay of many different actors (often with divergent agendas), the sheer size of many organizational systems, the myriad of expected and unforeseen organizational conditions the system must support, and the constantly evolving nature of the modern firm make these projects extremely challenging. These projects require technical expertise. They also call for a big dose of managerial skill and informed involvement by general and functional managers.

FULFILLING INFORMATION PROCESSING NEEDS

In Chapter 2, we stated that the primary reason why modern organizations introduce information systems is to fulfill their information processing needs. Information systems leverage IT at their core to optimize the manner in which the firm captures, processes, stores, and distributes information.

How does the firm go about introducing the information processing functionalities needed to fulfill its information processing needs? How do information systems come to be in modern organizations? At the most general level of analysis, this process has two main components: technology development and information system deployment.

- *Technology development.* Modern information systems are built on an IT core. Whether the technology is acquired and integrated into the existing firm's infrastructure or it is custom built by (or for) the organization, generating the IT core is a prerequisite to delivering the needed information processing functionalities.

- *Information system development.* Creating the needed IT core is not sufficient to fulfill the information processing needs of the firm (see Chapter 2). The firm must successfully integrate the technology with the other components of the organization (i.e., people, processes, structure) to develop a working information system. This is the implementation process.

The technology development and implementation processes are intertwined, not sequential. Because of systemic effects (Chapter 2), the components of an information system must interact with one another without friction. Thus, the design of a new software program (i.e., technology development) must take into account how the technology will be employed (i.e., processes), by whom (i.e., people), and with what purpose (i.e., structure). That is, technology development must take into account future implementation as it is being designed.

Three Approaches

There are three general approaches to the acquisition of information processing functionalities and the introduction of IT-based information systems. Note that each of these approaches encompasses both the technology development and implementation processes. However, the critical differences among them pertain to how the technology components, and more specifically the software that defines the capabilities of the system, are designed and developed.

1. *Custom design and development.* With this approach the organization implements a software application that is expressly made, whether internally or through outsourcing, for the unique needs of the firm.

2. *System selection and acquisition.* With this approach the organization implements an off-the-shelf software application that is mass produced by a vendor.

3. *End-user development.* With this approach the organization uses a software application created by its end users, rather than the firm's information systems professionals.

We describe below the advantages and risks associated with each approach. We also introduce the most prevalent methodologies used to articulate the information systems design and development process in each case. Our objective here is not for you to become an expert in systems design and development. Rather, it is to help you nurture an understanding of the process so that you can successfully take part in it.

Make versus Buy

In some cases, custom developing the software at the heart of a new information system is not an option for your firm, it is a necessity. This is the case when the system must enable a new initiative and no market for such a product already exists. For example, when Amazon first introduced its personal recommendation system (Figure 11.2), electronic commerce was largely uncharted territory and the firm was indeed shaping the online retailing industry. Waiting for an off-the-shelf product to be developed was not an option.

Typically, though, the firm will have to weigh the choice between custom development and purchase of the needed technology. Each approach offers some advantages and disadvantages.

Advantages of Custom Development   While pre-packaged software is available in the marketplace, in many cases the firm will still engage in custom design and development to capitalize on the advantages of this process. Such advantages include the following:

Unique Tailoring   The defining characteristic of custom-developed software applications is that they are molded to fit the unique features of the firm that commissions them. A quote by Bill Bass, former senior vice president for eCommerce at Lands' End, provides an apt metaphor: "Fitting 100 some million women in the U.S. in 8 or 10 basic sizes as well as they would like is really impossible."[2] When we purchase clothes in standard sizes, they often fit well in one area and less well in another. Typically we accept this substandard fit. Yet those who find it hard to

Figure 11.2   Amazon.com's personal recommendation system
(*Source*: Imagebroker/Glow Images)

[2]Ives, B., and Piccoli, G. (2003). "Custom-Made Apparel and Individualized Service at Land's End," *Communications of the AIS* (Vol. 11, Article 3) pp. 79–93.

locate fitting clothes (and can afford it) can purchase tailor-made garments—perhaps using the Lands' End Custom website.

The human body is unique and no two people are alike. The same holds true for modern organizations. Thus, off-the-shelf software will "fit" well in some areas of the firm but may create problems in others and require some adjustment from the organization.[3] Conversely, custom-made software, like a tailor-made suit, can be designed to fit perfectly with the organization's characteristics and needs.

Note that while every organization is unique, not all of its processes are. For example, while Lands' End and Eddie Bauer are two different organizations, they both provide e-mail for their employees and do so in a very similar fashion. Standard mail server software will likely serve the needs of both firms quite well (Figure 11.3). Conversely, if the business processes that the software is designed to enable are unique and value adding (i.e., a source of competitive advantage), commercial off-the-shelf software may undermine their uniqueness and be detrimental to the firm.

Flexibility and Control   Custom-developed software applications offer the highest degree of flexibility and control to the organization. Because the project team builds the system from scratch, the software can be molded into any form the stakeholders (e.g., management, end users) would like it to take, and the firm owes no licensing fees to software vendors. Moreover, since the firm retains control over the code, the system can be evolved, at any time, in any direction the firm would like.

This level of control is not achievable with software purchased from vendors, since software houses need to develop applications that serve the needs of a large number of buyers. Moreover, the software house has to prioritize the features that will be coded into the upgrades. Typically they are the ones that have the broadest appeal, rather than niche requests from individual clients.

Advantages of Purchasing   As the software industry has evolved and grown dramatically over the last thirty years, the off-the-shelf offer has become comprehensive. Purchasing software from a vendor yields a number of advantages to the organization.

Figure 11.3   An open source mail server

---

[3] As we will see, this adjustment of the organization typically takes place during implementation when, taking the software as given, a working information system is developed.

Faster Roll-Out   An organization that purchases new software is typically interested in the information processing functionalities it enables, not in the IT itself. Thus, how quickly the firm can be "up and running" with the new information system is an important concern. Purchased software dramatically reduces the time it takes to obtain the software and begin the implementation process. Rather than engaging in the lengthy custom development process, the firm researches and evaluates existing packages before selecting one. Upon purchasing the selected application, the implementation phase is ready to start.

Knowledge Infusion   Another advantage offered by off-the-shelf applications is access to the expertise coded in the software. Because software programs can enable and constrain the manner in which users complete a task or execute a business process (see Chapter 2), an organization that purchases prepackaged software also acquires a "way of doing business." Consider the example of a call center operator who takes orders from catalog shoppers. The design of the application will determine the order in which the interaction takes place (e.g., greeting, items to be shipped, verification of address, payment), and what data are necessary to complete the transaction (e.g., no order can be completed without a valid phone number) (Figure 11.4).

This notion of knowledge infusion is now an important design and marketing tool for software vendors who proactively seek out best practices in order to code them into their applications. Returning to the call center example, an often mentioned best practice in call center operations is to enable personalized interactions with each customer. Thus, a call center software vendor may code a feature in its application that automatically brings up the customer's order history so that the representative may engage in informed conversation with the customer.

Economically Attractive   While it is always difficult to generalize when it comes to system design and development costs, purchasing off-the-shelf applications typically allows the firm to capitalize on the economies of scale achieved by the vendor. As with the example of mass-produced and tailor-made clothing, when a vendor can produce many units of the same software

Figure 11.4   Call center application
(*Source*: Blend Images/Image Source)

application, it enjoys declining fixed costs that, in turn, lower the unit cost. This is particularly true with software, a classic information good (see Chapter 4) characterized by very high costs of producing the first copy and negligible reproduction costs.

High Quality   A great deal of debate surrounds the issue of software quality, with the skeptics pointing to the many examples of pre-packaged applications that have significant bugs. Yet large software houses with mature products will point to their sizable testing budgets and large installed base of users as evidence that their applications have been put through the paces and thus all major problems have surfaced.

Buy and Make

The make versus buy decision is typically treated as a dichotomous one (i.e., the firm must choose one or the other approach).[4] Yet modern firms are increasingly adopting blended approaches, first acquiring systems and then modifying them extensively.

A Cutter Consortium survey found that, when asked about the degree of customization required by large off-the-shelf applications the firm purchased, less than 12% of respondents said they modified the software slightly or not at all. A quarter of them reported modifying the application "a great deal." Furthermore, half of the respondents reported that the degree of package customization they engaged in exceeded their pre-implementation expectations.[5]

Keeping with the current integration trends (Chapter 3), off-the-shelf applications are becoming larger and more complex, and are increasingly crossing departmental boundaries. Under these circumstances we can expect the need for extensive customization of pre-packaged products only to increase—a fact lost on unsophisticated general and functional managers who expect the application to work immediately after installation, the way simple personal productivity software does.

BUILD YOUR OWN: SYSTEMS DESIGN AND DEVELOPMENT

Until the rise to prominence of the software industry, the acquisition of pre-packaged software was the exception, rather than the norm, for most organizations. Its long tradition notwithstanding, designing and developing organizational software applications and information systems has always been a complex, failure-prone undertaking. Viewed by many as more akin to alchemy than to a reliable science, systems design and development continues to frighten non-IT managers, who perceive it as a minefield of technical, behavioral, and managerial challenges (see Figure 11.5).

In order to manage the risk and complexity associated with custom development, information systems specialists, academics, and consultants have contributed to the creation of a number of systems design and development methodologies.

Systems Development Life Cycle

The two dominant systems development methodologies today are the system development life cycle (SDLC) and prototyping. The SDLC approach is predicated on the notion that detailed justification and planning is the vehicle to reduce risk and uncertainty in systems design and

---

[4]To simplify the discussion, we discuss each approach separately as well.

[5]Ulrich, W. (2006). "Application Package Survey: The Promise versus Reality," *Cutter Benchmark Review* (6:9), pp. 13–20.

Figure 11.5   The SDLC as perceived by many managers

development efforts. Thus, spending considerable time up front, the project team improves the chances of solving the right business problem with the right information system design. For this reason the SDLC is a highly structured methodology where the outputs of one stage become the inputs of the next, and where the project team strives to keep changes after the project has started to a minimum.[6]

The SDLC methodology is articulated in three phases—definition, build, and implementation—each one further divided into three steps (Table 11.1).

Definition   The definition phase of the SDLC is concerned with clearly identifying the features of the proposed information system. The critical actors in this phase are the prospective end users and the general or functional managers who represent the main stakeholders.

From the information systems staff, systems and business analysts get involved. Systems analysts are highly skilled information systems professionals who are well versed in both technology issues and communication. Their role is to help users identify and articulate the system requirements and serve as a liaison with the technical staff (i.e., developers). Business analysts are individuals with expertise in business process redesign as well as technology. They help ensure that the business processes and software programs at the heart of an information system are jointly optimized and work smoothly together.

---

[6]The SDLC is often called the waterfall model because, as water flowing down a waterfall never flows upward, there should be no going back once a stage has been completed.

Table 11.1 Principal phases of the SDLC

Definition
Investigation
Feasibility analysis
System analysis
Build
System design
Programming
Testing
Implementation
Installation
Operations
Maintenance

Investigation   During investigation, proponents of the new system must identify what business issues the system will pertain to. Managers who envision new ways of operating are the driving force at this stage as they formulate the main goals, scope, and value proposition of the new system. This stage is typically very informal. The next stage brings a greater discipline to the analysis.

Feasibility Analysis   In order to ensure that scarce organizational resources are put to best use, the project team must heavily scrutinize the proposed project prior to giving the formal go-ahead. Specifically, the team must evaluate the technical, operational, and economic feasibility of the project.[7]

Technical feasibility is the evaluation of whether the proposed system is viable from an IT standpoint. The team must ask whether the state of the art in hardware, software, and telecommunication equipment is such that the proposed system will work as intended (e.g., it will have enough storage capacity and an acceptable response time). The history of new systems development abounds with examples of technology implementations that predated their time, thus undermining system success.

Operational feasibility, sometimes called behavioral feasibility, is the evaluation of whether the information system as a whole, not just the technology component, is viable. This analysis requires an evaluation of the other three components to make sure that employees have the skills necessary to utilize the new technology, and that they will accept (or can be given incentives to accept) the new work system. During this phase the project team must envision how business processes will be redesigned, and must foresee possible drivers of user resistance and rejection.

Economic feasibility is the evaluation of the financial viability of the proposed system. A number of techniques have been developed over time to justify the proposed investment, including ROI, payback, and net present value computations. Ultimately, evaluating financial feasibility consists of performing a cost/benefit analysis in order to ensure that the money to

---

[7]Note that the feasibility analysis for a new system is informed by its business case (Chapter 10), but there are differences. The business case mainly focuses on justifying the pursuit of the project (i.e., cost/benefit analysis), while the feasibility analysis looks comprehensively at all the factors that can hamper system success—technical, operational, and economic.

be spent on the system design and development project meets the firm's financial hurdles for investment. The business case provides the basis for this analysis (see Chapter 10).

The outcome of the feasibility analysis is a document culminating in a "go" or "no-go" recommendation. At this point the firm has invested a small amount of resources, relative to the full project cost; thus if the project is to be called off, this is an appropriate time to do so.

System Analysis   Once a decision has been made that the system is worth pursuing, the project team needs to identify and articulate the system requirements. Systems analysts and the stakeholders (i.e., end users, management) take center stage at this point. If the system is not simply automating existing tasks but is instead enabling redesigned business processes, business analysts will join the team.

In large systems implementations, it is impossible to involve all users at this stage; rather a subset of the user population joins the team, sometimes full-time. Note that it is critical to choose users who are representative of the broader population. That is, the team should include not only the users who are highest performing or most well versed with technology (so called super-users), but also underperforming and, most importantly, dissenting users (those individuals who may indeed resist rather than support the new system).

Another important aspect of user involvement is that it should not be "window dressing" or "impression management." Systems analysts must genuinely seek out and value stakeholders' input in the process. The system analyst is the specialist in this phase, not the user. It is therefore the system analyst's job to ensure a productive and comprehensive surfacing of requirements.

As the outcome of this stage, the project team produces the systems requirements document (Figure 11.6). This document details what inputs the system will accept, what outputs it will produce, what users will have access to what information, and so on. The document typically includes mock-up screens and scenarios (Figure 11.7) and is sent to the stakeholders for review and approval.

In a strict application of the SDLC methodology, once the stakeholders approve the document, the systems requirements are "frozen" and the cost of future changes, if any are requested, becomes the responsibility of the stakeholders. This step is necessary to minimize the impact of scope creep—the phenomenon by which stakeholders add or change requirements during the build phase of the SDLC, thus significantly increasing cost and considerably delaying development.

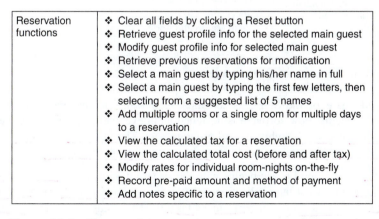

Reservation functions	❖ Clear all fields by clicking a Reset button ❖ Retrieve guest profile info for the selected main guest ❖ Modify guest profile info for selected main guest ❖ Retrieve previous reservations for modification ❖ Select a main guest by typing his/her name in full ❖ Select a main guest by typing the first few letters, then selecting from a suggested list of 5 names ❖ Add multiple rooms or a single room for multiple days to a reservation ❖ View the calculated tax for a reservation ❖ View the calculated total cost (before and after tax) ❖ Modify rates for individual room-nights on-the-fly ❖ Record pre-paid amount and method of payment ❖ Add notes specific to a reservation

Figure 11.6   User requirements

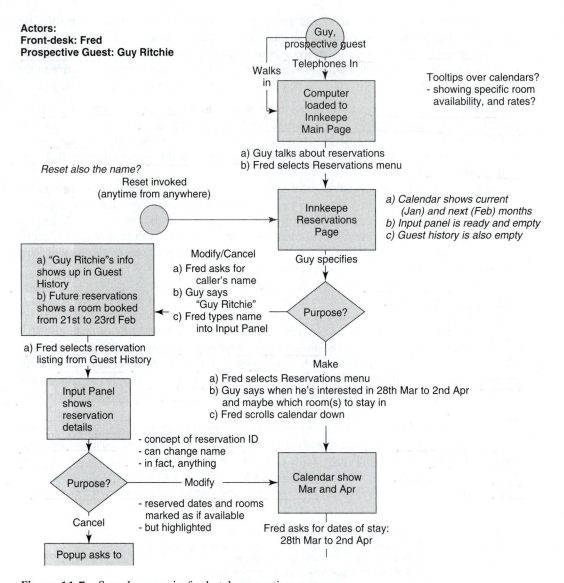

Figure 11.7 Sample scenario for hotel reservation process

Build The build phase of the SDLC is the most technical, and the one that most people picture when they imagine how software is designed and developed. This phase is the primary domain of developers: systems architects and programmers. The objective is to take the system requirements document and produce a robust, secure, and efficient application.

System Design The build phase begins with the system design stage. Taking the results of the definition phase (i.e., what the applications should do), architects create the structure of the system (i.e., how the application will perform its tasks). At this stage the team identifies what hardware will be used, what languages will be adopted, what data structures are needed, and so on. The output of this stage is a precise set of documents that programmers use to write code.

Programming   Programming is the process of translating the abstract software design into a set of commands or instructions that can be executed by the hardware. If the application requires the creation of new databases, their structure is also developed at this stage (Figure 11.8).

An important element of the programming stage, but one that developers often detest, is the documentation. Thorough and clear documentation is essential in organizational software programs because they are large, complex, and expected to last for a number of years. Without adequate documentation such systems become impossible to support and maintain, let alone upgrade and evolve over time.

Testing   While system testing is a process that programmers are constantly engaged in as they develop, formalized assessment of components and subsequently of the complete applications is an essential stage in the SDLC. While most non–IT personnel rarely think about testing, this stage can take as much time and resources as the programming stage. The testing phase is articulated in alpha testing, carried out by developers themselves, and beta testing, carried out

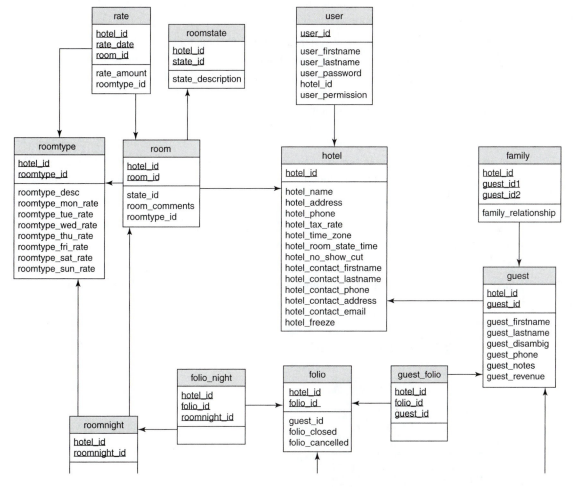

Figure 11.8   Database design underlying hotel property management system

by releasing the beta version to a limited set of actual users who use it and report any problems they identify.

Note that the objective of the testing stage is not to identify and correct all of the possible bugs plaguing the system, as this is uneconomical and rarely needed. Rather, the testing phase is designed to stress the system, to make sure that it can perform under production circumstances, and to correct the most important errors. The objective is to release the application when it is good enough, not when it is flawless.

Implementation   Once the software has been developed and tested, the project team needs to ensure that it is properly integrated with the other components of the information system. This is the implementation phase, an extremely delicate time when project management skills and executives' involvement are essential.

Installation   During the installation stage, the system is loaded on the production hardware and the databases are populated. Installation typically takes place during slow periods for the organization and, if at all possible, while the system is not needed (e.g., over a weekend, at night). If an existing system is being replaced, the firm migrates from the old one to the new one following one of four approaches (Figure 11.9):

- *Parallel.* The old and new systems are run for a time together. This approach is the most conservative as it offers insurance against failure of the new application. It is also the most costly as it requires significant redundancy of efforts. In some cases this approach is the only option (e.g., systems that must operate 24/7/365).

- *Direct.* The old system is suddenly discontinued and the firm cuts over to the new one. This is the most radical approach, but one that sometimes cannot be avoided (e.g., the old system stops functioning).

- *Phased.* The new system progressively replaces the functionalities of the old one. This approach is best suited to modular or componentized applications that can be rolled out in stages.

- *Pilot.* Well suited for multiunit operations (e.g., hotels, chain retailers), this approach allows the firm to run the new system in one business unit or in one of the firm's departments before rolling it out completely.

Beyond the technical aspects of the installation phase, there are two critical processes that take place at this time: end-user training and change management. End-user training typically

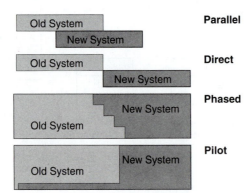

Figure 11.9   Migration approaches

occurs in formal settings, such as classrooms or make-shift computer labs. Change management is the process of smoothing the transition from the way the various stakeholders interacted with the previous system and carried out their work, to the new work practices. User resistance and inertia are the biggest dangers at this point. To the extent that stakeholders had been actively involved in the early stages of the SDLC and the design of the system, this phase will be less traumatic, thus minimizing risks of rejection.

Operations   At this stage the system is up and running, and the organization begins to use it. The project team is disbanded and the new system becomes a permanent asset of the firm to be maintained and managed.

Maintenance   Once the system is in place, and is up and running, both errors that had escaped the testing phase and enhancements that had escaped the requirements definition phase begin to emerge. Maintenance is the process of compiling this information, prioritizing requests, and implementing both fixes and improvements. Note that, as comprehensive and well designed as a new system may be, the organization is in continuous evolution. As a consequence, over time it is normal for a gap to emerge between the current system's functionalities and the firm's needs (remember this the next time you are tempted to ask, "What were they thinking when they designed this system?!?").

The functionality gap is closed on an ongoing basis by way of upgrades and additions until such ongoing maintenance becomes economically unfeasible and management makes the case for the development of a new information system. For this reason, some authors have begun to suggest that the traditional sequential SDLC approach needs to be reevaluated.[8]

Advantages of the SDLC Approach   The SDLC is a highly structured methodology that provides a systematic approach to reducing the uncertainty and risk associated with systems design and development projects. It clearly identifies roles and expectations for the members of the project team, and it offers a blueprint for how these individuals should interact. By demanding a thorough justification and requirements definition, it is particularly well suited for large-scale projects where changes that occur during development or implementation can be very costly.

The SDLC also offers a vehicle for communication and negotiation between the project team and the many project stakeholders. It does so by requiring evaluation and approval of deliverables for every phase, thereby stimulating discussion, facilitating the identification of priorities, and surfacing hidden trade-offs.

Limitations   While the SDLC methodology has evolved from the traditional waterfall approach into a more iterative process (e.g., spiral model) in which designers and developers are allowed some reevaluation of previous stages, the SDLC remains a highly structured approach. Thus, its critics point out that it creates substantial overhead in terms of time and cost, and does not enable the project team to properly address the inevitable changes that occur during the life of complex projects.

Prototyping

Recognizing the limitations inherent in the SDLC methodology, the prototyping approach is rooted in the notion that it is impossible to clearly estimate and plan in detail such complex

---

[8]Wagner, E., and Piccoli, G. (2007). "A Call to Engagement: Moving beyond User Involvement in Order to Achieve Successful Information Systems Design," *Communications of the ACM*.

endeavors as information systems design and development projects. Instead the team is better served by staying nimble and iterating quickly through multiple designs to zero in on the optimal one.

The growing acceptance of prototyping methodologies was enabled by tools that speed up the development process, such as nonprocedural programming languages. These tools allow developers to rapidly create working (or partially working) models of the proposed system and garner stakeholders' feedback about the system's design, functionalities, user interface, and so on.

Prototyping Life Cycle   One of the applications of the prototyping methodology is within the confines of the SDLC, as a way to elicit user requirements and seek input into the design of the user interface. The value of this approach stems from the fact that it is simpler for users to react to a prototype than it is for them to envision and articulate requirements in the abstract. Moreover, by involving users in the development of the front end of the application, the design team can foster their support and increase the chances of acceptance of the final system.

However, prototyping can be used as an alternative to the SDLC to develop a complete system according to the following steps:

Requirements Definitions   At this stage the development team seeks basic requirements. The degree of precision needed is much less than that needed in the SDLC because requirements are not frozen at this point. Rather, the understanding is that future feedback and modification will heavily shape the system.

Initial Prototype   Armed with the basic requirements, the team develops a first iteration of the system. The system could be only a shell (i.e., nonfunctional user interface), a partially functional application, or a "first-of-a-series" fully functional prototype.

Evaluation   At this time, the stakeholders review the prototype and provide feedback on the current design as well as requests for enhancements and new functionality.

Revision   Based on the feedback generated during the evaluation stage, the development team designs and codes the requested changes. This phase leads to a new prototype to be submitted to the stakeholders for evaluation. Note that at any time during these iterations the team and the stakeholders may conclude that no further investment in the project is warranted. In this case the firm stops the development effort.

Completion   Once the stakeholders and the development team are satisfied with the functionalities of the system, the iterative evaluation/revision process stops and the development team finalizes the system. At this stage the developers code important features that users typically do not request (e.g., security, administration). Documentation and testing follow, prior to the formal release of the system.

Advantages of the Prototyping Approach   Given the characteristics of the prototyping approach, systems developed this way tend to be more quickly delivered and closer to the users' expectations since the stakeholders are more involved throughout the development effort. Thus prototyping is best suited to smaller-scale projects and those that radically change the manner in which work is done. The prototyping approach also enables the firm to experiment with new technologies and new system functionalities because it requires a smaller investment of resources than the SDLC before the product can be evaluated—thus limiting the risk and sunk costs.

Limitations   The premium that the prototyping approach puts on speed and functionality development may cause the team to release a system that is lacking from a security, robustness, and reliability standpoint. Systems built using the prototyping approach are typically less thoroughly tested and documented than those using a more structured approach. Moreover, the rapid pace of iteration and release of new prototypes can mislead stakeholders who underestimate the complexity of software development. The consequence is rampant scope creep.[9] These limitations make the prototyping approach ill-suited for large-scale and complex systems development efforts.

Agile Development

A new breed of software development approaches has taken hold recently, in part due to the increasing popularity of prototyping. The software development approaches are collectively labeled as agile software development methodologies. A recent Cutter Consortium research found that over half of the organizations surveyed had already introduced agile methodologies (Figure 11.10).

The philosophy of agile software development has been captured in a document called the agile manifesto. The opening statement in that document reads: "We are uncovering better ways of developing software by doing it and helping others do it. Through this work we have come to value:

- *Individuals and interactions* over processes and tools
- *Working software* over comprehensive documentation
- *Customer collaboration* over contract negotiation
- *Responding to change* over following a plan

That is, while there is value in the items on the right, we value the items on the left more."

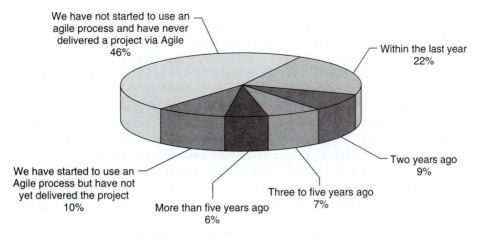

Figure 11.10   The state of agile methodologies used[10]

---

[9]Scope creep is a term that refers to uncontrolled changes in the magnitude of the project.

[10]Cutter Consortium (2007). "Making agility stick: What's working, what's not," *Cutter Benchmark Review* (7:7).

The agile manifesto clearly identifies the priorities and key characteristics of agile methodologies. First and foremost it is adaptability and speed. Agile methods do not call for the substantial amount of planning that characterizes traditional methodologies. Agile proponents believe that planning for all requirements and contingencies in all but trivial system developments is impossible. Significant planning will in fact backfire and limit the ability of the development team to adjust to inevitable new information. Agile developers therefore focus on developing applications with speed and releasing the system often—typically in less than a month. It is this rapid iteration of development and release that will surface accurate requirements and rapidly enable the development team to converge to a system that meets customers' expectations.

A second defining characteristic of agile development methodologies is team-work in open space offices that facilitate communication. Agile proponents advocate the use of small cross-functional teams with a customer representative, and daily face-to-face meetings. In order to organize the work and maintain the aggressive schedules that characterize agile projects, developers "chunk" the work into manageable yet self-standing components. The team then iterates through all of the phases of development—from requirements elicitation through testing and customer acceptance.

While agile development methodologies are still relatively new and in flux, they have gained acceptance within the software development community. As such you may find yourself partaking in agile development, as a customer representative on a cross-functional agile team.

Outsourced Development

Custom-designed software programs are increasingly developed by software houses that "fill in" for the firm's information systems professionals. These arrangements, typically called software development outsourcing, vary greatly, with some firms only outsourcing the programming and testing stages while others resort to an external provider to see them through the entire system development life cycle.

The outsourcing of software development projects has increased dramatically in popularity following the widespread adoption of the Internet. Software programs, as a classic information good (Chapter 4), can be designed and developed anywhere in the world. As a consequence, an increasing proportion of U.S. firms' custom software development is now done overseas. Consider virtual teams of developers as an example. Software projects are increasingly completed by development teams that work together but are not physically located in the same office. While cost considerations may come to mind as the principal reason to establish virtual teams, research by Cutter Consortium shows that over 85% of respondents saw the ability to pool the most qualified talent on the project as the principal driver for their adoption.[11]

With the widespread adoption and internationalization of custom software development, a set of tools to evaluate the quality of providers has emerged. The most popular, the Capability Maturity Model (CMM), ranks software development organizations according to their ability to produce quality software on a scale of 1 to 5 by evaluating a set of standard processes thought to determine software quality. Work on the Capability Maturity Model started at the Software Engineering Institute (SEI) at Carnegie Mellon University (CMU) in the early 1990s

---

[11]Piccoli, G. (2006). "Virtual Teams: No Longer an 'Emerging' Organizational Form," *Cutter Benchmark Review* (6:7), pp. 95–96.

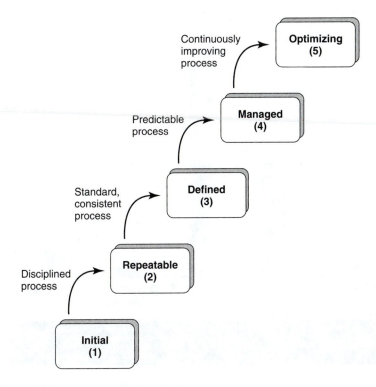

Figure 11.11 The five levels of software process maturity[12] (Image courtesy of Carnegie Mellon University's Software Engineering Institute.)

as a project funded by the United States Department of Defense (DoD). The DoD was looking to better understand how it could systematize software development processes so as to ensure reliable development and avoid both the failures and unpredictability that characterized it. A natural extension of this effort was to employ the CMM to evaluate vendors and software contractors. The CMM is based on the core notion that reliable and consistent implementation of a specific set of processes represents a higher level of software development maturity and, as a consequence, ensures higher quality software products (Figure 11.11).

The original CMM has evolved significantly over the years and, as a testament to its success, it is now used to evaluate and improve the quality of many other organizational processes (e.g., customer service, acquisition). Today software houses, particularly those engaged in outsourced customer development, seek CMMI certification[13] and you, as a buyer of their services, should ask for such information. The Software Engineering Institute at Carnegie Mellon is in charge of the certification process and periodically releases aggregate statistics (Figure 11.12).

One of the principal value propositions of custom software development outsourcing is in its superior cost/quality ratio. Firms in high cost of living countries, like North America or Western Europe, can outsource development to countries such as India, Ireland, or China, with a large pool of highly skilled software engineers and programmers, and a lower cost of living

---

[12]Paulk, M. C., Weber, C.V., Curtis, B., and Chrissis, M. (1993). "Capability Maturity Model for Software, Version 1.1." Technical Report (Carnegie Mellon University/Software Engineering Institute). CMU/SEI-93-TR-024 ESC-TR-93-177.

[13]CMMI stands for Capability Maturity Model Integration and it represents the current version of the CMM.

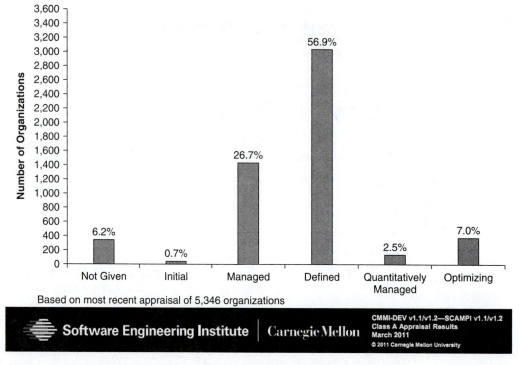

Figure 11.12   Process maturity level of appraised organizations (Image courtesy of Carnegie Mellon University's Software Engineering Institute.)

(i.e., lower wages). Outsourcing developments to these regions of the world enables the firm to receive superior-quality products at a fraction of the cost of internal development (Figure 11.13).

Buying Off-the-Shelf Applications

The SDLC provides the basis for the system selection and purchasing process that organizations use to design and develop information systems based on off-the-shelf software programs (Table 11.2). The systems selection process often starts when managers learn about the capabilities of a new application that is being advertised, described in the press, or promoted by consulting firms. Following the systems selection process is important because it enables a systematic investigation of these applications as well as competing products—thus ensuring that all issues are considered and the firm chooses the best solution for its current needs.

Definition

Both the investigation and feasibility analysis stages are qualitatively similar to those in the SDLC. At this time the proponents of the system articulate a vision for the proposed information system and evaluate its technical, operational, and economic viability. It is in the remaining stages of the definition phase that the major idiosyncrasies of the systems selection process occur.

System Analysis   During the system analysis stage, the selection committee focuses on eliciting the specific functionalities required of the proposed system. As with the SDLC, this phase entails

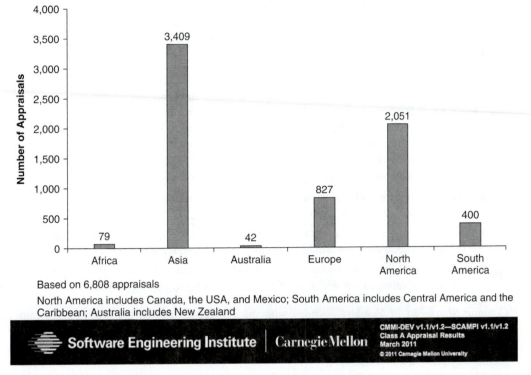

Figure 11.13 Distribution of CMMI rated firms in the world (Image courtesy of Carnegie Mellon University's Software Engineering Institute.)

Table 11.2 Phases of the systems selection processes

Definition
Investigation
Feasibility analysis
System analysis
Formulate evaluation criteria
Compile short list of vendors
Compile and distribute RFP
Evaluate alternatives
Negotiate contract

Build
System design (Customizations)
Programming (Customizations)
Testing

Implementation
Installation
Operations
Maintenance

the interplay of system analysts and stakeholders. However, the degree of precision and detail sought by the selection committee is less than that needed for custom development. The objective here is to have enough of an understanding of the systems requirements to formulate evaluation criteria.

Formulate Evaluation Criteria Systems selection is the structured attempt to evaluate all commercially available software solutions that can enable the proposed information system. In order to do so, it is necessary to develop a set of metrics that can be uniformly applied to all packages under investigation. The criteria must also be amenable to communication to software vendors by way of the request for proposal (RFP) process.

A common approach is to use the system requirements document to identify the features that appropriate applications should have, and group them into three categories:

- *Essential features.* Those capabilities that the system must have. Systems that miss any one of these features are automatically discarded.

- *Value adding features.* Those capabilities that, while not essential, offer significant advantages for which the firm would be willing to pay a premium.

- *Nonessential features.* Those capabilities that are "nice to have" but produce small tangible advantages for which the firm is not willing to pay a premium.

Compile Short List of Vendors Armed with the evaluation criteria, the selection committee seeks information about existing solutions. Web sites, trade press, vendor brochures, and trade expos are all viable sources of information. The information gathered is used to identify a preliminary short list of vendors.

This stage is important for two reasons. First, creating targeted RFPs that yield high-quality responses, and then evaluating those responses, is time consuming. Second, products that fail to meet necessary requirements can be identified fairly quickly, and vendors will appreciate not being asked to respond to RFPs that they have no chance of fulfilling.

Compile and Distribute the RFP The RFP is the formal communication document used to elicit substantial, detailed information from the short-listed vendors. Most organizations have a template for such documents. The RFP should explain what the selection committee has identified as the critical system requirements, the environment in which the system will be used, and any required performance metrics and expectations.

Upon its distribution to the short-listed vendors, those interested will respond to the RFP. The selection team should ask vendors to adhere to a template, making cross-comparison of the applications simple, and should ask for pricing information. Vendors should also provide such pricing information according to the firm's template, ensuring that the pricing mechanisms for the applications, any customization, and ongoing maintenance and upgrades are clear and comparable across vendors. Finally, the selection committee should specify a deadline by which vendors must respond in order to be considered.

Evaluate Alternatives Once all interested vendors have responded to the RFP, the competing solutions are evaluated using the criteria developed earlier. The selection committee compiles the list of top vendors and seeks any further information needed to make a final decision. This includes on-site demonstrations, evaluation of reference sites, and the like. The outcome of this stage in the selection process is a rank-ordered list of the acceptable candidates.

Negotiate Contract   Negotiations can be relatively quick and simple, or they can be a very involved process requiring input from professionals and legal counsel. The objective of the selection committee is to draft and sign a contract that provides the firm with the needed solution and insulates it from future risks. Common elements of negotiation are the components and magnitude of costs (e.g., installation, training, customization, maintenance, upgrades), the eventual liabilities and service-level agreements, control over the intellectual property, and the extent to which modifications are allowed.

Build

The build phase in the system selection process mirrors that of the SDLC but is much narrower in scope. When the software program is to be installed without configuration or customization, as is the case with simple applications, the firm can move directly to formal testing and implementation. However, as we mentioned above, it is becoming increasingly common for organizations that purchase off-the-shelf applications to configure and customize them extensively.[14]

To the extent that customization is necessary, the firm will engage in system design and programming of the required enhancements. This is where a tightly written contract becomes important, as the customization process can add significant time and cost to the project. The contract should specify who is responsible for customizing the application—the vendor, the firm, or a third party (i.e., independent consulting firm, integrator)—and the conditions of the customization effort (e.g., schedule).

Whether customized or not, the firm should test the system. In the case of off-the-shelf applications, the testing stage is mostly concerned with system performance rather than with the identification and correction of bugs.

Implementation

The implementation phase is also quite similar to the one described earlier regarding the SDLC. Installation is performed following one of the approaches described earlier. Interestingly, even within the same class of software applications (e.g., ERP), a firm may choose different approaches to move from the old to the new system. Note as well that the degree of process change and training required to get buy-in from users is typically greater when implementing off-the-shelf applications. This is because a pre-packaged program is not designed with the idiosyncrasies of your organization in mind. Rather the software house builds the program to appeal to the broadest market possible.

Asking for stakeholders' input during the selection and evaluation of competing solutions is one way to enroll them in the process and reduce rejection risks. However, you should still plan to invest considerable resources during the implementation phase to set up the application, train employees, and engage in change management—particularly when the application is larger in scope and forces a change in traditional work practices.

---

[14]Configuration is the process of tailoring a software program using built-in parameters. Customization is the process of changing the functionality of the software program beyond available options. Customization requires that the new functionalities be coded using a programming language.

END-USER DEVELOPMENT

As we discussed in Chapter 1, the ease of use of information technologies has steadily increased while their cost has declined dramatically over the years. These two forces have conspired to bring the power of software development to the masses in the form of end-user development. *End-user development* is an umbrella term capturing the many ways in which knowledge workers, not IT professionals, create software.

End-user-developed systems range from spreadsheet models (e.g., an ROI calculator written in MS Excel), to personal or departmental databases, to full-fledged software programs built with user-friendly computer languages (e.g., Visual Basic for Applications) or development tools such as fourth-generation languages. These "shadow systems" are now prevalent in modern organizations.[15]

The Benefits of End-User Development

The chief benefits of end-user development stem from user empowerment and the fact that some of the burden on typically overworked information systems departments is lifted. The benefits include the following:

- *Increased speed of development.* The user community typically must direct requests for new systems, and improvements to current ones, to the IS function. In turn, the IS function must prioritize the deployment of its scarce resources. As a consequence, those projects that end users can complete independently will be completed faster by virtue of not entering the cue.

- *End-user satisfaction.* One of the main problems with new systems is users' dissatisfaction or outright rejection. When users create their own applications, they are more likely to be satisfied with the result; they have either created the functionalities they wanted or have themselves decided what features to forgo.

- *Reduced pressure on the IS function.* End-user development can limit the number of requests the IS function receives, enabling them to be more focused on the projects that, because of their scope and complexity, really require their attention.

The Risks of End-User Development

Unfortunately, end-user development presents a number of difficult-to-manage risks that limit its value to the organization.

- *Unreliable quality standards.* There is a reason why software development is a lengthy process. Quality software requires a number of activities that may not be readily apparent but are necessary—such as testing, documentation, security, integration, and the like. Because of the limited skill set and knowledge of most end users, the quality of their work varies dramatically (Figure 11.14).

---

[15]Ulrich, W. (2006). "Application Package Survey: The Promise versus Reality," *Cutter Benchmark Review* (6:9), pp. 13–20.

Figure 11.14
Source: Fancy/Image Source.

■ *High incidence of errors.* Audits of spreadsheets used in organizations show that a sizable percentage, between 20 and 40% (sometimes 90%), of them contain errors. The focus on outcomes (i.e., what the program does) and rapid development typically conspire to increase the likelihood of errors in end-user-developed applications.

■ *Continuity risks.* Because end-user development often does not comply with traditional system development methodologies, it may be difficult for anyone but the individual who wrote the program to understand it, enhance it, and support it. Lack of documentation compounds this problem. A common scenario involves people like you, who develop great applications during internships only to see them fade into company oblivion once you leave the firm.

■ *Increased pressure on the IS function.* While end-user development can relieve some of the development demands on the IS function, it often creates more requests for assistance during the development process and, over time, more requests for help managing the applications after release.

SUMMARY

This chapter continued our discussion of the techniques and methodologies modern organizations use to introduce and manage information systems within the framework provided by the strategic information systems plan.

Specifically, in this chapter we focused on the three approaches used to introduce new organizational information systems: custom design and development, system selection and acquisition, and end-user development. We learned that

■ The astounding progress that has characterized information technologies over the last 40 years often misleads general and functional managers. Being mostly familiar with personal computing, they underestimate how much time and how much money it takes to build a stable, robust, and secure system that will work under a wide array of organizational conditions. In order to avoid these misconceptions, managers must become familiar with the process by which IT-based information systems come to be in modern organizations.

- Introducing an organizational information system is a two-step process requiring technology development and the implementation process. These two processes, while often described separately, are complementary and intertwined.

- Modern firms introduce new information systems using one of the following approaches: custom design and development, system selection and acquisition, or end-user development. The critical difference among them is the manner in which the software applications at the core of the information system are developed. In the first approach, IT professionals within the organization or who are contracted develop uniquely tailored software for the firm's needs. In the second approach, the selection committee chooses an off-the-shelf application. In the third approach, it is the firm's end users, rather than the IT professionals, who create the software.

- The main methodology for custom system development is the system development life cycle (SDLC). The SDLC, predicated on the notion that detailed up-front planning is the vehicle to reduce risk and uncertainty in systems design and development efforts, is best suited for the development of large, complex software applications. The SDLC is articulated over three main phases—definition, build, and implementation—and nine stages. The primary limitation of the SDLC is the creation of substantial overhead and rigidity that limit the project team's ability to address the inevitable changes.

- The prototyping methodology has emerged as a viable alternative to the SDLC. Prototyping is rooted in the notion that it impossible to clearly estimate and plan in detail such complex endeavors as information systems design and development

projects. Instead the team is better served by staying nimble and iterating quickly through multiple designs to zero in on the optimal one. Prototyping's advantages include user satisfaction (particularly for small-scale applications or those that dramatically change work practices), rapid development, and experimentation. The drawbacks include the risk of lower-quality systems than those developed using a more structured methodology, and scope creep.

- With the advent of the Internet and the growth of the software industry in countries with access to a large pool of talent and a low cost of living, it is increasingly viable to outsource development of custom applications.

- The software industry has grown to a point where almost any application a firm needs is available off the shelf. When building information systems around pre-packaged software applications, the firm must engage in a formal systems selection and acquisition process. Doing so ensures that the selection team evaluates all possible solutions and acquires the one that is best suited to the firm's needs. The selection and acquisition process mirrors the SDLC, with some important variations during the definition and build phases.

- The advent of powerful and easy-to-use computer languages and software development tools has enabled an unprecedented degree of software development by end users (i.e., non–IT professionals). The benefits of end-user development include increased speed, end-user satisfaction, and a reduced pressure on the IS function to develop new applications. The risks of end-user development include unreliable quality standards, high incidence of errors in the applications, continuity risks, and increased pressure on the IS function to support development and management of end-user applications.

STUDY QUESTIONS

1. Describe the reasons why general and functional managers often fail to understand the complexities of organizational information systems development. Can you provide an example from your own experience?

2. What is the difference between technology development and information systems development? What is the relationship between these two processes?

3. How do the three information systems development approaches in use today in modern organizations differ? Can you provide an example of each?

4. Provide arguments in support of both the make and buy approaches. What are the principal advantages of each decision? Increasingly firms approach information systems development as a "buy and make" process. What do we mean by "buy and make"? Why is this approach gaining increasing popularity today?

5. Describe the systems development life cycle (SDLC) methodology in the context of a "real" example. In other words, think about (or imagine) a situation where you proposed the need for a new information system.

For this system development effort, describe what happened (or should happen) during the definition, build, and implementation phases.

6. Repeat Question 5, this time using the prototyping methodology.

7. Repeat Question 5, this time using the systems selection and acquisition methodology.

8. Articulate the advantages and disadvantages of end-user development.

FURTHER READINGS

1. Paulk, M. C., Weber, C. V., Curtis, B., and Chrissis, M. B. (1995). *The Capability Maturity Model: Guidelines for Improving the Software Process.* Boston: Addison Wesley.
2. Pink, D. H. (2004). "The New Face of the Silicon Age: How India Became the Capital of the Computing Revolution." *Wired Magazine* (12:02).
3. Wagner, E., and Piccoli, G. (2008). "A Call to Engagement: Moving beyond User Involvement in Order to Achieve Successful Information Systems Design." *Communications of the ACM.*

GLOSSARY

- **Build:** The build phase of the SDLC is concerned with taking the system requirements document and producing a robust, secure, and efficient software application.
- **Business analyst:** Business analysts are individuals with expertise in business process redesign as well as technology. They help ensure that the business processes and software programs at the heart of an information system are jointly optimized and work smoothly together.
- **Custom software:** A software program that is created in single copy to address the specific needs and design requirements of an organization.
- **Custom software development:** The process by which an organization, or a contracted software house, creates a tailored software application to address the organization's specific information processing needs.
- **Definition:** The definition phase of the SDLC is concerned with clearly identifying the features of the proposed information system.
- **End-user development:** The process by which an organization's non–IT specialists create software applications.
- **Implementation:** The implementation phase of the SDLC is concerned with taking the technology component and integrating it with the other elements (people, process, structure) to achieve a working information system.
- **Off-the-shelf application:** A software program that is mass produced and commercialized by a software vendor.

- **Programmer:** A highly skilled IT professional who translates a software design into a set of instructions that can be executed by a digital computer.
- **Prototyping:** A systems development approach predicated on the notion that it is impossible to clearly estimate and plan in detail such complex endeavors as information systems design and development projects.
- **Software application:** A software program or, more commonly, a collection of software programs, designed to perform tasks of interest to an end user (e.g., write a memo, create and send invoices).
- **Software development outsourcing:** An arrangement where an external provider (i.e., a software house) custom develops an application for an organization.
- **System analyst:** A highly skilled IS professional whose role is to help users identify and articulate the system requirements.
- **System architect:** A highly skilled IT professional who takes the system requirements document (i.e., what the applications should do) and designs the structure of the system (i.e., how the application will perform its tasks).
- **System development life cycle (SDLC):** A software development approach predicated on the notion that detailed justification and planning is the vehicle to reduce risk and uncertainty in systems design and development efforts.
- **System selection and acquisition:** The process by which an organization identifies and purchases an off-the-shelf software application to address its information processing needs.

12

Information Systems Trends

What You Will Learn in This Chapter

In this chapter, we introduce some emerging and some enduring trends in information systems and technology management. Understanding these trends and technologies, the associated vocabulary, and the benefits and risks they engender for modern organizations is critical for you as a general or functional manager. You will hear much of this vocabulary from consultants, at conferences, and in the media, and you must learn to navigate it successfully. More importantly, as a manager you will be (or should be!) called on to participate in the debate about whether your own firm should embark in the type of initiatives described in this chapter. Understanding these trends is therefore a prerequisite to being an asset in the discussion.

Specifically, in this chapter you will:

1. Define the term mobile platform and its relevance in today's technology environment. Describe some of the emerging applications that leverage the mobile platform, as well as the key trends surrounding it.

2. Describe the importance of Green IS and energy informatics, the reasons for their emergence, and their potential impacts.

3. Define the notion of digital data genesis, the reasons for its emergence, and its potential impacts.

4. Define the notion of customer-managed interactions, the reasons for its emergence, and its potential impacts.

5. Define the term open source software and be able to identify the primary commercial models that have been crafted around the open source movement. You will also be able to articulate the principal advantages and risks associated with the implementation of open source solutions in modern organizations.

6. Define the terms cloud computing and software as a service (SaaS), understand their genesis, and discuss their principal characteristics.

MINI-CASE: IMPROVING ENVIRONMENTAL SUSTAINABILITY THROUGH SERVICE

Sitting at your desk in front of a blank document you recalled how you got here. Yesterday was a fantastic spring day in Milan and you felt like a caged tiger in that boardroom overlooking Piazza del Duomo. The temperature outside was 22 degrees Celsius (71 degrees Fahrenheit) and a cool breeze was clearing the crisp air. You had enjoyed bicycling to work that morning; it reminded you of biking to high school from your hometown. One of the few kids in your circle of friends without a moped or a scooter, you used to trek the 8 km (five miles) from your house to the school every day, rain or shine, warm or cold. Northern Italy had the kind of weather that made bicycling enjoyable for eight months out of the year and Milan is in the flatlands of the Po River valley, so bicycling was easy.

Coming out of your day-dreaming, you glance back to the room. The topic at hand is an old problem for the administration of the City of Milan: pollution. The City has tried all kinds of options to reduce emissions, from limiting traffic in certain areas, to alternating the use of cars between those with even and odd numbered license plates, to downright shutting down traffic in the city when the pollution numbers become too high. Your consulting firm has been involved in many of these changes. The latest in chronological order, a ticket for driving within the downtown area of the City called Ecopass—an idea borrowed from the City of London. The plan did not work as hoped, with residents complaining and some members of the board calling for the creation of classes (or levels) so that drivers would pay proportionally to how much their car pollutes. With all these exceptions, Ecopass soon became a logistical nightmare and its potential effect was drastically reduced. Hence today's meeting.

One of the options being discussed was to improve the bus system by increasing the number of busses on the road and increasing the frequency of their stops. This proposal was based on the well-known relationship between convenience and public transportation usage. The more stops and the higher the frequency of stops, the higher the number of people who would choose to take the bus rather than use their car. However, buses were also polluting vehicles; they are expensive to purchase and to operate. This option sounded to you like the usual incremental thinking. Solving the problem was not a matter of little tweaks and fixes, this city needed a radical shift.

While you were the youngest person in the room, still half in your spring day inspired day-dreaming you blurted out: "Why not use bicycles?" The room went quiet and everyone was staring in your direction. The first to speak was the Mayor herself. She said: "What do you mean?" Her voice was a combination of annoyance and intrigued curiosity. A bit tentatively you said: "Well... I mean... bicycles you know? Like they have in Paris and Copenhagen." Now fully focused, you were picking up steam, the power of your idea becoming clearer as you spoke: "We would need rental stations were people could pick up and drop off bicycles whenever they needed them, day or night. If we make this convenient enough I'm sure residents of Milan would be quite happy to contribute to reduce pollution in their city."

There was silence in the room. The first to break it was the Mayor again. She had looked at you and said: "Good idea. I want a feasibility study ready on my desk in one month." With that she shook your hand and left.

As you looked at your computer you recalled some of the considerations underpinning your intuition the day before. The initiative of the city was one focused on reducing pollution and improving environmental sustainability. Your job was to create a system that would encourage people to use bicycles instead of their cars or even the public transport systems. Some things worked in your favor. Italians in general were indeed environmentally conscious. They were also conscious about appearances and, while jumping on a bike may wrinkle their designer clothes, they would gladly do it if it could show others that they cared about their city. However, Milan was the bustling economic center of Italy, and people did not have time to waste. It was also the most technologically advanced city and Italy, for example, was projected to maintain the highest penetration of smartphones in the world (Figure 12.1).

You were convinced. The right design of the initiative would make it a success. Information technology would have to feature prominently in your design, no question. How? ...Well, that was the heart of the matter.

DISCUSSION QUESTIONS

1. What do you believe is the optimal design for your proposed bicycle rental system?
2. What is the role of information systems, if any, in enabling the design?
3. What are the main challenges you believe you will have to overcome in order to achieve widespread adoption?

continued

Smartphone Penetration Worldwide, by Region and Country, 2009–2014 (% of total mobile handsets)

	2009	2010	2011	2012	2013	2014
North America						
U.S.	32%	33%	37%	44%	51%	55%
Canada	30%	31%	34%	40%	47%	50%
Total	32%	33%	37%	44%	51%	54%
Western Europe						
Italy	36%	40%	47%	54%	63%	67%
Germany	17%	19%	22%	25%	29%	33%
France	16%	18%	21%	27%	29%	33%
UK	17%	18%	20%	23%	29%	32%
Rest of Western Europe	31%	36%	41%	49%	58%	64%
Total	25%	28%	32%	37%	44%	49%
Asia-Pacific						
South Korea	14%	15%	17%	21%	25%	30%
China	10%	11%	13%	15%	18%	21%
India	4%	5%	6%	8%	10%	12%
Rest of Asia-Pacific	8%	8%	9%	10%	11%	12%
Total	8%	9%	10%	12%	14%	16%
Worldwide	**9%**	**10%**	**11%**	**13%**	**15%**	**17%**

Source: Cisco Systems, "Cisco Visual Networking Index (VNI) : Global Mobile Data Traffic Forecast Update, 2009–2014" with Informa Telecoms & Media, In-Stat and Gartner, February 9, 2010

113396   www.**eMarketer**.com

Figure 12.1 Smartphone penetration as percentage of total handsets

INTRODUCTION

In this chapter, we discuss the most relevant and influential trends in information systems and technology management. We focus on those emerging and enduring trends that are capturing media attention and that consulting companies are promoting today. These are the trends that you will need to confront as you join the workforce in the immediate future.

This chapter is very important for you, as the ability to identify new trends is critical for successful managers. But the task of navigating the many emerging trends and identifying which technologies will succeed is no easy task. Even Bob Metcalf, a pioneer in networking technology, and the inventor of the Etherent protocol and the founder of 3Com Corporation, missed completely when in 1995 he proclaimed: "Almost all of the many predictions now being made hinge on the Internet's continuing exponential growth. But, I predict the Internet will soon go spectacularly supernova and in 1996 catastrophically collapse."[1] A good sport, Metcalfe admitted he was wrong and "ate his words" when he publically put the article in a blender and literally drank it after delivering the keynote speech at the Sixth International WWW Conference in December 1997.

---

[1]Metcalfe, R. (December 1995). "Column: From Te Ether," *InforWorld.*

We organize this chapter around the technologies at the core of each trend. This is a conscious approach that mirrors how decisions are made in modern organizations. Typically, an organization will become aware of an emerging information systems trend through publications, consulting companies, or conferences and events. The trend is defined by the functionalities of the technology at the core, or the features and characteristics of a new class of software applications—from which the trend typically takes its name and its impetus. It is critical for you to realize that, no matter how sophisticated a technology may be, in order for it to have a positive impact on the organization you must be able to design an information system around it (see Chapter 2). Thus, for each of the trends discussed in this chapter, we analyze the technology capabilities as a departure point to understand the organizational impacts that they engender.

THE MOBILE PLATFORM

Perhaps the most visible trend in computing today is the widespread adoption of the mobile platform. As of May 2010, 40% of American adults reported accessing the Internet through their cell phones.[2] The hardware has the form of cell phones or highly portable tablets. The cell phones, or more precisely the smartphones, have the ability to run an operating system and, therefore, software applications—just like any other digital computer. The commercial products we all know are the devices running the Google Android operating systems, and those running the Symbian OS, the iPhone, from Apple, and the BlackBerry from Research In Motion (RIM). But smartphones trace their roots to the efforts started in the early 1990s by the likes of IBM and Nokia to pack functionality into the portable phone—thus rendering it a multipurpose device rather than just a telephone. The history of the smartphone intersects with the rise, during the same years, of palmtop devices. These were hand-held computers known as Personal Digital Assistants (PDA), like those produced by Palm, Inc. (Figure 12.2) and later Handspring (Figure 12.3).

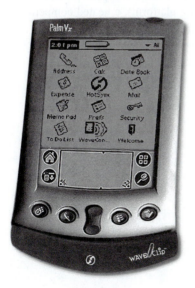

Figure 12.2   The Palm Vx

[2]Mobile Access 2010, Pew Research Center Internet and American Life Project. (Available 02/22/2011 at http://www.pewinternet.org/Reports/2010/Mobile-Access-2010/Summary-of-Findings.aspx)

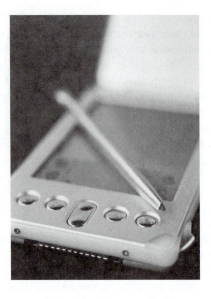

Figure 12.3   The Handspring Visor
Source: © PB Stock/Alamy Limited.

Those devices were conceived as computers with an operating system and, as a consequence, software developers recognized opportunities to build applications for the mobile platform.

As people were carrying around cellphones and PDAs, and hardware kept increasing in power, combining the two devices was a natural extension (and a very good example of the polymediation trend introduced in Chapter 1). While it is not our intent here to produce an exhaustive history of the smartphone, this brief discussion of its genesis helps you appreciate the context in which we have seen the rise of portable computers that look like cell phones and application stores where you can easily download software for your portable device. As with any platform, and more specifically with computing platforms, a heated competitive battle rages to establish a dominant operating system (Figure 12.4).

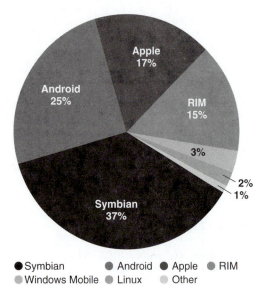

Figure 12.4   2010 Market share of smartphone operating systems (Created by Eraserhead1 at the English Wikipedia Project.)

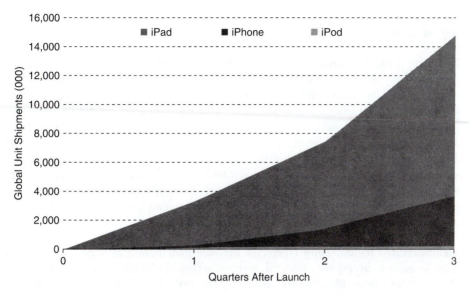

Figure 12.5   Cumulative units shipped in the first three quarters since launch

A recent development in the area of mobile computing is the rise to prominence of tablets, characterized by their lightweight, multi-touch input screens and sustained battery power. While tablets also trace their roots to earlier computing innovations, it was the launch of the Apple iPad in 2010 that established the category as it is defined today—a category created with unprecedented speed (Figure 12.5).

Many other manufacturers quickly followed suit, most notably RIM and Google Android. The last technological cornerstone of both the smartphone and tablets is the ability to connect to both Wi-Fi networks and cell phone data networks (e.g., the 3G and 4G networks). Thanks to its technological characteristics—portability and connectivity—the mobile platform gives users the opportunity for constant access to computing power and access to the data grid (Chapter 1). The success of the mobile platform was crystallized during the last quarter of 2010 when total shipments of smartphones surpassed total shipments of personal computers, with just over 100 million Smartphone units being distributed by the manufacturers globally.

Characteristics of the Mobile Platform

While mobile devices are digital computers, just like your desktop and laptop personal computers of old, vendors are trying hard to pass on the message that they are a new breed of devices. Leading this trend was Steve Jobs and Apple, who have been increasingly talking about the "post-PC era"—ushered in by the iPod—the first post-PC device—and subsequently by the iPhone and the IPod. As Jobs put it, when it comes to post-PC devices nobody cares that they are really a computer, all that matters is the user experience. . . and in that Apple is clearly leading the pack.

While mobile devices are architecturally like any other digital computer, they do have some peculiar characteristics that make them particularly appealing for organizations and end users. Particularly relevant are the characteristics that we could term ubiquity, identifiability, and context awareness.

Ubiquity   Ubiquity represents the idea that users of the device can access needed resources from (in theory) anywhere.[3] Mobile devices offer the highest level of potential ubiquity amongst commercially available information technologies because they marry portability with connectivity. Consider the travel industry as an example. As a travel industry executive envisioning opportunities to connect to and provide service to your customers, you would quickly realize that smartphones (and perhaps in the future tablets) are the only devices that travelers are all but guaranteed to be carrying during a trip. Those are the devices that enable the user to access informational resources anywhere they can find coverage for their data plans. Imagine then being without a hotel room as you land at the airport. No problem, simply geolocate your business meeting by typing in your address, search for hotels within a five-minute walk radius from that address, evaluate rates, and book. Now you have a room!

Identifiability   Identifiability represents the idea that mobile devices uniquely identify their user. In order to access the data grid, both smartphones and tablets utilize the cellular network and use a Subscriber Identification Module (SIM card). Each SIM card has a unique identifier, and since telephones are usually personal devices, each user can be uniquely identified to the network. This feature of the technology enables a wide array of strategies. Consider the example of a pizza chain such as Pizza Hut. Using your iPhone or iPod app you can create and order your own pizza. You don't have to specify the address and payment information because you are automatically identified. In fact, you could even save your favorite custom pizza orders and simply re-order them as desired.

Context Awareness   Context awareness is enabled by the fact that mobile devices can be geolocated. In other words, modern smartphones that incorporate a Global Positioning System (GPS) receiver can communicate their position to any software application running on them. Such applications can then make use of the location of the person carrying the device and infer the context in which the user is embedded at the time or the vicinity to other geolocated entities (i.e., a restaurant, a friend). You can quickly imagine many possibilities to craft business initiatives around the availability of this information. You can also quickly imagine many privacy violations and other abuses that these capabilities of mobile devices engender!

Mobile Commerce

With the increasing miniaturization of devices, digitization of content, and emergence of wide area wireless and cellular networks, organizations sought to extend their reach and use mobile devices for enabling transactions with customers. The term *mobile commerce* (or M-Commerce, mCommerce) refers to the ability to complete commercial transactions using mobile devices, such as smartphones and tablets. mCommerce has existed conceptually since the advent of

---

[3]We specify "in theory" because, despite technical feasibility, many users are constrained in their access to resources by their data plan.

electronic commerce, but it has recently received significant impetus as consumers have shown its viability by adopting electronic commerce and self-service through digital mobile devices.

Consider the following example. You booked your flight with Air France and forwarded your reservation to TripIt, the online itinerary management company. Before leaving for the airport for your 4pm flight, you receive an alert from TripIt informing you that your flight is delayed by 72 minutes due to some mechanical problem to your aircraft inbound from another airport. As a consequence, you decide to delay your departure from home to say goodbye to your kids coming home from school. After departure, your flight accumulates more delay and you realize that you will miss your connection. On the plane, which is equipped with Wi-Fi connectivity from GoGo Inflight, you check the TripIt App and see a list of alternate flights to your destination, which was automatically calculated by TripIt based on your itinerary and the delay information published by the airlines. The list shows you departure times, gates, flight status, and open seats. As you land you dash out of the gate like an Olympic sprinter to quickly reach the gate of the next best available flight (instead of cueing up at the transfer desk with non-mCommerce-enabled passengers!) and you are on your way to your destination with minimal disruption to your schedule. This scenario would appear quite futuristic just three years ago, but it is a reality today.

Another example is offered by local eCommerce players like Groupon or Living Social. Groupon, the leader in this market as of 2011, enables its members to see negotiated discounts (i.e., coupons) that only activate if enough people sign up (i.e., a large enough group). The discount and size of the group to activate Groupon, are set by those partner merchants. The idea of group buying has been around for a long time and early eCommerce players attempted to craft business models around it. The best example was Mercata, a venture backed by Paul Allen of Microsoft fame. However, Mercata did not succeed and, after burning through over $100M in venture capital investment, eventually had to close its doors. The success of this next wave of players is not guaranteed, but Google offered $6b for Groupon in 2010, (Groupon rejected the offer!) as a testament to the sentiment that this time around IT-enabled group buying represents a significant business opportunity. What has changed? The widespread use of social networking applications such as Facebook and Twitter, as well as the comfort that a large segment of the population has today with IT-enabled self-service, both play an important role. Most notably however, Mercata was an eCommerce venture, while Groupon and Living Social are mCommerce players. It is the prevalence of smartphones and the ability to leverage ubiquity, identifiability, and context sensitivity that seems to have drastically lowered the barriers to widespread adoption of group buying solutions.

Location-Based Social Networking

Social networking is now a staple of all aspects of life for Internet citizens (see Chapter 5). The rise to prominence of the mobile platform has enabled social networking firms to allow users to reach (some would say annoy!) their contacts more often and in a more timely manner using mobile versions of their service. Location-based social networking is an extension of mobile social networking whereby the geographical location of the user becomes an integral component of the service enabling efficient access to context-dependent services. Pioneers of this space, such

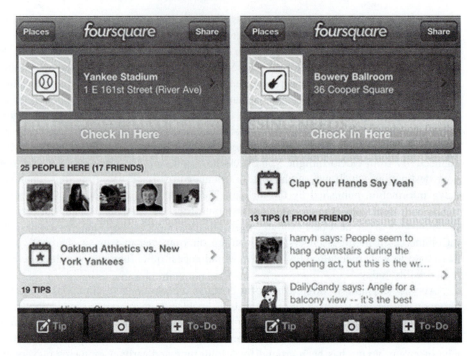

Figure 12.6   Foursquare   (*Source*: © Carolina Ruiz Vega/La Nacion de Costa/NewsCom)

as Foursquare (Figure 12.6) and Gowalla, enabled individuals to tap into their social networks while on the move. As such, location-based social networks represent an extension to the social context of the pervasive computing trend toward the widespread adoption of embedded sensors. They enable social network users to bridge the gap from access to their friends' ratings and reviews (what friends say), to their actual behavior (what friends do)—the ultimate high tech version of "voting with your feet!" Imagine this scenario: you are visiting a new city and you're hungry, but you are not sure what restaurant to take a chance on. Using location-based social networking, you can see what outlets are in the vicinity and read what your friends, or the extended Foursquare community members, indicate as the best spots.

Augmented Reality

Augmented reality is a field of computing that has recently received increased attention thanks to the launch of a few augmented reality applications for smartphones, such as Wikitude and Layar. In its simplest form, augmented reality consists of superimposing an information layer on top of a real image. Current applications use the camera, GPS receiver, compass, and accelerometer of modern smartphones to identify objects and then, using a database of entries downloaded to the device, superimpose contextual information on recognized objects. There is no consensus about the kind of applications that will benefit from augmented reality, but an intriguing example is offered by Italian gaming company Illusion Networks. The firm has created an impressive augmented reality application for the iPhone 3Gs called Voyager Xdrive (Figure 12.7). It allows travelers who are walking about in the Roman Forum to see a three-dimensional reconstruction

Figure 12.7 Voyager Xdrive in action (Image courtesy of IllusionNetwork.)

of the Forum the way it was during Constantine's rule (A.D. 320) and, for the buildings and monuments currently in view, to see and hear a description of them.

Augmented reality is not confined to the mobile platform. Car manufacturers, for example, are planning to use the windshield of a car as the surface on which to superimpose information layers. But on the mobile platform augmented reality may be extremely disruptive, mainly because it will further reduce information barriers and information asymmetry, and will do so "on the go" rather than forcing users to be sitting at a computer. Like the commercial Internet two decades ago, augmented reality has the potential to arm users with an unprecedented quantity of easily accessible and usable information. The difference is that such information will be available to them anytime and anywhere. Reconsider the example of the restaurant. As you are deciding where you want to go tonight for drinks to relax from a tough day on the road during your business trip to Chicago, in the lobby of your hotel—*The Ole Fogey*—you activate the Layar browser on your Android phone and scan the environment around you. You immediately see that two blocks over, at *The Edgy Hotel*, the bar is happening with a cool event—DJ MasterFun is in town. Ultimately, the night is a success, you unwind from your working day, and you promise yourself that on your next trip to Chicago you will book a room at *The Edgy*, not the old and stodgy *The Ole Fogey Hotel*. This example provides a glimpse into the power of augmented reality. This type of contextualized, real-time information access would not have occurred unless you had a portable instrument that worked seamlessly and easily at the moment you needed it (i.e., in the lobby of the hotel as you were making a decision). It is unlikely that you would have searched for the information about local venues on a laptop in your room, and even less likely that you would have done that from home prior to your trip. Yet, this information, and the ensuing experience, had a powerful effect on your travel experience (not to mention on brand perceptions and the brand development of the hotels involved!).

As John Doerr, partner at venture firm Kleiner Perkins Caufield and Byers put it recently: "We're at the beginning of a new era for social Internet innovators who are re-imagining and rein-venting a Web of people and places, looking beyond documents and websites."[4] While the mobile

[4]"Kleiner Perkins unveils new fund to invest in social web entrepreneurs," *Tech Journal South*, October 22, 2010.

platform is advancing rapidly and provides a wealth of opportunities, it is still unclear how organizations will be able to take full advantage of it. As with any technology, it needs to be evaluated in the context of its potential for value creation (Chapter 8) and appropriation (Chapter 9).

GREEN IS[5]

Environmental sustainability, the notion that it is imperative for the human species to take the lead in the conservation of the natural environment and the sustainable management of its resources, is now one of the critical items on the world's agenda. The impetus toward environmental sustainability has become a focus of the business and information systems community as well. In 2008, for example, technology advisory firm Gartner singled out "Green IT" as a primary strategic imperative for CIOs.[6] The report reasoned that, "The focus of Green IT that came to the forefront in 2007 will accelerate and expand in 2008. [....] Regulations are multiplying and have the potential to seriously constrain companies in building data centers, as the impact on power grids, carbon emissions from increased use and other environmental impacts are under scrutiny." This scrutiny is due to the fact that producers and users of IT negatively influence environmental sustainability because of environmental impacts related to the purchase, use, and disposal of IT (e-waste) and emissions from data centers using significant amounts of electricity. Thus, green IT initiatives are focused on minimizing the direct impact of IT production and use on the environment.

However, the exclusive focus on information technologies typical of the green IT movement is too narrow and should be extended to information systems, defined as those sociotechnical organizational systems designed to collect, process, store, and distribute information (see Chapter 2). Shifting the focus from Green IT to Green IS enables a broadening of the role of IT in not only minimizing adverse impacts on environmental sustainability, but also playing a proactive role in generating and implementing solutions. Consider the example of UPS, the global package delivery and logistic firm. UPS developed proprietary software to collect and record the state of its vehicles from a wide variety of data points produced in real time by the electronic components found in its vehicles. As a result, UPS was able to access more than 200 items of vehicle-related data, such as RPMs, oil pressure, seatbelt use, the number of times the truck is placed in reverse, and the amount of time spent idling. UPS captures this time-stamped data constantly throughout the day, augmenting it with location data (from GPS readings). The data collected provide 2,000 to 5,000 readings every day for each truck. Similar information is tracked for each package delivered, and the two sources of information are transmitted to a central repository where they are consolidated for analysis. With this information UPS can answer very specific questions of operational importance (e.g., what route did the driver take between the delivery at 125 Lenox Rd. and 15 Avalon St.?), and use the answers to work with drivers to reduce the distances they drive and the fuel they consume. These data are also used to improve safety by ensuring compliance with UPS and community safety standards (e.g., when did the driver fail to buckle up after a delivery?).

---

[5]Significant portions of this section are drawn and adapted from Boudreau, M.-C., Watson, R. T., and Chen, A. (2008). From green IT to green IS. *Cutter Benchmark Review*, 8 (5) and Watson, R. T., Boudreau, M.-C., and Chen, A. J. W. (2010). Information Systems and environmentally sustainable development: Energy Informatics and new directions for the IS community. *MIS Quarterly*, 34(1).

[6]Thibodeau, P. (2007). "Gartner's Top 10 Strategic Technologies for 2008," *Computerworld*, October 9.

The UPS example shows the power of information systems that are targeted to the challenge of reducing energy consumption and emissions. More broadly, it makes the case that information systems expressly designed to tackle the environmental sustainability challenge can help a firm limit its impact on natural resources while improving, rather than hampering the firm's quest for profits and growth. Recognizing this central role of information systems in the quest to foster sustainability, some scientists have advanced an even broader notion: Energy informatics, which is concerned with analyzing, designing, and implementing systems to increase the efficiency of energy demand and supply systems. Its core idea is:

$$\text{Energy} + \text{Information} < \text{Energy}$$

In other words, when augmented with information, energy systems will consume less energy.

DIGITAL DATA GENESIS

The attentive reader will notice that the central role that sensors play in the energy informatics paradigm is not constrained to energy efficiency and environmental sustainability problems. Rather, we are rapidly moving toward a world where events, transactions, and processes are all digitized. When a process (e.g., purchasing a book) is digitized, it is carried out through a digital computer (e.g., purchasing a book online). When an entity is digitized (e.g., an RFID-enabled gaming chip), we have the ability to access an informational representation of that entity (e.g., the position of the chip on the gaming table) and thus generate relevant data (e.g., how many times the chip has been played) from it. Interestingly, such data are natively generated in digital form. To understand this concept, consider the newest multibillion-dollar resort casino in the U.S.—Wynn Las Vegas. Historically, casinos have not placed significant value on customer data. Until the recent publicity given to CRM and BI practices (see Chapter 3), a large casino's standard operating procedure was to value customers on the basis of judgments made by hosts and pit bosses. This approach tended to give undue weight to the contribution of a few big gamblers—the so-called whales—while under-valuing the multitude of smaller, but often more valuable, players. With the advent of state-of-the-art digital slot machines, it became feasible and cost-effective to build comprehensive profiles of avid players, without disrupting their experience, in order to craft a targeted rewards strategy.

Casinos are now expanding their use of technology to capture valuable customer data by embedding radio frequency identification (RFID) transceivers in the chips used at table games. Embedding RFID transceivers in chips means that table games' data are generated in real time and with the outmost precision. Then they are recorded in an easily storable and retrievable format without interfering with the customer's enjoyment. Today, as gaming chips become digitized, monitoring, guessing, and data entry are unnecessary behaviors because data are "born digital" and can be automatically collected and stored in a computer. There isn't a universally accepted name for this trend; McKinsey, for example, uses the label "the Internet of things." We call this trend digital data genesis as it neatly captures the notion of creating data in digital form at their inception. However you want to refer to this trend, it is evident that the pace of digital data generation is accelerating rapidly as the number of connected physical devices increases

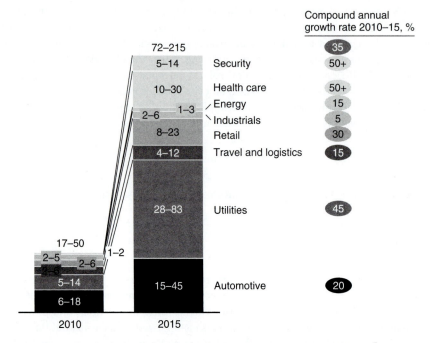

Figure 12.8 Estimated connected devices worldwide (in millions)[7]

(Figure 12.8). It follows that great opportunity exists for organizations for value creation fueled by this trend.

Beyond casinos, examples of digital data genesis are all around us. When we type search terms in Google we are generating data in digital form (i.e., data about what is interesting to us), when we place a call with our mobile phone we are generating data in digital form (i.e., data about our location, the person called, and the like), and when a smart electrical outlet (Figure 12.9) is recording power flow it is generating data in digital form (i.e., data about the electricity usage profile of the device that's plugged in).

In order to take advantage of the opportunities afforded by digital data genesis (DDG), a firm must develop a digital data genesis capability. Such capability consists of the threefold process of:

1. Choosing IT to generate and capture data in its native digital form.

2. Integrating IT in the business processes that generate the data of interest.

3. Managing the digital data so produced.

Note that the DDG capability is concerned with the generation and management of the data, not with its actual use in, for example, through analytical processes. In other words, DDG is a prerequisite to being able to compete on analytics, and the outcome should be measured by a consistent ability to generate data in digital form. There are countless examples of DDG.

---

[7]Adapted from McKinsey Report. (2011). "Big Data: The next frontier for innovation, competition, and productivity."

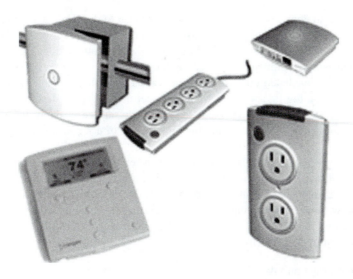

Figure 12.9 Smart electrical sockets, motion detectors, and thermostat by E3 Greentech

Consider, for example, Google's use of Gmail. Whenever you write an e-mail using Gmail, you are generating many forms of digital data. An interesting one is misspelling information. By monitoring common spelling errors, how they are corrected, and where in a sentence they appear, Google has been able to generate so much insight about the spelling process that in its (now defunct) communication product—Google Wave (Figure 12.10)—the spellchecker was able to confidently correct a large proportion of spelling errors automatically, without asking for user input.

Figure 12.10 Google Wave

A digital data genesis strategy requires a disciplined approach to digital data generation and capture, predicated on the recognition of the value of data and the consequent need to architect systems that originate it in a digital format. Take customer service interactions, for example. Customer service is increasingly computer-mediated, both online (e.g., e-commerce transactions) and offline. Every computer-mediated customer service transaction where digital identification of the customer occurs (e.g., a log-in, a swipe card, a customer number) provides an opportunity to capture data. The trend toward computer-mediated customer service is likely to accelerate with the increasing use of mobile technology and the high degree of accessibility and proximity it provides.

The pervasive and affordable network infrastructure ushered in by the Internet provides the second catalyst for digital data genesis strategies. This infrastructure makes it feasible for organizations to develop complete and centralized data stores of relevant data, regardless of their source or where in the world the underlying transactions occurred. Decisions about digital data genesis should be driven by the desire to seamlessly and unobtrusively collect data that answers basic questions about a transaction, such as:

- When did the transaction take place?
- Where did the transaction occur?
- What was the nature of the transaction?
- How was the transaction executed?
- Who initiated the transaction?
- What was the outcome?

While the digital data genesis has strong implications for analytics, much of the current attention to this trend mixes the two. This is a mistake, as digital data genesis enables transactional as much as analytical processing. Specifically, when massive amounts of data are created and captured digitally, it is possible to enable automatic transactions between systems or between systems and individuals. Specifically:

- Machine to Machine (M2M): IT-enabled everyday objects (e.g., utility meters) and pervasive connectivity (e.g., wireless networks) make it is possible to leverage data that is born digital to let the machine generating an event communicate directly with the other machines that can act upon that event. For example, agricultural systems today have sensors that measure the moisture and humidity of the soil and turn on automated sprinkler systems only when needed.
- Machine to Person (M2P): When the actuator[8] on the receiving end of the digital data generated by IT-enabled everyday objects is a person, rather than an object, we talk about M2P transactions. For example, users of the Trafikanten App in Oslo, Norway can identify the closest bus stop (or any other form of public transport) to her location, knowing with precision at what time the bus will arrive, rather than viewing static

---

[8]Strictly speaking an actuator is a device that converts energy (e.g., electrical current) into some kind of motion. A servomechanism to control the steering of an autonomous car is an actuator. We can extend the term to refer to devices that convert information into physical actions.

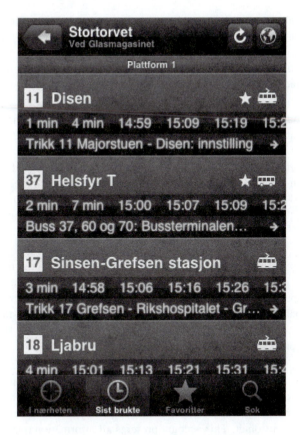

Figure 12.11   The Trafikanten App

timetables that do not take into account current traffic conditions (Figure 12.11). This is because each bus, as well as her smartphone, are digital data generators interconnected amongst themselves and with her.

Digital data genesis is a manifestation of the ongoing progression in IT adoption and use in organizations, rather than a revolution. However, digital data genesis suggests that there is value in proactively thinking about how to generate data from everyday transactions. This is a change in mindset from the traditional business intelligence approaches focusing on mining and extracting value from already available data that were generated as a byproduct of organizational transactions.

Analyzing Digital Data Genesis Opportunities

The proliferation of sensors and sensor data that produce usable information with unprecedented speed and granularity provides the opportunity to design information systems expressly designed to take advantage of this environmental change. At its most fundamental level, digital data genesis offers the opportunity to bridge the gap between the digital and physical world. In other words, as more and more physical activities come with an automatically generated information representation of the activity, it is increasingly possible to extract value from the symbiotic relationship of physical and digital systems. Consider the example described in the opening mini-case, where a layer of information could significantly improve the performance of a physical transportation system.

One approach to analyzing this symbiotic relationship between physical activities and information is through the lens of ubiquity, uniqueness, unison, and universality.

Ubiquity   Information access that is unconstrained by time and space ranks high on the ubiquity scale. Data that are generated natively in digital form are theoretically available in real time. Ubiquitous information provides opportunities for rationalizing the use of resources. Consider the example of a bus that automatically alerts you when it is five minutes away from your stop. Access to such information would allow you to leave the house at the optimal time, thus decreasing time spent in the cold and making the bus service more convenient to you—a result that, before the advent of ubiquitous information, could be achieved only by moving the stop closer to your house.

Uniqueness   Information access that is personalized and individually tailored to the needs of a person or other entity ranks high in uniqueness. In the age of customer relationship management and collaborative filtering (Chapter 3), we have become accustomed to receiving personalized service. Digital data genesis enabled unprecedented levels of uniqueness. Consider the music service Spotify, which can make music suggestions tailored to your individual needs because it has a complete informational representation of your music listening behavior.

Unison   Information that is consistent and devoid of redundancies ranks high in unison. At a procedural level unison translates into the standardization of the activities necessary to perform an activity. For example, a city transit system would be characterized by high degree of unison when it maintains one account per customer. This account presents all information relative to the person's interaction with the various transportation services (i.e., subway, bus, bicycles), using a consistent user interface on the many devices one can use to transact with the city transit (e.g., kiosks, website, mobile apps).

Universality   Information that is standardized and easily shareable across platforms ranks high in universality. A firm like TripIt has leveraged digital data genesis to achieve high universality when it devised a system to read travel confirmation e-mails from any travel provider and create a master itinerary for the traveler. At a procedural level universality describes the ease with which separate processes can interlock and coordinate. For example, the ability to pay a bill with a credit card when travelling abroad, and have that charge translated into our own currency automatically is an example of high universality.

As you become sensitive to the digital data genesis phenomenon, and you begin to see opportunities to harness data that are natively digital, you can focus on the dimensions of ubiquity, uniqueness, unison, and universality to maximize their value creation potential.

The Advent of Supercrunchers

Nobel prize winner Herbert Simon once stated that, "In an information-rich world, the wealth of information means a dearth of something else: a scarcity of whatever it is that information consumes. What information consumes is rather obvious: it consumes the attention of its recipients. Hence a wealth of information creates a poverty of attention and a need to allocate that attention efficiently among the overabundance of information sources that might consume it."[9] Digital data genesis exacerbates this problem by enabling the creation of unprecedented amounts of information. While this data, being in digital form, is amenable to being treated automatically by computers, some argue that the future belongs to individuals who are both creative and quantitatively oriented—so-called supercrunchers.[10] It is these individuals, the theory goes, who will be able to exploit the availability of data to their advantage and the advantage of their organizations by quickly and effortlessly testing their hunches and intuitions with data. As economics professor Hal Varian put it when he was serving as visiting scientist at Google: "The sexy job in the next ten years will be statistician... People think I'm joking, but who would have guessed that computer engineer would have been the sexy job of the 1990s!" If data is free and ubiquitous, as suggested by the digital data genesis paradigm, the ability to take advantage of such data becomes the valuable complementary scarce resource. Should you be positioning yourself to have such scarce ability!?

CUSTOMER-MANAGED INTERACTIONS

In Chapter 3, we discussed Customer Relationship Management (CRM). CRM has been, and continues to be, a major focus for organizations, particularly business organizations, but its limitations are now apparent. CRM is firm centric, only relying on transactional and behavioral customer data pertaining to the interactions of the customer with the firm engaging in it. CRM promises the ability to get to know customers intimately and be able to anticipate their needs. However, a firm engaging in CRM has a limited view of customers' actions and behaviors. Moreover, many events are unforeseeable or, when planned, only the customer knows about them. In response, the concept of customer-managed interactions (CMI) is emerging, promising to solve some of the limitations of CRM described above. CMI is predicated on a shift in the collection and control of the data. In the CMI approach, customer data are stored and managed by the customer—or on his or her behalf by an infomediary (see Chapter 5)—rather than by the firms who originally handled the transaction. Thus, customers maintain control over the decision to interact, the timing of the interaction, the channel to be used, and the data generated.

This approach solves the fundamental limitation of CRM initiatives because the customer's personal data warehouse holds a complete record of all relevant transactions, simplifies the data integrity and redundancy challenge, and, since the transaction is initiated by the customer, it reflects any unforeseeable or life-changing events that may be relevant.

When a customer is ready to transact with your organization, he or she will share the relevant data and his or her requirements with you and, perhaps, some of your competitors. Each of the interested organizations can elect to respond with an offer that the customer evaluates prior to making a selection (Figure 12.12). This scenario may appear overly futuristic, and in fact certainly is at this point for most goods. However, the process described above is no different from one that we are all very familiar with: the request for proposals (RFP) process.

[9]Simon, H. A. (1971). "Designing Organizations for an Information-Rich World," in Martin Greenberger, Computers, Communication, and the Public Interest, Baltimore, MD: The Johns Hopkins Press.
[10]Ayers, I. (2007). "Super Crunchers: Why Thinking-by-Numbers Is the New Way to Be Smart," Bantam Dell.

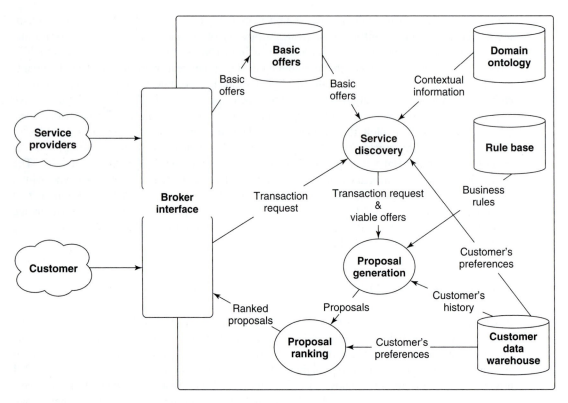

Figure 12.12 Customer interactions in the CMI paradigm

Today the RFP process is relegated to big-ticket items because the economics of the process are such that it is not feasible for most consumer goods. Yet as the price-per-performance of computing equipment continues to fall and IT becomes more and more pervasive, both in business and homes, we can envision a time when the RFP process becomes feasible for the majority of consumer goods: airline tickets, music CDs, books, home appliances, and the like.

Note that the CMI approach is not necessarily about the lowest prices. Conversely, for most industries and most organizations, CMI success will likely stem from the quality of the recommendation and the fit of the solution to the customer need. As the firm has access to much better customer data, it is reasonable for customers to expect much better-fitting solutions. The technology is now in place to support the move of CMI to the mainstream. The Internet has created the infrastructure for data transfer, the falling cost of storage justifies the development of comprehensive personal data repositories, and standards like XML provide the infrastructure for formatting messages among loosely coupled agents.

Consider, for instance, Quicken, the personal financial management software. While Quicken is typically focused on the financial side of the transaction, if you use credit cards as the exclusive form of payment and diligently download your statements to Quicken, you can develop a pretty comprehensive personal data repository. The leap to a situation where every transaction comes with an associated XML message describing it isn't big. For simple goods, such as airlines, this is already possible as the reservation fully defines the relevant characteristics of the product.

OPEN SOURCE

Open source software no longer qualifies as an emerging trend. Gartner estimates that by 2016 open source code will be present in the portfolio of mission-critical software (not just any application!) of 99% of Global 2000 enterprises—the biggest organizations in the world.[11] Indicating the consolidation of the trend toward open source software use, Gartner suggests that in 2010 only 75% of the Global 2000 relied on this class of software for mission-critical functionality. In a more general 2010 survey including organizations of all sizes, Gartner found that 46% of respondents had implemented open source solutions in a specific department or for a specific project.

The trend toward open source software use gained significant momentum with the emergence of the Internet, but it remains today an important, and evolving, IT opportunity for modern organizations. The open source movement has coalesced around the Open Source Initiative (OSI), an organization dedicated to promoting open source applications and system code, focusing on its benefits and qualities for the business community. In 2006, the OSI website captured the evolution of the movement: "Open source software is an idea whose time has finally come. For twenty years it has been building momentum in the technical cultures that built the Internet and the World Wide Web. Now it's breaking out into the commercial world, and that's changing all the rules. Are you ready?"[12]

Open Source: Definition

Open source software is often confused with free software—as in free of charge. In fact, licenses for open source software may or may not be offered at no cost (free of charge software is called freeware). Rather, the term *open source* is used to differentiate it from closed source, or proprietary, programs that prevent users from accessing and modifying the source code. The mission of the OSI captures this notion: "Open source is a development method for software that harnesses the power of distributed peer review and transparency of process. The promise of open source is better quality, higher reliability, more flexibility, lower cost, and an end to predatory vendor lock-in."[13]

Software programs are created by software engineers, who design the algorithm, and programmers, who code it using a specific programming language. The code generated by the programmers, which can be understood by anyone who is well versed in the programming language used, is called the source code (see Figure 12.13).

In order for the program to work, the source code has to be transformed (i.e., interpreted or compiled) into a format that a computer can execute, called the object code. Typically, when you purchase a software license from a software company (e.g., Microsoft Office, Oracle Database 11*g*), you are given the object code and the right to run it on your computers, but you are not provided with the source code. In fact, any effort to reverse engineer the object code to gain access to the source code is considered a violation of the intellectual property of the software house and will land you a well-founded lawsuit.

---

[11]Driver, M. (2011). "A CIO's perspective on Open-Source Software," *Gartner Research.*

[12]http://www.opensource.org/ (Accessed 06/12/2006.)

[13]http://www.opensource.org/ (Accessed 05/05/2011.)

```
dBDate = CDate(BirthDate)
dRelDate = CDate(RelativeTo)
iAns = Year(dRelDate) - Year(dBDate)

If Month(dBDate) <> Month(dRelDate) Then
    bSubtractOne = Month(dBDate) > Month(dRelDate)
Else
    bSubtractOne = Day(dBDate) > Day(dRelDate)
End If
```

Figure 12.13   Sample source code

Unlike proprietary software, open source programs are distributed with the express intent of enabling users to gain access to the source code and modify it. An open source license typically exhibits the following characteristics:

- *Free redistribution.* The software can be freely given away or sold.
- *Available source code.* The source code is published and freely obtainable.
- *Derived works.* Licensees can modify the software and redistribute it under the same license terms as the original.
- *No discrimination.* The license is available to any entity, including for-profit organizations and commercial users.
- *Technology neutrality.* The license, and all of its provisions, must be free of restrictions tied to the use of any technologies or type of interface.

Open Source Is Open for Business

Analysis of the open source licensing characteristics shows that the open source movement encourages, rather than opposes, commercial applications and commercial redistribution. This friendliness toward business applications has been the catalyst for widespread acceptance and growth of open source software as a viable alternative to proprietary programs.

A number of organizations have emerged in an attempt to capitalize on the open source movement. The following three models are currently being implemented:[14]

Sponsored Open Source   A number of not-for-profit foundations provide support and coordination to open source efforts. For example, the Apache Software Foundation coordinates enhancements to the Apache Web Server, and the Mozilla Foundation supports the development of the Firefox Web browser and many other products (Figure 12.14).

Some corporations also sponsor their own open source projects, typically "opening" their own software products by releasing the source code. The first example in this area was offered by Netscape Corp., which released the source code of its Web browser in 1998. More recently

---

[14]For a more in-depth analysis and treatment of them, see Watson, R., and Boudreau, M.-C. (2005). "The Business of Open Source: A Strategic Perspective," *Cutter Benchmark Review* (5:11) pp. 5–12.

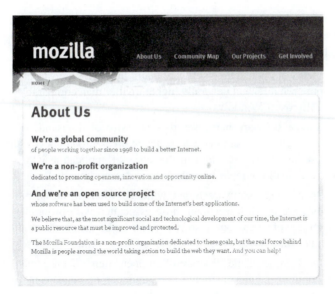

Figure 12.14   The Mozilla Foundation website

Sun Microsystems released the source code of its OpenOffice suite and NetBeans products, and in November 2006 even released the source code of its Java programming language.

Open Source Service   The open source service model emerged in the late 1990s with increasing attention being garnered by the Linux operating systems. While licenses to Linux had to be free, a number of firms, led by pioneer Red Hat, Inc., began charging for installation, support, training, and all the other ancillary services typically associated with software sales. Today a number of upstarts and established firms compete in this market, including big names such as HP, Unisys, and Novell. They support a whole stable of open source applications such as Linux (operating system), Apache (Web server), and MySQL (database management system).

Professional Open Source   The latest evolution in the open source model is professional open source. This label refers to organizations that, while being part of the open source movement and subscribing to the open source licensing terms, maintain fairly tight control over the software programs they sell. For example, a professional open source organization will have its own core set of programmers and developers who provide direction for the project. At the same time, though, the group will leverage the greater community of open source programmers, testers, and adopters. These organizations rely on their knowledge and understanding of the core source code to provide better services when a client adopts their software.

Advantages and Disadvantages of Open Source Software

As a general or functional manager, you will without a doubt be part of a system selection committee. Increasingly, such committees have the option of adopting open source software rather than purchasing proprietary programs. While decisions of this kind are very context specific, below we identify the main benefits and drawbacks of open source.

Advantages   The principal advantages of open source touted by its proponents are a function of the ability of open source projects to leverage a large community of developers, programmers, testers, and customers. These advantages include the following:

- *Robustness.* Proponents of open source software claim that mature projects (e.g., Linux) are more robust, more reliable, and generally higher quality than comparable proprietary applications (e.g., Microsoft Windows).

- *Creativity.* Open source software harnesses the creativity of thousands of developers around the world. As such, it is more likely to generate breakthrough new solutions (e.g., Firefox tabbed browsing, now a standard in this class of applications) than traditional products created by a small community within one software house.

- *Limited lock-in.* Open source software is not without switching costs, but supporters claim that such costs are much lower than those associated with proprietary software. For example, customers of open source software can make their own modifications to the source code rather than having to rely on the software vendor to do so.

- *Simplified licensing.* Because of the structure of an open source license, customers need not worry about complex legal constraints (e.g., number of concurrent users). They simply install as many copies of the program as they need.

- *Free license.* While not regarded as one of the chief benefits of open source by the open source movement, total cost of ownership is still an important factor to those firms that adopt open source applications. Because open source generally can be licensed for free, costs are lower than those associated with proprietary applications.

Disadvantages   Software is by no means simple (or cheap) to install and operate, and open source software is no exception. Thus, the skeptics respond by raising the following concerns:

- *Unpredictable costs.* Skeptics like to say that free software is like a free puppy—yes, you get it for nothing, but then you will encounter many (often unplanned) costs along the way. Thus, you need to carefully evaluate an open source installation based on total cost of ownership (see Chapter 10).

- *Support varies widely.* Depending on the product and where your firm acquired it, support can range from high quality to nonexistent.

- *Security.* Skeptics claim that publishing source code gives an advantage to those who want to break its security. Proponents of open source respond that a large community of developers will identify and close more weaknesses than a small team of company developers.

- *Compatibility.* Standardization of products using one or a few vendors simplifies compatibility and integration. There is no guarantee that open source solutions will be compatible with one another and/or with proprietary software.

- *The legal landscape.* Open source software requires that no portion of the code is protected by copyright. Recent court challenges have raised the specter that there is no way to ensure that copyrighted code will not make it into open source solutions, thus opening customers to liability. In response, some of the firms that support open source software (e.g., JBoss, HP, Red Hat) have adopted indemnification clauses in their licensing agreements.

In summary, the decision of whether to go with open source and with what products will depend on the characteristics of the organization and the maturity of the software program. Some products, such as the Linux operating system, are already so robust that in early 2005 the MIT Media Lab felt comfortable advising the Brazilian government to shun Microsoft products for open source software, contending that "free software is far better on the dimensions of cost, power, and quality."[15] Other products require a much stronger commitment in terms of support and investments. It is essential that organizations adopting such products have the expertise and resources to implement and maintain them.

SOFTWARE AS A SERVICE

Software as a service (SaaS) is not a new concept, but one that has gained significant currency with the renewed attention to outsourcing, the emergence of the open source movement, and the consolidation of the Internet as a viable platform for business operations. Software as a service is a software delivery approach in which a provider hosts the application in its data centers and the customer accesses the needed functionalities over a computer network. Thus, instead of licensing the application and requiring that the customer installs it, maintains it, and generally supports it, in the SaaS model it is the provider who performs these tasks. In other words, management of the application is outsourced to the provider, and the client simply takes advantage of the service. Perhaps the simplest example of SaaS is a class of applications you most likely use: Web-based e-mail systems such as Gmail (Figure 12.15).

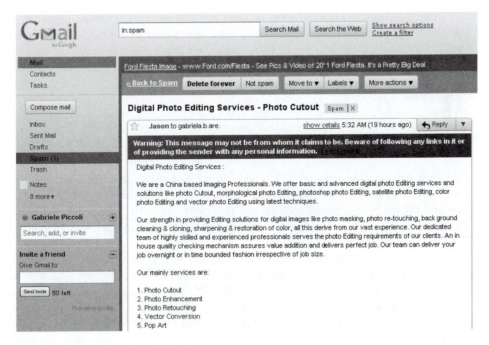

Figure 12.15   The Gmail client

[15]"MIT Urges Brazil to Adopt Open-Source," Reuters, March 17, 2005 (Accessed 02/06/2011 at http://msnbc.msn.com/id/7220913).

Figure 12.16   Transformer on the power grid (Image courtesy of ABB/Kuhlman Electric Corporation.)

The SaaS model focuses on the services (i.e., functionalities) being provided, not on the physical products (the applications) being sold. The metaphor for SaaS is the utilities we all use—such as electricity (Figure 12.16) or water. We don't worry so much about the generation of power and the management of the delivery system (i.e., the wires and transformers); we simply plug in our appliances and expect to access the service (i.e., electrical power) that comes through the wire.

Historical Context

Business Process Outsourcing   The idea of accessing software as a service provided by an outside firm is not new. The concept of business process outsourcing (BPO) has been around, on and off, since the mainframe era and the 1960s. In a BPO agreement, a client, say the local independent convenience store, engages a provider to supply and manage a given business process, say accounting and payroll.

In the traditional BPO approach, management at the convenience store would pass the provider the weekly time cards detailing hours worked by each employee, as well as invoices from suppliers and cash register records. The BPO provider would feed this information into its accounting and payroll applications and compute accrued vacation, benefits, and tax withdrawals, and cut the checks for the employees. The provider would also be able to produce financial statements for the business and accounting reports. In this case, not only the payroll and accounting software applications are outsourced, but the entire business process that they enable.

As the BPO model evolved over time, a number of other business processes became viable candidates for outsourcing. Today they include accounting, human resources and payroll, call center operations, and the like.

Application Service Providers   With the emergence of the commercial Internet during the dot-com days in the mid-1990s, application service provision emerged on the wings of the slogan "the network is the computer." This slogan captured the idea that, with the availability of widespread, increasingly reliable, and cheap computer networks (i.e., the Internet), it would not matter much where computer processing happened—at the user's workstation, on the firm's premises, or somewhere else in cyberspace.

Application service provision (ASP) is a software delivery model where a provider hosts and manages a standard application, say Microsoft Office, and enables clients to access it and use it over a computer network. This application is often purchased and licensed by the customer, but managed and supported by the provider on its infrastructure. Note that the term provider here does not necessarily imply an external vendor. For example, a retail chain—say Best Buy or Zara—may enable its shops to run the point of sale system (POS) directly from the chain's data centers using an ASP model instead of requiring each store to have a locally installed copy of the POS application. A defining feature of the ASP approach to software service provisioning is that each client will have access to a separate instance of the software application running on the vendor's remote servers. In the very early days of the ASP model the provider would run an instance (i.e., a copy) of the application for each client on a separate server (i.e., hardware). Later, with the advent of *virtualization* techniques, whereby a physical server is able to run multiple, independent instances of a software environment, the ASP vendors began consolidating servers and running multiple instances of their client software on the same hardware. However, each client accessed a separate instance of the application, even when the same application was being provisioned.

SaaS Today

Today, at least on the surface, the software as a service model has evolved to encompass the ASP model, as well as to include providers who develop applications with the explicit objective of hosting them and providing them as a service to clients—sometimes referred to as software on demand. Moreover, the SaaS movement has received further impetus from the increasing popularity of open source software, with providers who now deliver open source applications as a service.

However, true SaaS offerings are structurally different from the ASP approach, and this difference provides far superior economics. The difference is a technology architectural feature known as multi-tenancy. Multi-tenancy refers to the provision of applications that appear to be dedicated to a single user and customized to his needs. Instead the provider runs one copy of the application segregating data from user to user, and enabling each user to customize the programs' interface and features. Think again about your use of Gmail. You can modify the appearance (i.e., skins), some of the functionalities (i.e., incorporating Google Buzz), and you can certainly not read another user's e-mails! However, the provider is running just one single copy of the application (at least logically). This allows Google to reduce processing overhead, enjoy faster innovation cycles, and achieve practically infinite scalability.

While multi-tenancy sounds like one of those techie concerns that will quickly bore any executive or business manager, a minimal understanding of its characteristics, and clarity as to whether your vendor uses it or not, is a critical business concern. Multi-tenancy has significant implications for IT performance dimensions (deployment, scalability) that have significant direct impact on business performance dimensions (e.g., availability of service, customizability of the product, adaptability to customer needs).

Today there is a wealth of SaaS providers offering software programs ranging from basic personal productivity tools to highly specialized and customized applications. The advantages and disadvantages of the SaaS model parallel those that are inherent to any type of outsourcing agreement, with the added risks and rewards associated with the delivery of the application through a network.

On the positive side, SaaS applications reduce setup time and can be up and running relatively quickly. Their pricing can be more flexible, with charges based on actual usage rather than fixed licensing fees. As with any other outsourcing arrangement, SaaS reduces the number of local staff needed to maintain and support the application.

The above advantages come at a cost, of course. The chief limitation of SaaS arrangements is the added reliability risk associated with the availability of the Internet. If the firm's Internet connection experiences an outage, the applications become unusable, even though they are actually up and running. Another limitation of SaaS is that it is more difficult to integrate remote applications with the existing IT infrastructure of the firm and with its other applications. Thus, while there are providers who claim to offer ERPs on a SaaS basis, stand-alone applications may be most suitable to this model.

Finally, as with any other outsourcing arrangement, the performance of the firm is directly impacted by the performance of the service provider. For example, many Salesforce.com (Figure 12.17) customers blamed the firm for lost sales when Salesforce.com experienced

Figure 12.17   Salesforce.com's website circa 2005 (Copyright salesforce.com, Inc. Used with permission.)

an outage lasting almost a whole day on December 20, 2005—during the holiday season's final days.

CLOUD COMPUTING

To the skeptics, the term cloud computing is simply marketing veneer on the old SaaS concept. However, it is now becoming clear that cloud computing does represent a new approach to computing, one that brings together under the same umbrella many concepts that are indeed not new, such as virtualization, service-oriented architecture, and utility pricing of computing resources. The term cloud computing comes from the traditional icon used to diagram the telecommunication network, an icon then adapted to represent the Internet in order to provide an abstraction for all the technology and functionality the developers writing the diagram could assume to be working without worry about how they worked (Figure 12.18).

Now assume that to access a service, say the financial consolidation and analysis provided by Mint.com,[16] all you need is a personal computer equipped with a browser. Then you could argue that "the Mint.com service is in the cloud" and diagram it as in Figure 12.19. The diagram

Figure 12.18 Diagrammatic representation of the cloud

Figure 12.19 User accessing bank transactions through Mint.com

---

[16]Mint.com is a startup, recently acquired by Intuit for $170 million, that "brings all your financial accounts together online, automatically categorizes your transactions, lets you set budgets and helps you achieve your savings goals." Users log on and provide account information for their financial holdings and Mint downloads transactions from each one every night.

conveys the idea that, in order to gain access to the functionalities offered by the Mint.com service—consolidation of transactions, analysis of your spending patterns, status of investments and savings—the user need not concern herself with any of the specifics about how the data is collected from the financial institutions that have it, or how the data is stored, secured, and so on. In other words, the users simply access the service, and all of the complexities associated with creating, managing, and delivering it are addressed "in the cloud."

The simple example above conveys the essence of the cloud computing model, a computing delivery approach that divorces use of resources from the actual management of those resources. More precisely, however, the cloud computing framework focuses on resources rather than applications. That is, while the SaaS model focuses on the delivery of applications, the cloud computing model may provide any computing service. To readily appreciate the difference, consider one of the most prominent cloud computing offerings—Amazon Elastic Compute Cloud (EC2)—yes, the same Amazon that sells books! Amazon describes the EC2 offering in the following terms. "Just as Amazon Simple Storage Service (Amazon S3) enables storage in the cloud, Amazon EC2 enables 'compute' in the cloud. Amazon EC2's simple web service interface allows you to obtain and configure capacity with minimal friction. It provides you with complete control of your computing resources and lets you run on Amazon's proven computing environment." In other words, instead of accessing the functionalities of a full-blown application (as with SaaS), you are able to access computational or storage components—the building blocks of an application, if you will—that you can combine into your own offerings. But because these components are available in the cloud, you need not be concerned with their day-to-day management. . . as long as you trust the provider to do a good job for you!

Cloud computing parlance is differentiated along the three main elements of the system stack: Application, platform, and infrastructure. We can then speak of SaaS when referring to applications running in the cloud. The term Platform as a Service (PaaS) conveys the notion that what you are renting from the provider is not a full-fledged application, but rather a platform on which to build your own applications. In that case, you would be renting the use of hardware (the servers in a data center on which all this software runs) along with the functionalities of operating systems and utilities (i.e., storage, security, backup and recovery, application serving, and the like). Finally, at the level closest to hardware, we talk about Infrastructure as a Service (IaaS). In this case what you are renting is the use of hardware functionality—in essence computational power, storage capacity, and networking functionality.

Cloud computing is the latest in a long list of hosting models dating back to the 1960s and the concept of business process outsourcing. What is unique about cloud computing, however, is the notion that the utilization of, and payment for, the resources used by your organization is dynamic and agile. By agile we mean that an organization that sees a growing demand for its applications can scale the service relatively rapidly—Amazon suggests that they can scale their service in a matter of hours—and flexibly. This is significantly different from what happens if a firm owns its own data centers and has to acquire dedicated hardware to run its applications. Moreover, typical cloud computing providers adopt a utility billing model, whereby the user only pays for the usage of the service. Thus, as demand for the company's application subsides (e.g., imagine a retailer's website after Christmas, or the FIFA website after the World Cup Finals are over), and utilization drops, so does the cost of maintaining the service.

SUMMARY

In this chapter, we introduced some emerging and some enduring trends in information systems and technology management. Understanding these trends and technologies, the associated vocabulary, and the benefits and risks they engender for modern organizations is critical for you as a general or functional manager, as you will be called upon to participate in the debate about whether your own firm should embark in initiatives that leverage the technologies and trends discussed in this chapter.

Specifically, in this chapter we learned that:

■ The mobile platform represents the current frontier of technology adoption. Both individual users and businesses are integrating the mobile platform—in the form of smartphones and tablets—in their technology portfolios. While based on the traditional digital computer architecture, mobile devices offer peculiar characteristics such as ubiquity, identifiability, and context awareness. These characteristics make mobile "post-pc" devices uniquely suited to support emerging applications and uses such as mobile commerce, location-based social networking, and augmented reality—thus ushering in a wealth of opportunities for value creation.

■ Information systems can play a crucial role toward advancing the global imperative of environmental sustainability. Broadening our attention from Green IT, and its focus on reducing energy consumption of IT devices and data centers, to Green IS enables a broadening of the role of IT in not only minimizing adverse impacts on environmental sustainability, but also playing a proactive role in generating and implementing solutions.

■ The widespread adoption of information technology and the increasing computer mediation of organizational and social processes have created the possibility to utilize data that is born digital. The digital data genesis trend creates the opportunity.

■ In Chapter 3, we discussed Customer Relationship Management (CRM), its advantages and some of the principal limitations of CRM initiatives: firm centricity and limited predictive ability. In response to these limitations, the customer managed interactions (CMI) trend is emerging. In the CMI approach, customer data are stored and managed by the customer—or on his or her behalf by an infomediary—rather than by the firms who handled the transaction.

■ Open source software programs, those programs that enable the adopting firm to receive and modify the source code, are increasingly becoming a viable option for organizations. When weighing the decision to adopt open source instead of a proprietary software program, you need to evaluate the following advantages and disadvantages of open source projects. The pros include robustness, creativity, limited lock-in, simplified licensing, and free licenses. The cons include unpredictable costs, varying degrees of quality support, security concerns, compatibility concerns, and a potentially complex legal landscape.

■ Software as a service (SaaS) is a software delivery approach in which a provider hosts the application in its data centers and the customer accesses the needed applications' functionalities over a computer network. Instead of licensing the application and requiring that the customer installs it, maintains it, and generally supports it, in the SaaS model it is the provider who shoulders these tasks—customers simply gain access to the needed applications in much the same way they gain access to utilities (e.g., water, electricity).

STUDY QUESTIONS

1. Which of the trends associated with the mobile platform do you believe are most likely to become mainstream in the next three years? Why?

2. All too often organizations adopt an information technology or technology management fad without careful examination. Choose a specific organization and discuss how it could create value employing the mobile platform. Then identify an organization that is currently utilizing the mobile platform, but that you believe is wasting resources and will not benefit from the initiative. Explain your reasoning and discuss the differences.

3. Describe the concept of energy informatics. Describe where you believe energy informatics would have the strongest potential impact toward environmental sustainability.

4. How does the CMI trend respond to the limitations of Customer Relationship Management? Who would you think is best positioned to take advantage of the emergence of CMI?

5. What is open source software? What are the main advantages and disadvantages of open source software? When would you consider an open source software implementation in your organization? When would you not?

FURTHER READINGS

1. Watson, R. T., and Boudreau, M.-C. (2011). *Energy Informatics.* Athens, GA: Watson Press.
2. Watson, R. T., Piccoli, G., Brohman, M. K., and Parasuraman, A. (2004). "I Am My Own Database." *Harvard Business Review* (81/11), pp. 18–19.
3. Watson, R. T., Piccoli, G., Brohman, M. K., and Parasuraman, A. (2005). "Customer-Managed Interactions: A New Paradigm for Firm-Customer Relationships." *MIS Quarterly Executive* (4:3), pp. 319–327.

GLOSSARY

- **Augmented reality:** A field of computing concerned with superimposing an information layer on a real image, thus providing users with a simultaneous view of real objects and contextual information about those objects.
- **Cloud computing:** A general term referring to the ability to obtain and use computing functionality (e.g., storage, software) over the Internet.
- **Customer managed interactions (CMI):** A paradigm where the customer retains control over the decision to interact, the timing of the interaction, the channel to be used in the interaction, and the data generated.
- **Customer relationship management (CRM):** A strategic orientation that calls for iterative processes designed to turn customer data into customer relationships through active use of, and learning from, the information collected.
- **Energy informatics:** An emerging discipline that is concerned with analyzing, designing, and implementing systems to increase the efficiency of energy demand and supply systems.

- **Location-based social networking:** An extension of mobile social networking whereby the geographical location of the user becomes an integral component of the service, enabling efficient access to context-dependent services.
- **Mobile platform:** A platform is an underlying computer system on which application programs can run. With the term mobile platform, therefore, we refer to the hardware/operating systems combinations that enable mobile computing (e.g., Apple iPad/Apple iOS or Samsung Galaxy Tab/Google Android).
- **Open source:** A type of software licensing agreement that enables the licensee to obtain and modify the source code of the software program.
- **Software as a Service (SaaS):** A software delivery approach in which a provider hosts the application in its data centers and the customer accesses the needed applications' functionalities over a computer network.
- **Virtualization:** The process of enabling multiple instances of a software program to run on the same physical hardware as if each instance had its own dedicated machine.

13

Security, Privacy, and Ethics

What You Will Learn in This Chapter

This chapter discusses some important topics of managerial interest that are often delegated to IT specialists: security and IT risk management, privacy, and information systems ethics. The first objective of this chapter is to convince you that, as future general and functional managers, you will have to be involved in these decisions. The second objective is to help you gain an understanding of the circumstances in which choices and trade-offs are made so that you can actively participate in decision making. Specifically, in this chapter you will:

1. Learn to make the case that information systems security, privacy, and ethics are issues of interest to general and functional managers, and why it is a grave mistake to delegate them exclusively to IT professionals.

2. Understand the basic IT risk management processes, including risk assessment, risk analysis, and risk mitigation.

3. Understand the principal security threats, both internal and external, and the principal safeguards that have been developed to mitigate these risks.

4. Be able to identify the nature of privacy concerns that modern organizations face, and be able to articulate how general and functional managers can safeguard the privacy of their customers and employees.

5. Define ethics, apply the concept of ethical behavior to information systems decisions, and be able to articulate how general and functional managers can help ensure that their organization behaves ethically.

MINI-CASE: REINVENTRAVEL.COM COMES UNDER FIRE

As you watch the sun setting over the San Francisco skyline from your hotel room window, you can't avoid feeling that you really dropped the ball this time. You can still hear Clive Sturling, your CIO, as he tells you, "Don't worry about security, that's techie stuff, I'll take care of it. Just grow the business, that's what you are good at." You had not asked about security again after that conversation, perfectly happy to leave the "techie stuff" to him and that was before you launched the company over two years ago!

Well, it was him on the phone a minute ago, ruining what had been a perfectly good day. In a daze you replay the conversation in your mind: "We have been attacked," Clive had said. "It was a distributed denial of service attack, not much we could do with our current security infrastructure. The site was unavailable for about 70 minutes; it wasn't defaced or otherwise ruined, just down. I don't think many people noticed. The attack ended about an hour ago. I didn't want to call you before checking if they had compromised any files. It doesn't look like it."

Not much we could do? Isn't he the one who said not to worry about security? The site was down for "only 70 minutes." Does he know that in that amount of time ReinvenTravel.com typically processed 19,000 transactions? Granted, evenings were a bit slower, but there must have been at least 4,500 customers who noted the outage. Your emotions kept mixing at a dizzying pace. You were angry at Clive; you trusted him and he let you down. However, you felt sympathetic to his position as well. You had been the one who told him to "run IT on a shoestring," to help you speed the path to profitability as much as possible.

Oddly enough, as you begin to recover from the shock of the news, your college days flash into your mind, bringing a smile to your face. You had started in this field only three and a half years before, when you learned in one of your classes about the opportunity to revolutionize how people seek and purchase travel products. That day in your Information Systems class seemed like decades ago; now you were the CEO of a growing company with 52 employees, over 70,000 active customers and members, and revenues approaching $8 million. Clive had built the search engine in just eight months, alone! He was a wizard with that kind of stuff. Half the time you had no idea what he was doing. . . but that user interface, you certainly appreciated and understood that part of his work; everyone did! So far superior to anything that had been seen before. . . it was that fabulous demo that got you your first round of venture capital financing.

Financing. . . that word snapped you back to reality! You had to get ready for dinner. The meeting with your VC was in less than an hour, and you had yet to take a shower. With the first round of financing beginning to run out and minimal profits, a second round was a must. You had hoped to spend the evening discussing your plan for growing the customer base and beginning to monetize your membership, seeking their guidance and help with regard to the three potential partners you were evaluating. "Well, that ain't going to happen," you mumbled.

What should you do? Should you tell your VC about the denial-of-service attack? It may not be your choice; these guys liked to do their homework, and the odds were good that they were poking around the site when the outage happened. No time to call your legal counsel; you had to go it alone on this one.

Clive had been very unclear about whether an intrusion had occurred along with the denial-of-service attack. At this point you had little faith with regard to his staff's ability to find out; it seems that security and monitoring had not been ranking very high on their priority list! ReinvenTravel.com stored quite a bit of personal information about customers, including identifying information and credit card data. Should you communicate to the customers that an attack had occurred? Should you issue a press release? There was no evidence that security had been compromised, and even less that personal data had been stolen. A denial-of-service attack only made a Web site unavailable for some time. . . did it not? "No way, Clive and his staff would know if data had been stolen," you told yourself.

This was increasingly looking like a situation you were ill-prepared to address. But, as your father always said, "You wanted the bicycle? Now you have to pedal." As you began to feel the adrenaline pumping again, you exclaimed, "Here we go!" and jumped up from your chair. You had 55 minutes to develop your plan before dinner.

DISCUSSION QUESTIONS

1. Do you agree with the assessment that you had dropped the ball? Or are you being unduly harsh on yourself?
2. Who do you think should be making security calls at ReinvenTravel.com? Shouldn't this be the CIO's job?
3. What should you do tonight? Should you approach the topic at dinner or wait and see if anyone else raises the issue?
4. What should you do in the next few days? Should you issue a press release? Should you contact your customers directly? Should you focus on overhauling your security safeguards to prevent future similar problems and forget today's incident?

INTRODUCTION

This chapter focuses on three topics: information systems security and IT risk management, privacy, and information systems ethics. These topics, while distinct, are connected by a common thread. Information systems security, privacy, and ethical concerns were born along with the introduction of computer systems and information technology in organizations. However, the recent widespread adoption of the Internet and the proliferation of information for business use have dramatically amplified these threats. The computer security industry, for example, is estimated to be already in the billion-dollar range, with Gartner research estimating its size at about $16.6 billion in 2010. A ComputerWorld survey found that almost half of the organizations studied spend more than 5% of their IT budget on security. This level of spending notwithstanding, the 2006 InfoWorld Security Report found that over 50% of individuals in charge of their organization's security are at best "somewhat confident" in their enterprise's security systems. However, security breaches have significant business impacts. A scientific event study found that public traded companies that experienced security breaches lost an average of 2.1% of their market capitalization (an average loss of over $1.6 billion per incident).[1]

A failure in security, privacy, or ethics can have dramatic repercussions on the organization, both because of its potentially damaging direct effects (e.g., computer outages, disruptions to operations) and its increasingly negative indirect effects (e.g., legal recourse, image damage). Consider the following three recent examples:

Countrywide, at one point in time the biggest mortgage lender in the U.S. which is now part of Bank of America, notified customers in September 2008 that an employee had sold customer data to a third party—including highly sensitive information such as Social Security Numbers. The estimated number of records sold included up to 2 million customers. While the press release indicated that there appeared to be no evidence of malicious behavior (yet!) it offered to purchase on behalf of these customers a credit monitoring service for two years. While the Countrywide case was particularly egregious, it was one of 480 data breach cases reported that year alone[2], and the widespread occurrence of such incidents continues today. A similar fate befell online hotel review site TripAdvisor. While only e-mail addresses from the members mailing list were stolen, the incident reminded users of the difficulties in securing digital information.

In May 2011, WordPress.com, the leading blog-hosting site thought to serve the needs of 18 million publishers worldwide, was attacked by way of a distributed denial-of-service attack originating mainly from China. At first thought to be politically motivated, the attack crippled the substantial infrastructure of Wordpress for hours. A few years earlier, HostGator, a Web-hosting service firm that provides the tools for individuals and organizations to create and maintain a Web site, found itself under siege on a Friday afternoon. Customers began to (angrily) report that visitors to their legitimate Web presence would be automatically redirected to malicious sites that delivered viruses to the hapless visitor. It took HostGator over twelve hours to clean up the mess.

---

[1] Cavusoglu, H., Mishra, B., and Raghunathan, S., "The Effect of Internet Security Breach Announcements on Market Value: Capital Market Reactions for Breached Firms and Internet Security Developers," International Journal of Electronic Commerce, 9/1 (Fall 2004): pp. 69–104.

[2] Merle, R. "Countrywide says customer data were sold: Mortgage lender offers to pay for credit monitoring service," *The Washington Post*, Sunday, September 14, 2008.

RealNetworks, the maker of streaming audio and video products, faced significant backlash in the late 1990s when it was perceived as violating its customers' privacy. The company's new streaming audio/video player Real Jukebox was shipped with a feature that allowed it to capture information about what CDs the user was listening to, and send such data to RealNetworks servers over the Internet. RealNetworks contended that it was simply trying to provide its customers with a more personalized experience, and the feature could be disabled relatively easily. However, it faced significant backlash motivated by the perception that RealNetworks had attempted to collect the data surreptitiously, without the customer's express authorization. In other words, the company gave its customers reason to doubt its trustworthiness. A decade after the incident, multinational electronics firm Sony Corporation made the same mistake. In 2005 Sony embedded, without disclosure, rootkit when customers played one of 52 CD titles shipped that year. The software was designed to enforce copyright protection. While it created security concerns and drained resources from the users' system, the problem (as it was for RealNetworks 10 years earlier) was that it would install without seeking user's permission. In November 2005, Sony recalled the titles and backed out of the program.

ChoicePoint is a data collection company that accumulates public record information on all U.S. residents to resell it to organizations that use the data for research and marketing purposes, and to the government. In February 2005, ChoicePoint sold personal information on about 163,000 individuals in its databases to identity thieves posing as legitimate small businesses. While not a classic example of an information systems security breach (the company's computer systems and IT safeguards were not violated), the incident was certainly a security breach—the safety of thousands of private records was indeed compromised! Aside from the negative publicity that ChoicePoint attracted, the firm lost a lawsuit and was required to pay $10 million in civil penalties and $5 million in consumer redress to settle Federal Trade Commission charges that its security and record-handling procedures violated consumers' privacy rights and federal laws.

As we mentioned in Chapter 6, security, privacy, and ethics are areas where, as general and functional managers, you cannot abdicate your responsibility. Yet in order to actively participate in decision making on these three fronts, you must be able to understand under what circumstances choices and trade-offs are made, and what the principal threats and responses are.

IT RISK MANAGEMENT AND SECURITY

Information systems security refers to the set of defenses an organization puts in place to mitigate threats to its technology infrastructure and data resources. IT risk management is the process by which the firm attempts to identify and measure information systems security risks, and to devise the optimal mitigation strategy.

Security is an area that has increased in importance, along with the widespread adoption of information technologies and even more so with the development and growth of networks. More recently, security and IT risk management have come to the forefront of managerial attention because of the increasing threat of cyber-terrorism. For instance, Dennis Blair, the U.S. Director of National Intelligence, in written testimony to the U.S. Senate Select Committee on Intelligence in February 2010, stated: "Malicious cyberactivity is occurring on an unprecedented scale with extraordinary sophistication. . . Sensitive information is stolen daily from both government and private-sector networks, undermining confidence in our information systems, and in the very information these systems were intended to convey." As computer systems are increasingly underpinning the infrastructure of developed economies, they become legitimate targets of terrorism threats.

Why Is Security *Not* an IT Problem?

The pervasiveness and possible cost of the security threat should suffice to convince general and functional managers that security is a matter of strategic interest, not something that "the IT people should worry about." Speaking to the prevalence of such threats, a 2006 *InfoWorld* survey found that the 430 firms polled staved off a collective average of 331 network attacks in the previous 12 months.[3]

However, security should be on managers' radar screens also because of its peculiar characteristics that run the risk of leaving it underfunded, unless general and functional managers get directly involved in the threat assessment and mitigation process.

The game of chess offers a great metaphor for the information security management and IT risk management processes. In the game of chess the objective of the players, some more skilled than others, is to circumvent the defenses of the opponents in order to checkmate him. Security is a constantly evolving game of chess, one where current defenses, and their limitations, are the basis for future attacks. A difficult game, indeed. But what do you get if you win the security chess game? Nothing. In fact, the best security is the one that leads to nothing happening. As in the opening mini-case, all the "excitement" occurs when your security has been breached.

More specifically, security is a negative deliverable. In other words, all the money spent on managing IT risk and securing the firm's IT infrastructure and the data repositories produces no revenue and creates no efficiencies. It has no ROI. Instead it limits the possibility that future negative fallout will happen. As a consequence, it is difficult to secure funding for security efforts, a tendency nicely captured by Gene Spafford, a professor of computer science and security expert: "People in general are not interested in paying extra for increased safety. At the beginning seat belts cost $200 and nobody bought them."

Moreover, it is difficult to take credit for doing a great job when all you have to show for your efforts is that nothing bad has happened. This is particularly true when "lucky" firms around you also have not suffered an attack (or have yet to notice that one has taken place!) and skeptics in your organization can point to them as "proof" that you are overinvesting in security.

Consider the hurricanes that hit the coast of Louisiana and Mississippi in the summer of 2005 (Figure 13.1). One of the reasons for the devastation of the city of New Orleans was the underfunding of the levy system protecting the city. However, seeking funding for such a protective system is about asking for money for projects designed to avert a possible negative outcome that may occur sometime, at an imprecise moment in the future. This is a difficult task, and one that officials who are in power for relatively short periods of time have little incentive to fight for—particularly when many other (more appealing) projects compete for the same funding.

Because security is the type of investment that is difficult to gain funding for, particularly when competing for limited resources with projects that promise big results—efficiency improvements, revenue enhancements, and the like—it is all the more critical that it is not left to the IT group to make the case. General and functional managers must get involved in the security discussion, understand the threats, and assess the degree of risk that the firm should be allowed to take.

Forward-looking IT managers have begun to better "sell" security benefits. As Robert Charette, director of the Enterprise Risk Management and Governance practice of the Cutter Consortium, noted in an interview, "[Senior executives] don't care about the different levels

---

[3]Goodin, D. (2006). "Crisis in Confidence," *InfoWorld* (October 30). http://www.infoworld.com/article/06/10/30/
44fesecsurvey_1.html

Figure 13.1   Satellite image of Hurricane Katrina (Courtesy of U.S. Fish & Wildlife Service.)

of encryption—they care about the harm it will keep the company from suffering and how much it's exposed in the different scenarios."[4] Yet whether you are blessed with the help of "forward-looking" IT professionals or not, it is your responsibility as a general or functional manager to weigh in on the difficult trade-off decision between purchasing more security and accepting higher risks. If you are to do so, you must understand the basic threats and fundamental trade-offs engendered by computer security. This does not mean that you must develop an extraordinary amount of technical knowledge, as you will not be called on to personally implement the security measures. Instead you must understand the managerial process of IT risk management and information systems security decision making.

Risk Assessment

The risk assessment process consists of auditing the current resources, technological as well as human, in an effort to map the current state of the art of information systems security in the organization. An understanding of the current resources will provide an idea of the current set of vulnerabilities the firm is facing.

For instance, Dell is a firm with a very prominent Web site. Dell's Web site is not only the face of the company, but it is also one of its main sources of livelihood. If customers cannot access it, Dell loses revenue by the minute. Thus, for Dell the risks associated with a denial-of-service attack that brings the Web site down is a very tangible one. The same could not be said for the Boat Yard Grill, a restaurant in Ithaca, New York, and its website (boatyardgrill.com).

---

[4]Brandel, M. (2006). "Avoid Security Spending Fatigue," *Computerworld* (April 17).
    http://www.computerworld.com/securitytopics/security/story/0,10801,110504,00.html (Accessed 03/12/2011)

Figure 13.2   Microsoft France's website defaced

The risk audit is useful because it provides the basis for a risk analysis. Risk analysis is the process by which the firm attempts to quantify the risks identified in the audit. We use the word 'attempt' to stress that precisely quantifying the monetary consequences of some of these risks is impossible. What do you think is the value of the loss of customer confidence in the Visa and Mastercard brands after the February 18, 2003 announcement that an intrusion in their system allowed hackers to gain access to the accounts of 5.6 million customers? What is the value of the loss of confidence your customers may feel if they log on to your Web site one morning only to see it defaced with questionable pictures and comments? (Figure 13.2)

The impact of some security risks is harder to measure than others. However, the exercise is useful insomuch as rational decision making suggests that the amount you invest in security safeguards should be proportional to the extent of the threat and its potential negative effects. This is a critical point. Because security risks are really business risks—nobody would argue that loss of customer confidence is "an IT issue"—general and functional managers must be deeply involved in information systems security prioritization decisions.

Risk Mitigation

Risk mitigation is the process of matching the appropriate response to the security threats your firm has identified. As Bruce Schneier, the noted computer security and cryptography expert, aptly put it, "There are two types of encryption: one that will prevent your sister from reading your diary and one that will prevent your government."

Risk mitigation allows your organization to devise the optimal strategy given the set of security risks it faces. Such optimal strategy is the one that yields the best trade-off between the degree of security the firm attains and the total investment in countermeasures necessary to achieve it (Figure 13.3). The total cost for security is a combination of anticipation costs, those expenditures designed to anticipate and mitigate the threats (e.g., purchasing and installing antivirus software), and failure costs, the negative financial fallout ensuing from a breach of security (e.g., loss of revenue during a website outage).

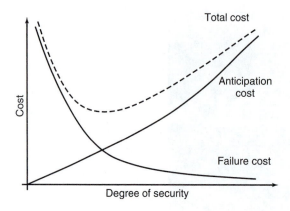

Figure 13.3   Cost/Security trade-offs

When faced with a security threat, the firm has three mitigation strategies available. Note than none of the three strategies described below is superior or inferior to the other in the absolute. The typical organization uses, consciously or unconsciously, a blend of all three.

1. *Risk acceptance.* This strategy consists of not investing in countermeasures and not reducing the security risk. The more an organization gravitates toward this strategy, the higher the potential failure cost it faces while minimizing anticipation costs.

2. *Risk reduction.* This strategy consists of actively investing in the safeguards designed to mitigate security threats. The more an organization gravitates toward this strategy, the higher the anticipation cost it faces while actively reducing failure costs.

3. *Risk transference.* This strategy consists of passing a portion (or all) of the risks associated with security to a third party (for example, by outsourcing security or buying insurance).

As the firm seeks to identify the optimal IT risk management and information systems security strategy, it will endeavor to identify the optimal blend of the three mitigation strategies. The ideal portfolio of security and risk management measures is based on the specific security threats the organization faces, as well as management's willingness to accept these risks. The major threats confronting the modern organization, and the safeguards available to respond to these threats, are discussed below.

The Internal Threat

Internal security threats are those posed by individuals who have direct, on-premises access to the firm's technology infrastructure, or those who have legitimate reasons to be using the firm's assets. Internal security threats are important because the firm that is able to secure its assets against improper internal use not only has mitigated an important risk, but is well on its way to mitigating the outside threat (i.e., the external threat can be seen a subset of the internal one). When addressing internal security threats, we can separate them into two broad categories: intentional malicious behavior and careless behavior.

Intentional Malicious Behavior   This type of threat is typically associated with disgruntled or ill-willed employees. This is a particularly troublesome threat because it is almost impossible to prepare for. Imagine, for example, that a member of the sales and direct marketing team is selling customer e-mail addresses to spammers. Unless this person makes a careless mistake or discusses his behavior with others, his actions may go undetected for a long time.

Careless Behavior   This type of threat is typically associated with ignorance of, or disinterest in, security policies. Consider the case of the U.S. Department of Veterans Affairs, where a laptop containing personal information on as many as 26.5 million veterans had been stolen from the home of an employee. The data, including names, social security numbers, and dates of birth, were not supposed to be transferred onto an unsecured laptop or taken off of the Department's premises. In this case, employee carelessness and lack of attention to existing procedures was the root cause of the failure.

Into this category fall a number of other behaviors that are more or less dangerous. For example, failing to modify default passwords, breaking the organization's policy on Internet and Web usage, not following guidelines about saving data on personal or portable devices, or failing to destroy sensitive data according to planned schedules.

The External Threat

Before the advent of the Internet and widespread connectivity, the importance of internal security threats far outweighed the danger posed by hackers and other outsiders. Mitigating the outside threat prior to pervasive networking simply amounted to physically securing the firm's IT assets. This is not the case anymore.

Today there is an incredible array of ways in which your firm's infrastructure can be attacked and compromised. Viruses, trojan horses, worms, time bombs, spyware, keystroke tracking tools, spoofing, snooping, sniffers—these are just some of the most popular examples of malicious code and techniques that modern organizations find themselves fighting off. Couple this seemingly unabated tide of new releases and new forms of harmful software with human threats like crackers, thieves, social engineers, and industrial espionage contractors, and you realize why security is continually ranked as one of the top worries for the modern CIO.

Those individuals who attack an organizations' IT infrastructure are typically called hackers. While some consider this a misnomer, contending that the term hacker simply means someone who possesses superior computer skills, the term has come to be associated in the media and general terminology with more or less maliciously intentioned individuals who attempt to subvert computer security defenses.

Below we address some of the external security threats confronting modern organizations.

Intrusion Threat   The intrusion threat is perhaps the most commonly envisioned when thinking about computer security. It consists of any situation where an unauthorized attacker gains access to organizational IT resources. Consider the following example. In the late 1980s a group of teenage hackers was found guilty of gaining unauthorized access to surveillance satellites and of using them for unauthorized purposes. As the story goes, the kids were discovered because the satellites were found marginally out of position at the beginning of every working day and the matter was further investigated. When the intruders' behavior was logged and monitored, it was discovered that upon taking control of the satellites, they were redirecting them on a nudist beach and taking pictures.

While the story screams urban legend, it is a great example of a (harmless) intrusion by individuals who did not attempt to inflict losses on the organization. Yet it is an intrusion nonetheless, as individuals without proper authority gained access to one of the organization's resources and used it for unintended purposes. More common, and less fun, examples include individuals who access private information by stealing or guessing legitimate passwords. This can be done by "sniffing" a network connection with specialized software and intercepting passwords that are not encrypted.

Social Engineering   An even simpler method is what is now called "social engineering," which is a fancy name to describe a very simple practice: lying to and deceiving legitimate users. Social engineering is roughly defined as the practice of obtaining restricted or private information by somehow convincing legitimate users, or other people who have the information, to share it. This is typically done over the telephone or other communication medium, and its success depends on the skills of the "social engineer," coupled with the gullibility and lack of training of the victim. Once the information has been obtained, say a password, the social engineer perpetrates the intrusion.

Phishing   The process of social engineering can be "automated" using a technique called phishing. Phishing consists of sending official-sounding spam (i.e., unwanted e-mail) from known institutions (e.g., Mastercard). The message indicates that the institution needs the recipient to confirm or provide some data and contains a link to a Web page, which is a copy of the original, with fields for providing the "missing" information.

The act of phishing is the act of collecting personal information, and a number of creative methods have been devised to direct traffic to the phony Web site (e.g., using links or fake promotions) and fool people into complying by crafting official-sounding messages from reputable institutions (Figure 13.4). Once on the target page, the user is asked to input some sensitive information—such as user name and password (Figure 13.5)—with the sole objective of stealing it for later use. While this appears simplistic, phishing has turned out to be a very effective way to obtain personal data—a 2004 study by Gartner estimated that almost 2 million people in the United States alone had had their bank account compromised in the past 12 months due to phishing scams.

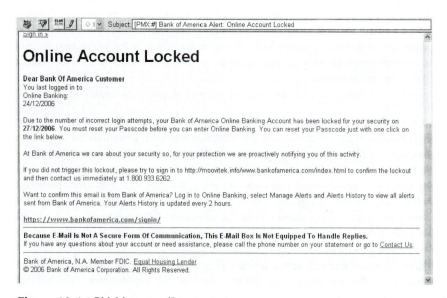

Figure 13.4   Phishing e-mail message

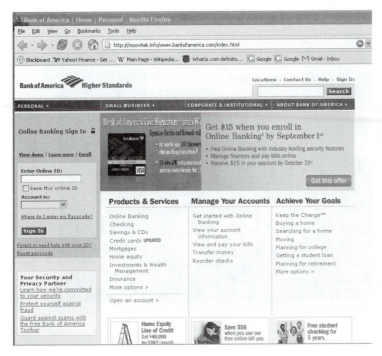

Figure 13.5 Capture page posing as a legitimate business

Note that the low degree of sophistication of the phishing e-mail in Figure 13.4—which hit my inbox with great timing as I was writing this chapter—led to warnings from both the e-mail client (Figure 13.6) and the Web browser opening the page (Figure 13.7). As in any high-stakes game of chess, the security game is replete with moves and countermoves, but a more sophisticated attack could likely have gone undetected.

Backdoors and Security Weaknesses   Another way to gain unauthorized access is to exploit weaknesses in the software infrastructure of the organization under attack. Commercial software typically comes with "backdoors." A backdoor is code built into a software program to allow

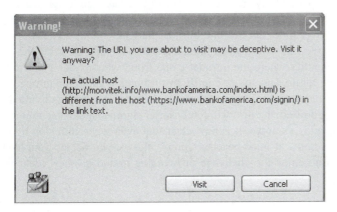

Figure 13.6   Warning message from e-mail client

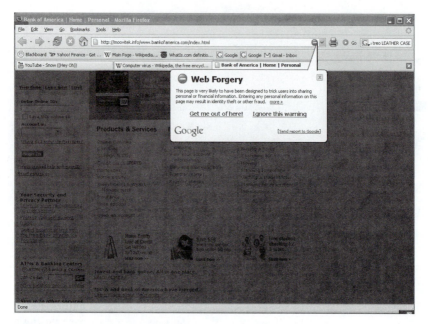

Figure 13.7   Warning message from browser

access to the application by circumventing password protection. Backdoors are built into software in the event that high-level accounts, such as administrative accounts, are for some reason inaccessible (e.g., the password has been lost, or a disgruntled employee is blackmailing the firm and will not unlock the software). While backdoors must be changed during the installation process, sometimes this step is forgotten and the default backdoor is allowed to exist while the program is operational. Hackers can then easily gain access to the application and take control of it, giving themselves high-level access rights.

Beyond default backdoors, software programs have weaknesses (i.e., bugs). Typically these bugs are annoying because they prevent the application from functioning normally. For example, a program will shut off unexpectedly, or freeze. At times though, they can be extremely dangerous as they create security holes that an ill-intentioned intruder can exploit.

The intrusion threat is particularly troublesome because it has significant and long-lasting potential impacts. First, it may go undetected for a long period of time, enabling the intruder to perpetrate her crime(s) over time. Second, the intruder may be able to gain access to private information and even steal records. Third, when intrusion is discovered, it will require a thorough investigation in order to identify where the intruder came from, whether she created backdoors that can be exploited in the future, and so on. Fourth, if information about the intrusion becomes public, something that is required by law in many states in cases where individuals' private information has been compromised, the firm will likely suffer significant damage to its reputation.

Going back to the opening example, it is now clear that even when intrusion by pranksters occurs (e.g., kids taking pictures of nude beaches, funny fellows who deface your Web site, or talented computer users who enjoy the challenge of breaking in and all they want is bragging rights with their friends), the expense in time, money, and trust recovery effort your organization must engage in can be quite high.

The Threat of Malicious Code   Another security threat that modern firms face daily is presented by malicious code—also known as malware. The term *malicious code* refers to software programs that are designed to cause damage to individuals and/or organizations' IT assets. Below we identify the main categories of malicious code and discuss their characteristics.

Viruses   Computer viruses are an increasingly pervasive security threat. By some accounts there are more than 350 new viruses being produced and unleashed every week. These viruses are more and more often produced by putting together "component parts," malicious scripts that can be assembled into complete viruses by relatively unskilled individuals—aptly called script kiddies.

A computer virus is a type of malicious code that spreads by attaching itself to other, legitimate, executable software programs. Once the legitimate software program runs, the virus runs with it, replicating itself and spreading to other programs on the same machine. By doing so the computer virus, much like a biological virus, is able to prosper. If the infected files are shared and executed by others, their machines will be infected as well.

Following the infection phase, the payload delivery phase occurs. The payload is the typically harmful set of actions that the virus is designed to perform. They may range from simply annoying the user (Figure 13.8)—a famous early virus dropped letters from the screen and nothing more—to wreaking havoc and bringing significant damage to the user—a popular one is the wiping out of all data on the hard disk. Some viruses deliver their payload immediately after infection, while others, known as time bombs, deliver it at a specific point in time or when a certain action is performed by the user. For instance, the Michelangelo virus discovered in 1991 was designed to deliver its payload on March 6, the birthday of the Italian master.

With the advent of the Internet and the widespread use of electronic mail, virus authors have found a new way to spread their "work." An e-mail virus is malicious code that travels attached to e-mail messages and has the ability to self-replicate, typically by automatically e-mailing itself to multiple recipients.

Trojan Horses   A Trojan horse is a computer program that claims to, and sometimes does, deliver some useful functionality. However, like the legendary war machine the Greeks used against the people of Troy (Figure 13.9), the Trojan horse hides a dark side and, like a virus, delivers its malicious payload. Unlike a virus, a Trojan horse does not self-replicate, but is passed on by those who share it with others.

Worms   A worm is a piece of malicious code that exploits security holes in network software to replicate itself. Strictly speaking, a worm does not deliver a payload, like a virus. A worm

Figure 13.8   The DROL virus

Figure 13.9   The Trojan horse as represented in the movie *Troy*
Source: © Travel Library Limited/SuperStock.

simply replicates itself and continues to scan the network for machines to infect. The problem is that, as the worm infects more and more machines on the network, the traffic it generates quickly brings the network down—with substantial damage. The original Internet worm, originating at Cornell University in 1988, was estimated to cost infected sites from $200 to $53,000 for repairs.

Spyware   Spyware applications have sprung up with the advent and widespread adoption of the Web. The term *spyware* suggests that the software runs without the awareness of the user and collects information. Broadly speaking, spyware is software that, unbeknownst to the owner of the computer, monitors behavior, collects information, and either transfers this information to a third party via the Internet or performs unwanted operations.

Typical examples of spyware include adware, software that collects information in an effort to use it for advertisement purposes by opening pop-ups or changing a users homepage; keyboard tracking, software that logs keyboard strokes in an effort to steal passwords and other sensitive information; and stealware, software that redirects payments legitimately belonging to an affiliate and sends them to the stealware operator.

While spyware differs from viruses, in that it cannot self-replicate, it can create significant problems for an organization. Beyond the malicious and often fraudulent effects of spyware, these programs divert resources and often slow down the user's legitimate work.

Denial-of-Service Attack   Denial-of-service attacks are particularly powerful today given the predominance of online operations and the number of firms that use Web sites and other online services for their operations. A denial-of-service attack is a digital assault carried out over a computer network with the objective of overwhelming an online service so as to force it offline.

Consider a website as the service of interest. A website is managed by a Web server that receives requests from clients all over the Internet and sends them the pages they request. When a Web server receives more requests that it can handle, it will attempt to serve them all but will begin to slow down, like a waiter who has been assigned too many restaurant tables and is scrambling to serve them all. If the number of requests is high enough, the service will likely shut down, thus becoming unavailable to legitimate traffic as well.

Denial-of-service attacks can be extremely dangerous because a skilled intruder will employ a denial-of-service attack to divert attention and then occupy resources of the attacked organization. While the firm is busy averting the denial-of-service attack, the intruder can exploit available security breaches or create backdoors to be exploited later.

Responding to Security Threats

The management of computer security is a continuous effort. The principal objective is to identify the different threats and develop safeguards that match up with them and limit their incidence of success.

Internal Security Threats   Prevention of internal threats is no simple feat since security products and technologies can only partially help. Prevention of internal threats requires the development and enforcement of security policies and auditing standards designed to ensure that such policies are understood and respected by those within the organization.

Security Policies   The most easily preventable security risks are those caused by ignorance of sound security practice. A security policy spells out what the organization believes are the behaviors that individual employees and groups within the firm should follow in order to minimize security risks. They include what computing services will be made available, and what computing services will not be made available within the firm. They specify what password standards the firm should follow (e.g., length, characters to be used, renewal schedules) and what rights different types of users will have. They specify the level of care that employees need to use with their passwords (e.g., do not share password with anyone, do not send passwords over clear channels such as unencrypted mail messages), what computing resources and what data should be accessible within the organization, and what data can be downloaded to personal devices and what needs to remain within the company. The policy should address legitimate uses of portable devices, what data can be downloaded to them, and how such devices should be secured by those who own them. A security policy may even address the level of care that employees should exercise when they leave the premises (e.g., not reviewing sensitive data on laptops while on airplanes).

Beyond having comprehensive security policies in place, the organization must audit them to ensure compliance. For example, accounts of terminated employees need to be swiftly deleted or made unavailable to prevent access from former employees who at best will see material they should not, and at worst will be able to damage company resources (e.g., delete data).

External Security Threats

Intrusion   A number of techniques and technologies to prevent intrusion have been developed over the years. The cornerstone of securing against intrusion is the use of passwords. Passwords ensure that resources are only made available to those who have the appropriate authentication levels. Thus, a password can be used to block unauthorized external users as well as discriminate to whom resources should be available among the legitimate users.

Organizations typically enforce standards to ensure that passwords are reasonably difficult to guess. For example, many security policies require that passwords have a minimum length; they use letters, numbers, and special characters; they don't use dictionary words, and so on. However, there is an inherent trade-off between the complexity of a password and human ability. In other words, if passwords are too difficult to remember, people will write them down, creating a new security risk! For this reason, the computer security industry is hard at work devising more

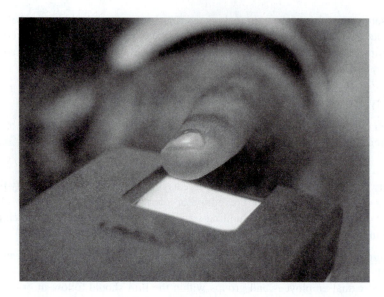

Figure 13.10
Fingerprint scanner
(*Source*: © Glyn Allan/Alamy
Images)

robust identification schemes, such as biometrics—the use of physical traits (e.g., fingerprints, iris scans) as a means to uniquely identify users (Figure 13.10).

A firewall is a software tool designed to screen and manage traffic in and out of a computer network. Thus a firewall is used to secure the perimeter of the organization's computing resources, employing a number of technologies and techniques. Firewalls can also be used to enforce security policies (for example, blocking traffic from Web sites deemed risky and blocking the download of some file types; see Figure 13.11).

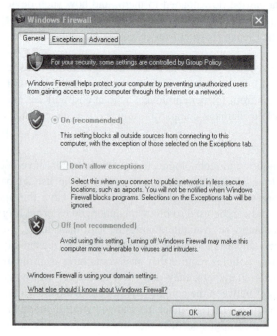

Figure 13.11   Microsoft Windows built-in firewall

Firewalls are a very important security tool, but you need to remember that perimeter protection is only as strong as its weakest link—much like the perimeter protection of a castle. For example, no matter how powerful your firewall is, if there are unsecured modems that an attacker can dial into, the network is not secure. Once an attacker gains access to the organization's resources through the unsecured modem, the strongest perimeter security is made useless—the intruder is working on the inside now.

Consider as well that any resource that is brought outside the perimeter is not secured by the firewall—hence the inherent danger associated with the proliferation of mobile devices. For instance, if an employee copies sensitive data to her laptop and then takes the machine on the road, the firm's firewall is useless in protecting such data. With data increasingly prevalent, and portable devices achieving widespread adoption, perimeter security is increasingly insufficient.

Another technique that has been developed to safeguard against the intrusion threat is encryption. Through the encryption process, content is scrambled in such a way that it is rendered unreadable to all recipients, except those who hold the key to decrypt it. Encryption ensures that if the wrong individuals gain access to the data, they will be unable to make out its meaning. Encryption techniques are used to secure transmissions as well as to secure stored data. Consider once again the example of the lost laptop discussed above. If the data it contained had been encrypted, the loss to the firm would simply amount to the cost of the asset—less than a thousand dollars in most cases.

Security policy and audits will help a firm ensure that no backdoors are left open after the installation of a new software program. With respect to security holes and weaknesses in software that are due to bugs, the IT staff in the organization must monitor bug reports and install patches—pieces of add-on code published by the software house that wrote the program designed to eliminate weaknesses that surface after the release of the software program. The problem is that many organizations lack the staff to constantly monitor this information and may fall behind in patch installations, thus opening the firm to unnecessary risks. To obviate this problem, many of the large software houses (e.g., Microsoft) have now developed patch management software that automatically alerts users to the availability of newly released patches—and, if configured to do so, downloads and installs them automatically (Figure 13.12).

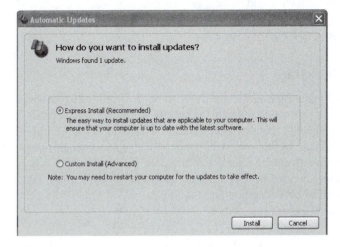

Figure 13.12 Automatic patch management software

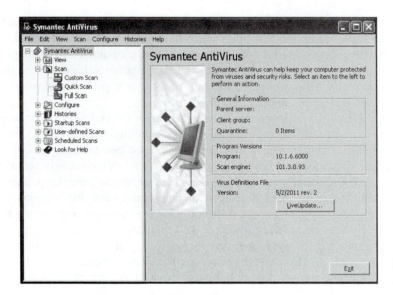

Figure 13.13
Antivirus software

Malware   Safeguarding against malware requires that the firm's IT professionals install the appropriate detection software (e.g., antivirus, spyware sweepers) (Figure 13.13). With the large number of new viruses being released, antivirus and other detection software is only as good as its most recent update. For this reason, organizations that manage their own networks are increasingly attempting to centralize these applications and push updates to individual users so as to ensure that safeguards against malware are up to date.

Training and policies can also be very helpful in mitigating the malware threat. Simple behaviors, such as not opening e-mail attachments from accounts you don't recognize (e.g., intriguing@sexylips.com), or limiting downloads from the Internet to trusted Web sites, go a long way in preventing infection.

Denial-of-Service Attack   Preventing a denial-of-service attack is very difficult. This is because in a well-orchestrated denial-of-service attack, the requests for the service are not issued from the same few locations, which would make it easy to recognize and block. Instead, in what's called a distributed denial-of-service attack, the attacker will hijack or spoof multiple machines and initiate the attack from these multiple locations.

Managing Security: Overall Guidelines

As a general or functional manager, you are not likely to be involved in the technical details of the procedures and safeguards chosen to mitigate the specific security threats identified in the risk assessment. However, you should expect to be involved in setting the agenda for how the overall set of risks is to be addressed. In this role it is paramount that you recognize one important characteristic of security investments: Security is a negative deliverable, one that produces no upside, but helps in limiting damage ensuing from an uncertain negative event. For these types of investments it is difficult to obtain appropriate funding.

Moreover, when it comes to security, it is impossible to ensure success. In other words, it is impossible to claim that the organization is absolutely "secure." Rather, it is possible to find out that the organization was not secure after a breach has occurred. Amid all these difficulties, general and functional managers play a critical role.

Have a Plan and Specify Responsibilities   You would be surprised to find out how many organizations do not devise formal plans to be enacted during an attack, or who fail to assign formal responsibility for security design and enforcement. This is particularly true for the design of new applications, as requirements requested by the business sometimes weaken the security of the applications. In this case the overall responsibility for security choices and trade-offs should reside with a business owner or other appropriate senior person, not with IT. When outside contractors are engaged in the development, security requirements should be spelled out in the contract.

A crisis management plan should specify who needs to be contacted in an emergency and what their roles should be. The plan must address questions such as what the first reaction measures should be (e.g., should the systems under attack be shut down or left operational). When and how should authorities, such as the FBI, be contacted? What will the firm disclose about the attack, if anything, and who should be in charge of press releases or of customer communication? What recovery plans need to be enacted under the various scenarios? In short, the plan should script all those decisions that are difficult to make when the firm is actually under attack.

Revisit Often   Security is a constantly evolving area for a number of reasons: first and foremost, the breathtaking pace of technical evolution. Every new technology and software program your firm adopts ushers in a unique set of security and risk management challenges that should be proactively addressed—whether that means taking specific steps to manage it or consciously accepting the risk. Thus, you must ensure that security audits and reassessment of security plans are done periodically.

Develop a Mitigation Plan   A well-architected security infrastructure and plan can go a long way toward tempering the many security threats modern firms face. But no matter how good your security is, there is always the chance that your firm will be successfully attacked and that your defenses will be breached. What you do in this case can be critical, particularly when you become vulnerable to an intrusion.

The first reaction to an attack is often to shut everything down. This is a mistake, since diagnosing where the attack is coming from, its severity, and its reach is much easier to do if the system is maintained operational and the attacker is kept unaware of the fact that you spotted the security breach.

The first order of business at this point should be to determine how the attack took place in order to eliminate its chance of occurring again. The next step requires an assessment of the damage, particularly as it pertains to the loss of sensitive data. A series of laws have been recently passed across the globe requiring firms to immediately notify those parties whose data may have been compromised. Whether this is a necessity or not in your jurisdiction, it is a wise move to immediately communicate the problem to those affected. As much as you would like to keep the matter private to avoid the negative publicity, people understand that security breaches do sometimes occur, but they will be much less forgiving if they discover an attempt to cover up the problem.

PRIVACY

Privacy concerns emerge in the relationship between individuals and organizations because, when dealing with business firms or nonprofit and governmental organizations, customers (and employees) often provide personal information under the assumption that the organization will take "good care" of it. We, as customers and/or employees, provide personal information in order to receive the benefits of the transaction (e.g., employment, value proposition). Yet a prerequisite to the transaction is that we hold some degree of trust in the organization that we are dealing with. We trust that our information is reasonably secure, despite many data breaches over the years (Figure 13.14), and the organization has taken steps to prevent unauthorized use of it by those who have no legitimate reason to access it.

In other words, we must have trust in the firm's information systems security. Even more importantly, we must trust that the organization will be a steward of our personal information

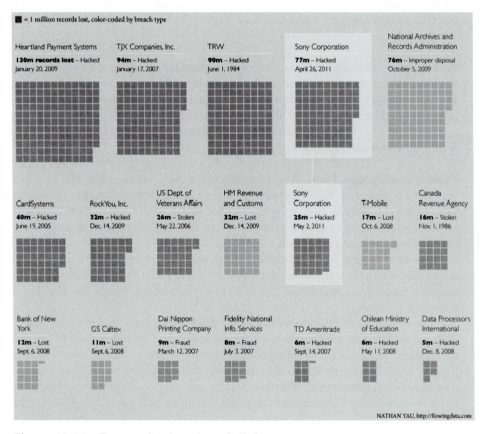

Figure 13.14 Greatest data breaches of all time

and that it will refrain from employing it in ways that will be harmful to us or our interests. For instance, even if we have great faith in the firm's security, we still must believe that the firm is ethical enough not to collect our data and immediately turn around and sell it to spammers in order to make a "quick buck"—as the employee of Countrywide did in the example discussed in the introduction.

Consider the following, more subtle incident: "In 2003, the public learned that JetBlue Airways had turned over records on more than a million of its passengers to a government contractor. The contractor sought the information to test a security application designed to identify suspected terrorists. However, the sharing violated JetBlue's privacy policy, which promised that the company would not provide personal information to third parties. The CEO issued a public apology and indicated that he had no knowledge of the data transfer at the time it was made. Nonetheless, JetBlue had to confront a lawsuit from privacy groups and passengers."[5]

What was the problem? After all, JetBlue was only trying to aid in efforts to prevent terrorist attacks and ultimately improve the safety of its own passengers! The problem is that JetBlue had not developed an appropriate process for dealing with privacy concerns in the face of the proliferation of customer data it stewards and the mounting number of potential (perhaps legitimate) uses of those data.

Privacy Defined

If there could be some doubt regarding whether computer security is an "IT issue" or a "business issue," there is no such doubt regarding privacy. Given the ethical concerns and the potential for liability associated with privacy, general and functional managers should be front and center in identifying and responding to the privacy concerns of the organization. This is not surprising when you consider that, by some estimates, nearly 80% of organizations collect information, and half of them indicate that this information is sensitive in nature.[6] But what is privacy exactly?

Privacy can be defined as the ability of individuals to control the terms and conditions under which their personal information is collected, managed, and utilized. Private information is that information that can be traced back to the individual—for instance, a person's name, picture, address, social security number, or medical history.

It is evident from the above definition that privacy is not security, even though there is much confusion between the two terms. Privacy subsumes security. That is, a firm that is unable to secure customer or employee data will not be able to ensure privacy. More specifically, privacy is about informed consent and permission to collect and use identifying information, while security is about safekeeping of the collected data.

Privacy Risks

Privacy risks are a byproduct of the success that firms have been enjoying with their use of information technology. In a world where competition is global and it is not possible to have a personal relationship with the thousands or millions of customers your firm is trying to reach, IT-enabled information systems have created the ability to "know" individuals we do not interact with directly.

---

[5]Culnan, M. J. (2006). "Privacy in Search of Governance," *Cutter Benchmark Review* (6:1), p. 5.
[6]Piccoli, G. (2006). "Doing Privacy Right: Using Data and Preserving Trust," *Cutter Benchmark Review* (6:1), pp. 3–5.

In many cases, these developments have been welcomed by those involved (e.g., customers[7]). Many of us enjoy the personal recommendations produced by online retailers or online services (e.g., Spotify), or the fact that we don't have to repeat our preferences every time we book a reservation with the same hotel chain or airline. But these very advances in technology that allow us to better compete and better suit our customer needs create the potential for highly damaging privacy violations.

Function Creep   As we discussed in Chapter 4, information is not consumed by use and can thus be employed multiple times in different applications and for different purposes. For example, information about the number of soda cans sold by a vending machine can be used to compute revenues at one time and forecast future sales at another.

Function creep occurs when data collected for a stated or implied purpose are then reused for other, unrelated, objectives. In the case of the soda vending machine, this is not a problem, but when individuals' personal information is concerned, privacy issues take center stage.

Consider the famous example of Eckerd Corporation, the U.S. drugstore chain. Eckerd settled a lawsuit with the Florida attorney general's office contending that the firm had engaged in deceptive trade practices and breached customers' privacy by sending unsolicited promotions based on the prescriptions customers had filled in the past. The firm now obtains express permission from customers before sending them marketing material on behalf of pharmaceutical companies. It also endowed a $1 million chair in ethics at Florida A&M School of Pharmacy as part of the settlement.

While the above incident could be ascribed to the heightened sensitivity surrounding medical information, the quick backpedaling reaction and image damage the firm suffered are not much different than what was experienced by RealNetworks in the case described in the introduction to this chapter. At the heart of both cases is a perceived breach of trust due to the fact that information the customers had provided with one intent was being used for other aims. The intention of the firm may be a good one—to provide valuable personalized information, for instance. However, the customers' perceived loss of control over their personal data opens the door to concerns of abuse and negative reactions.

Proliferating Data Sources   Perhaps even more difficult to manage than the potential for function creep is the dizzying proliferation of data sources and technologies that generate customer data. Consider modern cellular phones. Such devices enable a fairly precise estimation of their physical location. This capability can be life saving in the case of 911 calls. Yet the potential for privacy invasion is just as significant. Can you imagine walking down a street and being pestered with "eSolicitations" from "nearby businesses"?

Beyond technology advances and the adoption of devices that surreptitiously generate the data, modern consumers themselves seem to revel in providing more and more information on a voluntary basis. Whether this is plain old self-expression, the need to feel part of a community, or the fact that we are becoming increasingly used to voicing our preferences to get tailored offers, is irrelevant. The amount of personal information individuals are posting to sites like Facebook, YouTube, or Flickr is unprecedented—not to mention the use of geolocation services

---

[7]While the arguments here can be extended to other entities, such as employees or suppliers, we use the example of customers throughout for simplicity.

Check out the same results on Twitter search

Why

Hey, do you have a Twitter account? Have you ever noticed those messages in which people tell you where they are? Pretty annoying, eh. Well, they're actually also potentially pretty dangerous. We're about to tell you why.

Don't get us wrong, we love the whole location-aware thing. The information is very interesting and can be used to create some pretty awesome applications. However, the way in which people are stimulated to participate in sharing this information, is less awesome. Services like Foursquare allow you to fulfill some primeval urge to colonize the planet. A part of that is letting everyone know you own that specific spot. You get to tell where you are and if you're there first, it's yours. O, and of course there's badges..

More Info

Home
Why
About

Made Possible By

Forthehack

Foursquare
Twitter
@boyvanamstel
@frankgroeneveld

Figure 13.15   PleaseRobMe.com

like Foursquare or Facebook Places. The point about over-sharing was made in a very powerful manner by the site PleaseRobMe.com, which scraped Twitter feeds that were pushed through Foursquare to show how easy it would be to identify the empty houses of the "over-sharers" and, potentially, go and rob them (Figure 13.15). You can see how for organizations navigating this landscape in a legal and ethical manner without missing opportunities for business success is becoming increasingly difficult.

Improving Data Management Technologies   Not only is personal data easier to generate than ever before and proliferating, but it is increasingly simple, and cost effective, to merge data repositories. Consider one of the most celebrated examples of the successful organizational use of customer data: Harrah's Entertainment, Inc. Harrah's collects individual demographic data that its customers provide when signing up to its loyalty program, and individual behavioral data when its customers stay at property, gamble, and redeem offers. Harrah's also collects non-gambling data from external data providers such as Acxiom. It then merges all this information in its data warehouse to develop a complete profile of each customer.

The development of data management technologies enables initiatives of this kind and has created an unprecedented level of opportunity for data-driven strategies. It also creates much pressure for, and risk of, function creep if not managed carefully.

The Legal Landscape   In an environment as difficult to navigate as privacy, it would be quite helpful to have comprehensive legal guidance. Unfortunately, though, with some exceptions, information technology evolution outpaces legal development. To further compound the problem, the Internet has all but destroyed traditional geographical boundaries, making legislation difficult to enforce and easier to circumvent.

It used to be that a community, a state, or an entire nation would be able to easily regulate behavior within its jurisdiction. For example, if a state did not want to allow its residents to gamble, it would simply not issue gaming licenses. Today this level of legislative control is no longer possible, when everyone with a computer can travel to any Web site in the world with the click of a button.

Safeguarding Privacy

Fair information practices have been proposed as a basis for privacy governance. Fair information practices are based on the five principles of notice, choice, access, security, and enforcement.

- *Notice* refers to the right of individuals to be informed when their personal data is being collected, and to be informed about how it is or will be used.

- *Choice* calls for the ability of individuals to be informed of, and object to, function creep, whether within one firm or across firms who share information (Figure 13.16).

- *Access* refers to the right of individuals to be able to access their information and correct any errors that may have occurred in their records.

- *Security* calls for organizations that house individuals' private information to ensure its safekeeping and to protect it from unauthorized access.

- *Enforcement* calls for organizations that collect and use private information to develop enforceable procedures to ensure that the above principles are upheld.

Noted privacy expert Mary Culnan offers the following straightforward guidelines for organizations that seek to comply with the above fair information practices: Say what you do, do what you say, and be able to prove it.[8]

Say What You Do   This first guideline requires that the firm develop a codified set of policies and procedures for safeguarding privacy. It also requires that the firm communicates these policies to affected individuals (e.g., customers, employees). Being able to follow this guideline is predicated on the firm's ability to audit and identify the personal information it collects and stores. It also necessitates a clear understanding of how the information is used today, how it may be used in the future, and whether it is transferred or otherwise shared with partners.

Do What You Say   The second guideline requires that those who represent the firm know, understand, and can enact the policies the firm has developed. Ensuring this level of compliance requires both training, so that the employees are aware of the policies and know how to best enact them, and follow-up, so that procedures are audited and behavior is monitored.

Be Able to Prove It   The third guideline requires that the firm document its policies and the processes it has developed to ensure privacy. This guideline acts as a sort of insurance against possible privacy violations. It enables the firm to demonstrate that it takes privacy concerns seriously and has been diligent in minimizing the possibility of privacy violations.

---

[8]Culnan, M. J. (2006). "Privacy in Search of Governance," *Cutter Benchmark Review* (6:1), pp. 5–13.

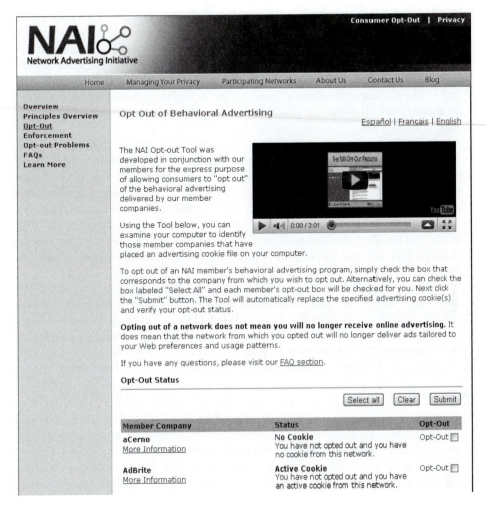

Figure 13.16 Privacy control tool for opting-out of targeted advertisement based on Web browsing behavior

ETHICS

Many of the judgment calls about privacy that were discussed in the previous section are really ethical choices. But what is ethics? What does it mean to be ethical? How do you as a general or functional manager ensure that the people you manage act in an ethical manner when it comes to information systems use?

Ethics: Definition

Webster's Dictionary defines *ethics* as "the discipline dealing with what is good and bad and with moral duty and obligation." Ethics is the branch of philosophy that concerns itself with morality by studying right and wrong and attempting to draw a distinction between good and evil.

Examples of unethical behavior in business abound. The corporate scandals that have led to the demise of one-time stock market darlings like Enron Corp. and Global Crossing in the U.S., or Parmalat in Italy, have clearly shown that we cannot assume that all of today's managers are equipped to make appropriate ethical choices. These corporate scandals have led to legislation,such as the Sarbanes-Oxley Act in 2002, which increases the scope of management and director's responsibilities, as well as the reporting requirements that public firms have to comply with. However, unethical behavior in business circles has roots that go beyond a legislative vacuum.

While many react with outrage to unethical behavior, arguing that "everyone knows what's right and what's wrong," this stance oversimplifies reality. Because of the intense technical training that most business and management schools focus on, the fact that managers will make ethical decisions is often mistakenly taken for granted. Most managers are ill equipped to make ethical decisions because they typically lack formal training in the area, and because their attention is usually on the objective they are trying to reach. Aptly capturing this dilemma was a former CIO at Metro-Goldwyn-Mayer Studios: "When your job is building the best-performing database you can, you don't always think about the ethical implications of how that data will be used."[9]

Moreover, aside from those spilling over into illegal behavior, ethical choices are rarely straightforward. In fact, ethical dilemmas are typically rooted in the choice between multiple suboptimal courses of action that force well-intentioned individuals to make difficult trade-offs.

Fortunately, many business and management schools are formally introducing ethics into the curriculum. This education is necessary to enable future business leaders to confront ethical dilemmas and develop a sophisticated understanding of ethics before joining the workforce.

Information Systems Ethics

Information systems and new technologies, with their penchant for enabling new ways of doing business, constantly introduce the potential for ethical dilemmas. Moreover, because of the rapid pace of the evolution of IT and the slow pace at which legislation is passed, formal explicit rules lag behind the possibilities offered by new technologies. Ethical guidelines fill (or should fill) the void, providing direction in the absence of explicit laws. Consider the following scenarios:

- As you are driving home, you hear a song from your youth. You had totally forgotten about that one head-banging band... memories of friends and happy times fill your mind. As you walk into your house, you think about downloading an mp3 version of the song from one of the many file-sharing networks available today on the Internet. While you know that downloading the song is "technically" illegal, you are confident that you will not have the time and interest to find and purchase the CD. You just want to listen to the song again and daydream a bit more... and what was the name of that other hit the band had...?

- As the IT director for your organization, you have some leeway with the priorities you assign to various projects. You recently reallocated resources and delayed the CRM implementation to speed up the ERP roll-out that is already running considerably behind schedule. You have reason to believe that Jack, one of your project managers, forwarded your e-mail about the shift of resources to the VP of marketing.

---

[9]Wilder, C, and Soat, J. (2001). "The Ethics of Data," *InformationWeek,* May 14. http://www.informationweek.com/837/dataethics/htm (Accessed 03/07/2011).

As the IT director, you are well aware that all company e-mails are backed up on the mail server, and you know the backdoor that enables access to every account. As you walk over to the mail server late one evening, you tell yourself that it is critical that a General be able to fully trust his troops... you must find out whether you can trust Jack.

■ It was your college-days dream, running your own company! ReinvenTravel.com had been it for the last four and half years. An industry magazine called it "the intermediary that reshaped how people buy travel." But now your dream had turned into a nightmare. After filing for Chapter 11 bankruptcy protection and trying to restructure, it was clear that ReinvenTravel.com would not make it.

The decision was tough. You had been offered $7.2 million by your largest competitor—MightyTravel—for the preferences and historical transaction data of your customers. While you never liked the folks over at MightyTravel, they assured you that they would use the data to offer a more targeted and personal travel experience to your former customers. Your privacy policy never explicitly addressed what you would do with customer data, and the $7.2 million will allow you to honor salary and pension commitments to your employees. As you sign the contract, you reassure yourself, thinking that your customers will appreciate receiving more targeted offers from MightyTravel... everyone prefers targeted offers... right?

What is common to all three scenarios is the fact that each of the ethical dilemmas they capture would not have been possible just a few years ago. New technologies brought them about as a byproduct of their enabling new ways to collect, process, store, and distribute information. More importantly, all three scenarios paint an accurate picture of typical ethical dilemmas: The appropriate course of action is far from clear and no choice is without a negative impact on other individuals.

Ensuring Ethical Uses of Information Systems

There are no silver bullets to ensure ethical behavior in the context of organizational information systems. Developing a culture of ethical decision making is critical. Such a culture should create the preconditions for and reward behavior that strives for harm minimization, respect, and consistency. Professional communities, such as the Association for Computing Machinery (ACM) or the Association of Information Technology Professionals (AITP), have attempted to create an ethical culture that goes beyond individual organizations by promulgating codes of ethics. For example, the ACM first introduced its code of ethics in 1992 with the following preamble:

"Commitment to ethical professional conduct is expected of every member (voting members, associate members, and student members) of the Association for Computing Machinery (ACM).

This Code, consisting of 24 imperatives formulated as statements of personal responsibility, identifies the elements of such a commitment. It contains many, but not all, issues professionals are likely to face. [....]

The Code shall be supplemented by a set of Guidelines, which provide explanation to assist members in dealing with the various issues contained in the Code. It is expected that the Guidelines will be changed more frequently than the Code.

The Code and its supplemented Guidelines are intended to serve as a basis for ethical decision making in the conduct of professional work. Secondarily, they may serve as a basis for judging the merit of a formal complaint pertaining to violation of professional ethical standards."[10]

Ethical dilemmas typically pit the interest of one person or group (e.g., shareholders) against that of another (e.g., customers). Applying the principle of harm minimization, one needs to weigh the relative impact that the decision will have on all individuals affected and strive to moderate damage to any one individual or group. The principle of respect requires that information systems decisions be made in an effort to treat each of the affected parties with the utmost consideration. Finally, the principle of consistency provides a test for evaluating decisions. It requires a person confronted with an ethical dilemma to consider whether he would approve if everyone else made the same choice he is considering.

A practical, and pragmatic, approach to foster a culture of ethical decision making is to establish an information systems ethics code of conduct. A code of conduct, typically used by professional associations, offers two advantages. On the one hand, it communicates to all parties the organization's principles of ethical information systems use. Thus, it can be used as an educational mechanism to point employees in the right direction. On the other hand, it identifies the firm's formal stance, thus enabling detection of, and distancing from, unethical choices made by any member of the organization.

 ## SUMMARY

In this chapter, we focused on three topics of interest to general and functional managers: information systems security and IT risk management, privacy, and information systems ethics. A failure in security, privacy, or ethics can have dramatic repercussions on the organization, both because of potentially damaging direct effects (e.g., computer outages, disruptions to operations) and increasingly negative indirect effects (e.g., legal recourse, image damage).

In this chapter, we sought to convince you that, as future general and functional managers, you will have to be involved in these decisions. We also helped you gain an understanding of the circumstances in which choices and trade-offs are made so that you can actively participate in decision making.

- Information systems must be secured against both internal and external threats. The internal threat is due to either ill-willed or careless members of the organization and is mitigated by way of security policies and training. The external threat comes from skilled individuals, referred to as hackers. The external threat takes the form of malware, intrusion attempts, and denial-of-service attacks.

Each of the threats is matched by the appropriate safeguard.

- Information systems security and risk management are not "IT issues." Because of the impact of the security breaches on the current and future viability of the organization, it is critical that general and functional managers take an active role in security decision making. This is done by participating in risk assessment, the process designed to evaluate the potential impact of threats confronting the firm, and risk mitigation, the process of identifying the appropriate response to these security threats. This involvement is necessary in order to make the appropriate trade-off decision among risk acceptance, risk reduction, and risk transference.

- Privacy concerns, like security threats, need general and functional managers' full attention. This is because privacy, like security, is a negative deliverable. That is, investments in privacy help the organization avoid a possible negative occurrence (e.g., lawsuit, loss of customer trust, negative impact on the firm's image) rather than generate

---

[10] ACM Code of Ethics and Professional Conduct. http://www.acm.org/about/code-of-ethics/#sect2 (Accessed 05/05/2011).

benefits, such as improved efficiency or increased revenues.

■ In order for the firm to safeguard the privacy of its employees and customers, it must subscribe to fair information practices. Fair information practices are based on the five principles of notice, choice, access, security, and enforcement. Moreover, the firm should produce a codified set of security policies, monitor and enforce compliance with them, and document both the policies and the processes it has developed to ensure privacy.

■ The recent flurry of corporate scandals has ignited interest in business ethics. When it comes to information systems, ethics becomes a crucial guiding light for management behavior as legislation often lags behind technology improvements. Thus, developing a culture of ethical decision making is essential for modern organizations.

STUDY QUESTIONS

1. Imagine that you have just been hired by a retail financial institution. How would you explain to your CEO that she needs to get involved in information security decisions?

2. What are the three costs associated with information systems security? What is the relationship among them?

3. Define what is meant by internal and external threats. How do the two differ? How are they related?

4. Define and provide an example of each of the different types of intrusion threats. Describe the appropriate countermeasure for each of your examples.

5. Define and provide an example of each of the different types of malicious code threats. Describe the appropriate countermeasure.

6. What is a denial-of-service attack? Why are these attacks particularly dangerous?

7. Imagine that you have just been hired by a retail financial institution. How would you explain to your CEO that she needs to get involved in privacy decisions?

8. How is privacy defined? What are the principal privacy risks? Can you provide examples of each one?

9. What is ethics? What are the principal challenges associated with information systems ethics?

FURTHER READINGS

1. Austin, R. D., and Darby, C. A. (2003). "The Myth of Secure Computing." *Harvard Business Review*, June, pp. 120–126.
2. Dutta, A., and McChronan, K. (2002). "Management's Role in Information Security in a Cyber-Economy." *California Management Review* (45:1), pp. 67–87.
3. Purcell, R., and Fusaro, R. (2000). "Chief Privacy Officer." *Harvard Business Review*, November/December, pp. 20–22.
4. Wilder, C., and Soat, J. (2001). "The Ethics of Data." *InformationWeek*, May 14. http://www.informationweek.com/837/dataethics.htm (Accessed 06/07/2007).

GLOSSARY

■ **Backdoor:** Code built into software programs to allow access to an application by circumventing password protection.

■ **Biometrics:** In the context of computer security, the term biometrics is used to refer to the use of physical traits as a means to uniquely identify users.

■ **Denial-of-service attack:** A digital assault carried out over a computer network with the objective to overwhelm an online service so as to force it offline.

■ **Encryption:** A technique designed to scramble data so as to ensure that if the wrong individuals gain access to the data, they will be unable to make out its meaning.

- **Firewall:** A hardware or software tool designed to screen and manage traffic in and out of an organization's computer network.

- **Hacker:** The term hacker simply means someone who possesses superior computer skills. It has come to be associated in the media and general terminology with more or less maliciously intentioned individuals who attempt to subvert computer security defenses.

- **Information systems security:** The set of defenses an organization puts in place to mitigate threats to its technology infrastructure and data resources.

- **Intrusion:** The intrusion threat consists of any situation where an unauthorized attacker gains access to organizational IT resources.

- **IT risk management:** The process by which the firm attempts to identify and measure information systems security risks, and to devise the optimal mitigation strategy.

- **Malware:** The general term malicious code, or malware, refers to software programs that are designed to cause damage to individuals and/or organizations' IT assets.

- **Phishing:** The process of collecting sensitive information by tricking, in more or less automated ways, those who have it to provide it thinking that they are giving it to a legitimate concern.

- **Privacy:** In the context of information systems, privacy is the ability of individuals to control the terms and conditions under which their personal information is collected, managed, and utilized.

- **Risk analysis:** The process by which the firm attempts to quantify the risks identified in the risk assessment.

- **Risk assessment:** The risk assessment process consist of auditing the current resources, technological as well as human, in an effort to map the current state of the art of information systems security in the organization.

- **Risk mitigation:** The process of matching the appropriate response to the security threats your firm has identified.

- **Social engineering:** The practice of obtaining restricted or private information by somehow convincing legitimate users or people who have it to share it.

- **Spyware:** Software that, unbeknownst to the owner of the computer, monitors behavior, collects information, and either transfers this information to a third party via the Internet or performs unwanted operations.

- **Trojan horse:** A computer program that claims to, and sometimes does, deliver some useful functionality. But the Trojan horse hides a dark side and, like a virus, delivers a malicious payload.

- **Virus:** A type of malicious code that spreads by attaching itself to other, legitimate, executable software programs.

- **Worm:** A piece of malicious code that exploits security holes in network software to replicate itself.

INDEX